Home Is Where
the (He)art Is

The Bucknell Studies in Latin American Literature and Theory
Series Editor: Aníbal González, Yale University

Dealing with far-reaching questions of history and modernity, language and self-hood, and power and ethics, Latin American literature sheds light on the many-faceted nature of Latin American life, as well as on the human condition as a whole. This series of books provides a forum for some of the best criticism on Latin American literature in a wide range of critical approaches, with an emphasis on works that productively combine scholarship with theory. Acknowledging the historical links and cultural affinities between Latin American and Iberian literatures, the series welcomes consideration of Spanish and Portuguese texts and topics, while also providing a space of convergence for scholars working in Romance studies, comparative literature, cultural studies, and literary theory.

Titles in Series

Sergio Waisman, *Borges and Translation: The Irreverence of the Periphery*

Stuart Day, *Staging Politics in Mexico: The Road to Neoliberalism*

Amy Nauss Millay, *Voices from the* fuente viva: *The Effect of Orality in Twentieth-Century Spanish American Narrative*

J. Andrew Brown, *Test Tube Envy: Science and Power in Argentine Narrative*

Juan Carlos Ubilluz, *Sacred Eroticism: Georges Bataille and Pierre Klossowski in the Latin American Erotic Novel*

Mark A. Hernández, *Figural Conquistadors: Rewriting the New World's Discovery and Conquest in Mexican and River Plate Novels of the 1980s and 1990s*

Gabriel Riera, *Littoral of the Letter: Saer's Art of Narration*

Dianne Marie Zandstra, *Embodying Resistance: Griselda Gambaro and the Grotesque*

Amanda Holmes, *City Fictions: Language, Body, and Spanish American Urban Space*

Gail Bulman, *Staging Words, Performing Worlds: Intertextuality and Nation in Contemporary Latin American Theater*

Anne Lambright, *Creating the Hybrid Intellectual: Subject, Space, and the Feminist in the Narrative of José María Arguedas*

Dara E. Goldman, *Out of Bounds: Islands and the Demarcation of Identity in the Hispanic Caribbean*

Eva-Lynn Alicia Jagoe, *The End of the World as They Knew It: Writing Experiences of the Argentine South*

Sharon Magnarelli, *Home Is Where the (He)art Is: The Family Romance in Late Twentieth-Century Mexican and Argentine Theater*

Raúl Marrero-Fente, *Epic, Empire, and Community in the Atlantic World: Silvestre de Balboa's* Espejo de paciencia

http.//www.departments.bucknell.edu/univ press

Home Is Where
the (He)art Is

The Family Romance
in Late Twentieth-Century
Mexican and Argentine Theater

Sharon Magnarelli

Lewisburg
Bucknell University Press

Associated University Presses
2010 Eastpark Boulevard
Cranbury, NJ 08512

The paper used in this publication meets the requirements of the American National Standard for Permanence of Paper for Printed Library Materials Z39.48-1984.

Library of Congress Cataloging-in-Publication Data

Magnarelli, Sharon, 1946–
　　Home is where the (he)art is : the family romance in late twentieth-century Mexican and Argentine theater / Sharon Magnarelli.
　　　　p.　cm.
　　Includes bibliographical references and index.
　　ISBN 978-0-8387-5707-9 (alk. paper)
　　1. Mexican drama—20th century—History and criticism.　2. Argentine drama—20th century—History and criticism.　3. Family in literature. 4. Women in literature.　I. Title.　II. Home is where the art is.
PQ7189.M294　2008
862′.6409355—dc22　　　　　　　　　　　　　　　　　　2007042820

For Lou

Contents

Acknowledgments

In many ways this project began back in 1984 when I was awarded a Fulbright Fellowship to do research on theater in Argentina. From that point on, my interest in Spanish American theater has continued to grow, and I am deeply indebted for that "foundational" opportunity. More recently, a sabbatical leave from Quinnipiac University along with numerous research grants from both the Research Committee and the College of Liberal Arts at Quinnipiac have provided me with both release time and several types of funding, and it is thanks to their generosity that I have been able to complete this project. I am also grateful to my many colleagues in the field of Spanish American theater who offered helpful comments after listening to portions of this project that I presented at various conferences. I would also like to acknowledge and express my gratitude to the playwrights whose works I have included in this study; they have been generous with their time—meeting with me and/or answering my questions—and in many cases they made their works available to me, often before they were published.

Some of the chapters included here were first published as articles. I would like to thank the following publishers for granting permission to republish those materials:

"Authoring the Scene, Playing the Role: Mothers and Daughters in Griselda Gambaro's *La malasangre,*" *Latin American Theatre Review* 27, no. 2 (1994): 1–27. Permission granted by Stuart Day, editor.

"*¿Homo sapiens?* by Marcela del Río: Who Framed the Family?" in *Studies in Honor of Donald Shaw,* ed. Susan Carvalho (Newark, DL: Juan de la Cuesta, 2006), 293–320. Permission granted by Thomas Lathrop, editor.

"Papeles maternales: Griselda Gambaro y Hugo Argüelles," in *Imagen del teatro,* ed. Osvaldo Pellettieri (Buenos Aires: Galerna, 2002), 75–81. Permission granted by Osvaldo Pellettieri, editor.

"Simulacra and Commodification in Diana Raznovich's *Casa Matriz* (or Whose Life Is This Anyway?)," *Letras Femeninas* 32, no. 1: 169–87. Permission granted by Carmen de Urioste, editor.

"Sub/In/Di-verting the Oedipus Syndrome in Luisa Josefina Hernández's *Los huéspedes reales*," *INTI* 40 (Fall 1994): 93–112. Permission granted by Roger Carmosino, editor.

"Teatralidad y familia en *Escarabajos* de Hugo Argüelles," in *Tendencias críticas en el teatro,* ed. Osvaldo Pellettieri (Buenos Aires: Galerna, 2001): 53–64. Permission granted by Osvaldo Pellettieri, editor.

Introduction

LINKING THEATER WITH FAMILY AND HOME MAY SEEM ECCENTRIC AT first, perhaps even perverse. After all, contrary to viewing television from the safety of our homes, to experience theater we are required to leave that secure site and venture out into the streets. Once at the theater (in whatever form it may take), our encounter with the art form transpiring before our eyes is shared with dozens, if not hundreds, of strangers, who surround us, often in silence and darkness, and who, at the end of the performance, will disappear from our life as quickly as they slipped into it a couple of hours earlier, taking with them that brief sense of community we theoretically experienced as spectators. Nonetheless, I am convinced that the fact that contemporary plays so often revolve around the middle-class, nuclear family and/or are set precisely in the family home cannot be irrelevant.[1] Indeed, it seems possible that at times such a focus has been chosen precisely to re-instill that sense of security and community we seem to lose en route to the theater, as it clearly does in the case of Roberto Cossa's *El saludador* (The Greeter or The Waver), a play in which spectators are afforded a distinct sense of settling in at home and participating in a communal, neighborhood experience.[2] At the same time, the focus on home and family seems designed to shore up our waning sense of family in the late twentieth and early twenty-first centuries, when, or so we have been told, the nuclear family and family values as we have come to know them are disappearing. In response to this sense of loss, which, as many scholars have cogently argued, is more imagined than real since the storybook families that are being lost have probably always been the exception rather than the rule (if they ever existed at all), some theatrical works offer us an idealized, mythologized pseudomirror of what we think our family is, what it should be, or what we would like it to be. Most works, however, provide something of a negative pseudomirror: underscoring the dysfunctional elements of family, they empower us with a certain sense of relief and superiority by reassuring us that as imperfect as our own families might be, they are certainly far better than the one portrayed onstage.[3]

11

What interests me most as I examine the manipulation of images of family and home in Mexican and Argentine drama of recent years are three interrelated aspects. First, what insecurities on the part of audiences are assuaged by means of theater's spotlight on family and home, or, on the contrary, what anxieties are created or aggravated? Second, which unexamined and perhaps even unacknowledged images of family are uncritically accepted, while, on the other hand, which are challenged, how and why? Third, what are the implications of theater's trope of family for the larger sociopolitical body? There can be little doubt that our perceptions of family and home are of particular cultural import since as tropes they have come to have sociopolitical, national, or even international ramifications far beyond those individual units we label home or family. In fact, many of the plays I analyze link, subtly or not so subtly, notions of home and family to sociopolitical, historical issues, underscoring the fact that certain images of family are perpetuated by political leaders precisely so that they can be carried over to and influence our perception of other sociopolitical institutions. Indeed, it cannot be irrelevant that in times of weakening power, political leaders turn to and exalt the glories of family and home. For example, both Mexican and Argentine government officials have resorted to extolling virtues of the family at those very moments when both their power and the institutions they support (and, conversely, on which they and their power depend) have seemed most vulnerable. I think, specifically, of the Proceso (the military dictatorship of the late 1970s and early 1980s) in Argentina, the period of the Mexican Revolution (1910–20s), and more recently the 1980s and 1990s in Mexico when the hegemony of the PRI (Partido Revolucionario Institucional [Institutional Revolutionary Party]), Mexico's ruling political party since the time of the Revolution) was being challenged.[4] During each of these periods of "crisis," political leaders directed attention toward family values (although, of course, the question of whose family values never arose). It would appear that this focus on family values served, in part, to divert attention from national problems, but also, and again in part, to provide a mechanism for proposing that what appear to be (and are) institutional, governmental problems would be easily remedied and disappear if only each family unit would subscribe to and enforce appropriate family values. Translate: what is wrong with the national government is not the fault of its leaders and institutions but rather of its citizens who do not have their own families under proper control. To what extent, then, is theater complicitous in this process and to what extent does it encourage the spectator to see the process, the attempt to shore up the threatened fortress, for what it is? If, as Donzelot has argued, families are consistently regulated and policed to ensure their proper conformity to social norms, to what extent does theater participate in or, on the contrary, diffuse this policing, this normativization and valorization of family?[5] Yet, at the same time, and inversely, I also explore the motives on the part of theater for linking itself with family and insisting on theater in terms of this familial, communal experience.[6] National or even international politics aside, what theatrical needs are met or apprehensions allayed by focusing on the home rather than on the elsewhere? Why this investment in home and family on the part of theater?

My study comprises two levels. On the thematic level, I examine a number of dramatic works from the second half of the twentieth century in terms of their inversions of or deviations from the traditional romance plot, in which the son leaves the home in search of adventure and/or the father. Conventionally, his adventures result in his identification with the father and/or his becoming a (the) father himself once his adventures have won him the hand of a (the) girl. That is to say, the traditional romance plot is already implicitly predicated on the family: starting with leaving the "original" family and ending with forming a "new" family, with a new head/patriarch, but one who for all intents and purposes will echo the father and perpetuate the status quo. In the contemporary works I have studied, quite the opposite is the case. Although the central trope of family still provides the anchor for the action, the end results are notably different. In Hugo Argüelles's *Escarabajos* (Dung Beetles), for example, the actor-son rejects the father and identifies with the mother, who is metaphorized as the Medea he plays onstage.[7] Thus, in what becomes a trope redoubled, he plays (becomes) his mother or, at least, his reading of her. Furthermore, his choice of males as objects of erotic love effectively precludes his becoming a father and thus in any way mirroring his own father/victimizer, while his specific choice of a lover maintains him clearly in the role of victim that he associates with his mother (and this in spite of the fact that Medea is most often read as the victimizer and not as the victim that she also was). In *La esfinge de las maravillas* (The Sphinx of Marvels), by the same author, the adopted son abandons the home, the father, and indeed the mother, after she undergoes a lobotomy (ordered by the father) that destines her to a vegetative existence.[8] Once out of that space (the home) and that web of relationships, the son will continue, it would appear, his philandering ways, but without benefit of parallel structures; that is, he will father children with various women, allow those women to support him, but not recognize the children as his own, not become a (the) father in the sociopolitical sense. Furthermore, in our last glimpse of the shattered remains of what we had readily recognized as and labeled a family, it seems clear that power relations and gender roles have shifted dramatically, for the daughter has assumed the patriarch's former position and now overtly manipulates and controls him as he had earlier manipulated and controlled others. While the family is shattered and shown to be inadequate to the desires/needs of its members, and although the work offers no remedy, replacement, or alternative to the institution, the question of family is revealingly linked to yet another institution: that of theater. In Sabina Berman's *Entre Villa y una mujer desnuda* (*Between Pancho Villa and a Naked Woman*), fathers are absent or ineffective, and numerous gender and generational roles are turned on end.[9] Epitome of hypermasculinity, the fictional Pancho Villa fathers endless children but still looks to his mother for her blessing—her approval and confirmation of his worth. Meanwhile, Gina, the protagonist, defies generational norms and couples with her son's best friend in what blurs the line between sons and fathers (or husbands). In Marcela del Río's *¿Homo sapiens?* (Homo Sapiens?) family roles are presented as consciously theatrical, and the traditional bourgeois family is displayed in a zoo cage, object of observation, amusement, and disdain.[10] While Luisa Josefina Hernández's *Los huéspedes reales* (The Royal Guests) examines the potential romance triangle among father, mother, and daughter, there is no son, and the daughter's decision at the end to remain with the mother in the family home after the father's suicide, rather than venturing out into the world prepared for her by societal norms (that is, rather than allowing her hand to be won and marrying the conquering hero/son), again challenges or even inverts the traditional romance plot (along with Freudian interpretations of it) in its gesture of turning inward rather than outward.[11] In Cossa's *El saludador* the prodigal father returns home to find that his wife and son have survived quite nicely without him and that his presence is, by and large, superfluous. In the final compromise, as the family becomes a cooperative, he is allowed to stay in part because he owns the family home, the space/place of the play, but mostly because the wife/mother needs a regular, dependable sexual outlet (a privilege traditionally reserved only for males). In Eduardo Rovner's *Volvió una noche* (*She Returned One Night*), the father is barely mentioned, and it is the mother who has returned from the dead to teach her adult son his proper place in the world and enforce her mores. Thus, he must come to some kind of resolution with her rather than with the father.[12] And, in Diana Raznovich's *Casa Matriz* (*MaTRIX, Inc.*) as well as in two plays by Griselda Gambaro, *La malasangre* (*Bitter Blood*) and *De profesión maternal* (Of the Maternal Profession), the traditional family romance is rewritten in a way that focuses on the mother/daughter relationship, a relationship that has far less frequently been the central one in literary or theatrical works.[13] Indeed, in both *Casa Matriz* and *De profesión maternal,* as in *Volvió una noche,* the father figure has quite literally been written out of the script.

To me, the common denominator in most of these works is the implicit or explicit focus on either the mother and the daughter (implicitly a future mother herself) or the attempt to rethink and recast the relationship of the "child" (male or female) with that mother. For the most part, throughout the centuries, in psychoanalytical as well as literary discourse, the mother has been either overly idealized in the form of the self-sacrificing, all-suffering mother or else cast as the wicked other, source of all evil: Eve, Medea, psychoanalysis's castrating mother, and so on. Yet these Spanish American works, written by both males and females, seem to defy these traditions. For example, in Gambaro's *De profesión maternal,* as well as in the two plays by Argüelles, the mother is neither self-sacrificing nor wicked, but (often like the daughter) simply does not know how to play the familial role society has assigned to her. My questions are why and how has the family romance changed at the end of the twentieth century? What are the similarities among the plays; what are the differences?

I employ the term *family romance* on several levels and with several meanings. First, I borrow it from Marianne Hirsch, who borrows it from Freud.[14] According to Hirsch, "In Freud's terms, the family romance is an imaginary interrogation of origins, an interrogation which embeds the engenderment of narrative within the experience of family. Through fantasy, the developing individual liberates himself from the constraints of family by imagining himself to be an orphan or a bastard and his 'real' parents to be more noble than the 'foster' family in which he is growing up. The essence of the Freudian family romance is the imaginative act of replacing the parent (for boys clearly the father) with another, superior figure."[15] The two aspects of this definition that will prove most constructive in the coming discussion are the notions of the embedding of narrative within the experience of family and the quest to invent, imagine better parents/origins. In this sense, then, and in light of my comments above, the plays analyzed here represent a certain expansion of the Freudian notion of family romance insofar as while the characters may reject the literal parent (particularly the father), the plays often challenge, if not openly reject, socially acceptable parental images per se. That is, it is not only the individual parent that is refused but also the sociopolitical concept itself. At the same time, however, and in many ways paradoxically, as the familial metaphor is applied (within the plays) to larger sociopolitical institutions, the Freudian thrust of imagining better parents, in the form of better political leaders or more noble, less reprehensible (and violent) national origins (which are frequently imaged in terms of birth), maintains its currency in particularly pertinent ways. For example, the del Río play opens with a parade (which we do not see, but which is described to us) that effectively functions as a review of Mexican history and culture, but it is one in which the Mexican government (the controlling party, the PRI) would rewrite the metaphoric birth of the nation by imagining its origins not as the forcible rape and conquest of the native women and lands by the Spanish conquistadors and colonizers, but rather as a peaceful (and desirable) love affair that produced the mestizo people. It is the myth of the loving family itself that the playwright interrogates on both the personal and the public levels.

I also employ the term *family romance* as Hirsch herself does. Specifically, she aims to "retain the Freudian definitions as reference points but reframe them to be more broadly applicable."[16] In this sense the term evokes "the discursive and imaginative role that the family plays in our narratives and the particular shape and nature of familial structures . . . The family romance is the story we tell ourselves about the social and psychological reality of the family . . . and about the patterns of desire that motivate the interaction among its members."[17] It is this definition that perhaps most closely frames my approach to the plays analyzed here. Part of my focus will be the question of desire since erotic desire within the family structure (in the sense of the Freudian perception of desires within the family, the Oedipal/Electra complexes) is repeatedly an underlying motif in these works, although I would argue, as Doris Sommer does in regard to Latin America's foundational fictions, that erotic desire functions in unexpected ways to shore up the fantasy of familial bonds, which are then extended to include the fantasy of national bonds.[18] We find the question of erotic desire in the triangular relationships among the family members of *Los huéspedes reales, La esfinge de las maravillas,* and *La malasangre.* As we will see, however, not all desire in these plays is erotic in nature. Indeed, desire functions on a number of levels. Within the plays desire (erotic or not) often proves to be closely tied to questions of the empowerment of the subject as the character seems to desire what would confer power on him/her or, inversely, what would disempower the other. One of the motivations of a number of the plays seems to be to propose the possibility of desiring differently.[19]

But, for me romance is also and necessarily a reference to the narratives bequeathed us, those cultural, historical, and literary tales that surround us and shape our perception of society and our roles within it, whether the fairy tales of our childhood, the foundational fictions of our adolescence, or any of the other narratives that reach us via the numerous media available today. All of the plays I examine challenge the familial images perpetuated in these narratives and lend a new shape to the traditional family romance. Surely this is related in part to the question of postmodernism. If as Lyotard has proposed, the postmodern age challenges or debunks the grand narratives—the narratives of mastery and the master (read, the master's?) narratives—, then surely the works I am studying are complicitous with this tendency insofar as they remap the positions and authority of the parents (real or metaphoric).[20] But, as I hope to demonstrate, this is only one aspect, for at least some of the works I analyze reveal far more subtle complexities as they question (in ways perhaps unthinkable during the first half of the twentieth century) family relationships and the discourses that have both portrayed and perpetuated them.

Thus will be the thematic focus of my analysis. But, at the same time I shall be examining how the works and their implied performances manipulate spectators into a position that encourages us to support and perpetuate the family relationship portrayed in the work or, on the contrary, to challenge or even reject it.[21] If we acknowledge that theater is always and necessarily complicitous in shaping social relationships (either by resisting the status quo or by perpetuating it) and that theater is less an imitation of reality than an interpretation of it, then our questions must be, how does any given work encourage spectators to leave the theater and perform citationally, to repeat the portrayed roles in our own lives outside of the theater, or on the contrary to opt for other possibilities in our citational performances.[22] How does the work situate spectators so that we will identify or disidentify with the family represented? At the same time, however, I also discuss the plays in terms of audience desire. As Herbert Blau has theorized, "The audience . . . is not so much a mere congregation of people as a body of thought and desire. It does not exist before the play but is *initiated* or *precipitated* by it; it is not an entity to begin with but a consciousness constructed."[23] The question then will be how do the plays construct the audience and its desires? If we accept that, as Gladhart has phrased it, "Theatrical spectatorship is not innocent, in that a deliberate choice has been made to view this show, this stage," then how do the desires of the audience influence the performance and vice versa?[24] To what extent do the implied desires of the audience mirror the desires performed onstage? To what extent is audience desire offstage shaped by the family desires represented onstage?

Although my analyses of ten plays written and performed between 1956 and 1999 have taken me in any number of directions, I have also found notable points of contact, and this in spite of formidable divides on a number of levels. Obviously, the plays I have chosen are distanced by the continent of physical space that separates Argentina and Mexico and that functions as a trope for many other divides, such as the very different cultures and master narratives of the two countries, the more than forty years of history that separate the first play from the most recent, the genders of the playwrights, their socioeconomic status, and their sexual preferences. Nonetheless, all of the works I study in some way stage the constructedness of the notion of family and/or attempt to deconstruct that constructedness to allow us the opportunity to glimpse (or at least imagine) relationships based on different premises. I use the term constructedness in the sense that Judith Butler uses it, which is to say not as something strictly artificial but rather as something that is "constitutive, that is, ha[s] this character of being that 'without which' we could not think at all."[25] Indeed, as Donzelot has convincingly documented, families (or at least the images we have of them) are constructed through relations of power and normative constraints (as is gender, according to Butler).[26] These points become particularly pertinent for the study that follows when we recognize the close interdependence between family and gender. Gender surely begins at home: not only is the family home the training ground for future gender roles, but those roles are rehearsed and played out most fully there. While not always explicit, each of the plays somehow stages the concept that family, as we conceive of it today in the Western world, is neither natural (a given in nature), eternal, nor inherent, but rather a construction (which according to most scholars dates from the 1600–1700s) and one that has met and continues to meet numerous sociopolitical needs, as scholars as diverse as political scientist Jacques Donzelot, philosopher Elisabeth Badinter, and psychiatrist Ann Dally have all contended.[27] Thus, each play evokes the contingency of the institution we call family and the myths that surround it. On some level then, each undermines our "dreams" of family, our wishful thinking.

My study comprises two parts. The works analyzed in the first section are all fundamentally naturalistic in style and for the most part portray what we might call the traditional nuclear family unit: mom, dad, child(ren)—a definition/image of family that, let us not forget, was brought from the Old World to the New and imposed on the native populations (along with monogamy, property rights, and so on) as part of the Conquest and the European colonization of the New World during the sixteenth, seventeenth, and even eighteenth centuries. It is also a definition/image that continues to be perpetuated today by means of what we might call a global neocolonization that is being effected by mass media and international commerce. In many cases the plays of the first part focus on the events leading up to the disintegration of the family unit and the reshaping of the remains. The Hernández play, for example, takes us to the father's suicide and the new family composed of mother and daughter. Once Dolores is dragged off the stage at the end of *La malasangre,* the spectator must recognize that familial relations, which here provide a metaphor of the nation's sociopolitical relations, have been broken and cannot be repaired; "big daddy" will now have to look elsewhere to tyrannize those he would pretend to adore. At the end of the inner play of *Escarabajos,* the family disintegrates, and the mother will die shortly thereafter. The del Río play seems to end circularly where it began: the television is turned on once more, and recent events of revenge, betrayal, and murder are elided or forgotten. Although *El saludador* maintains the family unit at the end, it is now restructured as a cooperative. What each play implicitly evokes is a certain anxiety in regard to "typical" or traditional family portraits. Each is riddled with doubt and uneasiness about marriage, home, and family. And although each reaches some sort of narrative closure, there is frequently a tacit challenge to that very closure. The fact that the playwrights have chosen to focus on processes of disintegration suggests that something is inherently wrong with the family, or at least with its traditional depiction. For example, one might well ask what Argüelles means to suggest in *Escarabajos* by having the fifty-five-year-old protagonist remember his mother and family in terms of the exception rather than the rule: that is, in terms of the two years they lived with the father (and thus constituted the mask or farce of a typical family unit) rather than the twenty years they lived without him, apparently in relative happiness, in a different (nontraditional but not uncommon) sort of family unit. Along the same lines one might also question how the family in *¿Homo sapiens?* can carry on at the end as if nothing had happened. In the latter, although the audience is not witness to the actual disintegration, it seems clear that the sham cannot continue. The foundation of the family, built as it is upon layers of dirt that hide the putrefaction and worms (a metaphor from one of the characters), is sure to give way at any moment.

I title the second part of the study, "After the Great Divide," in reference to Huyssen's study on postmodernism since the plays of the second part are marked by postmodernist tendencies in several ways.[28] Significantly, with one exception, the plays I analyze here in the second part all begin after the disintegration, on the other side of the great familial divide, in what might well be read as a typically postmodern gesture.[29] In these plays, the traditional, nuclear family unit no longer dominates. In *Entre Villa y una mujer desnuda,* the female protagonist is divorced, and her son lives in the United States. Her lover Adrián is separated and apparently has only minimal contact with his wife and child. Historical figure, Pancho Villa, father of numerous offspring scattered throughout the countryside, has seen his mother only a half a dozen times in eighteen years and early in the play kills the woman with whom he might have started a family, thus precluding any potential family ties. *Volvió una noche, Casa Matriz,* and *De profesión maternal* all elide traditional, nuclear family units, for the "children" have already grown up. Furthermore, in the Rovner play, the mother is already dead. In the Gambaro play, mother and father had separated some forty years ago, and now mother and daughter, reunited after all that time, discover the ambiguity or even meaninglessness of those familial terms. In the Raznovich play, there is no reference to Bárbara's "real" family. Instead, she hires a substitute mother as a birthday present to herself, a rented mother whose job it is to play the chosen role in a way that will please her audience (Bárbara) and give that audience the show it has paid for and expects to see— surely an enlightening, self-reflexive comment on the image of family portrayed in theater. Revealingly, then, in all three plays emphasis is given to the degree to which the image of the mother is part and parcel of the dominant imaginary.

The fact that most of the plays of the second group begin well beyond the point of disintegration that marks the end of the plays in part 1 does not mean that we are necessarily witness to some type of reintegration, however. On the contrary, and again in what might be considered good postmodern form, in these plays disintegration is considered a way of life, and the historical and sociopolitical contingency of the family is underscored. Even though at the end of *Volvió una noche,* Manuel may be about to begin a new family unit, it is clear that it will be as ephemeral and contingent as the previous one. But, and more important for my focus here, the fact that these plays underscore the contingency of the family unit does not mean that the image or the trope of family has been erased. Quite the contrary, while the traditional family may no longer be a presence on the stage, its specter definitively lives on.

As a result of this specter, a critical element in my analyses of these works is the question of memory. Maurice Halbwachs has noted that memory is always related to family, class, or religious affiliation, and I would note that religious affiliation is often imaged and perceived in familial terms.[30] In recent years, as scholars have analyzed nation and other imagined communities, they have come to recognize the importance of memory—selective remembering and selective forgetting—in the construction of those communities. Yet the importance of memory in our most basic imagined community—the family—has seldom been recognized, much less explored, and this in spite of the fact that the community we call family is every bit as constructed and invented as are others such as nation. One of my other concerns will be the extent to which theater replicates or reinforces our fractured memories and that to which it contests them. Paradoxically, although *family* tends to conjure up warm, fuzzy images, the Western tradition has a long history of familial conflict, starting with Cain and Abel and continuing through Abraham and his grandsons (Esau and Jacob)—memories we seem to push aside as we remember family. Freud, of course, further unsettled our notions of family in the early twentieth century with his focus on conflict and competition within it. If we acknowledge that theater (like any art form or any master narrative) creates memory as much as it reflects it, it becomes of paramount importance to investigate which of our memories theatrical works select, which they reject, and why? Which constructs are allowed to count as memories, which are not? Reformulating the questions that Butler asks about bodies, we might well query, what are the constraints by which memories are materialized, which memories come to matter?[31] Cossa's *El saludador,* del Río's *¿Homo sapiens?,* Rovner's *Volvió una noche,* and Berman's *Entre Villa y una mujer desnuda* are among the plays that overtly stage memory and underscore the selectivity involved in both individual and collective memory. But, at the same time, memory is also pivotal to the coming analyses insofar as any reaction to an art form, but perhaps particularly to theater because of its ephemeral character, is already necessarily a memory as we re-member (put the parts, body, back together, re-form, refashion) what we saw or what we think we saw.

It is important to note, however, that although the family and the home provide the backdrop in all of the plays analyzed in the coming chapters, in many of these works the theme or message of the play rests not with the family per se, but elsewhere. In other words, the playwrights have employed the trope of the family to communicate a message that is not necessarily related to the family. Indeed, as Graham-Jones points out in her study of Argentine theater under dictatorship, "family dynamics functioned as a metaphor for multilevel power relations . . . The enclosed space of the home effectively, and frequently, represented the country under dictatorship."[32] She later adds, "in contemporary Western theatre, a common synecdochic stand-in for the social structure has been the family."[33] Similarly, Laura Mulvey has noted that the home is a social and mythologized space that can "draw attention to the way that oppositions of inside/outside have given order and pattern to the centrifugal/centripetal tensions in urban, industrialised, capitalist life."[34] As she later observes, "The social sphere of the family provides a ready-made *dramatis personae* of characters whose relations are by very definition overdetermined and overlaid with tension and contradiction . . . At one and the same time, the family is the socially accepted road to respectable normality, an icon of conformity, and the source of deviance, psychosis, and despair."[35] Still, although the playwright's message(s) may be found elsewhere, as I will argue, the use of the trope of family to communicate this elsewhere, this other message, is, in and of itself, significant and reveals much about our often unacknowledged and unchallenged images of family. Indeed, one might well ask the significance of reverting to family, what Donzelot has deemed the basic unit employed to shore up Western society, in so many of our metaphors, but particularly in those related to sociopolitical and/or religious institutions.[36] Let's think, for example, of the family of man (repeatedly mentioned in del Río), the family of God (i.e., the Trinity, which becomes the trope for the model family, with God, the father, at the head), the national family, and so on. Clearly, one of the problems of this metaphorization of family is that in its emphasis on similarities it tends to erase differences. As a result, we come to expect all the qualities of one term of the equation to be applicable to the other; that is, rather than being like family, nation comes to equal family and vice versa, and the multiple shapes or forms that the family might take are reduced to one. Thus, my approaches to the plays in the coming chapters will endeavor to take both aspects into account as I attempt to analyze the family without losing sight of the play as a whole and its other messages. At the same time, I try throughout to balance, not lose sight of, the specific, local, sociopolitical, and historical contexts of the plays even as I focus on the more universal (in terms of the Western world, of course) trope of family.

As might be expected, issues of space/place will provide a focal point for many of my analyses. Space is always paramount in theater insofar as by definition the genre necessarily entails the use of space, the stage. In all these plays, in which the theatrical stage represents (becomes) the family home and vice versa, the complicity of theater in shaping both our past memories and our future perceptions of those collective communities we call theater and family surfaces and becomes one of the thematic focuses. For example, in the del Río play, the fact that the family home is a cage in a zoo signals the potential of the home to function as a trap, in both senses of the word (something that lures us in and something that restrains us) while it characterizes the spaces of both home and theater as ones of observation and surveillance. In the Cossa play, the patio wall that marks the division between inside and outside, family and global issues, "us" and "them," dominates the stage. The division between the family living room and the outside patio in *Escarabajos* is revealingly edged with parasitic plants while the other section of the stage is occupied by a theater dressing room, thus provocatively dramatizing a disquieting interrelation among the three. During the course of Laura Yusem's production of *De profesión maternal,* the mostly bare stage, which represented the family living room, was repeatedly "populated" with chairs, carried in, carried out, continually moved, and rearranged, indexes perhaps of the continually shifting familial, gender positions we occupy and of the contingency of the structures themselves and theater's investment in them. In *Volvió una noche* characters that are already dead come and go through the walls of the family home, thus underscoring the degree to which the past, memory, and prior cultural mores infiltrate our present. And, finally, in *Entre Villa y una mujer desnuda,* the living room of Gina's apartment serves as the stage for her erotic trysts with Adrián as they struggle to form (or avoid forming) a family unit as well as for Pancho Villa's battles (erotic and otherwise), again highlighting the continuation and influence of the past in our present.

I have limited my study to Argentine and Mexican theater and, with the exception of Luisa Josefina Hernández's *Los huéspedes reales* from 1956, to plays from the last two decades of the twentieth century. Restricting the study in this way is admittedly arbitrary, as limitations, boundaries, and demarcations inevitably are, arbitrary but necessary from a practical standpoint. Surely, I might well have chosen other geographic areas. I chose these two, in part because of their accessibility to me. Since I am a North American who frequently visits Buenos Aires and Mexico City but who does not live there, accessibility is a major factor. I also limited my analyses to plays whose texts have been published. At the same time, my focus has admittedly been theater performed in the urban centers, not that of the provinces, again primarily for reasons of access. In addition, I might well have chosen a different time frame. Again, I was motivated in large degree by accessibility, since I wanted to deal with the plays not exclusively as texts but also as performances, productions, and stagings. I have been able to attend productions of most of the plays. Nonetheless, I have imposed far fewer limits in terms of theory and employ a number of theoretical approaches. In each case my theoretical approach is informed by the play; I have chosen to fit the theory to the play rather than to force the play into a theory.

With the exception of the first chapter, the essays in this study were written over a ten-year period from 1991 to 2001. Since the start of my project, interest in Spanish American theater, theater by female playwrights, the performance of gender, and the motif of family have grown, and numerous excellent studies have appeared in recent years that focus on varying aspects of these topics. Diana Taylor's 1997 *Disappearing Acts: Spectacles of Gender and Nationalism in Argentina's "Dirty War"* analyzes the gendering of national identity in political spectacles as well as theatrical productions in Argentina during the period from 1976 to 1983. Examining Argentine theater of the same period in *Exorcising History: Argentine Theater under Dictatorship* (2000), Jean Graham-Jones sees family relations as a metaphor for national politics. Similarly, Camilla Stevens, in *Family and Identity in Contemporary Cuban and Puerto Rican Drama* (2004) views the family story onstage as a metaphor for the national community and relates it to the struggle for national and cultural self-definition as she explores Puerto Rican and Cuban drama from two decades (mid-1950s to mid-1960s and mid-1980s to mid-1990s).[37] Other critics have focused on performance as a structuring theme and have examined works from numerous Latin American countries: Catherine Larson (*Games and Play in the Theater of Spanish American Women*) and Margo Milleret (*Latin American Women on/in Stages*), both of whom focus on women dramatists, as well as Amalia Gladhart (*The*

Leper in Blue: Coercive Performance and the Contemporary Latin American Theatre).[38] In each of these three works, the critic devotes part of the study to questions of gender as performance. Although there are thematic overlaps between my study and the ones mentioned above, only one of the plays I analyze appears in those books (*Casa Matriz*). My study differs from the others in that I have neither limited my focus to one country nor attempted to incorporate representative works from many countries. While I too am interested in questions of gender as well as familial roles as performance and as metaphors of national or international politics, I examine other ramifications of the motif. Furthermore, I have limited my study to just ten plays by eight playwrights so that each work can be analyzed in depth. I am less interested in a survey of the motif's presence in Spanish American theater than in how the motif contributes to the individual play and how it seeps into that work even when the playwright's focus seems to be elsewhere. My goal has been to explore how the works avail themselves of the motif to communicate their larger message and simultaneously mirror that motif back, challenging our perception of it, in a gesture that underscores the interdependence between our sociopolitical structures and theater. Not only are the plays complicitous in shaping the perceptions of family they would seem only to reflect, they also draw on the image of family to comment on theater per se.

The dramatists included here are ones whose work I have long admired. Although some of them also work in other genres, they are dramatists first and foremost. All are highly regarded in their respective countries, have received critical acclaim, having won multiple prizes, and have had significant success in the stagings of their plays. Although Spanish American theater is generally not well known outside of Spanish America, several of these playwrights, such as Gambaro, Berman, Rovner, and Raznovich, are indeed known in other parts of the world and have had plays produced in other countries. Others, unfortunately, are not well known outside of their own countries, although they certainly deserve to be. In addition, many of the playwrights discussed have taught or otherwise influenced successive generations of playwrights. I have provided details of the dramatists' careers at the start of each chapter.

This study begins with Mexican Luisa Josefina Hernández's 1956 play, *Los huéspedes reales* in chapter 1 as a way of demonstrating that although the notions I discuss in the other plays may appear new, they indeed have a history and are not, strictly speaking, an "invention" of the last few years of the twentieth century. In fact,

Los huéspedes reales does much to lay the foundations for recasting and refiguring the Freudian notions of family that have become so widely accepted in the twentieth century. Specifically, I analyze the work in terms of its refusal of the Oedipal family romance and argue that the visible ordinariness of the setting strongly contrasts with the sense of discomfort and uneasiness that characterizes audience reception. In this way, Hernández challenges the notion of theater as a mirror of nature and suggests that "nature" (in this case the patriarchal family structure) is a sociopolitical invention that has been disguised as nature, beginning with the Greek classics and continuing through Freudian psychoanalysis.

Chapter 2 centers on *La malasangre* (1981) by Argentine Griselda Gambaro. In the play the family structure is a metaphor for the political climate in Argentina at the time of the Proceso. My focus is on the mother-daughter relationship as I examine the women's role-playing and their complicity with sociopolitical power(s) as embodied in the familial image of the patriarch. Victims of the patriarchal power(s), they nonetheless repeat, within their own relationship, the role of victimizer, author(iz)ed by the patriarch and our sociopolitical structures. Each woman is ultimately characterized by her desire to disidentify with the other female and associate herself with the powerful male (the father) in the hopes of gaining some scraps of his power. Thus, the play demonstrates that what has been comprehended as a problem on the personal, family, or gender level is in fact a generic problem, synecdoche of the larger issue of the abuse of power in Western society and (inter)national politics.

Escarabajos (1991) by Mexican Hugo Argüelles is the focus of chapter 3. Like Hernández, Argüelles turns to classic Greek theater (in this case *Medea*) for his structuring metaphor. In this chapter I demonstrate the interconnectedness of memory, mirrors, mother, myth, and metatheater within the play. I argue that by means of the frame play, which is set as the protagonist is about to go onstage to perform his version of Medea, Argüelles highlights the theatrical, mythical misreadings that have framed or been superimposed on the face of the family. At the same time, the play suggests that if theater is a looking glass, it is one (like Snow White's looking glass as analyzed by Gilbert and Gubar) in which the king's (the patriarchy's) voice reigns and from which that voice controls the self-images we find there.[39] By adjusting the "mirror" of theater, the play underscores the bias, the vested readings, that frame any artistic production and the distortion that results when art reflects not life but other art, other theater, other performances, when memories, collective or individual, but especially those of family, are reproduced, cited.

Chapter 4 looks at the seduction that occurs both onstage and off in Argentine Roberto Cossa's *El saludador* (1999). I argue that both the stage (theater) and the family home here become ambiguous places of memory and seduction as Cossa employs the conventions of naturalistic theater to destabilize both those conventions and the old discourse (myths, memories, seduction) of family. As audience expectations are continually thwarted and figurative language is literalized in this play, the audience finds itself cast in the role of neighbor and/or member of the theatrical family. Nevertheless, although the audience is seduced by the naturalistic stage and the familiar setting, the repeated breaching of the theatrical fourth wall ultimately produces a literalization of the power of theater to seduce us, to make us part of its "family" and collective memories.

My analysis of Mexican Marcela del Río's 1991 *¿Homo sapiens?* in chapter 5 examines the figure of family in terms of Mexican history and demonstrates the ways in which sociopolitical structures are predicated on the creation and perpetuation of very specific images of family, images that, as the play posits, are fashioned and reinforced via public spectacles (another form of theater) such as parades and political gatherings. Del Río makes visible the institutions that have long framed and controlled our images of family. By adjusting the theatrical frame, reframing the family, as del Río does, the play allows the audience to perceive the family differently and recognize it as a sociopolitical construct that responds to specific political and economic ends. The private and the public (national) loving "families of man" are shown to be empty signifiers, tools to achieve the vested interests of certain members of those families. Similarly, theater is shown to be a frame that can function as a cage (maintain us within the status quo) or as a tool of revelation.

In chapter 6, I turn again to Mexican history and theories of nation to examine *Entre Villa y una mujer desnuda* (1993) by Mexican Sabina Berman. The play revisits one of the beloved myths of the Mexican Revolution, Pancho Villa, and demonstrates that issues of family are intricately related to history and national agendas. In my analysis of the play, I argue that both family and myths of nation have been instrumental in channeling desire and maintaining the status quo, the dominance of the nation's "fathers." Berman's utilization of an embedded play dramatizes the extent to which history and its master narratives populate our present and control our performances inside and outside the home. Furthermore, by emphasizing multiple, fragmented families onstage, Berman reminds us that the national family offstage is equally multiple and fragmented, not the neat homogeneous unit that is often depicted.

Theories of performance and performativity provide the theoretical foundation for chapter 7, where I examine motherhood as performance in two plays: *De profesión maternal* (1997) by Griselda Gambaro and *La esfinge de las maravillas* (1994) by Hugo Argüelles. Although these are two very different plays by playwrights with dissimilar styles, they do depict motherhood in surprisingly similar ways. In both, the presumably biological instinct proves to be more acquired than natural. I argue, borrowing from Butler's theory of gender and performance, that in both plays we find that "what passes as 'maternal instinct' may well be a culturally constructed desire which is interpreted through a naturalistic vocabulary."[40] In both plays, motherhood is shown to be a role, a performance, and one that, like any other, needs to be learned and rehearsed until the actor finally gets it right. At the same time both plays underline the complicity of theater and art in the tragedy that results when this normative role proves to be impossible to embody.

In chapter 8 I turn to postcolonial theory to explore the intricacies of Eduardo Rovner's *Volvió una noche* (1993). Theorizing that the family provides the basic paradigm of the colonial endeavor as it transmits cultural mores and polices our desires, encouraging us to desire what our culture would have us desire, I argue that the mother in the play embodies the notion of transculturation. However, even as an index and perpetuator of culture, the mother, like culture itself, is never monolithic but comprises contradictory characteristics to begin with, always already a palimpsest, a transculture in the process of yet another transculturation. The play teaches us to laugh at and empathize with the anxiety and discomfort that transculturation and finding ourselves in liminal positions often cause us (inside the home or out), whether we try to cling to past traditions and ignore assimilation and new mores, or vice versa, embrace the new and reject the old. Significantly, however, we find that in this play theater, like home and the family, functions as a contact zone, where transculturation occurs in both directions.

Finally, in chapter 9 I look once more at the performance of motherhood as I analyze Argentine Diana Raznovich's *Casa Matriz* (1989). In this play, mother is again shown to be a theatrical role and one tied not only to various art forms but also to consumerism and economic interests—production as well as reproduction. Specifically, the mother here is a commodity that one buys or rents, and by implication possesses and controls. On the surface the mother/

actress has been hired to fulfill the desire(s) of the audience and provide it with the show it wants to see. However, as I argue, the buyer's (and by implication the audience's) control is a sham, and its desires are in fact manipulated, shaped by the product rather than vice versa. Thus, I read the play as a scathing comment on theater's role in selling certain images of family.

Home Is Where
the (He)art Is

1

The Family Unit(ed) or the Holy Trinity

1

Sub/In/Di-verting the Oedipus Syndrome in Luisa Josefina Hernández's *Los huéspedes reales*

I HAVE CHOSEN TO BEGIN THIS STUDY OF THE FAMILY ROMANCE WITH Luisa Josefina Hernández's play, *Los huéspedes reales* (The Royal Guests) (1956), for several reasons.[1] First, its early date reminds us that issues of family are not new and in many ways not very different from what we will find in plays written almost half a century later. Second, her fame and success in a field that has traditionally been dominated primarily by males are particularly noteworthy. Her name was one of the few female names that inevitably came to mind for many years when we thought of Mexican theater. But, even more important, as a professor of dramatic composition for several decades in Mexico's largest university, she has surely impacted a generation or more of contemporary Mexican dramatists.

The play's dramatis personae comprise six characters: the protagonist, Cecilia; her mother, Elena; her father, Ernesto; her fiancé, Juan Manuel; and her two friends, Isabel and Bernardo. The action of the majority of the work revolves around the events leading up to and her reservations about her impending marriage, which mandates her departure from the childhood home and role. The play ends with her return to that home two days after the wedding and her father's subsequent suicide. During the course of the play we watch tensions mount among the characters, particularly between her mother and father, as Hernández dramatizes and implicitly challenges the tenets of family life in a most unsettling manner.

The play opens as night begins to fall in a comfortable, middle-class living room, marked more than anything by its complete normality. The first words are spoken by the protagonist Cecilia, "Bueno, Isabel . . . ¿Por qué te *molesta?*" (Okay, Isabel . . . Why does it *bother* you?) (*HR,* 84, emphasis added) to which her friend responds, "A ti debería *molestarte,* no a mí" (It should *bother you,* not me) (*HR*, 84). Thus, already in the opening moments of the play, characters twice use the term that epitomizes the work: *molestar,* to bother, to disturb; from the Latin *molestus,* heavy, hence painful, troublesome. Surely, *Los huéspedes reales* is a disturbing, troublesome play, marked by an abnormality that contests the visible ordinariness of the setting. The work is rendered even more troublesome by the fact that one is encouraged to read it as a contemporary version of the Electra complex.[2] Although such a reading is in many ways valid, perhaps even incontestable, it nonetheless occasions a sense of dis-ease, dis-comfort (at least in this critic), for while the focus on the Electra, implicitly incestuous, relationship between Ernesto and Cecilia *might* explain the twisted love/hate attachment between mother and daughter, there are too many elements of the play still left unexplained: among them, the unusual friendship between Cecilia and Isabel; the perversely destructive, if indeed socially "normal and natural" relationship between Juan Manuel and his lover; the convoluted bond between Elena and Ernesto; the mercurial rapport between Cecilia and Bernardo, which oscillates between platonic friendship and eroticism. None of the relationships of the play fall into the category of what we would like to label "normal"; much about the play is disturbing. Why?

Until relatively recently Western thought has been dominated by what Jacques Derrida has labeled phallogocentrism, in which the spoken word and the masculine have been consistently privileged in our history, philosophy, and sociopolitical structures.[3] Similarly, our literature and our literary criticism have been dominated by what might be called the Oedipus syndrome, a fixation that manifests itself in two modes: first by a privileging of the masculine as both writers and readers are immasculated, forced into reading and writing like men, and second, by an insistence on perceiving Oedipal relationships everywhere and then basing our literary analysis on that perception. Critic Judith Fetterley has analyzed the process of immasculation that informs our reading of texts as we are all, male and female, coerced into the role of "male" readers.[4] Parallel and simultaneous to this immasculation, there has been a perceptual and analytical emphasis on the father's position and power, which has led us to view him as the center or mediator of all desire, relationships, and action.[5] In the Oedipal syndrome we not only privilege but also become obsessed with the fictive father's symbolic phallus while we tend to efface or condemn all else, including the fictive mother and the feminine.[6] Like Freud, whose Oedipus complex was founded on a mythic, literary construct, we have formulated our cognizance of the literary world on a metaphor based on another metaphor and thus redoubled the fictive edifice, perhaps blinding ourselves (like Oedipus) as we bury ourselves in mythic chimeras. As a result we have often focused on only one half of the perceived, perceiving, and perceivable world: the masculine, the paternal, the phallic.[7]

Doubtlessly, the problem of immasculation (in both its manifestations) has affected women writers as much as readers since the former have often been told that they have to write like a man in order to be published, read by men, and thus be successful. Or so it has seemed. I suggest, however, that at times the immasculation has been only skin-deep and that beneath the visible surface there can be found a contravention of this process in texts that divert, subvert, and even invert the Oedipus syndrome while apparently affirming it.

A case in point is Luisa Josefina Hernández's *Los huéspedes reales,* a work that structures itself on the tension between the visible and the invisible, the spoken and the unspoken, on a number of levels as, wittingly or not, it diverts, inverts, and subverts the syndrome it seems to perpetuate. Most critical readings of *Los huéspedes reales* have immasculated, metaphorically at least, both the protagonist Cecilia and the playwright by emphasizing the potentially incestuous relationship and positing that the central object of desire is the father's phallus. I suggest, however, that the play's phallocentric ideas and the Electra complex are undermined or negated as much as they are supported. In fact, much as the society it portrays, the work proffers and endorses contradictory discursive fields as it sketches a site of resistance, albeit unwittingly, in which societal norms and models for normal or natural interpersonal relationships are questioned.[8] In this manner, *Los huéspedes reales* simultaneously colludes with *and* contests the Oedipus tradition on which those interpersonal relationships are perceived, hence the reader's troublesome sense of dis-ease.[9] The fact that all characters prove ill-adapted to ideal societal family and gender roles delineated by readers of Freud may point more to the inadequacy of the roles themselves than to some tragic flaw on the part of the characters. Indeed, Hernández's theatrical mirror discretely calls attention both to the inadequacy of drama as a mirror of reality and to the artificiality of the nature that mirror would pretend to reflect.[10] In this chapter I propose to read the play not as a mirror of the Oedipus tradition but as a potential site of resistance, reappropriation, and rereading of that tradition.

Let us note first that since Cecilia, the purported Electra here, does not aim to kill her mother (as in the Sophocles play) nor has her father been murdered by the latter, we must presume that the Electra evoked by most critics is the potentially incestuous Electra of psychoanalysis's Electra complex, not that of the classical myth, in which there seems to be no suggestion of incest or erotic desire between father and daughter.[11] In their search for a feminine counterpart to the Oedipus complex, in which the son wishes to eliminate the father and usurp his patriarchal, phallic position by marrying the mother, Freud's followers, among them Jung, labeled the potentially incestuous relationship between father and daughter and the resultant jealousy toward the mother, the Electra complex.[12] As described by psychoanalytical theory, the daughter wishes to replace (become?) the mother (as wife of the father). Although the Electra complex is one limited to females, the object of desire, the focus of attention, is still the metaphoric or virtual phallus, just as it is in the Oedipus complex.[13] Significantly, then, both the Oedipus and the Electra complexes are constructs (psychological myths?) that privilege the masculine.

By centering on the relationship between Ernesto and his daughter and labeling it "unnatural" or incestuous, critical analyses of *Los huéspedes reales* have also privileged the masculine and implied that the object of desire, which motivates all action in the play, is the symbolic or literal phallus of the father. I suggest, however, that the primary concern of the play is less Ernesto and phallic desire than Cecilia and, specifically, her rejection of both the phallic and the limitations imposed by gender roles. At the same time, I propose that all the action of the play revolves around her and the rite of passage (marriage) she undergoes. The work is clearly structured to begin and to end with her: she is the first and the last character to appear onstage and to speak. Indeed, her centrality is marked as early as the opening stage directions (which for the theater audience are unspoken and perhaps invisible), which describe the setting as the living room of Cecilia's house (*HR*, 84)—and each scene begins with a similar description. In a patriarchal society such as the Mexican and in view of the fact that Cecilia is presented as a young woman only twenty years old, it would be more appropriate to designate the home as that of Ernesto, that of Ernesto and Elena, or even that of the parents of Cecilia (the latter, had Hernández wished to draw more attention to Cecilia). The fact that the playwright specifically and repeatedly labels it Cecilia's home suggests, first, that Cecilia is the most important character in that house and, second, that there is a special tie between Cecilia and that house, whose two doors signal her two options: one leads to the interior of the house, the other, outside (*HR*, 84). Similarly, Cecilia has two options: she can pass from inside to outside, take her assigned position (that of wife and future mother) in a new home under the auspices of the husband and the sociopolitical structure of adulthood, or she can turn inward, refuse to pass, and turn back instead to the security of the childhood home and the pseudo gynecocentric world it implies.[14] She opts for the latter, making the final words of the play particularly significant: "Queremos estar *solas* . . . Y esta vez, el camino es largo, largo, largo" (We want to be *alone* . . . And this time the road is long, long, long) (*HR*, 138, emphasis added). The home, traditional center of matriarchal influence (and initial infant attachment according to Freud), will finally belong exclusively to and be dominated by the women, in fact, not just in appearances. But, as suggested by Cecilia's image of the long, long road, a relationship between mother and adult daughter, unmediated by the father, will not be an easy one, for it is one that has yet to be staged, written or imagined, described or prescribed.

In addition, except for scenes 3 and 5, in which Bernardo appears, all the scenes of the play take place in the closed, protective environment of the house.[15] Thus, it would not be difficult to understand the house as a synecdoche of the childhood Cecilia does not wish to leave. Indeed, as the moment for her departure nears, the stage directions describe her as having the most terrified face on earth (*HR*, 118), because in her own words, "llegó un mensajero envuelto en una capa de terciopelo y montado en un caballo blanco para anunciarme que debo partir" (a messenger arrived wrapped in a velvet cape and mounted on a white horse to announce to me that I should leave) (*HR*, 109). Later she recognizes that everyone wants her to go (*HR*, 119). Furthermore, after the marriage ceremony (the rite of passage), Ernesto notes that the house was the only thing Cecilia had and accuses Elena of having taken everything away from her without knowing if she was giving her anything in return (*HR*, 130), although, of course, the same accusation might be made of him when he commits suicide and leaves her fatherless.

Unlike the purported, if indeed metaphoric, object of desire in the Electra complex, an erotic relationship, with either her father or Juan Manuel, would more often than not seem to be precisely what Cecilia does not desire.[16] She yearns for permanent childhood and perhaps impossible, fairy-tale love, but not erotic, phallic love. Indeed, Hernández discourages our interpretation of Cecilia's desire as incestuous by having her recognize that she and her father are playacting when they talk about their love and by having her laugh

at it: after they recite the lines they *would* say in a love scene, Cecilia reacts by laughing and asks Ernesto if they really said those
things when he was twenty (*HR,* 100), certainly not the words of a
young woman trying to seduce her father and gain his sexual favors
(as some critics have implied), although perhaps the words of one
who recognizes the playacting involved in assuming adult gender
or sex roles.[17]

John Kenneth Knowles has attributed the tension and lack of
tranquillity that permeate the work and mark Cecilia's interaction
with the other characters (those bothersome elements) to Cecilia
being constantly under the influence of *sinrazón* (unreason or il-
logic), adding that she recognizes that she is totally absorbed by
love for her father and is willing to remain with him forever, at any
cost.[18] I suggest, however, that the *sinrazón* that dominates Cecilia
may well be the sociopolitical structure that requires the daughter,
in this case an only child and the center of the tiny universe of the
home, to give up this privileged position and to exchange it for that
of wife, subject (in the society portrayed) to domination and perhaps even abuse (psychological if not physical) by the husband, in
this case a particularly odious one. As Cecilia observes, she is
going to marry the person she most despises and cannot do anything to prevent it (*HR,* 109). It is the home itself and all it symbolizes (the past world of privilege) that Cecilia does not wish to leave
as much if not more than it is her father. Her resistance to the sociopolitical structure is particularly apparent near the end of the play
when she insists, in unequivocally nonerotic terms, that she is in
love with her house and her bed where she sleeps alone (*HR,* 135).
Let us note too that, although Cecilia repeatedly assures Ernesto
that they will die together, when he does die, she does not consider
suicide, but rather life, specifically among women (*solas,* alone,
without males) in the now maternal home. Thus, the conclusion of
the play, when she apparently decides to stay with her mother,
marks a site of resistance to the Oedipal syndrome as it signals the
possibility that her actions have been motivated by desire for self-
determination (which would include not relinquishing her privileged position in the home) and/or for a relationship of equality
with her mother or others, even as she recognizes how long the road
to those goals will be.[19]

Cecilia's resistance to the phallocentric is subtly portrayed as
early as the opening scene. There she interacts with two female
characters, Isabel and her mother, and wonders about the female's
preoccupation with the males and why they talk about them so
much (*HR,* 84) while recognizing the potential perniciousness of

those males to the rapport among females—"¿No te perjudicaría que yo tuviera un novio visible?" (Wouldn't it be detrimental to you if I had a visible boyfriend?) (*HR*, 85). Although males may motivate much of their discourse here, those males are distinctly and significantly absent, as they are again at the conclusion of the play. It is interesting that the male's invisibility here, his nonpresence, tacitly empowers the females and enables bonds between them, much as, I suggest, Ernesto's final suicide, nonpresence, will empower the wife and daughter and furnish the stage on which a different relationship between them might begin to be enacted.

The question of invisibility also underlines the play's resistance to traditional sociopolitical and gender roles insofar as only certain roles, certain possibilities—the phallocentric—are seen, can be seen, can be staged (because they have already been written, prescribed). Others are hidden from view in a complex game of hide-and-seek that simultaneously evokes and denies their existence. For example, after Ernesto's suicide, Cecilia states to Juan Manuel that this is a matter between her and her father and that she does not want him to see what will follow (*HR*, 138). What follows, what is a matter for her and her father, and what she (and perhaps Hernández) does not want seen, what is visually censored here (again perhaps because it has not yet been written, imagined) can only be a new or different rapport with the mother in the microcosmic world of the house of women. Similarly, also left essentially invisible (censored, unstaged) are Isabel's feelings for Cecilia, which are evoked only indirectly or articulated to an often absent Cecilia, in a pertinent play of revealing and concealing. As Isabel says, "Siento afecto por ti, Cecilia. Lamento que a veces . . ." (I feel affection for you, Cecilia. I am sorry that sometimes . . .) (*HR*, 86). Later, alone in Cecilia's room she whispers, "¿Por qué no aceptas que te quieran? Yo siempre te he querido mucho y nunca me has prestado atención" (Why won't you let yourself be loved? I have always loved you a lot and you have never paid attention to me) (*HR*, 124). She continues, "Si no sabes querer a las personas, deberías por lo menos apreciar su cariño . . . Vuelve en ti, Cecilia, no estés loca, Cecilia, por favor sé feliz" (If you don't know how to love people, you should at least appreciate their affection . . . Come to your senses, Cecilia, don't be crazy, Cecilia, please be happy) (*HR*, 124). Thus, Isabel's discourse, although frequently silenced (censored) by Elena, as is Cecilia's, asks Cecilia to be happy (as Ernesto also does) and not be crazy by rejecting that visible role that society has determined should be hers. Still, by positing that it is crazy to resist the dominant mode, her speech subtly proposes that the craziness is in the eyes of the beholder. In this respect another, different possibility is put forth: that the *sinrazón* may exist not in Cecilia but in the social structure that would impose very specific and limited gender roles and (perhaps as a result) discourage interpersonal relationships that are not triangular, mediated by, and centered on a male (father, husband, boyfriend). And, in spite of Elena's apparent willingness to impose the societal role on Cecilia, there are moments of the play that also point to her own resistance or potential resistance to the imposed gender roles. As she argues, in a statement whose multiple negatives mark the resentment and the resistance, "Durante veinte años no he pensado sino en ti, a nadie he servido sino a ti, no he salido a la calle más que contigo" (For twenty years I haven't thought of anything except you, I haven't served anyone but you, I haven't gone outside except with you) (*HR,* 113). Ernesto, however, views her dedication to him differently; he sees it as a trap embroidered with complex designs to prevent them from advancing to the future that he admits he neither needs nor wants.

At the same time, it cannot be irrelevant that both Elena and Ernesto acknowledge that Cecilia is incapable of loving anyone. Even her relationships with Bernardo and Ernesto, the two males for whom she does demonstrate some degree of fondness, are alternately marked by attraction and rejection and echo the antagonism between Elena and Ernesto that becomes visible during their various encounters. Although Elena recalls a past when their relationship was based on some mutual affection and perhaps even desire, Ernesto's discourse refutes that memory and functions as a weapon to hurt her. What is perhaps most unsettling throughout the play is the rapidity with which all the characters convert (by means of their speech) from visible victim, brunt of others' verbal aggression, to victimizer, verbal attacker.

Similarly, the most mistreated character of the play, Juan Manuel's lover, also takes her turn as aggressor when her speech avoids censorship and she makes visible her invisible relationship with Cecilia's fiancé. In fact, the question of appearances (or visibility) and female empowerment (or lack thereof) along with the question of phallic, heterosexual eroticism are brought to the foreground when his mistress phones Cecilia from a *casa de citas* (hotel that rents rooms by the hour), locus of illicit eroticism. The call highlights both the erotic that will structure Cecilia's future with Juan Manuel and the latter's capacity for oppressive and deceitful behavior (which again juxtaposes the visible and the invisible). Although Hernández overtly portrays Juan Manuel as a contemptible character with whom marriage should be unthinkable, his behavior, while exaggerated and made to appear particularly loathsome, is not totally alien to Mexican society's expectations of the male, that is, to his prescribed role as husband and father. As Elena notes with subtle irony, the male is expected to be unfaithful (*HR,* 103). And he is expected to dominate or even hurt her with her implicit consent or at least her silence (*HR,* 103). Thus, Juan Manuel has apparently only performed as he has been taught. As a result, he is not only not ashamed of the psychological havoc he has wreaked on his lover but, in fact, proud of having reduced her to a lesser being: "además *es culpa mía* que se encuentre como ahora, casi enloquecida . . . *Ahora no es nada . . . ya no es una persona*" (in addition *it is my fault* that she is in the state she is in, almost crazy . . . *Now she is nothing . . . she is no longer a person*) (*HR,* 91, emphasis added). Who could blame Cecilia for not choosing this future?

Again, perhaps Cecilia's problem is less incestuous desire for her father than her reluctance to accept an adult woman's role (wife and mother) and follow social mandates that disadvantage her. Poignantly, after her father has urged her to comply with "nature," to marry and seek her "felicidad de buena ley" (genuine, legitimate happiness; perhaps understood as mandated happiness) (*HR,* 136), she acknowledges that what he has called fraud is a fraud, but it is completely real and cannot be erased (*HR,* 136). Earlier, Cecilia insisted that if she were to marry, the chain of betrayals would begin, suggesting that she would do to her children what her parents are doing to her (*HR,* 117) because she is on the road to what should not be, and she does not know how to avoid it for there are forces that are pushing her (*HR,* 110). As a result, the ulcer, the sore, the Oedipus syndrome, the metaphoric journey on the metaphoric social road that prescribes and restricts gender role possibilities, will be perpetuated infinitely. I suggest, then, that the erotic, incestuous relationship that defines the Electra complex is negated more often than it is affirmed in Cecilia's character, if indeed not in Ernesto's, which may explain his suicide.[20] Let us recall that in the final scene Ernesto overtly reveals incestuous desire for Cecilia when, according to the stage directions, he looks at her as a man looks at a woman (*HR,* 136). Her reactions to him have generally been interpreted as an indication of her incestuous desire. Nonetheless, they might alternatively be interpreted as her comprehension of the agency of his erotic desire in her power over and conquest of the male other (in this case so that she can stay in her home, and paradoxically, in her nonerotic state).

On several occasions Knowles substantiates his Electra complex theory by referring to Cecilia's manipulative powers that make her worthy daughter of her mother.[21] Nonetheless, she is unquestionably more a mirror reflection of the males of the text since wife is precisely the role she wishes to avoid. The irony implicit in the text's resistance to the Oedipus syndrome is that in the Oedipal narrative the son would become (assume the place of) his father; in the Electra complex the daughter would become (assume the place of) her mother as erotic companion of the father. But such is exactly what Cecilia does not want. In this family romance, Cecilia seeks not to be her mother but, on the contrary and in the words of Marianne Hirsch, to disidentify with the mother.[22]

At the same time and perhaps even more important, Cecilia might well be designated worthy daughter of her father, for like him she wishes to halt the flow of time. Ernesto arrests the process by committing suicide; Cecilia attempts to halt it by forestalling the rite of passage and remaining in her nonphallic state within the pseudo gynecocentric home as daughter, not as wife. Early in the play her position is made clear when she insists, "no voy a crecer nunca" (I'm never going to grow up) (*HR,* 99). Later she is even more specific and adamant: "quiero quedarme aquí, *detenida,* como para que no me pase nada" (I want to stay here, *arrested/unmoving,* so that nothing happens to me) (*HR,* 116, emphasis added) and, like a child, promises Ernesto that if he will stop the process, she will be good (*HR,* 117). That is, she would have them remain forever like father and daughter in a state of permanent status quo, Garden of Eden, where being is static, not fluid, not a process of becoming, and definitely not phallic. Even Ernesto's words highlight her desire to freeze time: "El mal no es nuestra cercanía, es tratar de confundir y *detener el curso de las cosas*" (The evil/wrong is not our proximity, it is trying to confuse and *stop the course of things*) (*HR,* 117, emphasis added). Their sin will be to attempt to negate the course of events by refusing to follow the process of sociopolitical norms (considered natural although strictly cultural, manmade), by means of which the daughter must abandon her privileged position in the childhood home and exchange it for one of complicitous submission in the home of the husband.[23]

Significantly, however, her father is not the only character to whom she expresses a desire to halt the flow of time and remain as they are. As early as scene 3, after acknowledging her sexual inexperience, she dreams aloud to Bernardo, wishing that they could stay as they are (sexually inexperienced?) forever, living a century in this street (*HR,* 98), a street that perhaps evokes a certain freedom from familial, patriarchal society's roles. When again, at the end of the work, Cecilia reiterates her desire to stop the inevitable process and remain a child, Ernesto responds, "Eres una mujer y quieres ser una niña, eres mi hija y quieres hacer papeles de esposa" (You're a woman and you want to be a child, you are my daughter and you want to play the roles of wife) (*HR,* 136). Ironically, however, the roles Cecilia wishes to fulfill are those of mother: fix breakfast, take care of his clothes, sew on his buttons, read to him (*HR,* 135)—that is, play house. Since she refers to herself as his *niña* (little girl) and yet is capable of mothering him, keeping him dependent, it is perhaps logical that he should conclude that he is no longer a man (*HR,* 137).

Nonetheless, in the Oedipal syndrome the object of desire is not only the literal phallus but also the perceived power and position of the father. In this respect Hernández's work also marks a site of rereading, for Ernesto is anything but powerful. Indeed, throughout he is shown to be ineffectual and powerless, as incapable as Cecilia of assuming his assigned role within societal gender arrangements, in his case that of patriarch. Instead of taking care of and controlling her, he is faced with being taken care of and controlled by her as he is reduced to the role of a child. Thus, the rite of passage implicit in the marriage ceremony has been inverted, for Cecilia has not gone *out,* left the parental home for the home of the husband, to assume the socially acceptable (and visible) role of mother of another (a procreative, sexual being within society), but rather has turned back, inward, to assume that role (invisibly as it were) within the parental home but without the concurrent sexuality and procreativity (indeed, insisting that she is her own daughter [*HR,* 136]) of the visible role prescribed by society—prescribed and thus visible. It would appear then that the problem of all the characters is double: to find and enact the prescribed, visible role appropriate to the specific point in time while neither anticipating nor betraying the future.

Still, like many critics, Ernesto reproaches, not himself, but Elena for the catastrophe that results from Cecilia's marriage to Juan Manuel, even though he had refused to take action to stop that wedding. He himself articulates early in the play, although paradoxically in the third person and in the past tense (not unlike the tendency we find in psychoanalytical narrative), his decision to do nothing: "No quiso intervenir" (He refused to intervene) (*HR,* 94). As is typical in our Freudian, Oedipal systematics, the father's culpability is overlooked here and blame is placed on the child, who is accused of an Electra complex, or on the mother, who is accused of being a castrating female or of having insisted that the daughter live in and adjust to the phallocentric society that has been historically (if indeed patriarchally) prepared for her—the society that the mother is impotent to change for either herself or her daughter.[24] As Elena express it, *like all women,* Cecilia had to make a new home with a man (*HR,* 130, my emphasis). In this manner, Elena recognizes that within the sociopolitical structure roles are fixed for each stage of life, prescribed according to gender, and inescapable.[25] Yet, critics of the play have accepted Ernesto's accusations and words as more valid than Elena's in spite of the fact that he is a man who hits his wife (*HR,* 131) and calls his daughter a whore (*HR,* 137). Meanwhile, Elena believes she has only fulfilled her role and wants to continue to occupy her place (*HR,* 112), like the one Cecilia is to assume with Juan Manuel—"ese lugar preparado hace tanto tiempo" (that place prepared so long ago) (*HR,* 102).[26] And just as Cecilia would avoid her future role as Juan Manuel's wife and mother of his children, Elena, who is certainly not to be idealized in her maternal role, would abandon that role and return to her earlier role as young wife, before Cecilia's birth; as she states in another observation fraught with negatives, "Tengo la sensación que desde que ella nació no hemos estado juntos nunca . . . No hemos puesto atención en nuestros sentimientos y en nuestros deseos sino en ella, siempre en ella" (I have the feeling that since she was born we haven't ever been together . . . We haven't focused on our feelings and our desires but rather on her, always on her) (*HR,* 102).

I have discussed elsewhere the relation between marriage and the rite of passage.[27] It is important for our purposes here, however, to recognize that the rite of passage marks the preparation for and the assumption of adult gender roles and sexuality (children are usually, if indeed erroneously, considered asexual), as defined by the given society. As a result, the effects of this rite of passage on the male and the female differ significantly. Theoretically, the ritual, the marriage, will offer the son passage from his adolescent role of semidependence to one of power and supremacy. In primitive societies, the rite of passage signals the boy's acceptance into manhood as he leaves the world of the women and enters that of the men.[28] Metaphorically at least, he will realize the desires of the Oedipus complex: he will visibly become the (a) father as he marries the (a) mother (to be). He will gain a father's control of the (a) mother/wife and the children. Within the world of the new family, he will assume the power and role, the phallic position, he believes his father already has and will imitate, reflect him.

Within the context of the Hernández play this change of male

status is made apparent when Juan Manuel announces their marriage by stating that he is going to invite her to a faraway place
forever (*HR,* 89), a statement that heralds permanent, major change
and movement from the inside to the outside (a faraway place).
Then, when Juan Manuel informs Cecilia that he wants to marry
her, he revealingly adds that they will make a home together, have
several children, bring them up (*HR,* 90), thereby signaling the start
of the process (the road repeatedly evoked) that will preclude the
prerogatives she has enjoyed in her privileged position as only
daughter in this family. At the same time, he also alludes to the
beginning of what she later calls the fraud—the education of children to conform to the same old patterns.[29] Ironically, of course, the
activities to which he refers are ones for which society will hold
her responsible while overlooking and perhaps even condoning his
inactivity and lack of participation, just as so many critics have
overlooked Ernesto's lethargy and subsequent willingness to cast
all blame on Elena.

Even more important, throughout this scene the stage directions
and other kinesic indicators consistently mark Juan Manuel as a
contemptible being. This is the first time he has spoken with Cecilia
since she learned of his mistress, a factor that seems to have motivated his decision to announce his marriage plans to her, but, instead of offering her some form of explanation or even consolation
for this breach, he employs a diversionary technique and announces
that he has a surprise for her. In this respect, he uses the word to
hide rather than to reveal or communicate, even when he states his
intention to reveal. Ironically, of course, she has already received
the surprise in the form of the phone call (discourse that does discover). At the end of a dramatic delay, when he finally tells her
what he has in mind, both his discourse and the kinesic code belie
his sincerity. Not only does Hernández have him prevaricate, when
he tells her that he has never been able to think about anyone but
her (*HR,* 90), she also has him follow his words with an inappropri-
ate gesture—laughter. To add insult to injury, he assures her that he
could not marry anyone else because she is so simple—a strange
but revealing basis for a marital relationship, which again signals
the confrontation of contradictory discourses that suggest that the
future wife must be an eternal child, but one who has abdicated her
earlier privileges. Cecilia's responses, however, bring both his duplicity and the paradox of societal expectations into focus. She
forces him into the explanation that he, as the stage directions note
in a curious paradox of visibility and invisibility, "*pensaba pasar
por alto*" (*planned to ignore*) (*HR,* 90). Cecilia makes him articu-

late, make visible, what he and much of our androcentric society would prefer to leave invisible, unarticulated—that their relationship (a product of contradictory expectations) will be based on both an imbalance of power and insincerity (role playing).[30]

The imbalance of power in their relationship (an imbalance that seems to structure all the relationships of the play) and his sense of prepotency continue to surface as he tells Cecilia she understands nothing, as he articulates, perhaps unwittingly, his perverse pleasure at the destructive power he has wielded over his lover, as he speaks to her as one might to a child, and as he reminds her of her own impotence, telling her that women like her cannot do anything (*HR,* 92). Admittedly these concepts are taken out of context, but nevertheless, viewed in juxtaposition to each other, they do reflect a pattern. This pattern continues in his question to her about whether she will know how to administer all that he will give her, a gift he expects her to accept without complications (*HR,* 90). The question itself, of course, implies some form of innate incompetence on her part; he will give, she will receive (preferably eagerly) and administer (but probably poorly). That is, she will be kept in her childlike state, but the few privileges that accompany that state will be taken away. At the same time, because of the deceptive nature of his own discourse and kinesics (his theatrical performance), he misreads her reactions, both verbal and physical: he views her anger and aggression with self-flattery and interprets them as signs of her love for him rather than her disdain since it is inconceivable to him that anyone might perceive him differently than he views himself. He expects her to be a mirror to reflect and glorify his image, his assumed role. Revealingly, the theatrical role he assumes even within the play creates the world as he would have it rather than mirroring nature. While he cannot or will not see beyond the mirror of his own reaction, the play itself resists his reading and bothers us.

Later he will become bothered himself, annoyed with her when *"le parece que se pone en cuestión su autoridad de futuro marido"* (*it seems to him that his authority as future husband is being questioned) (HR,* 105), that is, when she resists, refuses to accept "without complications" the assigned role with all its inherent contradictions, and Elena will have to warn her that she is forgetting her position (*HR,* 106). Thus, Hernández clearly establishes the despicable nature of Juan Manuel's personality and the fact that the marriage ritual will provide him with dominance over Cecilia as it forces her into a less than desirable role/position. As Isabel notes, offering to flee from this future with her, "Ya no podrás escoger nada ni hacer nada. Todo estará hecho y decidido" (You will no longer be able to choose or do anything. Everything will be done and decided) (*HR*, 119). In this future, Cecilia's status will be that of a possession; as Juan Manuel states, she is "todo lo que no he *tenido* nunca . . . La idea de *tener* un hogar, una casa decente con una mujer virtuosa es lo que me ha dado fuerza . . . Estoy orgulloso de ser aceptado por la única mujer que considero digna de ser mi esposa" (all that I have never *had* . . . The idea of *having* a home, a decent house with a virtuous woman is what has given me strength . . . I am proud of being accepted by the only woman I consider worthy of being my wife) (*HR*, 101, emphasis added). Indeed, let us not forget that one of the reasons Juan Manuel has chosen to marry Cecilia is that his mistress is a woman who betrayed the future (*HR*, 91), betrayed *his* future: she is already married, possessed by someone else. Nonetheless, at the same time, Juan Manuel's words about Cecilia are subtended by two implicit ironies. First, he has not been accepted by her, and second, he wants to have a home with a virtuous woman but feels no need to be virtuous himself. That is, the image of himself he wants her to reflect will be a mythic and distorted one. Hernández, however, offers a subtle explanation for this exaggeration of self-importance and self-imposition on the part of Juan Manuel, who declares that he wants his home with Cecilia to be everything his own has not been. In his own words, "yo crecí en el más completo desorden . . . mi padre no supo ser un padre y mi madre no pudo resistir a . . . tantas cosas" (I grew up in the most complete disorder . . . my father did not know how to be a father and my mother could not resist . . . so many things) (*HR*, 101). Lest the same occur in the new family, he will assume an overly compensatory, dictatorial, patriarchal role and play the role (in the most theatrical sense) he thinks should be that of the male. Again, while the society portrayed would reduce the possibilities for adult roles to two—mother or father—the fact that none of the characters can fill the roles as scripted suggests the play's resistance and challenge to the roles.

It seems clear that it is the phallocentric future of society's gender arrangements that Cecilia rejects: "Lo de siempre. La interminable cosa que a todo el mundo le sucede: lo que no puede evitarse" (The same old thing. The never-ending thing that happens to everyone: what cannot be avoided) (*HR*, 98). She spurns the future, the empty dishes at the metaphoric banquet, the role playing without love, which leaves one hungry, as is Elena: "un banquete para huéspedes reales. Cubiertos de plata, vasos de oro, un clavel rojo cerca de cada plato . . . ¡y las fuentes vacías!" (a banquet for royal guests. Silver cutlery, gold glasses, a red carnation near each plate . . . and the platters empty!) (ibid.).[31] Disidentifying with and rejecting the predetermined adult role in society, that of wife and mother (particularly as enacted by her own mother), Cecilia herself sums up her position: "la hija soy yo. Yo soy la niña, la mimada, la irresponsable" (I am the daughter. I am the child, the pampered one, the irresponsible one) (*HR*, 135). Cecilia would be (remain) her own creation, her own possession, and repudiate the cultural gender definitions. Let us recall that in the first scene the male is defined by his capacity to possess or have women when Elena assures the young women that the man who does not *have* women is less manly (*HR*, 87, my emphasis). The implication is that in order to be a woman, Cecilia must be possessed.[32] Indeed, as Ernesto states in the final scene when Juan Manuel tries to return Cecilia to him as if she were merchandise purchased at a store, "¿No es suya? ¿No la quería usted?" (Isn't she yours? Didn't you want her?) (*HR*, 134). Nevertheless, the complexity of the Hernández work rests in the tension between the visible and the invisible, between contradictory discursive fields, for as defined by Elena the man not only has women, but is had by them: "Con ellas vive, por ellas se doblega, a ellas se entrega" (He lives with them [women], he yields to them, he surrenders/devotes himself to them) (*HR*, 87). Thus, nothing is as simple as it seems; all is marked by tension-producing contradiction. It is perhaps this very tension—not always visible—that bothers us as the play simultaneously supports and undermines the contradictory positions and discourse that shape our extratextual world.

Ironically, of course, in the final analysis the rite of passage, the wedding, does take place, and although Cecilia later returns home, seemingly turning back in time (as Elena would also), home is no longer the same after Ernesto's suicide. Now she will have to begin what she labels the long road, the inevitable and interminable state of becoming, but now in a gynecocentric environment in fact, not just in appearance. Thus, as I stated at the beginning, she rejects the symbolic phallus as implied in both an erotic relationship and societal gender roles, specifically the traditional feminine role of submission, a role that, revealingly, her mother rarely assumes as anything more than the most superficial mask. Indeed, Cecilia's calm in the face of her father's suicide suggests her recognition that now she will be able to remain in her home, in her childlike state, for now her mother will accept her. Could this be what she desired all along? Is this what must not be seen, what must remain invisible in the end?

And what is this long road to which Cecilia refers? The answer perhaps is to be found at the end of scene 5, the halfway point of the play. Here Cecilia speaks with Bernardo of her desire to remain forever in the street, just as they are. They have decided not to become lovers (again to remain just as they are, avoiding, rejecting the erotic) but to enjoy the little time they have left before her marriage, in their platonic adolescent state, in some sense outside of the normal flow of time, pretending that it is not inevitably moving forward. As Bernardo proposes, first employing the path/road image, "Caminemos por el sendero de la sinrazón . . . Ya sabemos que el orden, de algún modo, ha de restablecerse" (Let's take the path of unreason/illogic . . . We already know that order, somehow, will reestablish itself) (*HR,* 112)—there is no escaping the sociopolitical structures. But Cecilia images the path/road, the flow of time, less unidirectionally, imagining a river (traditional image of time) that flows forward and backward at once, as well as a wind that blows from north to south and vice versa, and a street that goes up and down at the same time (ibid.). And because the road here is described as short, it presumably does not require all their effort. On the other hand, the road evoked in the final scene is long and thus will require all their effort, perhaps more than anything because it goes against what is considered the natural flow of time and the grain of society with its imposition of phallocentric relationships (adulthood, erotic relationships, abandonment of the home of the parents to become parents). In this way, the play's conclusion marks the site of resistance. Not only does it avoid the narrative closure of traditional literature ("and they lived happily ever after"), but it also highlights that the end is not *the* end but rather *an* end, and specifically one that marks the beginning of the struggle and emphasizes the immensity of the effort that will be required to change gender arrangements and conceive of new possibilities both inside and outside of literature.

Frank Dauster is certainly correct in his analysis of the ritual form in the play and in his emphasis on the feast.[33] I would only expand his choice of myth, for *Los huéspedes reales* might also be read as a modern rendition of the story of Iphigenia, the other daughter of Clytemnestra and Agamemnon, the daughter who believed (as did her mother) that she was going to her wedding when in fact she was going to be sacrificed for the "good" of society, for the war effort.[34] Cecilia, of course, is more perceptive than Iphigenia and recognizes the metaphoric death inherent in the ritual marriage. When Juan Manuel announces that he is going to invite her to somewhere far away and forever, she cynically wonders if they are going to attempt suicide together (*HR,* 90). She further highlights the death motif when she questions, before consenting to the marriage, if the other woman (his lover) will inevitably die (*HR*, 105). It is significant, too, that in the story of Iphigenia, once the process is set in motion, Agamemnon, not unlike Ernesto, is too weak and cowardly to confront society (in Agamemnon's case, the army), acknowledge that the sacrifice is wrong, and act with strength and conviction to prevent it. In both cases, the paternal figure is impotent to provide the protection the daughter needs—the metaphoric phallic power and discourse are a sham, as Jacques Lacan has long insisted. Ultimately, both Iphigenia and Cecilia go to the sacrifice with courage. Iphigenia is saved by the goddess Diana. Whether or not Cecilia is saved we cannot know, for the play ends as Ernesto commits suicide. Because he precludes the future and metaphorically substitutes for Cecilia as the sacrificial victim society seems to demand, he cannot be killed (in the future) by the unfaithful and treacherous Clytemnestra, as was Agamemnon in a later installment of the Greek myth. In this respect Hernández precludes a simplistic reading of the ancient myths, recognizing that it is merely a question of where we focus, where we arbitrarily establish our beginnings and endings in our attempt to provide an illusory mirror of progress. Different starting and ending points would produce quite a different, even contradictory myth. Thus, we might perhaps better label the principal conflict in the Hernández play as that between Cecilia and the phallocentric, patriarchal society, of which Ernesto is but a feeble, ineffectual representative.

Again we return to the notion that nothing is quite as it has appeared. Everything has been marked by contradiction. What appeared to be love was not. What seemed to be hatred between mother and daughter may not have been. What we interpreted as the object of desire, the phallus, was precisely what was not desired. The banquet, symbol of social ritual and role playing, was empty, foodless—a signifier that negates itself. And most important, what we labeled natural was not. The marriage, part of the "natural chain of events" is shown to be a process of socialization, inevitable perhaps, but man-made and supplemental. In his analysis of the play as a classic tragedy, Knowles posits that the principal movement within the genre is the reestablishment of the order and equilibrium lost when a "natural law" has been violated.[35] As Hernández shows, however, the law is anything but natural. The reflection itself is inevitably distorted. Surely, the theatrical mirror here reflects not nature but the sociopolitical inventions we have designated as natural.

2

Authoring the Scene, Playing the Role: Mothers and Daughters in Griselda Gambaro's *La malasangre*

ONE OF THE MOST RESPECTED PLAYWRIGHTS IN ARGENTINA, GRISELDA Gambaro is perhaps best known for her four early plays: *El desatino* (The Blunder), *Las paredes (The Walls), Los siameses* (The Siamese Twins), and *El campo (The Camp),* written and staged between 1963 and 1968.[1] As these works indicate, her principal thematic concerns are oppression—political or interpersonal, direct or indirect—and our capacity to victimize others. Indeed, Gambaro maintains that the only two postures available to human beings are those of oppressor or oppressed.[2] She carries this notion further in some of her plays by dramatizing the possibility that one assumes the role of oppressor in response to one's prior experience as the oppressed. Nonetheless, Gambaro's early plays were criticized for her apparent lack of concern with the oppression of women. The playwright responded to that criticism by proposing that to speak about women, there is nothing better than to speak about relations among men.[3] Significantly, however, her later works evince a higher incidence of female characters, a change that seems motivated by her recognition first, that our sociopolitical structures and their tendency for biological essentialism mark women as more likely victims of oppression, and second, that women rather than men might represent the norm, human beings in general, "everyperson."[4]

Particularly successful in bringing female characters from the wings to center stage are four of her works from the 1980s: *El despojamiento (The Strip), Real envido* (Royal Gambit), *La malasangre (Bitter Blood),* and *Antígona furiosa* (original title maintained in translation). Although the immediate, historical referent for each is unquestionably the sociopolitical situation in Argentina during the late 1970s and early 1980s, the plays also address the question

53

of oppression in more universal terms.[5] At the same time, however, if indeed more subtly, all four also probe the position of women in contemporary society and portray the female as an actress. Although not always conscious of it, the woman in these Gambaro works is inevitably compelled to assume a sociopolitically acceptable role predicated on oppression and victimization, generally her own.[6] In the coming pages I would like to examine *La malasangre,* written in 1981 and staged in 1982. In it the two female characters serve dual functions. First, they depict "everyperson" and what Gambaro perceives as "everyperson's" alternately subject and object relation to oppression and the abuse of power. At the same time, however, they function as synecdoches, in both the biological and the sociopolitical realms, of what are specifically feminine roles, mother and daughter, roles which, as Gambaro demonstrates, are just that in the sociopolitical arena: parts to be played.[7] Gambaro is not to be accused of biological essentialism here, however, for her point is that although biological factors may mark the actor/actress's suitability for a given role, the role itself is still unquestionably superimposed, an assumed mask, created by and dependent on perceptions that have been framed and limited by an often unacknowledged agent (director/author).[8] And while dramatizing the role playing of the female characters, Gambaro subtly underscores the fallibility and fragility of the roles as author(iz)ed by our sociopolitical structures.[9] We find not only that we paradoxically perceive the mother role alternately as both the romanticized, perfect Madonna (the ideal that Dolores perhaps would become) and the Freudian castrating mother (the reality that the mother seems to have become), but that the images themselves are projections, literary creations, author(iz)ed by either fear or wishful thinking. No female is either, yet every female at times assumes each of these antithetical roles.

Set around 1840 at the height of the Rosas regime in Argentina, *La malasangre* is the dramatization of totalitarian power both inside and outside the family and again portrays the capacity of the victim to convert to victimizer. Although the entire play takes place within the family home (revealingly decorated completely in shades of red), spectators soon learn that the father, ironically named Benigno, the good father/god, rules with an iron fist in both arenas.[10] Outside he beheads those who oppose him, and their bloody heads, euphemistically dubbed melons, are paraded through the streets. Inside, with the help of his henchman Fermín, he tyrannizes his wife, daughter, and the latter's tutor. The play opens as Benigno is about to choose a new tutor for his daughter, Dolores. He selects Rafael from among the group of candidates, believing that his hunchback will prevent the wife and daughter from becoming physically attracted to him (as he suspects they were to the last tutor). Dolores's initial antagonism toward Rafael is followed by a series of antithetical gestures (often inherently theatrical) that sometimes would seduce him, sometimes spurn him. She eventually charms him into falling in love with her perhaps because as she had earlier acknowledged, once her father forbids something she wants it even more (*LM,* 72). Although Rafael recognizes that she fell in love too quickly (*LM,* 81), he succumbs to the allure of her plan to escape from the father's realm of influence to an idealized paradise across the river. The mother discovers their plans, reveals them to the father, and Rafael is killed. In the last scene his body is returned to Dolores, for which she is grateful, in a thinly veiled allusion to the "disappeared" in Argentina. Finally, having reviled the mother for her role in the atrocity, Dolores defies the tyrant himself, screaming that she hates him and is no longer afraid. She is dragged out of the room, and the play ends with the father's reference to the silence that remains after her prolonged scream.

Like *El despojamiento* and *Real envido, La malasangre* offers us a spectacle of the female characters in their roles as actresses, in both senses of the word, although in this play, the women's status as dramatis personae might be easily overlooked.[11] Since their roles are precisely the ones we expect of women (mother and daughter), we perceive them as natural and tend to forget they are roles. Nonetheless, in *La malasangre* the unnamed mother is a role player so completely absorbed in and by her role as victim, object of both physical and verbal violence and oppression, that she is seldom capable of perceiving the possibility of any other role for either herself or other women, including her daughter, part and potential mirror of herself. Like the young man of *Las paredes,* she would probably serve as her own jailer once the prison doors were opened. But the mother here is ostensibly even more despicable than the victimized protagonists we encounter in other Gambaro plays, for while they help no one, they harm only themselves, or so we might have been inclined to believe. Gambaro proposes here, however, that by passively accepting our role as victim on one stage (in this case in the family drama), we facilitate the continuation of that role either on another stage (the public, the national) or in another person when we readily convert into the oppressor or the oppressor's lackey, deluded into believing that by doing so we derive some of his power. When the mother of *La malasangre* does act, she betrays her daughter, bars her escape from that tyrannical environment, and perpetuates the system of oppression that also subjugates her.

More important, in this work Gambaro dramatizes the link between political oppression outside the home and the oppression of women inside it. Etymologically the term *violence* is related to violation, and it is significant that in *La malasangre* much of the oppression and violence carries sexual, erotic overtones and borders on violation.[12] In fact, the patriarch, the father, specifically employs erotic gestures to reduce his victims (male or female, political or interpersonal) to the (perceived) state of mindless, physical objects. He accomplishes this principally by the (mis)use or (mis)appropriation of ostensibly normal gestures that may not be immediately identifiable as oppressive. For example, laughter, normally a kinesic sign of merriment or delight, indicates both violence and violation as it is employed here first by the father and later by the daughter. Spasmodic, almost machinelike, and forced, the father's laughter is juxtaposed with physical violence in the opening scene as Fermín brutally mistreats one of the candidates. Each successive time the father laughs, he intends to dehumanize or violate another character, often but not necessarily female. His ever-inappropriate laughter functions to underline his own superiority and to objectify others as he converts them into inferior things, mere actors, almost automata on whom he can impose a role and whom he can direct, in the most theatrical sense.[13] Thus, he laughs as he orders his wife, "Traete tu bordado y sentate allí . . . Pero te autorizo a ausentarte" (*LM,* 66) (Bring your needlework and sit down over there . . . But you can leave anytime) (*BB,* 118).[14] Similarly, he laughs when he commands Rafael to disrobe and later when he forces him to dance with Fermín.

I would suggest that Benigno's laughter mirrors his propensity for decapitating his enemies, "los salvajes, inmundos, asquerosos" (*LM,* 71) (those filthy, disgusting beasts) (*BB,* 122), that is, those to whom he would deny the status of full personhood.[15] In this play, the decapitations literalize the perceived, metaphoric separation of mind and body that has structured Western thought since the time of the ancients and that in many ways parallels the separation of spirit and flesh (as religious discourse is wont to label it).[16] However we label it, the possession of a mind/spirit is presumed to distinguish the human being from the animal and the latter's implicit inferiority. On the one hand, the decapitations of the play signal censorship insofar as the tyrant denies the other the use of his/her head both literally and metaphorically. Without a head one cannot think, speak, see, hear. But at the same time, without a head one cannot be intellectual rather than carnal (*puta* [whore], as the father labels the mother), that is, have access to what is implicitly a superior category and full human status. In this respect, the father's laughter and statement to the mother that she should bring her embroidery but she can leave anytime reinforce this separation by reminding her (and the spectator) that she is mere flesh, destined for mindless activities (embroidery). Even more revealing, this mindless activity, the embroidery, simultaneously, if indeed metaphorically, beheads her in another way, for it distracts her by keeping her from thinking and from seeing (other than her embroidery). In fact, in scene 7 her concentration on her needlework prevents her from seeing Juan Pedro's erotic assaults on Dolores. Yet the mother apparently fails to recognize both the ploy and the role into which she is cast, the metaphoric decapitation (do not see, do not think, do not speak other than what the tyrant would have you think, speak, see) that disempowers her. But the metaphoric beheading is bidirectional and effects the other characters (as well as the spectator), for by means of her embroidery (literal or metaphoric) the mother becomes the agent who perpetuates, albeit unwittingly, both the tyrant's mores and that which he would have others see. As we know, embroidery makes more esthetically pleasing, pretty, what is not. Such is precisely the function of her verbal embroidery when, in reference to the literal beheadings that Benigno frequently orders, she assures Dolores, "Quien te oye puede pensar que corta cabezas todo el día. Es bondadoso. *No le gusta hacerlo* . . . Se le oponen y no lo dejan elegir" (*LM,* 84, emphasis added) (Whoever hears you would think he cuts heads off all day long. He's good-natured. *He doesn't like to do it* . . . They go against him and give him no choice) (*BB,* 133, emphasis added).[17] Obviously, her words here, like so many others in this text (*melons,* among them) fail to encompass reality. On the contrary, they distract from, embroider, and cover that reality, for, as Benigno earlier stated, if indeed in another context, he has already chosen (*LM,* 63). He does elect or choose, and what he chooses, metaphorically and literally, is his own head with its implicit superiority over the others whom he defines as mere (inferior) body. And, more specifically what he has overtly chosen here is the tutor, who in turn will act as his agent and presumably oversee, choose, what goes into Dolores's head. By means of both his laughter and the decapitations, Benigno author(ize)s his version of reality, the official one that affirms his superiority, his possession of a head. Similarly, Benigno metaphorically beheads the candidates in the opening scene. By discussing only their visible, physical attributes, he converts them into or perceives them as bodies separated from minds, and this in spite of the fact that they are potential tutors, not lovers: he notes that one is good-looking and accuses his wife of liking the face of another (*LM*, 60).

The sexual innuendoes and erotic gestures that punctuate the work highlight the similarities among the metaphoric decapitations. Indeed, Benigno emphasizes the affinity among the women and the other potential victims when he notes that Dolores needs a "mano fuerte en guante de seda. Es lo que necesitan las damas . . . Y no sólo las damas" (*LM*, 89) (strong hand, soft touch [literally, in a silk glove]. That's what the ladies need . . . And not only the ladies) (*BB*, 138). And this strong hand in a silk glove often controls by means of gestures that eroticize the other, reducing him/her to a body without a mind. Significantly, although the play opens with a scene replete with Christian symbolism, the erotic soon comes to the forefront. Benigno is entirely motionless (*LM*, 59) and is looking out the window when the mother enters with wine, symbol of blood, perhaps hers, and utters the ambiguous words, "Acá está el vino" (ibid.) (Here's the wine) (*BB*, 112).[18] Does "Here's the wine" (sacrificial blood) refer to the wine decanter or to herself, supplier of that sacrificial blood? His sarcastic response as he asks why two glasses and who is drinking with him (*LM*, 59) not only reinforces her servitude and denies her equality with him but also provides the motif that will be kinesically repeated throughout the play as characters are elevated or demeaned in status according to whether they are allowed (almost ritualistically) to partake of wine or drink, suggesting perhaps that only those with heads can drink.[19] Metaphorically, she may be the bearer of the wine/sacrificial blood, but she is not allowed to participate in the ritual by consuming it or receiving its benefits, for she is perceived as carnal (body/matter) rather than intellectual or spiritual (head/mind).[20] Furthermore, his sarcastic question to the mother about who is drinking with him is followed by his observation that it would be better if she did not think (*LM*, 59), as he metaphorically beheads her again, perceives her solely as a biological role, flesh. The erotic is further foregrounded with his gesture of physical violation, for he rudely touches her breast (*LM*, 60) as he ironically calls her his wise little wife, doubly emphasizing her corporeality and lack of mind or intellect. His fear that she might find one of the candidates attractive leads him to call her a *puta* (ibid.) (whore) (*BB*, 113) and decree that she will look only at his face.

While casting her as mere biological, unthinking presence, he would control not only her actions but also her field of vision; like Natán of *Real envido*, she will see only what the "king" decrees.[21]

And what the king decrees is that she see, focus on, only his face, his head, the fact that he has a mind and by implication the status of full personhood that he would deny her. The motif of fields of vision (perceptions) and their limitation by the despot evokes the overt issue of censorship as well as the more covert issue of how we see or perceive anything, of how perspective or vision (for example, our image of mothers and daughters and their respective roles, again as bodies, physically defined, rather than as minds, philosophically or psychologically defined) is limited, defined, and controlled by sociopolitical institutions (church, state, educational systems). In her assigned role, whore, the mother will say and see only what Benigno deems appropriate. But in fact, the framing, the limitation of perception extends far beyond his immediate control over the mother. When Benigno first calls the mother a whore in the opening moments of the play, certainly spectators can see that it is he who behaves lasciviously, not her. Nonetheless, the imputation of the epithet *whore* to her tends to shift the perceptual frame (as it does in real life) and encourage spectators to shift the blame along with it and view her rather than him as licentious and reprehensible. As he states, "Yo dicto la ley" (*LM,* 60) (I dictate the law) (my translation). His word is law, the official version; all will be seen as he dictates.[22] But, the dictation/diction precedes the law; the word precedes the fact. He encourages all to perceive her according to his terms, that is in strictly erotic terms, without a head.

In this way, the term *whore* here not only leads us to focus on the mother's carnality and guilt but also calls to mind her capacity to "sell out," to be a willing collaborator with the despot. But what Gambaro dramatizes here is a metonymic inversion, for (1) collaboration has been confused with and projected as the erotic, and (2) at this point, her complete collaboration is still wishful thinking, projection on his part, for while she is subservient and obeys for the most part, she does not directly collaborate until the end, and even then as we will see, not quite completely. Nonetheless, and unlike the male collaborator Fermín (who is never referred to in erotic terms), the female collaborator is "feminized down to the very bottom [of the ladder of hierarchically ordered positions in relation to the ultimate power], the place of the prostitute."[23] In *Real envido* (written the year before *La malasangre*) Gambaro demonstrated that the use of the same term to refer to unrelated signifieds leads us to confuse the two and erroneously impute all the qualities of one to the other.[24] Indeed, one of the problems with metaphors is that we tend to perceive only similarities and lose sight of the differences. Similarly, here Benigno's use of *whore* in reference to her "willing" sellout carries with it and inflicts on her all the erotic connotations of the word, erotic connotations that are not valid but that serve to degrade her more as they cast the shadow of blame and prurience on her while deflecting attention from his responsibility. As Susanne Kappeler has noted,

> the willing victim is termed whore, a name of unambiguous femininity. We use the term prostitution metaphorically to describe collaboration, libertinism, selling out. The different terms in this system of masculine semantics carry . . . connotations of differing degrees of blame. This naming is based on the look at the represented scenario, with the customary focus on the hero and his objectified victims . . . and so leads to the absurdity of blaming the victim . . . Responsibility has been hidden in favour of blame . . . The categories of slave-complement to the master, of the woman-masochist-complement to the male sadist, are the result of conditioning . . . an invention and creation of the master-mind . . . They are engendered by the master plot, with which the responsibility remains.[25]

In this way Benigno casts the mother in the erotic role to degrade her and keep her in her place while metaphorically washing his hands of his responsibility for her degraded position and his role in it as he would lead all to view her role (whore, carnality incarnate) as natural. Again Gambaro highlights what happens when the tyrant imposes (and others accept) metaphors that are only half valid: others are blinded into seeing only half-truths, framed segments of the larger picture, which benefit those in power and elide (remove from the frame) their responsibility in acts of oppression.

Significantly, this pattern of reducing the other to mindless flesh is repeated in scene 7. This time the agent is Juan Pedro and the object, the daughter Dolores (who is soon to be his wife). At one point he grabs her breast (*LM*, 91), at another he throws himself on top of her and paws her (*LM*, 100), at still another he presses her hand against his penis (*LM*, 101). The repetition of the kinesic signs emphasizes the similarities between the father and the suitor. Specifically, Benigno has chosen (again note he is always the one who chooses/elects) the suitor, who with his daughter will form the future couple, the future mother and father, and who, like Benigno, will decorate his house entirely in red and control every aspect of their shared life. Juan Pedro even assures Dolores that her tutor is "superfluo. Ya sabe lo que una mujer debe saber y el resto . . . se lo enseñaré yo" (ibid.) (superfluous. You already know what any woman should know and the rest . . . I'll teach you) (*BB*, 149)—that is, her head will be controlled by him, now taken out of the father's

hands and placed in his. Juan Pedro's lewd, brutally lascivious gestures toward her mirror Benigno's toward the mother and similarly
function to reduce her to an erotic object, a toy, each time his "audience" (the mother) looks away and he can drop his mask of ideal
suitor. His physical attacks, like the father's laughter and metaphoric beheadings, function like the internal frame in René Magritte's painting *Les liaisons dangereuses* (The Dangerous Liaisons).
In that canvas another painting/mirror within the painting frames
the female subject in such a way that only her naked body is visible;
her head is elided, left outside the frame, ostensibly of no relevance.
Similarly, the framing gestures of both men in the Gambaro play
would remind mother and daughter alike of their incompleteness,
that they are flesh, body not mind, and specifically flesh that is vulnerable to the attacks of the patriarch or patriarch-to-be. As Dolores
is repeatedly sexually assailed by Juan Pedro while her mother "ab-
sents herself" in her embroidery (also metaphorically leaving her
head outside the frame), Gambaro has Dolores arrive at the realiza-
tion that "nada es tan simple como uno cree. Y nada tampoco tan
complicado" (*LM*, 101) (nothing is as simple as one thinks. And
nothing is so complicated either) (*BB*, 148). She indirectly acknowledges that her father is not unique, that his erotic aggression
toward her mother epitomizes a pattern that conflates the terms of
eroticism and victimization and spills over into the public arena.
But like her mother in her role of blindness, Dolores "plays dumb,"
consciously assumes the role of the mindless fool, already decapi-
tated:

> Rodeada estoy de imbéciles
> y simulo que soy tonta
> los imbéciles me creen
> y me hago la marmota. (*LM*, 89)

> [I am surrounded by imbeciles
> and pretend I am stupid
> the imbeciles believe me
> so I keep on acting dumb.] (*BB*, 138)

In the society portrayed, in which the powerful males are ever
willing to oppress others through the instrument of the erotic (a separation of mind and body), to be a female in the private sector (in
the family) is to be perceived only in the physical role, as a body
without a mind.[26] Whether mother or daughter (preparing to assume
the role of wife and mother), the female is cast into a carnal role,
labeled and metaphorically perceived as a whore. In this manner,

Gambaro demonstrates how language is used to violate by imposing metaphoric blindness. The powerful devise linguistic frames
that behead both viewer and viewed and encourage us to see the
female only as body, the erotic incarnate. Thus, violence, aggression, and oppression are camouflaged, veiled under the guise of
eroticism. At the same time, Gambaro theorizes that our fields of
vision are inexorably controlled as some members of society are
marked for victimization. As Dolores ironically notes, "Sólo el
poder otorga una pureza que nada toca" (*LM*, 99) (Only power con-
fers untouchable purity) (*BB*, 147). Notably, the imperfect, impure
other is marked by either excess or deficiency, often biological
since the biological is the most visible. As females, Dolores and her
mother are perceived as biologically lacking (not male) and thus
suitable victims of oppression, which will manifest itself first in the
arena of eroticism and then in more general terms. Similarly, because of his biological excess, his hunchback, Rafael is also marked
as a suitable recipient of oppression even though he is male. Indeed,
Benigno treats Rafael as he does his wife, framing and foreground-
ing his carnality and physical imperfection. Their first scene together is punctuated with erotic undertones as Benigno presses
Rafael into a role of inferiority, carnality, and submission, demanding, with a certain lechery, that he remove his clothes (*LM*, 63).
Later the "request" is repeated in similar terms: "(*Vagamente las-
civo*) ¿Y . . . y lo que le pedí . . . ? (*Bajo*) Desnúdese" (*LM*, 64)
([*Vaguely lascivious*] And . . . my request . . . ? [*Softly*] Get un-
dressed) (*BB*, 116). Of course, once his desire is fulfilled, that is,
once Rafael has submitted to his vaguely erotic request and unveiled his excess, his hunchback, Benigno assures him that he finds
it disgusting (*LM*, 65).[27] Lest we fail to recognize the use of ostensibly erotic gestures as means of oppression here, Gambaro underlines the issue of the erotic by having the father hum his refrain,
"La madre se me calienta, la hija se me enamora" (*LM*, 62 and 65)
(The mother gets sexually aroused on me, the daughter falls in love
on me) (my translation), almost immediately. Later, Benigno casts
Rafael in the role of the female (mere body, inferior or insignifi-
cant) to humiliate him in scene 5 where he forces him to dance with
Fermín.

Again, Gambaro portrays this biological essentialism as a form
of linguistic and mental framing that encourages us to perceive the
other as an object, a body without a head, as in the Magritte painting. Significantly, however, the decapitation is bidirectional. Not
only is the victimized other metaphorically beheaded, but the observer is also blinded, made incapable of seeing. Just as the father

would limit and control the mother's field of vision as he casts her in the role of whore, his epithet shapes our perception of her. Similarly, the father's repetition of the refrain, "The mother gets sexually aroused on me, the daughter falls in love on me" (cited above) comments on the patriarchal perception of female sexuality. The young woman, the daughter, falls in love while the older woman, the mother, becomes sexually aroused. The suggestion is that the patriarch perceives the two expressions as signifiers of the same responses or emotions, separated only by time. Yet the tune, coupled with his previous jealousy, evokes interesting possibilities. By using *me* in each of the propositions, he places himself as the indirect object, suggesting that the daughter's love and the mother's passion are both somehow related to him, although it is not clear whether he has motivated their responses, will suffer/enjoy the results of those responses, is simply acknowledging his authorship of the respective roles, or some combination of the above. At any rate the juxtaposition of the two erotic propositions posits a close, almost mirror relation between the two female characters, a bond cemented by their individual relationships (implicitly erotic) to him. Although we expect a close relationship between a mother and a daughter, we do not expect that it will be depicted in terms of sexuality, nor that the fulcrum of that bond will be the father/husband. And yet, how many psychological schools have told us just that as they have expressed the relationship between mother and daughter in terms of competition for the paternal phallus?[28]

Gambaro posits a new twist to this concept, however. *La malasangre* acknowledges the competition between the two women as they alternate in their collaboration with the despot, but Gambaro proposes a different basis for that competition and shows that it is not limited to women. The play emphasizes that the competition is merely perceived in sexual terms because the patriarchy ascribes sexual terminology to nonsexual situations, thus framing and controlling perceptual fields in order to reduce the other to the status of inferiority, carnality, potential victim. The play dramatizes, however, that the competition between mother and daughter is not for the phallus in the sense of sexual favors of the father (which may well be wishful thinking on the part of the patriarchy). Here the spectator finds no Electra complex, penis envy, or desire for the phallus, à la Freud and Lacan. While the competition may seem to manifest itself in these terms because of what we have been taught to perceive (in this case by the patriarch who has set the scene in motion and framed it to his advantage), the competition is in fact based on a desire for some of the power and status he has, luxuries (including a mind and the status of full personhood) that one might acquire by identifying closely with the ruling class. In this respect, the mother parallels the father's henchman, Fermín, the father's ally, ever ready to perform his dirty work, often conceiving of it even before the father does, for both support the oppressor and perpetuate his oppression on others and, by implication, themselves in the hope (delusion) of acquiring some of his power.[29] Of course, the difference is again one of perception, naming, and framing, for, while Fermín is seen as a henchman or collaborator, the mother is imaged as the more gender-specific and erotically defined whore that "gets sexually aroused on me." On the other hand, the daughter, while often equally complicitous, is viewed as "daddy's little girl." She is more easily controlled, and, since she is not yet fully developed in erotic terms, rather than being sexually aroused, she falls in love, preferably with someone in daddy's image and chosen by him (as Juan Pedro is). Her acknowledged inferiority and submissiveness to the despot saves her from decapitation and "carnalization" by the father but not by the future husband.[30] Early in the play the daughter identifies closely with the father when her authority has been challenged by Rafael. In those scenes she openly assumes the role of "daddy's little girl," reverts to childish actions and speech (thus paradoxically marking not only her identification with him but also her submissive position), and attempts to be supported by or vicariously acquire some of his power and authority. When she cannot assume a role of overt authority, she resorts to the childish, feminine charms (theatrical role) that she has been taught in order to direct Rafael's speech and actions.

In this manner, Gambaro underscores the metonymic inversions on which two misconceptions are based. The female characters desire not the father himself (anymore than the male characters, Fermín or Rafael, do here) but what he symbolizes: economic security, status (including full personhood), power, and the right to choose. And, by means of this family drama, which becomes a national drama, Gambaro demonstrates that some of the actions we have been taught to perceive as erotic are, like rape, aggressive acts of oppression and dominance, intended to demote the other (usually female but not necessarily) to an object (body), marked by either excess or deficiency in comparison to the established, if indeed arbitrary, norm.

Ultimately, the opening scenes, like the scene of the dance where the father controls the rhythm of their movements and their partners, illustrate the relation between the all-powerful father and his subordinates, particularly women, whom he continually objectifies

by negating their separate and independent existence as he controls
their every move (their bodies) as well as their discourse. Noting
that her father calls hatred, love, Dolores recognizes, "Y lo más cu-
rioso es que . . . también [mi madre] llama amor al odio de mi
padre. Y a veces . . . hasta yo lo llamo de la misma manera" (*LM,*
95) (What's even more curious is that . . . she [my mother] also
calls my father's hate, love. And sometimes . . . I even think of it
the same way) (*BB,* 143). Her observation reflects the vast range of
the father's influence and control as well as the similarities between
mother and daughter. In addition, it verbalizes her own ambivalent
position as she alternately embraces her father's mores, playing the
role of pampered, dutiful daughter, metaphorically dancing to his
beat, and defies those mores. In spite of appearances to the contrary
then, Dolores mirrors her mother as well as her father. Like the
mother, she too assumes the assigned role in the father's presence
and is sometimes complicitous in the oppression (hers and others)
but sometimes rebellious. Although the father's label *whore* encourages spectators to think of the mother as despicable and totally
under his control, and although she is generally visibly obedient,
hesitant, and self-effacing, like the daughter, she at times does attack or defy the patriarch. For example, in response to his epithet,
whore, she orders him not to insult her (*LM,* 60). When challenged,
she softens the imperative to, "Te pedí que no me insultes" (ibid.)
(I asked you not to insult me) (*BB,* 113), but the assertive words
have already been spoken and cannot be taken back anymore than
they can later when Dolores recognizes that Rafael has been beaten
because of her words. We witness in both female characters, then,
an ambivalence, a fluctuation between two levels of discourse and
thus two levels of acting between which the limits are not clear. By
staging this fluctuation, Gambaro subtly destabilizes our perception
of the roles and the sociopolitical structures on which they are
based as well as our confidence in what (we think) we see, reality
as framed by the patriarch. The roles as author(iz)ed continually
crack, for both female characters are alternately victim and victimizer. Surely, Gambaro's point is to demonstrate how Benigno accomplishes this without seeming to. He would have others perceive
their roles (as either victim or victimizer) as inherent or natural to
them and not author(iz)ed by him, as if they had nothing to do with
him.

The mother's subsequent utterances continue to allude to her dual
role, foreshadow the conclusion of the play, and again evoke the
similarities between mother and daughter. Banished from Benigno's presence in the first scene, she pauses at the door to observe

softly that she hates him (*LM*, 61), words that anticipate Dolores's in the final scene. When confronted by Benigno, she recants by saying that she did not mean to say it, again heralding the final scene when she suggests to Dolores that she did not mean to do what she did: "¡Se me escapó todo de las manos!" (*LM*, 108) (It got out of hand) (*BB*, 155); similarly, Dolores surely did not mean for Rafael to be killed in the end. When Benigno applies more physical force, the mother recapitulates completely and tells him she loves him (*LM*, 61); that is, she tells him what he wants to hear just as she will in the end. Obviously, the father can and will use his authority, in the form of physical violence if necessary, to control the discourse of others, so that he will hear only what he wants to hear: "Yo tampoco entiendo lo que no me gusta oír" (ibid.) (I don't understand what I don't like to hear) (*BB*, 113), as he will in the final moments of the work when he silences his daughter. But let us not forget that he may be able to silence the women, but, in the process, they have both already spoken the destabilizing words, "I hate you," and, once uttered, those words cannot be erased. The silence that oxymoronically shouts at the conclusion of the play is surely the echo of what the despot did not want to hear, the unwanted element that encroaches into his painstakingly framed world and threatens to undermine it, and that, once articulated, must leave its trace.

The play suggests that the two antithetical role models for women as scripted by the patriarch and Western civilization, one embodied by the mother (whore/castrating mother) and one by the daughter ("daddy's little girl"), may be less diametrically opposed than might be immediately apparent. In different ways both would (perhaps must) collaborate with the tyrant, assume the role he assigns them. For that reason the mother's entrance is fraught with signifiers of her denigrated and abased position. She appears powerless before the father and, except for the gestures of defiance already noted, generally seems either impotent or unwilling to break out of the role he has assigned her. Dolores's first appearance onstage contrasts sharply with her mother's role of timidity, self-doubt, and self-effacement. She is described as defiant (*LM*, 66), and she is intentionally rude to Rafael as she alludes to his servility and his defect: "Es mejor morirse de hambre que aceptar lo que no merecemos . . . O lo que merecemos por taras" (*LM*, 67) (It's better to die of hunger than to accept what we don't deserve . . . Or what we merit because of physical defects) (*BB*, 119). The last statement may be equally intended to refer to her mother and her subservient position since her next speech is punctuated with irony and insults for her mother: "Mamá te mandaron a buscar tu bordado . . . ¡Vaya, perrito!" (*LM,* 67) (Mama, weren't you told to go look for your needlework . . . Get going, little puppy) (*BB,* 119).[31] Nonetheless, Dolores's ostensible dissimilarity from her mother in terms of strength and overt hostility is the result of her comprehension of the differences between the mother and father and her desire to disidentify herself from the former. She cannot (or will not) identify with that debased character anymore than the spectator can. As a result, Dolores logically identifies more with the father; she may hate what he does and the fact that he cuts off the heads of those who oppose him, silencing them as he silences the women, but his position is still preferable to that of her mother. Her identification with the tyrant may manifest itself as defiance of him and the oppression of others (Rafael, her mother, and at moments even Fermín) but her motivation mirrors her mother's, for both would acquire some of his power, follow his model. Still, their choice of a role model is predicated on no choice.

We find in Dolores's initial actions a strong tendency to imitate the father even in her early treatment of her mother. Since they are both women—biologically similar—and both victims of the patriarchal despotism—socially similar—one might expect some form of identification between the two, some measure of camaraderie, but the opposite is true since Dolores would step out of the mirror and disidentify with her mother and her fate.[32] Thus, her behavior wavers between her defiance and her imitation of the father, his cruelty, lying, and pretense as indicated by the stage directions that refer to her sweet hypocrisy: she is described at various times as having a poisonous sweetness (*LM,* 69), a suspicious sweetness (*LM,* 84), a feigned sweetness (*LM,* 88), as well as a sugary smile (*LM,* 89). At other times her discourse is punctuated by kinesics designated only by some form of the term *sweet,* a sweetness that directly emulates the father's behavior, also frequently marked by stage directions that employ similar terms, and evokes the sweet melons, heads severed from bodies. Dolores would cast herself not as his victim but in his role. Again, Gambaro reminds us of the potential for violence, aggression, and cruelty in us all, even those of us who mirror the victim as the daughter mirrors the mother (in spite of the former's refusal of that identity) as well as our potential for misreading the signs of sweetness, perhaps just as we often misread the signs of eroticism. All is often not what it seems; we consistently (mis)recognize our identity with the victim, a (mis)recognition that leads us to (mis)identify with the oppressor.

But stage directions calling attention to Dolores's feigned sweetness diminish as the work progresses, and she seems to become less imitative of her father. At the end of scene 2, not irrelevantly, the scene where Fermín presents her with a sweet, bloody melon, Dolores causes Rafael to be beaten. Rafael had rejected her advances and not allowed her to play (in either sense of the word) with him; specifically and not unlike her father, what she wanted to play were erotic games. Angry, she assumes the role of indulged child, but her recognition of the consequences of her role playing produces a change in her demeanor from scene 3 on as her rebellion takes a new tack, and her sweet hypocrisy is limited to her interactions with her father or her suitor, Juan Pedro. At the same time her discourse toward Rafael and her mother (before the final scene, of course) becomes less antagonistic. Inversely, her mother's attitude toward her becomes increasingly assertive and finally openly inimical, a change visually, if indeed metaphorically evoked in the action (openly evocative of a bullfight) that opens scene 4: "*La madre sostiene un vestido entre los brazos . . . Cuando la madre se acerca con el vestido y lo acomoda para que coloque la cabeza, Dolores se inclina y sale por el otro lado*" (*LM*, 83) (*Mother holds a dress in her arms . . . When Mother approaches with the dress and holds it out so Dolores can put her head through, Dolores bows to her and takes off in the other direction*) (*BB*, 133). In this manner, the kinesic indicators evoke the adversarial inclination that informs their relationship and more subtly, more metaphorically, Dolores's interest in keeping her head out of her mother's hands.

The bases for this change are multiple. First, the mother knows that Dolores has caused Rafael to be beaten and openly criticizes her for it, stating that she should not have done what she did, even as she recognizes that there are many ways to hit/hurt someone (*LM*, 76). At the same time, the mother may fear Dolores's growing power, which has resulted from her (mis)identification with the father and her playacting, and fear that this power, which Dolores has already (mis)used against Rafael, may be directed toward the mother herself. At the same time, Dolores may provide a mirror in which she recognizes her own debauched identification with the father. It is at the start of scene 3 that Dolores's ambivalence toward her mother and vice versa is most apparent, for here, after each insult, Dolores uncharacteristically begs her to stay rather than ordering her out of the room as she so frequently does. Yet each of these requests is answered with a curt, "No."

It is not until the final scene, however, that the mother overtly adopts Fermín's role as the father's henchman. Yet she answers Dolores's charges that she denounced them by responding that she thought it would be better (*LM*, 106), words that recall the opening moments of the play and the father's perhaps all too premonitory reprimand to the mother that it would be better if she did not think (*LM*, 59). After Dolores assumes the father's role and beheads the mother in a parallel manner, "Si nunca pensaste nada. ¿'Cuándo' empezaste a pensar? ¿Para qué?" (*LM*, 106) (You never thought anything. When did you start to think? Why?) (*BB*, 154), she articulates her perception of the betrayal and the competition: "Envidiosa. Aceptaste todo desde el principio . . . Miedo de vivir hasta a través de mí. Humillada que ama su humillación" (*LM*, 106) (Jealous. You accepted everything from the beginning . . . Afraid of living even through me. A humiliated person who loves her humiliation) (*BB*, 154). Ironically, Dolores, who has repeatedly (mis)treated her mother according to the father's example, nonetheless expects more from her, expects the protection and camaraderie that she herself has been unwilling to offer. She emulates the father whose epithet *whore* projects the blame on the other as it absolves the self. Inversely, by having the mother respond with words that echo the father's near the beginning of the play—"No quiero oírte, no entiendo" (*LM*, 106) (I don't want to listen to you, I don't understand) (*BB*, 154)—Gambaro again highlights the capacity of both women alternately to be victimized by, yet (mis)identify with, the tyrant. Although Rafael is dead, Dolores's defiance, her rebellion against her father, continues at the conclusion, manifest not only in her words, but also in the fact that it is now she who laughs rather than he, as she affirms her right to see and speak (metaphorically she affirms her possession of a head). She now kinesically evokes her sense of superiority and degrades, dehumanizes him. Her laughter is followed by her use of the diminutive, *papito* (little daddy or daddy dear), used with disrespect, not affection, and by her declaration, "¡En mí y conmigo, nadie ordena nada! . . . ¡Ya no tengo miedo! ¡Soy libre!" (*LM*, 109) (No one gives me orders any more! . . . I am not scared anymore! I'm free!) (*BB*, 157).[33] Tragically, however, the price of her freedom is death, literal or metaphoric, hers or Rafael's, for as the earlier scene with the dead bird suggested, the patriarchy can surround itself only with what is already dead, metaphorically or in fact. At the same time I would again note the similarities, albeit unwitting, between father and daughter. For example, in spite of the mother's rhetorical embroidery to the contrary, when Benigno chooses, someone dies, someone is beheaded; and someone dies the two times Dolores chooses in this play: the former tutor, chosen by Dolores, has disappeared from the scene, and Rafael, with whom she chose to escape, also dies.

To date critics have read the conclusion of the play with optimism, proposing that Dolores will break the pattern of oppression.[34] They view her, unlike her mother, as having undergone a spiritual conversion that will allow her to be free because she is not afraid. Indeed, Gambaro's words on the back cover of the Ediciones de la Flor edition suggest that she meant for the play to be read in that way. There she indicates that she tried to tell a story that would pass through that zone where absolute power fails if the conquered face it with courage and dignity.[35] And although I certainly would agree that in the final moments, after Dolores has realized the tyrant's power to hurt her (if indeed via the body of Rafael) rather than someone else, she does manage to "recapitate" herself, get her head back so that she can think, see, and speak, I find little in the play to encourage us to believe that she will continue to speak significantly more loudly than her mother, whose occasional defiance of the father has accomplished little other than to victimize her even more. In fact, the play concludes after Dolores has been dragged out of the room, perhaps to her own death, imprisonment, or disappearance, and the father/despot remains onstage, alone and unmoving as in the beginning. Little has changed.[36]

Furthermore, I find nothing in the text to suggest that had Dolores been able to escape to the "paradise" across the river she would have produced a significantly different structure, for as Peggy Kamuf has argued, "Unlike material conversion, which is the process of transforming one substance into another, spiritual conversion can only be understood as the function of a reevaluation, that is, it is not the terms themselves which are changed but the values or meanings assigned to them: negative value replaces positive value or positive negative."[37] I propose, then, to look more closely at Dolores's conversion and to read less optimistically. As noted, although early in the play Dolores frequently imitates her father, she later abandons this ploy and attempts to rebel against him with Rafael, who is in every way her father's opposite; his deformed body defies the beauty of classical, symmetrical form, but he is beautiful on the inside, morally good or so the later scenes of the play would lead us to believe. The two would escape to a place across the river where nothing is painted red, and silence is not imposed: "Donde nos sirvan dos tazas de chocolate y podamos beberlas juntos. Donde no griten melones y dejen cabezas. Donde mi padre no exista. Donde por lo menos el nombre del odio sea odio" (*LM*, 96) (Where they'll serve us two cups of hot chocolate and we can drink them together. Where they don't shout about melons and leave heads behind. Where my father doesn't exist. Where at least hate will be called by its real name) (*BB*, 144). While we would definitely want to support Dolores's agenda here, we must not be overly simplistic about it. It is not irrelevant that in order to author(ize) her Eden across the river, Dolores would have to assume what had been her father's position at the start of the play—theatrical director—certainly with more benevolent goals, but director nonetheless. As the quotation indicates, she would escape to or create a world where she, rather than her father, would author(ize) actions, speeches, and existence. She would assume not the role he has assigned her but the role he has deemed his own, that of author/director. But with what model or experience would she accomplish this? Mother? Father? Fermín? Rafael? Note too that like her father's mandates, her statements tell less what she will do across the river than what "they," someone else, will do: serve, not shout and leave, not exist. I suggest then that Dolores's lack of role models, her ignorance of how to do otherwise or be different from her father (or for that matter, her mother) would cripple her even if she could reach her paradise across the river.

It cannot be irrelevant that when Dolores first appears onstage, the stage directions refer to her fragility, a fragility that she manages to surmount by means of pride and an arrogant scorn (*LM*, 66) and describe her as defiant. At the end we find the following stage directions in reference to her: "*salvaje . . . masculla con un odio contenido y feroz . . . Furiosa . . . Ríe, estertorosa y salvaje . . . Desafiante*" (*LM*, 109–10) (*savage . . . mutters, containing a violent anger . . . Furious . . . Laughs out loud wildly . . . Defiantly*) (*BB*, 156–57). Again, little has changed since the opening of the play, and her role here differs little from that of defiance in the beginning, although she has unquestionably graduated from "daddy's little girl." But since Benigno thrives on beheading the *salvajes* (savages), as she is twice described, who defy him, she certainly is/will be beheaded, metaphorically if not literally: she is silenced and her body (the physical) is dragged offstage as Benigno glances at the body of Rafael and utters the final words, "Qué silencio" (*LM*, 110) (What silence) (*BB*, 157)—surely one imposed by him with his final metaphoric beheading.

Furthermore, it is important to recognize that Dolores has undergone several "mini conversions" throughout the course of the play but always reverts to her former, oppressive behavior. For example, in scene 3 she is first disparaging toward Rafael in spite of the fact that she has caused him to be beaten, then apologetic, then antagonistic again. And although in some of the later scenes she seems to empathize more with her mother, her treatment of her in the last scene surely echoes the father's: she orders her out of the room, demands she stop crying, and hurls the designation "algodón sucio" (*LM*, 110) (filthy yellow-belly (*BB*, 157) at her. Like the father's epithet *whore*, this one also suggests collaboration, unchasteness, and guilt (the mother's). To further emphasize that the blame lies with the mother, Dolores accuses her of having done this to her (*LM*, 106). While I certainly concur with Gambaro and her critics that for Dolores to break the silence is a first and crucial step toward significant change, that step is neither easily nor quickly accomplished. On the contrary, it is a difficult, lengthy, and prolonged step (as is the final scream), and more important, only the first of many. Still, this first step (like the play itself) is one that calls for a reassessment of the ways we use language and of the extent to which we alternate as its subjects/agents and as its direct or indirect objects.

In addition, the relationship between Rafael and Dolores, the potential future family unit, is not to be romanticized. Although toward the end their relationship appears to be of fairy-tale dimensions, it has in fact been based on a struggle for dominance and control, just as all the depicted relationships are. Early in the play, Dolores mocks and degrades Rafael, and later he, her. At their first meeting, she is openly hostile to him for no apparent reason other than to demonstrate her superiority. Although he initially resists her erotic advances (which mirror the father's) as well as her reduction of him to an inferior role or plaything, he eventually succumbs to her, as he did to the father. In both cases his initial negatives evolve into acquiescence: he repeats the words each wants to hear and performs the acts (perhaps in the most theatrical sense) each wants to see. In this respect, although the roles might be inverted, it seems their relationship would differ little from that between the parents or even between Rafael and Benigno. Indeed, in Rafael's last appearance alive onstage, he literally puts his head in Dolores's hand: as the stage directions note, "*Dolores extiende la mano hacia el rostro de Rafael . . . Rafael se inclina y apoya su rostro en la mano*" (*LM*, 104, emphasis added) (*Dolores reaches her hand out toward Raphael's face . . . Raphael leans forward and rests his face in her hand*) (*BB*, 152, emphasis added). Revealingly this action is preceded by his statement that it is not just her that he is choosing; he also opts for heads on shoulders (*LM*, 104), a repetition of Dolores's earlier words, thereby signaling her success at casting him in the desired role. This less-ideal aspect of the liaison between Dolores and Rafael is elided or forgotten later in their more idyllic love scenes, as it often is in the world outside the theater too. We all want to find fairy-tale endings even if we have to distort events to engineer them. We want comedy (cf. the father's laughter) even when there is only tragedy. At the same time, although the new couple gives lip service to equality and nonoppression, it seems likely that Dolores would impose her will and assume the father's role as she disidentifies with and distances herself from her mother and her role as the oppressed. Even if the gender roles of power could have been inverted in the paradise across the river, there seems little reason to conclude that the structure would alter significantly. Dolores perhaps is truly her father's daughter as her laughter at the end may reflect. But how can it be otherwise? From where would she have learned any other behavior? She recognizes the evil of her father's ways (or even her mother's) but has no models by means of which to overcome them effectively.

But even this reading of the play errs by omission and utopian blinders, for it is important to recognize that while Rafael is unequivocally a victim here, like both mother and daughter, he is not incapable of violence and aggression himself, for like them he too lacks positive role models. In scene 2 he strikes Dolores and in scene 3 he physically (and violently) forces her to sit down (*LM*, 79). Surely, no character in the world of *La malasangre* is without sin; all are capable of cruelty and violence to the other. All would assume the father's role in both the microcosm of the family and the macrocosm of the larger sociopolitical situation, national or international. Gambaro's world is not divided into "good guys" and "bad guys"; all characters are both, enmeshed in that human inertia that Gambaro has so frequently criticized. According to her, man is a very passive being who has difficulty accepting his responsibility in regard to others and in regard to himself, and our turning inward and not accepting the responsibility that is ours has always concerned her because that attitude leads to destruction and death.[38] If there is any conversion on the part of Dolores, it rests in her final assumption of her responsibility in Rafael's death and her recognition that nothing can change until the punishment "belongs" to someone, in some sense to us all as we waver between victim and victimizer, ignorant of any other way to be. As Dolores says in response to her mother's "Se me escapó todo de las manos" (*LM*, 108) (It got out of hand) (*BB*, 155), "es lo que pasa, se escapa todo de las manos y el castigo no pertenece a nadie. Entonces, uno finge que no pasó nada" (*LM*, 108) (that's what happens, it gets out of hand and no one's at fault. Then you make believe that nothing's happened) (*BB*, 155). Thus, Gambaro proposes, it is essential to recognize and accept responsibility for the metaphoric beheadings that deprive others of their personhood and not mimic Juan Pedro whose response to his lascivious brutality toward Dolores (his metaphoric beheading of her) is to act *"como si el gesto no hubiera tenido nada que ver con él"* (*LM*, 91–92) (*as if the gesture had nothing to do with him*) (*BB*, 140). Dolores, on the other hand, does seem to assume her responsibility in the end even as she recognizes "No bastaba pegarte, jorobadito. *Pero no fue por tu joroba* . . . Todos debemos vivir de la misma manera. Y quien pretende escapar, muere" (*LM*, 109, emphasis added) (It wasn't enough to beat you, dear hunchback. *But it wasn't because of your hump* . . . We must all live the same way. And whoever tries to escape, dies) (*BB*, 156, emphasis added). As I earlier posited, the physical, biological mark is just an arbitrary designation of a victim, but one from which the tyrant will let no one escape alive, with personhood intact.

Although both mother and daughter are decidedly victims, products of an oppressive society, created by and for it, Gambaro underscores the ambiguity of women or men who eternally face equally negative alternatives. For example, in spite of the betrayal that leads to Rafael's death and Dolores's despair, the mother is not without some human decency and redeeming value as is evidenced in the final moments when the father raises his hand to strike Dolores, declaring that he will beat the daylights out of her (*LM*, 110). At this moment the mother intercedes and receives the blow intended for Dolores, significantly the only blow throughout the work that the father delivers himself. Any grace she might have been afforded by this act of generosity, however, is soon dissipated as she then helps Fermín drag Dolores out of the room, kinesically converting again into the patriarch's confederate.

In *La malasangre* Gambaro uses what contemporary critics might call the family romance with its inherent role playing and power plays on the private level to dramatize oppression and less recognized role playing on the public, national level. Or is it the other way around? Throughout the play, Gambaro posits that what has been comprehended as a problem on the familial, personal, or gender level is also a generic problem, a synecdoche of a larger issue or structure on the level of Western society and (inter)national politics. Surely, one of the questions implied in the silence with which the play concludes is, given the family drama of interpersonal oppression on which society is based, what else can we expect in the larger theater of sociopolitical structures? All that remains at the end is silence, for there is nothing left to say. We have yet to author(ize) that viable alternative across the river.

3

The Family Romance in *Escarabajos* by Hugo Argüelles: Repositioning the Mirror

> I, the horrible Medea! And now try to forget her!
> —Anouilh, *Medea*

Memory, mirrors, mother, myth, and metatheater all become inextricably interconnected in *Escarabajos* (Dung Beetles) (1991) by Mexican Hugo Argüelles (1932–2003), in ways that are not only surprising but definitively memorable, even haunting.[1] Just as it would be difficult to rise to the challenge of Anouilh's Medea to forget her, spectators cannot easily erase the final image of the Argüelles play from their minds: Jaime smeared with theatrical makeup in a garish (re)creation of Medea. In this chapter I would like to look at what happens when memory, metatheater, mirrors, myth, and mother converge. More specifically, what happens when theatrical, mythic misreadings are superimposed on the face of the family and the looking glass (like Snow White's) becomes the place where the self seeking itself finds only the locus from which the patriarch(y) speaks?[2] What happens to perceptions of family when the mirror of art (in this case, theater) mirrors or imitates not life per se (à la Aristotle), understood as autonomous and distinct from theatricality, but theatricality itself, specifically the theatricality of everyday life and of our place within the family romance as produced and directed by that patriarch(y)?[3]

A prolific dramatist, Argüelles has received relatively little critical attention outside of Mexico. Critics in Mexico have generally examined his work within the context of naturalism (with its designated goal of depicting the realities of nature and society) and have focused on his plays as scathing critiques of middle-class Mexican mores, viewing his works as psychological or sociological studies that hold a mirror up to society.[4] Nonetheless, I hope to show that the society reflected in *Escarabajos* is distinctly theatrical, a series

of performances on the part of the characters. That is, the play spotlights the theatricality, the performativity, and citational performances (in the words of Judith Butler) that are ingrained in that
family structure.[5] In this way, Argüelles inverts the Aristotelian pre-
cept and demonstrates that life imitates art, specifically classical
Greek theater. Or perhaps better expressed, Argüelles dramatizes
our tendency to perceive life—rewrite or recast reality as it were—
in terms of art, as we consciously, or more often unconsciously,
conform to and cite previously authorized models. The protagonist,
Jaime, defines, rewrites, and frames his own life in terms of Greek
tragedy, but specifically Greek tragedy as it has been re-viewed, incorporated, and rewritten in contemporary theater, where the classical metaphors have been re-metaphorized, distanced from their
"original" renditions in a gesture that obscures their status as metaphoric, fictional constructs and only partial (in both senses of the
word) reflections of reality. Yet, not unlike Jaime, as Argüelles dramatizes, in the world outside the theater, we have come to view and
perhaps even live our interpersonal relationships in terms of the
family romances of Oedipus, Electra, Medea, and company. As
Kintz has cogently argued, one of the functions of Greek tragedy
(perhaps particularly *Oedipus*) was to organize "cultural representations of marriage and gender," that is, the family.[6] Indeed, the
theatrical structures in this play, particularly the nonverbal semiotic
indicators (icons and indexes), underline not only the inescapability
of those citational performances but also the seams and problems
that inevitably characterize them.

According to Judith Butler, performativity is neither a singular
nor deliberate act, but, "a reiteration of a norm or set of norms."[7]
As she argues, borrowing from Jacques Derrida, a performative
succeeds because it is in some way identifiable as a citation, identifiable as conforming to an iterable model.[8] Yet, as the North American theorist further asserts, these acts take on the appearance of
actions freely chosen to the extent that they hide the conventions of
which they are but a product.[9] I am not suggesting here that as icons
of human beings Argüelles's characters are necessarily consciously
performing a role or assuming a mask that covers or disguises some
essential personality or nature (although at times they do acknowledge their role playing). Rather, I am suggesting that, as Butler has
argued and Argüelles dramatizes, there is no essence or nature
thinkable or representable apart from theatricality and performance.
The Argüelles characters are thoroughly penetrated by the theatrical mode and never stop playing a role, and this even within the
supposed reality of the family drama. Significantly, however, even

as he dramatizes that old plays are firmly entrenched in our contemporary attitudes and performances, Argüelles underlines the fact that the readings on which our familial performances or citations are predicated are frequently misreadings, readings that are distorted because they are necessarily partial and vested—we read and see what meets our or someone else's (often the patriarch[y]'s) interests. Thus, Argüelles demonstrates that in so many ways our classical signifiers (Medea, Oedipus, et al.) fall into the category of what Murray (following the theories of Laplanche and others) has labeled enigmatic signifiers or specters, signifiers that have been designified or have lost their signifieds but without losing their capacity to signify.[10] In other words, the addressee knows that they signify (they signify *to* the addressee) but s/he does not necessarily know *what* they signify. They maintain the power to signify but only traces of the original signifieds.

As suggested, a middle-class family romance comprises the core plot of *Escarabajos*.[11] The play is a composite of two parts, one might well say two distinct plays, that are staged in physically and temporally discrete spaces. The inner play, the family drama, written in 1959, takes place on the main, center stage.[12] This play is inner or internal in two senses of the word: in the metatheatrical sense insofar as it is framed by Jaime's monologues and in the psychological sense insofar as it dramatizes his memories, presented in a naturalistic style. Reminiscent of a drawing-room comedy, all the action of the inner play occurs in the family living room, stage, as I will argue, of the familial role playing. The frame play, Jaime's monologues, which were added in 1991, are staged on a platform, physically higher than the main stage and somewhat to the side.[13] For me, the monologues provide both structure and dramatic interest to a work that might otherwise be unmemorable. In the coming pages, I will focus primarily on the frame play since the monologues that frame the play also frame (in both senses of the word) our reading or interpretation of the inner play. Without those monologues I think we might well interpret the action (anecdote) of the family drama quite differently. And, as I will argue, without the frame of Greek tragedy, the protagonist Jaime might also remember and interpret his family history differently. Thus, the two frames are interdependent.

The inner play, set in 1959, is a type of flashback that dramatizes the conflicts that arise when a *casa chica* (house where one's lover and illegitimate children live) becomes too large because the family refuses, first, to perform a proper desire for the patriarch and, second, to remain neatly contained within the rigid mold (performance) of a proper model family as defined by society and interpreted (directed and enforced) by that patriarch.[14] In the play's prehistory, Elvira was abandoned by Mauro, the father of her two children, Leticia and Jaime. Mauro subsequently married a wealthy woman, but the original family was reunited when he sent for them twenty years later. As the inner play opens, the family has been living together again for two years; Leticia and Jaime, now in their twenties, are resentful of their father's domineering control over them all and of their mother's complete, servile devotion to him. That play concludes when, after pressure from his wealthy wife (with whom he has no offspring), encouragement from Jaime and Leticia, along with his subsequent recognition that they will never conform to his paradigm of an ideal family that adores, respects, and obeys him, Mauro decides to abandon Elvira once again. Lest there be any doubt about the centrality of the family to the play's thematic crux or Argüelles's perception of that sociopolitical institution, Leticia links the dung beetles of the title to the family:

A veces, fantaseo con una idea: pienso en ellos [her family] como si fueran una familia de escarabajos, sí, esos insectos que tenázmente [sic] van formando una gran bola de mierda que trasladan de aquí para allá . . . para luego comérsela . . . Y también para cerrar la entrada de sus nidos. Muchos se quedan detenidos ante la inmundicia que formaron . . . ante la enorme cantidad de mierda acumulada . . . que los fijó, que los detuvo para siempre.

[Sometimes, I fantasize with an idea: I think about them (her family) as if they were a family of dung beetles, yes, those insects that tenaciously form a big ball of shit that they carry from here to there . . . in order to eat it later . . . And also in order to seal the entrance to their nests. Many remain immobile when faced with the filth they formed . . . when faced with the enormous quantity of accumulated shit . . . that immobilized them, that halted them forever.] (*E,* 125)

While this is certainly not an attractive picture of family, I will argue that the *bola de mierda* (ball of shit) that the dung beetles carry everywhere and that ultimately paralyzes them functions as a metaphor for the citational roles imposed on all the members of the family and perpetuated by theater.

Meanwhile, the frame play, staged on a physically higher level and to the side of the main stage (off center as it were), provides the first scene, the last scene, and two more brief scenes that interrupt the family drama. It is set thirty-two years later in 1991, in Jaime's shabby, run-down dressing room. Now a middle-aged, mediocre actor, he has been able to survive, in his own, revealingly ironic words, "siendo el mejor maquillista del teatro experimental mexicano . . . Y desde luego, ayudándome otro poco con la venta de las enciclopedias" (by being the best makeup artist in Mexican experimental theater . . . And, of course, helping myself a bit selling encyclopedias) (*E,* 32). Obviously, these words juxtapose two seemingly incompatible fields of knowledge and thus foreground the inevitable seams as Jaime straddles or inhabits (and is inhabited by) two contradictory discursive fields: the encyclopedia with its hegemonically approved and accepted (white, Eurocentric, patriarchal) collection of facts, and experimental theater with its implicit alternative culture and lifestyle and its attendant challenge to the supposed knowledge represented by the encyclopedic archive.[15] Even more important is the fact that Jaime has earned his living not as an actor, but as a makeup man—one who covers up surfaces and hides or overwrites one possible perception with another (something that he does literally and figuratively throughout the play). His monologue, a running commentary on the family drama and something of an epilogue to the events of that drama, is directed to his now-deceased mother, who, in his words, let herself die after Mauro's second abandonment. Jaime talks to his mother (or, more accurately, to her ashes in a jute bag on his dressing table) as he applies his makeup (which, significantly, he mixes with those ashes) and prepares for what he labels the most important role of his life—Medea in a daring transvestite version of Anouilh's play of the same name.[16] The play ends as Jaime leaves his dressing room, exits the visible, concrete stage, to enter the other (invisible) stage as Medea.

The semiological indicators of the play (icon, index, and symbol) invite us to recognize theater (or theatricality) as both the form and the content of the work.[17] For example, the fact that the inner family drama of *Escarabajos* is framed by and in some sense contained within Jaime's monologue with its overt references to theatricality, implicitly signals that the actions of that inner play should be understood as shaped and limited by theatricality. By hyperbolizing the theatrical frame, Argüelles not only questions how meaning is produced by representation, he also makes a spectacle of spectatorship. We watch Jaime watch himself first in the mirror in which he is making himself up and then in the internal scenes from his youth, which are ultimately his own creations insofar as they are psychological projections (just as the Medea he is creating in the mirror is his personal invention). Indeed, I would argue that the positioning of the dressing room and its ever-important mirror at an angle to the main stage invites, even forces, us to reconsider the positioning of that theatrical mirror that is the main stage and our position in relation to it. Clearly, we cannot observe both stages or mirrors without shifting our position, both physically and psychologically, a shift marked and facilitated, to be sure, by the spotlights.[18] Furthermore, both mirrors are directly linked to memory. The main stage overtly presents Jaime's memories of a few months of his youth as the family situation reached crisis proportions and culminated in his mother's death. But, his dressing room is also the site of memories for, as he applies his makeup and prepares for his role as Medea, he states that he wants to remember his mother during the two hours that it takes him to get ready for the performance each night. That memory (again specifically of his mother) is precisely what we see mirrored on the main stage, projected in the inner play, the family drama. In this way the addressee of the frame play is the subject of the inner play, and mother is re-created, remembered on two different stages.[19] What is most significant, however, is the emphasis on the framing and the mirroring. Although in narrative we expect to find and even question the controlling voice or perspective that has selected and framed the tale, in theater the framing apparatus is usually not seen and rarely questioned. In *Escarabajos,* however, Argüelles underscores the framing apparatus, making visible the generally invisible controlling perspective (in this case that of the mature Jaime) that necessarily structures and frames everything we see in the theater, including the family drama. But, as I have suggested, Argüelles also provides another layer of frame, which suggests that Jaime's frame has already been framed.

Significantly, Jaime's first words (to the audience, to his mother's ashes, or to himself) are "A ver . . . vamos a ver" (let's see . . . we're going to see) (*E,* 31), words that underscore the ideology of presence and visibility on which theater has been traditionally predicated, but what is it that we are going to see? What we see is his reflection in the mirror, framed by that mirror as he sits at an angle to the audience, with his back partially to us, and puts on his makeup.[20] In this way, what we see overtly marks the role playing or theatricality of it all. Significantly, however, in none of the multiple theatrical mirrors presented in the play can we find what we might be wont to label an "original" image, an image that predates the mirror, the representation, the theatrical greasepaint, and that is not already fully penetrated by theater. In fact, from his early years (even in the inner drama) Jaime is repeatedly shown to be rehearsing a role. In other words, he never escapes from and perhaps (within the representational economy of the play) never exists independently from the theatrical frame or performative citations. Not irrelevantly, as the lights go down in the dressing room and our attention is diverted to the main stage living room, Jaime as a young man is again framed. He is outside of the family living room, in the garden (if indeed one distanced from the idyllic Eden), framed through the window at the back of the stage, at the bottom of which is "una jardinera, adornada con *plantas parásitas* y de sombra" (a window box, adorned with *parasitic plants* and shade ones) (*E,* 27, emphasis added). Jaime is not only physically separated from the principal action (the family living room), but he is viewing as he is viewed, framing as he is framed, spectacle and spectator at once. And, significantly, this opening scene of the family drama mirrors the frame play inasmuch as he is again preparing for a theatrical performance, rehearsing his lines, thereby underscoring the theatricality of the family drama.

In this way Argüelles introduces a protagonist who continues to act, to play a role throughout the work, on both the conscious and the unconscious level, on both the stage of his dressing room and that of the family living room. As Jaime notes, what matters most to him is "convertir[se] en otros seres . . . y así no tener que vivir [su] propia realidad . . . tan frustrada y desagradable" (become other people . . . and thus not have to live [his] own reality . . . so frustrated and unpleasant) (*E,* 32–33). What Jaime never seems to recognize, however, is that as he converts into other people, he only moves from one theatrical frame (play if you will) to another, equally restrictive and equally predetermined. His statement, "Soy actor y no voy a ser otra cosa en mi vida" (I am an actor and I am not going to be anything else in my life) (*E,* 132), should be taken quite literally. In the frame play he moves from the literal stage (his dressing room) to the invisible stage where he will play Medea. It is surely significant, however, that even in that frame play, when he is in his theater dressing room, he plays the role of actor. In addition to talking to his mother (imagined audience) about his upcoming role as Medea, he seems to be trying to convince her (and himself as well) that he really is an actor and deserves the title or designation. Similarly, in the inner play he moves from the garden where he rehearses his lines to the living room where his manners, actions, or bearing are described as *"tan pronto infantiles como* cuidadosamente estudiados" (*one moment childish the next* carefully assumed) (*E,* 53, emphasis added). In other words, inside or out he is playing a role; he may perceive himself as beyond the control of his father, having rebelled against the latter's indictment to become what he should be, but he has merely moved from one looking glass, one play, to another. Significantly, however, both looking glass scripts are still authored in the final analysis by the same patriarch(y), the metaphoric law of the father, and are controlled by his voice—but more of this below. In this way the play calls attention to the frame itself, marks its own theatricality, and thereby questions the basic premises of representation, reminding us that the supposed mirror of art is itself a representation, a product of ideology, chosen and positioned by someone for some purpose, never innocent, anymore than Hamlet's mirror of nature was unmotivated (designed as it was to "catch the conscience of the king"). Furthermore, as Victor Burgin has noted, "what we see and the way we see it . . . has a history. It, like everything else, is a product of representations, whose effects come to be 'seen' as natural."[21] The mirror of art, like the window at the back of the stage that serves as a visual frame, is shown to be metaphorically adorned with shadowy plants (hidden motivation, unseen apparatus and agenda) as well as parasitic plants (ones that feed off of other entities, destroying the other to reinforce the self).

At the same time, the mirror in which the middle-aged Jaime applies his makeup functions as an index that points to the character's search for himself in and via that mirror, both the literal one and the one metaphorically figured in the internal play. What he seeks is a suitable image or reflection, suitable in that it has been previously authorized and thus is citable, as well as one that will please his audience, give his audience the show they have come to see. In this mirror, Jaime not only seeks, but he also creates the image that will please the audience—both the internal audience (himself) and the external one. Specifically, he "puts on" his mother's ashes and incorporates her into his performance (his personal creation, as he calls it) just as numerous vested readings have been incorporated into familial performances both on- and offstage. Yet, what he incorporates are specifically her ashes, remains destroyed beyond recognition (as the final image of Medea will be in *Escarabajos*). In this way Argüelles seems to be suggesting that the roles we cite and assume outside of the theater may equally be defined as the rubble or ashes of some other misdirected reading. Even more revealing is Jaime's statement that he wants to remember (recreate?) his mother so that she can help to provide both the source and the explanation for his personal experiences.

The originality of the Argüelles play resides in the fact that the immediate "source" of the performative citations that Jaime recites (cites anew) is his mother rather than his father. He is adamant in his conversation with the latter that he does not want to resemble him: "Eres la última persona a quien le haría caso" (You're the last person I would listen to) (*E*, 132). He later speaks of "¡ . . . la repugnancia de irme convirtiendo en alguien como tú! ¡El asco de saberme tu hijo . . . y el miedo de no poder ser . . . como yo quiero . . . !" (the repugnance of becoming someone like you! The disgust of knowing I'm your son . . . and the fear of not being able to be . . . as I want . . . !) (*E*, 134). Clearly, then, this is anything but an Oedipal endeavor: first, Jaime achieves no discovery or insight at the end, and second, he identifies not with the father à la Oedipus (or at least à la Oedipus as retold by psychoanalysis) but with the mother. Although there is significant antagonism between him and the father, he certainly does not want to become him, replace him, or sleep with the mother. The father is not the model on which he bases his citations; the mother is, if indeed the mother already framed by the patriarchal looking glass (that is, the mother performing as patriarchal society has said she should, as I discuss below) and then perceived and (re)mirrored by Jaime himself in the form of Medea. Furthermore, the source of the approval he implicitly seeks is also the mother's rather than the father's.[22] Several times in his opening monologue, addressed to his mother, he implicitly seeks that approval or collusion: "Me comprendes, ¿verdad? Sí . . . tú siempre estuviste de mi lado . . . ¿Te gusta la idea? Sí . . . me imagino . . . o quiero creer que sí" (You understand me, right? Yes . . . you were always on my side . . . Do you like the idea? Yes . . . I imagine so . . . or I want to believe so) (*E*, 32). Indeed as he notes, "siempre (¡siempre!) sentí la necesidad de tu compañía en cada una de mis actuaciones" (always [always!] I felt the necessity of your company in every one of my performances) (*E*, 31). In this respect, then, Argüelles encourages us to reconsider the authority (implicitly patriarchal) of the psychoanalytical narratives (based as they are on Greek myth and tragedy) that have presumed to mirror our reality.

Nonetheless, the paucity of the repertoire of potential images and roles at Jaime's disposal is indexed in the makeup pots and the bag with his mother's ashes, both of which are significantly limited and finite. Indeed, he notes in his opening monologue, "cada noche tus cenizas irán formando parte de esa creación mía . . . hasta que un día desaparezcan todas convertidas en parte de un rito teatral" (every night your ashes will form part of that creation of mine . . . until one day they all disappear, converted into part of a theatrical ritual) (*E*, 32). In this way, by using up and exhausting the ashes Jaime metonymically displaces the mother and continues the process of destruction she had begun when she "killed" herself. But, again, displacement and distance are the key words, for the Medea (mother) Jaime creates is the product of his perhaps unique reading or memory, just as his mother's suicide is also a product of his reading or memory insofar as even he acknowledges that she did not really kill herself; although she had attempted suicide (and failed) three days earlier, she ultimately died of sudden heart failure. Thus, Argüelles underscores the links between citational performance and memory. In order for a performance to be cited it must be remembered, but memory, as we know, is necessarily selective and partial (again in both senses of the word). As a result, the citational performance that Jaime creates with Medea (already repetition, citation) is indeed a grotesque one.[23] But, again, this too points to Argüelles's message in regard to the grotesqueness of the roles all the characters (and perhaps the audience) citationally perform. Furthermore, I would argue that the result is grotesque in part because what Jaime puts on and incorporates is a necessarily selective and hence distorted reading or memory of Medea perpetuated by other distorted readings, but all of them motivated by a vested interest, as I will argue below.

Clearly, Jaime's search for and performance of previously authorized images, in turn, evoke the extent to which each of the characters in the inner family drama does exactly the same. Specifically, the makeup Jaime uses to create that image, makeup that already evokes a theatrical mask, is also an index of the makeup his mother uses in the inner play in her attempt to create an image, perform a citation that will please her audience. In her case, the audience is Mauro, and the performance with which she hopes to please him is that of the still youthful, sensuous, and desirable woman who, more importantly, is also desiring, that is, capable of performing a proper desire for him, one that in turn will be reflected back from him in the form of his own passion aroused—a result never achieved in this play.[24] As she enters the stage for the first time, she is described as, "*consciente de su agradable aspecto . . . Muy pintada . . . marcando su evidente sensualidad*" (*conscious of her nice appearance . . . Very made up . . . accentuating her evident sensuality*) (*E*, 41). Nevertheless, it is important that we recognize that in both cases, that of the mother and that of Jaime, the audience for whom they perform is at least twofold. Again emulating the larger structure of the play, their audiences are both internal and external, for both observe themselves even as they are viewed by others. In other words, each is a spectator (and specter) of him/herself as well as a spectacle for the other.[25]

Revealingly, what I call Elvira's performance has been read, or misread, by the character of the frame play, the mature Jaime, as an indicator of her passion for Mauro à la Medea. That is, he has failed to perceive the mirrored surface as mere theater, performance, or role. For example, as Jaime exclaims in his monologue to his mother's ashes, "¡Y ahora será como si los dos formáramos parte de 'Medea'! . . . ¿qué mejor ejemplo que el de la pasión que vivió mi madre . . . para partir de ahí . . . a las complejidades de tal personaje? . . . ¡Y qué mejor que mezclar tus cenizas en mi maquillaje, para que así, fueras formando parte de esta 'Medea' . . . !" (And now it will be as if the two of us were part of "Medea"! . . . what better example than that of the passion my mother lived . . . to start from there . . . to the complexities of such a character? . . . And what better than to mix your ashes in my makeup, so that you will be a part of this "Medea" . . . !) (*E*, 32). That is, her passion has been read or re-membered through and mediated by the mirror of art. Yet, it is precisely this reading that Argüelles challenges in the play. In spite of the fact that within the representational economy of the play, it is the adult Jaime who frames the family drama with his monologue and, in the production I saw, at least, is placed on a physically higher plane that would seem to evoke his superior vision, this superiority is precisely what is placed in doubt. In fact, I would suggest that his superiority should be viewed as ironic, for there is little in the characterization of Jaime that would encourage us to accept his interpretation of events. Indeed, in the final moments of his last monologue he himself underscores his unreliability and bias, suggesting that all he has said up until this point has been self-deception. In reference to the role he is about to perform, he asserts, "¡Y voy a obtener un gran triunfo! ¡Y ya no voy a engañarme nunca más!" (And I am going to achieve a great triumph! And I am never going to fool myself again) (*E*, 149). But, of course, his "great triumph" (like his mother's) is predicated precisely on playing a role. Similarly, the semiological indicators in the text, especially the redoubling of the metaphoric mirror of theater, invite us to read Elvira's performance as just that, as her performance of the role assigned her within the patriarchal family.[26] And there can be little doubt that the role she has been assigned is precisely that of performing desire for the patriarch. The fact that Argüelles presents Jaime as totally enveloped in and circumscribed by the theatrical frame leads us to reason that he necessarily views all aspects of life through the filter of the roles perpetuated and framed by theater and that the filter has prevented him from seeing his mother's citational performance as just that. Yet, in this case, it is important to recognize that the theatrical filters through which he has chosen to see love or passion are filters that, in the words of Susan Carlson, "deflect considerations of money, class, or power," considerations that are clearly fundamental in this play and that are underscored in the family drama.[27] As Sandra Cypess has discussed in her analysis of another Mexican play, the Medea myth focuses not only on themes of love, exile, betrayal, and death but also on racism (Medea was different, from elsewhere, not welcomed by the Corinthians) and economics or greed (Jason was motivated by his lust for gold).[28] Clearly both of these motifs are repeated in the Argüelles play: Elvira is not from Mexico City (where the action takes place) but from Veracruz, where people are often less European looking, noted for their darker skin, while Mauro's double abandonment of her is predicated on his lust for gold (that of his wealthy wife) as well as his desire, like Jason's, to marry into a higher socioeconomic class.[29] By reading her performance in terms of passion, Jaime can elide other socioeconomic issues, perhaps the very ones he would prefer not to acknowledge in his own life, where he is reduced to selling encyclopedias to make ends meet, to promulgating the very archive of knowledge that would maintain him (a non-European, homosexual who rejects the patriarchal model) in a marginalized if not oppressed position. In addition, Argüelles dramatizes Jaime's double movement here, a movement that points to, in the words of Butler, "the reiterative and citational practice by which discourse produces the effects it names."[30] On the one hand, Jaime imitates and incorporates his mother's role into his own, but on the other, he projects that theatrical role or mask back onto her. Then, once he has projected it back onto her, he gives it another twist and ends up reading her as the source of the role. He enacts a metonymic inversion that blurs the distinction between citation and original, spectator and spectacle, and effectively produces the effect that he seems to cite as the original.

At the same time, Elvira's performance points to and mirrors Mauro's (and/or vice versa). The middle-aged Mauro of the inner play, not irrelevantly, is approximately the same age Jaime is in the frame play and seems every bit as mediocre as Jaime, if indeed in different ways. Mauro's motivations for reuniting the family, a family that held no interest for him for twenty years, a family that he abandoned for a wealthier woman in a superior social position (like Jason in the classic *Medea*), are relatively transparent. According to him and, unlike Euripides' Jason, who left the family "for the good of the children," Mauro reunites the family "for the children." Twenty years later, like Jaime, he now needs to *convertirse en otro* (become someone else) and perform a different role, if indeed a commonplace one, already framed by prior representations—that of patriarch, surrounded by his loving, adoring family who will care for him in his old age and for whom his word is law.[31] Let us note that it is this very position of supremacy and power that is lacking in his marriage: there he has no children over whom to lord, and he is in a position of social and economic inferiority in relation to his wife. That is to say, he has a vested interest in reuniting the family, for it provides him a starring role as well as a stage, an audience, and a supporting cast for a satisfactory citational performance— that of the omnipotent patriarch—and in this way to avoid facing his own mediocrity.[32] As I have argued elsewhere, without a son to envy and confirm his patriarchal position (and, I would add here, a woman to perform desire for him), a male's role as patriarch has little validity, resonance, and consequence; he cannot find himself in the metaphoric mirror.[33] But, more than anything, and like El- vira, he is motivated by a fear of being alone, a fear that we see played out also in Jaime in the frame play.

Nonetheless, Argüelles portrays the woman, Elvira, as willing to rejoin him for parallel motives. As an unmarried mother in a tradi- tional society, she has no socially validated position, no authorized role to perform, regardless of how much of a farce her role within the family romance may prove to be. As a result, Elvira's perform- ance must be read as such, as a show motivated not so much by passion as by social scripting and ambition.[34] Rejoining Mauro, she is afforded a role (if indeed merely a supporting one, not a leading one as his is), while at the same time, she achieves some degree of economic stability, for her children and for herself in the coming (her later) years. Surely, both parents are merely citing and per- forming previously authorized roles in which they have a vested in- terest—domineering patriarch and woman whose only admissible role is that of wife and mother, under the tutelage of the patriarch as she performs a proper desire that is indispensable to him. Yet, in the Mexican middle-class society of the late 1950s, how would ei- ther gender have imagined a different citation to perform? And, what would they have gained by trying to? In this respect, Argüelles dramatizes how Elvira's very "passion," her desire, has been so- cially (pre)scripted and dictated. But, at the same time he under- lines the degree to which theater itself is complicit in establishing and perpetuating vested norms. Let us not forget that quite literally Medea has always been (p)(re)scripted by a man (be it Euripides or Anouilh) and often played by a man (Greek performers were all male). What is more, Anouilh's Medea is a re-scripting of Euripi- des', which in turn is a rewriting of the even earlier myth(s). Per-

haps Medea has never been anything but man-made, always framed
(literally and figuratively) by a male (as she is here, by Jaime who
would assume her role, incorporate her, devour her as a parasitic
plant might). Perhaps she has always embodied the performance of
the passion that the patriarch would like to be able to incite and has
come to believe he does incite, a citation of a citation designed to
please her audience.

At the same time, Jaime's monologue and re-view of his earlier
family life might be seen as an attempt to justify, or better yet, re-
classify, rename, his family's mediocrity and by implication his
own. Jaime perceives the citational performances, his mother's as
well as his own, in terms of passion. Nevertheless, where he sees
passion, we, the external audience, see only mediocrity, characters
trapped in grotesque roles, as they drag around the baggage of so
much theater, the *bola de mierda* described by Leticia. And, the
process by which he re-views his family life consists of several
steps. First, he identifies his mother with Medea, misreading her
sociocultural and economic necessity as passion rather than mediocrity, in much the same way as Medea's fury—the fury of a woman scorned—and her refusal to play the proper subservient
feminine role have traditionally been read as passion rather than
strength and defiance. Then, Jaime identifies himself with his mother's perceived passion and by implication casts himself in Medean
terms, thus embodying a metaphor of a metaphor, at the same time
as he metonymically confuses source and citation, spectator and
spectacle. He then takes it a step further and compares the passion
he feels for his homosexual lover with the passion Medea supposedly felt for Jason, and then conflates that lover, who has abandoned him for a wealthy woman and a bourgeois heterosexual life,
with Jason and in turn with Mauro. Thus, in so many ways
"Medea" here functions as a specter, a signifier that haunts family
or interpersonal relations even though its signified remains shadowy and unsettled.

Nonetheless, Jaime's gesture here evokes a more universal one as
Argüelles implies that society in general constructs its self-image
in much the same way, casting itself within the chosen frame, viewing itself through a filter, so that it can see itself as it would like to
see itself. Let us not forget that Medea is already a representation,
a fiction, someone's re-creation of what he saw, or thought he saw,
or would have liked to have seen. But Jaime's interpretation of
Medea as an index of passion is a further framed, vested representation that focuses on only one trait of a very complex character while
eliding other traits and irreconcilable contradictions, as for exam-

ple, her anger, her fury. Yet, the personality characteristic that Jaime emphasizes is the one with which he can (and indeed wants to) identify since he associates Medea's passion with his own for his lover. By presenting this unilateral perception of Medea as projected and framed by Jaime, Argüelles questions the meaning of referentiality and seems to acknowledge that, as Butler has phrased it, "the ideal that is mirrored depends on that very mirroring to be sustained as an ideal."[35] Thus, Argüelles evokes the complicity of theater in sustaining our ideals (theatrical though they may be). Revealingly, Argüelles's grotesque mirror destroys that ideal in the end.

In order to better understand Argüelles's point and grasp the significance of his resorting to Anouilh's Medea rather than Euripides', we will need to return to the sources and see how Euripides' and Anouilh's plays differ, and how, in both, Medea might (perhaps should) be read, re-membered, or framed differently, as other than an index of passion. In both plays, Medea had abandoned her homeland for Jason and, at the start of the plays, has in turn been abandoned by him. In Euripides' *Medea,* the first several pages are devoted to describing her state of depression, her lucklessness, her hatred, and her fury.[36] Since she mentions only once that Jason meant everything to her, her famous passion would seem to be a bit difficult to document. But, she is unquestionably furious. I would suggest that her fury (like Elvira's in the final moments of the Argüelles play) might well be read as motivated by socioeconomic exigencies rather than by passion. As a foreigner, abandoned by Jason, Medea no longer has a role or place within Greek society, and as a result she finds herself, quite literally, unclassified and declassed—in theatrical terms, without an authorized role to perform citationally. Her actions, killing Jason's bride and her own children, are obviously designed to punish him for his (socioeconomic) betrayal. Her objective is clearly not to win him back (which would likely be her goal were she motivated by passion). Indeed, she is explicit that she killed the children to hurt him and that it was his lust (not hers) and his new marriage that slew them.[37] She is also most critical of his expectation that she, like any "good" woman, should be a subservient doormat to him.

Jason. Because your love was scorned you actually thought it right to murder.
Medea. Do you think a woman considers that a small injury?
Jason. Good women do. But you are wholly vicious.[38]

Since Medea will not accept the status quo, the role assigned her by the patriarch(y), she is defined as a bad woman. It is important to note, too, that Medea also resolves to kill the children to "save" them, so that they do not "fall into the murderous hands of those that love them less than I do."[39] In the end, Medea flies off on her magic chariot to bury the children elsewhere, "where no enemy may violate their tombs and do them insult."[40]

Surely, this picture of Medea is quite different from Jaime's portrayal of his mother who, as a woman scorned, killed, not the children, but herself (in one of Jaime's versions at least) as she directed her fury inward rather than outward. Unlike Euripides' Medea, Elvira never challenges the status quo nor proffers any threat to it. But, let us not forget that Euripides' portrayal of Medea, like Jaime's of his mother, is a definitively framed one, one that incorporates only a segment of a longer narrative. Like Anouilh, Euripides focuses only on the disintegration of Medea's relationship with Jason. Their courtship, years of happiness, and so on, are omitted as are their lives after the breakup: Euripides' play ends as Medea goes off to Athens where she marries Aegeus and starts a new life.[41] In Jaime's case, that is, in his memories of the inner drama, we are also presented with the events leading up to the final crisis. What happened during all those years after Mauro's first abandonment is left in the shadows, and one must wonder why Elvira did not commit suicide then had she felt the great passion Jaime attributes to her. Surely in all three cases we are led to question why the frame or the mirror has been placed where it has.

Anouilh's rendition of the myth unequivocally announces that what Medea feels is not passion but "newly born hatred": "Oh, my newly born hatred . . . ! How soft you are" (perhaps better translated, "how new you are").[42] She continues, "I am listening to my hatred . . . Oh, sweetness! Oh, lost strength! . . . I have found myself again . . . Now again I am Medea! I am no longer that woman bound to the smell of a man, that bitch in heat who waits."[43] Later, she adds details, "Jason, you put her to sleep, but now Medea is awakening again. Hatred. Hatred! . . . I am reborn."[44] Thus, Anouilh suggests that while her lust for Jason controlled her, she was not herself, not Medea. Now that she hates, she is; thus this Medea is an index of hatred and fury rather than passion, memorable for her destructive actions at the end when she is reborn as Medea. In her final speech she concludes, "I am Medea at last and forever! . . . I, the horrible Medea! And now try to forget her!"[45] Anouilh's Medea (like the other characters of the play) is marked by a self-consciousness of the theatricality of her role and by the fact that her role is

memory, repetition, citation, a pre-scription that meets sociopolitical needs.[46] Let us add too that the question of passion or desire is
put to rest early in the play when the nurse states unequivocally,
"You no longer love him, Medea. You have not desired him for a
long time now."[47] But what we certainly have in Anouilh's play, as
in Euripides', is an impressively strong woman who acts, who takes
matters into her own hands and resolves them as she sees fit, destroying as she goes. She is a character who stands in sharp contrast
to Elvira, although the latter does display fury, if indeed only at the
end when she attacks Mauro screaming words that indeed echo
those of the two Medeas,

> ¡Cállate, no me vas a ordenar, no vas a gritarme, no lo soporto más, me
> he aguantado tantas cosas, pero ya no! ¡Ya no! ¡infeliz! ¡Te he dado lo
> mejor de mí misma y me has deshecho la vida, miserable! Tú eres el
> único culpable de que no pudiéramos vivir juntos, por qué [*sic*] eres un
> cabrón, estúpido y mezquino, pero ya no voy a aceptar tus desprecios,
> ¡desgraciado! ¡ya no! ¡ya no!

> [Be quiet, you are not going to give me orders, you are not going to
> shout at me, I am not going to take it anymore, I have put up with so
> many things, but no more! No more, you wretch! I have given you the
> best of myself and you have destroyed my life, wretch! You're the only
> one who is to blame that we couldn't live together, because you are a
> bastard, stupid and mean, but I am not taking your contempt any longer,
> swine, not anymore, not anymore!] (*E,* 146)

It is precisely the strength of the two Medeas, their ability to defy
the patriarch who would take advantage of them (in the form of
Mauro or Jaime's homosexual lover) that both Elvira and Jaime
lack. Indeed, her fury is directed inward, suggesting that the only
way she can live up to her words of defiance is by ceasing to exist
at all. The suicide of Anouilh's Medea on the contrary seems more
an act of affirmation. After proclaiming herself the pawn of the
dirty games of the gods and declaring that she has found her scep-
ter, symbol of the power that was forfeited when she left her homeland to follow Jason, she kills herself with the same sword that she
had used to kill the children and "collapses in the flames," thus
achieving the finale she herself had put forward early in the play
and doing what the king had refused to do: "Let there be only one
thing left of Medea: a big black spot on this grass and a tale to
frighten the children of Corinth at night."[48] Anouilh's Medea,
scripted in the twentieth century, when magic chariots no longer
whisk one away, must kill herself, write herself out of one tale in

order to write herself into another. But that other tale, that tale of fury and strength that would frighten children, seems to have been misread or shunted aside to allow the patriarch(y) (who would see himself as inspiring her passion) to continue to occupy center stage.

Why then is Medea read as an index of passion while the complexity of her characterization by both Anouilh and Euripides is overlooked—by Jaime as well as society (theatergoers) in general? Is it possible that society would prefer to look the other way and not understand the fury and hatred in a woman who recognizes that she has been wronged by society and by the gods—gods who in the Anouilh version are closely linked to men? As Anouilh's Medea tells Jason in what must be understood as a critique of self-serving patriarchal society, he has Heaven on his side and the police as well.[49] In the same speech she underscores the patriarchal foundations of those, like Jason, who have been right since the beginning of time because they speak like their fathers and like their fathers' fathers.[50] In so many ways these classical tragedies have molded or modeled the world in their own image.[51] But, at the same time, and this may well be the most original aspect of the Argüelles play, the Mexican dramatist proposes that the reverse occurs simultaneously: contemporary society or individuals read, re-member, and thus mold the classical texts in their own image(s). Like any reader, Jaime "discovers" in the text of his familial memories and in those of the Medea plays a reflection of himself and his relation with his lover, who, as noted above, is conflated with both Jason and Mauro, just as Jaime conflates himself with (his reading of) Medea and Elvira. His memories and his readings, and by implication his performative citations (conscious, in his theatrical roles, or unconscious, in his interpersonal relations) of earlier texts, are not only framed by but clearly a product of his present experiences. That is, he has produced, re-membered, a family romance to reflect and justify his present. Thus, Argüelles underscores the complexity of citational performativity: the present is not merely a product of the past, but that past, the memory of that past, our telling and citing of that past at least, is equally a product of the present. Even though Jaime is determined not to be like his father, the patriarch, we might well argue that his reading, memory, and eventual citation of his mother is equally, if indeed differently, self-serving; he sees what he needs to see to find and justify his own self-image, overlooking all the heroine's qualities except passion. In spite of his defiance of the patriarchal norms, he still falls victim to the patriarchal mirror. By citing his mother (as he has re-membered her) and accepting his victimization within that script (a victimization that neither fictional

Medea accepts), he unwittingly authorizes and perpetuates the patriarchal norm. Indeed, reading Medea as an index of uncontrollable passion and desire for the patriarchal male centralizes that patriarch (be it Mauro or Jaime's lover), provides the audience (be it Jason, Mauro, or the male, patriarchal theatrical audience) with exactly the felicitous self-image it seeks, continues to provide acceptable (acceptable to the patriarch of course) citations to be performed by both males and females, and does very little to challenge the status quo. Jaime is as trapped in the patriarchal looking glass as was the "wicked" queen, Snow White's stepmother (and, of course, as was Snow White herself), for all he finds there are images that serve the patriarchy and oppress him.[52] As a homosexual in a heterosexual masculinist society, he is perhaps as marginalized and feminized as is a female.

Argüelles, however, unlike Jaime, challenges that looking glass, that patriarchal norm. By hyperbolizing the frame, the Mexican playwright has forced us to see it and to question the vested interests that have placed it here and not elsewhere, that have made it reflect this rather than that. As Moses Hadas notes in his introduction to *Ten Plays by Euripides,* Euripides retained the old stories and the great names but then imagined them as contemporaries and thus deflated the heroic outlook.[53] Argüelles similarly deflates the heroic patriarchal looking glass as he implicitly encourages us to ask the questions that Kappeler asks of pornography: "who is holding the mirror, for whose benefit, and from what angle."[54] What sociopolitical, economic, or ideological goals are met by choosing, perpetuating, representing one story instead of another? What meanings are reproduced through these specific representations and to what ends? It cannot be irrelevant that Argüelles has chosen specifically to have his character prepare for Anouilh's rendition of the myth, not Euripides'. In an earlier play, *Medea y los visitantes del sueño* (Medea and the Dream Visitors) (1967) Argüelles availed himself of the Euripides version.[55] There Medea's monologues, combined with those of other memorable female protagonists of the Western tradition (Phaedra, Laurencia of *Fuenteovejuna,* Lady Macbeth), serve to foreground feminine strength and women in starring roles. At the same time the play highlights the power of theater to engulf us as it overpowers and becomes more "real" than supposed reality. To be sure, the characters overpowered by the magic of theater in that play are actors, but as I have argued, all the characters of *Escarabajos,* actor Jaime as well as the rest of his family, come under the influence of theatricality and are quite literally engulfed in it, in part because they consistently fail to question it, as I think Argüelles does. Insofar as he has chosen specifically Anouilh's version of the myth, he emphasizes the rewriting involved, the repeated distancing from any original image— reminding us that the rewriting works both forward and backward. In this way what is foregrounded is the enigmatic signifier or specter that continues to haunt our citational performances even though its signifieds are far removed.

The final image of the play is that of Jaime now grotesquely made up as Medea, about to go onstage. That image is accompanied by the words, "¿Ves? ¡Ya soy cada vez más tú y cada vez más 'Medea'! Por tanto . . . ¡Gracias mamá . . . ! ¡Va por ti!" (You see? I am already more and more you and more and more "Medea"! For so much . . . Thanks mama . . . ! This one's for you!) (E, 149). In this way Argüelles signals the unacknowledged grotesqueness of representations whose theatricality and framing apparatus have traditionally gone unmarked. The grotesque results when the frame of art is situated such that only one characteristic of a complex, if indeed contradictory, character is centralized, brought into focus, while all other qualities are elided, left outside of the frame, so that we cannot or need not see that complexity nor those contradictions. By providing us with two metaphoric mirrors (one of which, the frame play, includes a literal mirror), and placing them at an angle, a slant from one another, Argüelles underscores the bias, the vested readings, that frame any artistic production and the distortion that results when the mirror reflection is cited or reflected anew, when memories, collective or individual, especially those of the family, are reproduced. Medea, like the enigmatic signifier, the specter, theater in general, continues to signify to the audience, but what it signifies is always open, subject to change, subject to the control of the mirror and the framing apparatus (theater, playwright, and so forth). By moving one of the mirrors to the side of the stage, off center, Argüelles calls into question the mirror of the center stage and its role in our family dramas and romances.

4

The Family Drama:
Ambiguous Places of Seduction and Memory
in Roberto Cossa's *El saludador*

EL SALUDADOR (THE GREETER OR THE WAVER) (1999) IS ONE OF THE
more recent works of Argentine Roberto Cossa, whose long, successful career as a playwright began in 1964.[1] Pellettieri has situated his work in the category of *reflexive realism,* positing that he
(like others in that category) understand art as commitment, designed to encourage social change.[2] For Woodyard, Cossa has consistently "balanced his theater between considerations of aesthetics
and form and his concern over sociopolitical issues in his country."[3] As we will see, *El saludador* is no exception. Nonetheless,
while other critics have expressed a confidence that the play com-
municates a clear message to the spectator, I am not so sure. For
me all the elements of the play point to ambiguity, an ambiguity
that is directly tied to questions of family and theater.[4] As I will
argue, throughout the play Cossa avoids assigning single meanings,
single interpretations, and instead repeatedly allows the "instrument," the theatrical sign to signify in more than one direction. As
a result, the play wavers between the stance of *either/or* and that of
and/also while the figure of family is yoked to mutually contradictory referents (safe haven versus entrapment, conformity versus individualism, idealism versus pragmatism). Cossa employs the
conventions of naturalism to seduce his audience but simultaneously subverts those conventions and the old discourse of family.
In this way the play stages the problem of interpretation: how to
interpret old images (e.g., family) in a changing world. The space
of the play, both the fictional space of the family home and the theatrical stage itself, become ambiguous places of seduction and
memory.

Cossa's plays have long depicted the middle-class Buenos Aires
family, although one might well argue that in many of his works

95

the family is the medium more than the subject of his message.[5] Most would probably agree that in the majority of his plays the members of the family unit prove to be significantly dis-united when not openly antagonistic toward each other.[6] What is more, when his plays do not end in death, they frequently end with pessimism, inaction, or impotence in the face of social forces that overwhelm the individual. On occasion (for example, *De pies y manos* [Hand and Foot]), they even end with violence. One of the major differences in this recent dramatic piece is that the familial antagonism is resolved in a nonviolent, less pessimistic compromise at the end, and the family reintegrates, although now under the guise of a cooperative.

The plot of this hilariously funny three-character play is relatively simple. At the start of the play, Saludador has just returned home to his wife, Marucha, and their son, Vicente, after some ten to fifteen years during which he roamed the globe and involved himself in any number of causes meant to right the wrongs of the world.[7] Apparently he has had no contact with the family during his absence, for, as Marucha notes, "Al menos me podrías haber avisado . . . Un telegrama. Una carta. Una llamada de teléfono" (You could have at least let me know . . . A telegram. A letter. A phone call) (*ES,* 107). He insists that while away he always wanted to return home and thought about them continually, but things got in the way. One time, for example, he had his ticket, but the plane made a stop in Mexico, and he just could not resist the temptation to embrace all those Zapatistas. In his absence, Marucha has established a life and routine and has raised their son without Saludador's emotional or financial support. In fact, Vicente does not even recognize his father and greets his returns with questions like, "¿Quién es este señor?" (Who is this man?) (*ES,* 116). Although Saludador is determined to settle back into the family fold at the start of the play, Marucha is not willing to have him. In a surprise, but uproariously funny conclusion to the first scene, she cons him into the lemon tree near the patio wall and throws him and his possessions over. This motif, which provides much of the humor of the play, is repeated on two of his next three returns. Each time he is thrown over the wall, he apparently goes back to his life as an advocate of whatever the most recent international cause might be, only to return home again eventually. Each successive return is marked by the loss of one or more limbs: the first time he has lost an arm (because he waved to the "wrong" side in Angola); the second time, a leg (lost in a benefit game for the dying in Biafra); the third, the other arm and leg, as well as an eye (voluntarily "lost" during his tenure as president of the world association of organ donors to provide an example for the rest of its members).[8] Now limbless, on his final return he enters, not over the wall as he has on each previous occasion, but through the wall, in a miniature motorized car. The play concludes when, rather than throwing him over the wall once more as the audience is expecting, Marucha decides to let him stay. Her decision is based on his assurance that he has not lost anything else, "de lo que no se ve" (of what you don't see) (*ES,* 116), because as she tells the audience with her now characteristic, strong sense of pragmatism, "Necesito sexo . . . Me calienta. En todo lo demás es un ingenuo, pero en el sexo . . ." (I need sex . . . He turns me on. In everything else he's a child, but in sex . . .) (ibid.). As a result, they form a cooperative, settle into a domestic routine, and he now spends his days greeting (*saludando*) their neighbors rather than the international masses and great names of history as he had done in his charitable pilgrimages. Order is restored, but it is a variation on the previous order.

Meanwhile, the action of the play is repeatedly interrupted as Marucha violates the theatrical fourth wall and turns directly to the audience to discuss her concerns and engage us in what appears to be a dialogue but what is ultimately only a monologue, since no one in the audience actually asks the questions she answers or responds to hers. At the same time, a concurrent subplot develops as Marucha coaches Vicente in his endeavors first to land a job and later to get a promotion. Significantly, her lessons center on the notion of ambiguity and her repeated advice, "No te olvides. Ambiguo" (Don't forget. Ambiguous) (*ES,* 110). As I have suggested, ambiguity (from the Latin *ambigere,* to go or to take in two directions) is a key concept in this play.[9]

Since Cossa has emphasized on more than one occasion the importance of space in the creation and shaping of this work, I would like to focus on the setting, the space/place of the play, to orient my exploration of seduction, memory, and family.[10] The play's single setting is the patio of the family home, one of modest construction in a neighborhood of Buenos Aires or nearby. Although this is not the family living room, which provides the setting for many of the other works analyzed in the course of this study, it is still in many ways the heart (in spatial terms, at least) of family life. It is, as the stage directions specify, where the family has breakfast and even their main meal in the summer—that is, locus of family gatherings and interaction, literal and figurative get-togethers. In addition, it is where many household chores are performed. Marucha works here throughout the play (often hanging or folding laundry), always dressed in her apron, symbol of her sociopolitical, socioeconomic role as housewife, homemaker, index of the unpaid (and often unacknowledged) domestic labor on which the functioning of the household and the family depends.[11] There is a door to the rest of the house, as well as (and more importantly in metaphorical terms) a staircase, not very high, that leads up to Vicente's room. The location of that room near the center of the patio signals the centrality of the son to the family (indeed without him the family as such would not exist) while its physically elevated position evokes the family's aspirations: the mother's, that he will rise above their perilous socioeconomic circumstances; the father's, that he will prove ideologically superior to the bourgeois materialism embraced by the society in which they live. Finally, that very important wall over which Saludador is repeatedly evicted, about two meters high, runs along the back perimeter of the stage.

The patio, synecdoche of the family home, which in turn functions as a metonym of the family itself, provides the stage (literally and figuratively) for the actions to come. Insofar as those actions revolve primarily around seduction and memory, the play figures both the family home and the stage as loci of memory and seduction. Significantly, however, this is a completely naturalistic setting in every way, one that the audience has seen, lived in, or visited.[12] In fact, as the audience settles into its theater seats and views the open stage, there is a sense of familiarity, of settling in at home. Unpredictably, however, this completely (unremarkable) naturalistic setting is the locus of hyperbolized and patently unrealistic events, events that do not fit into the logic of the naturalistic setting but rather challenge many of the assumptions underlying its naturalistic mode. (We may occasionally feel the urge to throw our spouses and their accompanying baggage over the wall, but we do not act on those fantasies, nor do we consciously give our limbs in the name of humanitarian projects.) Indeed, I would argue that the use of the naturalistic setting of the home is a statement on the Western tendency to see home and family as natural, normal, inevitable arrangements as opposed to the constructions and conventions that they are. The unnaturalistic events that occur onstage clearly disrupt that kind of thinking. The end result, then, is that expectations are repeatedly turned on end as figurative language is literalized. A certain indeterminacy of meaning reigns as Cossa challenges not just notions of family and related sociopolitical issues, but also those of theater itself (particularly naturalistic theater), suggesting that naturalistic theater and the old images just do not work any more (or at least not in the same way), and this in spite of their pervasiveness; like Saludador, one cannot go home, either to old images or to the naturalistic stage with its unacknowledged assumptions and unexamined notions of both theater and family.

Indeed, the opening scene of the play, in which Saludador's first homecoming is staged, undermines a number of the unquestioned and perhaps even unacknowledged expectations and assumptions on which naturalistic theater depends. First of all, the initial dialogue between Marucha and Saludador (and, let us not forget that dialogue is the axis on which naturalistic theater revolves) ultimately proves not to be a dialogue. It may look like one insofar as the two characters alternate as speakers, but, as in Marucha's dialogues with the audience, the characters are not responding to each other. What we witness might better be labeled two, juxtaposed monologues, narrative renditions of two separate pasts, histories that occurred at the same time but in different places and that are patently subject to more than one interpretation. He narrates his adventures abroad, the success and warmth with which he was urged to remain elsewhere. She, without warmth and not wanting him to stay, recriminates him for his absence and the hardships that absence created. If she is unimpressed by his "successes," he is equally unmoved by her problems. They are patently not hearing each other in this opening "dialogue." Second, the family to which Saludador is returning does not fit into the traditional image of family, at least not in the logic of the naturalistic stage. Indeed, his absence has explicitly refuted that image, if family is to be defined as mom, dad, and children, since one element of that unit has been missing, and not due to circumstances beyond his control, but by choice. Furthermore, insofar as his absence has allowed (indeed, forced) them to survive without him, it also renders his presence and participation in this family unit contingent and nonessential. And, if his participation is superfluous, then family (which in Western culture is imaged in predominantly patriarchal terms) needs to be delineated, imaged in a new way, as I think it is to some degree at the end, when the family becomes a cooperative. In many ways, then, right from the beginning the play metaphorically pricks a hole in the bubble of the myth of the traditional patriarchal family and deflates it, a deflating that is dramatized onstage when Saludador first sees his son, Vicente, early in the play. Here Saludador's language and gestures reflect his initial expectation of the mythic family (unconditionally loving, timeless, and unchanging). We watch as that expectation (myth) inflates with anticipation (via the diminutives of affection) and then deflates when confronted with reality:

Saludador. (Grita) ¡Vicentico . . . ! ¡Vicenti-qui-co . . . ! ¡Vicenti-qui-
qui-co . . . !
Marucha. (Hacia la habitación) ¡Vicente!
*Desde la habitación aparece VICENTE, un muchachón casi veintiañ-
ero, agitado por la gimnasia.*
Vicente. ¿Qué pasa, mamá? ¿Quién grita?
Saludador. (Se va desinflando) Vicenti-qui-qui-co . . . Vicenti-qui-co
. . . Vicenti-co . . . Vicente . . .

[Greeter. (Shouts) Vinnie . . . ! Little Vinnie . . . ! Itty bitty Vinnie . . . !
Marucha. (In the direction of the room) Vincent!
*Vincent comes out of the room; a young man almost twenty years old,
he's been exercising.*
Vincent. What's going on mama? Who's shouting?
Greeter. (He deflates) Itty bitty Vinnie . . . Little Vinnie . . . Vinnie . . .
Vincent . . .] *(ES,* 107)[13]

Other expectations are similarly negated or at least foiled in this
opening scene. Although many twentieth-century plays have centered on the homecoming of the prodigal son, this is a homecoming
of the prodigal father, but, like the dialogue, the homecoming is not
a homecoming on a number of levels.[14] First, as noted, there is no
welcome; Marucha does not warmly embrace either him or his return. This prodigal father (who has metaphorically spent his inheritance in the form of his limbs) does not receive the warm embrace
that the prodigal son received (nor can he give one in the end, for
he has no arms). And, unlike the prodigal son who acknowledged
the implications of the ideologeme, *son,* and recognized that he was
not worthy of being called that, this father never wonders if he is
worthy of being called father. On the contrary, when some form of
dialogue is finally established a bit later in the first scene, he insists
on his prerogative to return to his former place and occupy it anew,
in accordance with his memory of it. Responding to Marucha's
query about why he has returned, he states unabashedly (no prodigal son remorse here), "Volví para estar con mi familia" (I came
back to be with my family) *(ES,* 108). Still the ensuing dialogue
challenges his (and probably the audience's) assumption that he has
a family and/or a place within it.

Marucha. Esta no es más tu familia.
Saludador. Marucha . . . vos sos mi familia . . . El Vicentico es mi fa-
milia.
Marucha. Hace años que no sabés si tu hijo existe.

[*Marucha.* This isn't your family anymore.
Greeter. Marucha . . . you're my family . . . Vinnie is my family.
Marucha. For years you haven't known if your son existed.] (*ES*, 108)

And let us not forget that the home Saludador comes back to here is literally and figuratively a stage, as Marucha's "conversations" with the audience remind us, and one on which he would have them all continue in the old family drama he remembers.

Saludador's memory to the contrary, this is certainly not a family in any traditional sense of the word. It is significant too that in spite of his insistence that he has returned to be with his family, on none of the three occasions when she throws him out, over the wall, does Saludador attempt to get back into the house (via wall or door). He may have passed through the home, but he has certainly not come home in the traditional sense. Now, although the final homecoming is ostensibly successful insofar as he is allowed to stay, it too is a misnomer, for he still is not coming *home,* in the sense of returning to things and places the way they were. On the contrary, the family (and by implication the home) is transformed into a cooperative in which the son provides a salary from his job outside the house, the mother provides the domestic labor, and the father supplies merely the physical shell or structure, the house, which he owns and has refused to sign over to her, the place and stage of this family drama. Clearly, what was is no longer. At the same time, the audience's desire, as we settle into the theater, to return to a safe haven, a secure, crystallized past (a desire that clearly mirrors Saludador's) is similarly frustrated in this play, for our imagined homecoming also proves to be limited to its shell, a hollow and ambiguous place/space—the theater itself.

As noted, the most important aspect of the setting, in terms of the action as well as the play's iconicity (which is the essence of naturalistic theater) is the wall at the back of the stage. That wall and the image of someone being thrown over it are precisely the seminal images from which the play was constructed.[15] The comic effect of Saludador being thrown over the wall is a function of both its hyperbolic nature and its repetition.[16] Yet, clearly that action is an example of what I have labeled the highly improbable events staged in the play. It could not, would not, happen in the real life evoked by the naturalistic setting. It is, like so many aspects of the play, a humorous literalization of a metaphor, in this case, some variation of "throw the bum out," and ultimately functions to challenge the iconicity (metaphoricity) of naturalistic theater, that mirror of nature that stresses similarities and downplays differences and thus ultimately prescribes as much as it describes. Still, while unrealistic, this action provides a hyperbolized enactment of the desire most spectators have probably felt at some point in their lives—in fantasy at least, and irrationally to be sure—to throw something or someone out, out of our space and out of our sight, and thus eliminate the problem from our lives and change our world (on either the sociopolitical or the personal level). It is an urge/fantasy on which we do not act, but surely we are amused (seduced) by seeing it literalized onstage by Marucha, who not only feels it but acts on it (although, as in a comic strip, he suffers no physical harm but rather bounces right back each time). After the first time Saludador is so unceremoniously rejected by Marucha, we come to expect him to be thrown out, as he is literally two more times. That expectation is thwarted the final time, but more of this below. The hyperbolic nature of this literalization intensifies in his third ejection. This time, and in what might be viewed as a prefiguring of his final return, he does not just go away, disappear from Marucha's and the audience's view, as he has before. On the contrary, after he has been thrown over the wall (this time with the help of Vicente), he reappears above the wall, "*como catapultado*" (*as if he were catapulted*) (*ES,* 114). Old images are not so easy to dispose of; they resurface in the most unexpected places. With each catapulted reappearance he comments on the conversation between mother and son until "*Marucha le tira un botellazo, como a un muñeco de un parque de diversiones*" (*Marucha throws bottles at him like at a doll in an amusement park*) (ibid.). Once Vicente exits, Marucha continues throwing glasses and bottles over the wall, asserting her authority and prerogatives, reminding Saludador and the audience that this family will no longer echo the patriarchal model; times are changing here as well as out there in the world that he roams: "¡Callate, vos! Que yo soy la que se banca esta casa . . . La que mantiene un hijo . . . ¡Tu hijo! . . . ¡Así que la que decide aquí soy yo!" (Be quiet! I'm the one who holds this house together . . . The one who supports a son . . . Your son! . . . So the one who decides here is me!) (ibid). In this way, family gender roles are destabilized, disrupted; the wife is no longer the *muñeca* (doll), toy, or plaything of the patriarch. This is no *Doll's House,* and Nora does not have to leave here; the patriarch does (if indeed only to return again and again). Similarly, the notion of the female as a sexual object or toy is inverted in the end when Marucha allows Saludador to stay specifically so that she will have a sexual outlet; thus the male is cast in the role of sex object rather than the female. At the same time, the gender roles that have been the cornerstone of the patriarchal family are turned on end here. Mother and son throw the father out (rather than him, with his patriarchal prerogatives, forcing one of them out), and in the end, the son provides financial support for the father (rather than vice versa), who continues in his prodigal ways, wasting his days greeting neighbors and discussing his latest cause with them: how to correct the problem of dog excrement in the streets.

Now, the hyperbolic literalization of the metaphor that the scenic space (the patio wall) provides for within the home and on the stage, is repeated in the unseen, unstaged, strictly narrative global space of Saludador's wanderings, which might similarly be read as literalizations of metaphors: to be "over the wall," "off the wall," or "climbing the wall."[17] Saludador is literally over (beyond) the wall in his global pilgrimages and off the wall in the exaggeration of his commitment to various causes (in his idealism run amok).[18] The fact that inside that wall he is so easily seduced by Marucha and led to a position that allows her to throw him over it surely evokes the ready seduction that the various causes have held for him (and, as I will argue, that both naturalistic theater and the figure of the family have held for us all). In both cases, Saludador displays a certain innocence and/or willingness to be seduced that we might well associate with the spectator's willing suspension of disbelief in the theater. Indeed, according to his reports to Marucha, he has been involved in activities that include at least twenty different locales and/or causes, ranging from Biafra to Cambodia to Cuba to French Canada, to name just a few. Revealingly, however, his causes always center on the other, the foreign, the not domestic (either in terms of home or nation), while he shows no concern for the latter: for his family's economic problems (caused in part, at least, by his dedication to "more important" causes) or for his nation's sociopolitical and socioeconomic problems (which, in turn, have impacted this specific family). The group closest to home that interests him is the Wichi community, still an exotic other even though it is included within the geopolitical boundaries of Argentina.[19] While many (probably most) of his causes will seem of value and well intentioned to the at least semiliberal spectator, they are, nonetheless, repeatedly marked by questions of perspective and how to know what the issues are and/or which side is the "right" side— hence the arm lost waving to the "wrong" side, lost at least in part because, in his innocence, he does not comprehend the complexity of the power struggles or the issues. Saludador consistently fails to perceive that there will always be more than one side, perspective, in any issue and that those perspectives might not be mutually exclusive (either/or); on the contrary, and as the play repeatedly demonstrates, there may indeed be no clear-cut right or wrong side (as is the case at home, in the two very different ideological stances embodied by the two parents). Like everything else in the play (including the figure of family), sociopolitical struggles are often marked by ambiguity, metaphoric walls that have two sides—it is all a question of where (on which side of the wall) one is positioned.

While his ingenuity at home is reflected in his ingenuity abroad, it seems clear that it is the other, the foreign, the exotic (rather than the local or home) that holds the most seduction for him and that he values the most. The paradox, however, is that he approaches the other, the foreign, as if it were home, the local, the family. Excentric though he is in each case, he tries to literalize the metaphor and make the world his home, his family, and thus demonstrates the problems inherent in taking the notion of family with its dream of homogeneity (similarity, "us" as opposed to "them") and metaphorically imposing it elsewhere, outside the concrete family unit (and perhaps even inside it). His unarticulated perception of the world as one big family, ready for and in need of his embrace (and vice versa), leads to his failure to differentiate between and among places and cultures (even individuals), viewing them all as the unfortunate other who needs his help, casting himself as "big daddy," who is watching and knows what they need, what is "best" for them.[20] In many ways then, unintentionally to be sure, he repeats the colonizing gesture of which Argentina itself (indeed, Latin America in general) has been victim and underlines the potential (if indeed unwitting) perniciousness of the humanitarian endeavor. While his intentions are good (as are those of many humanitarian causes), we must remember that, at best, such causes often venture precariously close to what might well be labeled colonialism (first, in their tendency to erase differences and, second, in their often unacknowledged presumptions of cultural superiority—"father knows best") or, at worst, just a thin mask for colonialism (cf. the Crusades). Indeed, let us not forget that the thanks Saludador has gotten—or perhaps better expressed, the price he has paid—for meddling in the affairs of others is the loss of his limbs. In economic terms (which evoke the economic basis of many goodwill movements), his potential *plusvalía* (added value, surplus value, or capital gain), becomes a *minusvalía* (lost value) (wordplay intended).[21] In this way, the play raises the question of how to understand events and places, the inside or essence of the matter, when one is clearly outside, other, and perhaps has no right to intervene.

At the same time it lays bare the danger of imposing the metaphor of family with its implicit tendency to blur difference and overemphasize similarity, even with the best (or at least most innocent) of intentions. Thus, Cossa dramatizes the complexity of negotiating between overemphasizing and underemphasizing difference (inside the family and out). Overemphasis casts the other as a totally foreign, antagonistic alien with whom one has nothing in common and cannot identify or empathize; underemphasis erases difference and reduces the other to a reflection of the same/self, running the danger of prescribing rather than describing and forcing the other into the homogeneous (and fantasized, idealized) mold of metaphor (resemblance, family).

Saludador's idealism is hyperbolic in quantity (he has embraced far too many causes) and in what would appear to be its indiscriminant heterogeneity (from socialism to ecology to defending the rights of aborigines), but, paradoxically, it is this very heterogeneity that he would dismiss or perceive as homogeneity. The fact that Saludador chases after so many different causes (chimeras?) suggests that it may be less a question of political conviction than a way of life, and one that is specifically outside the confines (wall) of the family, that is to say, ex-centric. Paradoxically, however, it is his very ex-centricity that provides him the raw material to create memories and narratives that centralize him, place him center stage, as it were. Significantly, the play opens with narrative: Saludador tells Marucha about his "success" in Cuba and how everyone, including Fidel Castro, wanted him to stay because they loved him so much. In this way his narrative emphasizes his ex-centricity even as it centralizes him. The story is about him, about his centrality as an object of love and admiration in Cuba and is a tool to seduce Marucha, to get her to focus on, centralize, and love him, embrace him as he has embraced so many causes. But, of course, the extent to which he is a reliable narrator, to which his interpretation of events is valid, and to which he perceives either differences or resemblances, remains in question.

The suggestion is that the fact of being a cause may be more important than the goal, objective; the label/image (preserve of shaky myths though it may be) overshadows the reality. Although Saludador is shown continually crossing space, walls, both literal and figurative, very little has been accomplished. By his own reports, he has been witness to the great moments in contemporary history, the great transformations (in his words) that are taking place beyond the patio wall, but for the most part he has been an observer on the sidelines. As in the final scene, his activity has been limited to greeting, waving (*saludar*) and hugging (literally and figuratively, embracing, *abrazar*), albeit at the end without arms with which to wave or embrace literally and in what undermines the label as it highlights its status as wishful thinking.[22] Surely, such is also the case with the label/image, *family,* which is perhaps as arbitrary (distanced from the signified) and tenuous as is Saludador's very name. We all know what family is supposed to be (or at least we think we do, although as I will argue below, our perception is often bidirectional and contradictory even if not acknowledged as such) and are drawn by its paradisiacal allure, but we seldom (never?) actually find that ideal family in the world outside of fictional representations, the mirrors that reflect our desires more than nature. In fact, it is often the case that, rather than providing a citational model (à la Butler), our image/myth of the ideal family (like most mythic ideals) functions as a standard against which our own families and experiences seldom measure up very well.[23]

Indeed, Saludador's name encompasses a number of ambiguities and highlights the arbitrariness of the sign, which can evoke multiple, and at times contradictory, signifieds. He has no proper name; he is designated in the play text and the program merely as Saludador, index of his activity—which again, like the family, is not what its name suggests. Although throughout the text the stage directions and other didascalia refer to him only as Saludador, it is not until the end of the play that he is so baptized by the neighbors, according to Marucha, because he spends his days greeting them. The paradox is that the verb *saludar* is generally a reference to a physical activity (to wave or to salute, the latter carrying a certain military, political connotation) as well as to a verbal one (to say hello). Obviously his lack of arms truncates the greeting. At the same time the verb is related to *salud* (health), and etymologically to greet one is to wish one health. To the extent that it is from the same root as the Spanish *salvo* (safe), it is also to wish someone safety and/or perhaps by implication to save someone (or something) as Saludador continually attempts to do in his goodwill pilgrimages, albeit without results. Thus, the idealistic *salvador* (savior) has been reduced to a mere *saludador* (greeter, waver), an empty signifier (as empty perhaps as that of family). The play suggests, however, that this may have been his place, his role, all along.

In many ways (unexpectedly to be sure), Saludador reflects the theater spectator, sideline observer of the (re)production of moments in history, but distanced from them. Also like him, the audience escapes to the comfortable world of naturalistic theater perhaps in order to escape from the realities of home, politics, economics, and so on, outside the theater—an escape to the representation of an idealized figure of home, which is so distinct from the pragmatic, day-to-day experience of home. Paradoxically, our presence in the theater is an escape to a world of resemblances, a world we can comprehend (unlike the one outside the theater from which we are escaping), a safe haven of limits and boundaries, preestablished rules, which is precisely what the family is (or so we are told). Like Saludador, who assures Marucha that the world is in transformation (*ES*, 109) but who expects his home and family to remain the same, outside of history and change (hence the gift for a five-year-old that he brings home for his twenty-year-old son), we expect family and theater (and particularly family as presented in naturalistic theater) to remain the same, with rules we understand. These expectations are definitively thwarted here on several levels as Cossa evokes a familiar (and the familial) system of signs and icons to discredit that very system in the end.

Significantly, the principal icon exploded in this play is the wall, the major actant in the comic effect of the play as well as in the development of plot, as it marks both visible and invisible boundaries between inside and outside, moderation and exaggeration, which are repeatedly traversed. In keeping with the system of icons with which spectators are familiar, that wall visually evokes the perceived isolation of today's nuclear family. Historians tell us that since the Industrial Revolution the family in Western society has gradually become smaller and more isolated. The family was once characterized by its greater extension, comprising not only what is today's nuclear family (mom, dad, children, or some combination thereof) but also other family members (grandparents, aunts, uncles, cousins) as well as servants, and frequently embraced several generations.[24] Even when all the various family members did not live in the same house, they generally lived nearby, frequently interacted, and formed part of a larger community. As we know, such is seldom the case today in Western urban centers (and let us not forget that Cossa is specific that the action takes place in or near Buenos Aires).[25] With the passage of time, changing lifestyles, professional mobility, and so on, much of this sense of community has been lost (if it ever did in fact exist and is not merely a collective memory of a paradise lost), and the nuclear family has come to find itself pretty much enclosed within the four walls of the home, isolated in what it perceives as its privacy and safe haven, but certainly not unaffected by events outside those four walls, as Cossa demonstrates.[26] I would argue that the setting here functions as an indicator of this perceived and probably mythic isolation, due in large part to the predominance of the wall, a wall that ostensibly marks the division between family (private) world and external (public) world, but, as I hope to demonstrate, that division is charged with ambiguities and contradictions.

First, it is particularly significant that this is a patio wall, that is, a wall that in many ways is more ambiguous than others. The external wall of a house would proffer a somewhat more definitive line of division between what we have been taught to perceive as diametrical opposites: inside and outside, public and private, culture and nature, opposites that tend to blur or melt into each other in this play in spite of the dominating presence, visibility of that wall. But, a patio wall is already outside and, on the one hand, represents another division, and thus might be read as another layer, another line of defense if you will, to isolate and protect the family, assure its unity and mark where difference (not family) begins. Specifically, this is a *muro,* an exterior wall, with etymological links to the older term and acceptance *muralla,* which according to Corominas means thick, exterior wall, especially one that *protects* a fortified place (emphasis added).[27] That connotation is surely destabilized here by the fact that this family is not protected from outside influences and problems; the metaphoric wall of protection is repeatedly breached. Yet, on the other hand, a patio is an intermediary, ambiguous space: neither inside nor completely external to the home. It is out of doors, outside the primary structure of the house, but still partially within the family's control. While the fact that the patio is out of doors evokes nature and a certain freedom (surely more imagined than real) from sociocultural restraints, this patio, marked and limited by the wall, is a controlled nature—appearances to the contrary, it is marked and traversed by the sociocultural, and thus simultaneously subverts the myth of family as natural, reminding us that, while we tend to image family as a natural construct, it is (at least at this point in history) a thoroughly cultural creation, neither prior to nor independent of culture, discourse, and representation. Further marking its status as acculturated nature (oxymoron intended), the patio contains potted plants, well taken care of according to the stage directions, and a cultivated lemon tree with its sour fruit, and all that might evoke. In this respect, the patio and the wall that marks its outer edge are ambiguous, on the one hand, neither here nor there, on the other, both here and there, or better yet, an indicator that the two are not so easily separated. Thus, in so many ways the wall undermines the myth or dream of the isolation of the family. Just as Saludador scales or passes through the wall, bringing the outside with him, the patio, the family, the domain of the private, are thoroughly penetrated and determined by the public, the outside, existing notions and representations of family. And, let us not miss the paradox here: the patio's fourth wall is definitively the fourth wall of theater, the one through which the audience peers, in what provides another visual link to the complicity of representation in our perception of family. But, more of this below.

Second, as the events of the play demonstrate, the family cannot stand as an isolated unit but rather is necessarily impacted by events in the macrocosm, their sociopolitical context, which as Cossa suggests, becomes ever larger and more global. The economic problems Marucha has faced at home have been provoked by those of the country, which in turn are shaped by global problems. Similarly, the causes that Saludador embraces have affected or will affect both Argentina and the individual family unit. In this respect, the isolation indexed by the wall is wishful thinking, a myth, a dream, perhaps not unrelated to Saludador's often mythic causes. It is an ideal or an image that, again, just does not work any longer, and this in spite of its hegemonic hold. Indeed, each of the characters is what s/he is precisely because that figurative wall has been penetrated, sociopolitically, socioeconomically, and ideologically. He is an idealist because those ideas are floating around out there, because there are revolutions and causes of which he is aware. She is a pragmatist because her family is plagued by the economic problems of the world, which have trickled down to her microcosm. The wall ultimately indexes less the isolation of the family than the patriarchal structures and discursive frames (myths) that cast the family gender roles in such a way as to perpetuate the division into pragmatists and idealists. He can go out into the larger world with his idealism and fight revolutions precisely because she holds down the home front, the pragmatic, feeds his son, and then him when he finally does return. This notion is reinforced by the fact that, as I mentioned earlier, although he would change the world, he wants nothing to change at home. Paradoxically, then, that conservative structure (home, the family), mired in the practical, often perceived as an impediment to progress and idealistic goals, is precisely what sustains that idealism. As the play demonstrates, it is the basic configuration of the family on which the rest of the sociopolitical agenda depends. This notion is visually underscored in the final scene when Saludador is perched on top of the patio wall, facing outward—his focus is outside the home, but he is supported by its structure.

Cossa has made reference on a number of occasions to the fact that revolutions inevitably fail, suggesting that such is due, in part at least, to a lack of practicality. As I have been arguing, this lack of practicality (on the part of the idealist, who in this play as in many others is definitely imaged as male) seems built into the structure of the family unit, to the extent that the pragmatic aspects have often become the domain of the female. If one assumes that each individual begins with a measure of idealism and a measure of practicality, it would seem that the contemporary, Western family structure pushes some individuals in one direction and some in the other precisely because of this familial, domestic(ated), gender-linked, division of labor. While idealists make revolutions, the rest of the world still has to figure out how to eat and survive, and that responsibility often falls to women as a result of the initial organization of the family.[28]

In fact, the etymology of *family* may be as revealing as that of *saludador*. The term comes from the Latin *familia,* the group of slaves and servants belonging to a person, which in turn comes from *famulus,* servant, slave.[29] Thus, Saludador can work for revolution because his basic needs are taken care of by others (in this case, the female of the family, whose domestic labor, until the end, apparently is not valued).[30] It cannot be irrelevant either that Saludador returns home, this time for good, only once he can no longer take care of himself (due to his missing limbs), only once he is rejected by others who are afraid of him and will not take care of him or embrace him, only once he is reduced in many ways (but certainly not all, he is definitely not castrated, literally or figuratively) to a level of infantilism. What is more, family is imaged throughout the play as a source of nourishment (literal). Although in his idealist rhetoric Saludador would help the poor and theoretically feed the hungry, he often focuses (childlike) on his own hunger and even acknowledges (if we are to believe his report) that he never stopped thinking about his beloved *milanesas* (breaded cutlets), which he made famous throughout the world. Indeed, at home he is shown whining that he is hungry and cajoling Marucha into making "milanesas como me gustan a mí" (breaded cutlets the way I like them) (*ES,* 108) (a meal to which he would contribute nothing either in terms of labor or economics). And on at least one occasion abroad, he reports that locals (far poorer than he) fed him.[31]

This ideological linking of the female with the home is underscored in the kinesics of the play. As noted, Saludador comes and goes over or through the wall. In the final scene he is perched on the wall, saying hello to the neighbors in a gesture that again marks his ex-centricity and the ambiguity of the wall as border: simultaneous mark of division and convergence (inside and out). Vicente similarly exits the space of the home to go to work and interact with the larger world; much more pragmatic, however, he utilizes the door. Marucha, on the other hand, never leaves the home, never leaves the stage that is the home and that inversely evokes the home as a stage.

The permeability of the wall and of the image of family is underscored at the end when Marucha decides they will become a cooperative. The old myth of family as an independent unit, safe haven, secure and isolated from the world falls apart. The family is intrinsically neither isolated nor safe. And, in response to Marucha's unconvincing series of clichés about the "nature" of family and why she is going to let Saludador stay ("Porque sí. ¿Por qué la gente se casa . . . ? ¿Por qué tienen hijos . . . ? ¿Por qué viven juntos? La vida es así. Nacimos para vivir en familia" [Just because. Why do people get married . . . ? Why do they have children . . . ? Why do they live together? That's how life is. We were born to live in a family]), Vicente observes rightly, "Nosotros no vamos a ser nunca una familia" (We're never going to be a family) (ES, 116). In some sense in the end, rather than throwing Saludador over the wall once more, they throw out the traditional image of family and reinvent. The notion of cooperative (as opposed to family), an alliance freely chosen and not necessarily to the exclusion of other alliances, functions as a marker of shifting identities and signs, a recognition of differences (including those within), even as it subtly acknowledges that the resulting unity is neither natural, inherent, nor stable, but contingent and in a permanent state of flux. Unlike our ahistorical myth of family, this cooperative unit is no longer ahistorical, apolitical, or universal but spatially, temporally, and ideologically positioned. But, let us not be too optimistic and overlook the fact that what they invent is not so much an invention as a reproduction, a commodity from the outside, a product of the idealism floating around out there, brought into the house, at least in part, by Saludador and his socialist leanings.[32] And that invention implies quite a different and more extended or inclusive concept of family as it redefines traditional family gender roles, but only to a limited degree, for many aspects will not change. She still provides the labor while he passes his days waving to the neighbors. Although the cooperative limits the male, patriarchal prerogatives on which the traditional notion of family is structured (it is Marucha who decides he can stay), and although the value of her domestic labor is now acknowledged, the patriarch, stripped of his appendages (with the notable exception of the one that marks his masculine privilege—the phallus), will contribute little to the cooperative other than sex and the four walls, the house that he rhetorically assures her is hers, but which he has refused to sign over to her. The cooperative may provide a new form for old experiences, but it leaves a large segment of the old ideological construct securely intact.[33]

One must not miss the paradox of this question of property and papers. On Saludador's second return, Marucha tries to seduce him (quite literally) into signing over to her the papers to the house, paradoxically the four walls that idealists like him see as an impediment to progress and their idealistic goals and the same house that he has not cared to live in or maintain while on his charitable missions—the same house that stands as a symbol of the familial and domestic responsibilities he has not cared to shoulder and that she has had to assume in his absence. Although he insists that papers mean nothing and that it is her house, he himself refers to it as "Mi casa" (My house) (*ES*, 111). In the heat of the erotic seduction, he promises her anything she wants, but he still has enough presence of mind to use the excuse of his missing arm in order not to sign and thus ensure that what he has labeled "her" house or even "their" house is still definitively and legally *his* house. In this way our attention is drawn again to the misconceptions that surround our notions of family as well as its status (not always visible) as a guarantor of the patriarchal system and privileges. As noted, he and the son come and go from the home/stage, which she never leaves, which surrounds her, and in which she is central (literally and figuratively). Similarly, we tend to associate home with women. Old adages have assured us that "a woman's place is in the home" and that the home is the domain of the female. What is underscored here, however, is that if this is her domain, it is so only to the extent that the propertied patriarch allows it to be. The patriarch ultimately limits and frames her reign. In the end, the patriarch may be maimed, but he is certainly not impotent (again literally or figuratively). She may be the *ama de casa* (housewife, literally mistress of the house) but he is definitively the *dueño* (owner).[34]

The question of property and the paradox of how deeply ingrained that question is in our society (even in idealism and socialist causes that would seem to disallow private property) are highlighted by the fact that Saludador uses religious and socialist rhetoric to justify his return to his position as patriarch, head of the family, propertied landowner. Specifically, before returning home for good, he has consulted with the Vatican, where he is assured that God is everywhere, but particularly in his little house (with his family), with the Jewish leader in Jerusalem, who tells him to return to the home of his ancestors, and with comrade Massimo D'Alem, who had earlier affirmed, "la propiedad privada es un robo" (private property is robbery) but who now assures him, "No nos referíamos a la casa propia . . . Hasta te diría que tampoco a la casa de fin de semana . . . El robo empieza del country en adelante" (We weren't talking about one's own house . . . I'd say not even the weekend house . . . The robbery begins with the country house and beyond) (*ES,* 116). The inveterate idealist, who would right the wrongs of the world, finds justification for coming home and reassuming control of his family and property (and in some sense perpetuating what some would call the wrongs and injustices of the world) in those doctrines and discourses that have long been used to justify (again not always visibly) the patriarchal privileges inherent in the patriarchal system, which is based on the familial arrangement (and ruled over by the father).

Revealingly, the home/patio, which is the stage (and the two are irrevocably fused together here), is the locus of memories and seduction, in a subtle evocation of the seduction of memory, and again evokes the family and the seductive value of that collective memory. It is in the patio that Saludador remembers and recounts his foreign ventures. In what provides a double distancing and framing factor, he remembers himself remembering: framed within his memories are his recollections of remembering the home and the family (along with the *milanesas* [breaded cutlets] that function as an icon of both). He also recounts the seduction of staying away (Castro asked him to stay, the crowds cheered him, and so forth). Since as we have seen, home is not the home he remembered, we might well question the authenticity of his other seductive memories. Perhaps it is just the allure of being elsewhere, wherever one is not at the moment, an allure (seduction) based on inaccurate or partial (ambiguous, mythic) memory. Surely, we are seduced in much the same way by traditional (naturalistic) representations of family, which generally locate or position the ideal elsewhere: temporally, in the past (the paradise lost) or in the future (the homecoming), or spatially elsewhere, in some other house, never in our own, which always seems far less idyllic.

At the same time, the patio is the locus of Marucha's seduction of him. In order to get him to do as she wishes (position himself so that she can throw him over the wall, sign the papers to the house, and so on), she seduces him with memories of a shared past that may or may not have existed. What is clear is that the patio, the present, is riddled with the past and memories just as the patio/home is perforated by the elsewhere. In one case she remembers and recounts the seduction of their wedding night; in another, she

remembers the time he won the championship in the card tournament and they carried him on their shoulders (cf. the seminal image
on which the play developed). In each case, the fact that Saludador
does not remember the events she describes suggests that they may
well be inventions. Still, inventions or not, those memories seduce
Saludador, and he accepts them not only as valid but also and significantly as his own, as we too perhaps do when similarly seduced
by the naturalistic stage and the collective memory of family depicted there.[35] Indeed, his easy seduction, perhaps particularly in
the champion scene, may well point to his repeated desire to be the
center of attention at home and abroad. It would appear that any
memory that centralizes him will do, whether the Cuban crowds
cheering him and urging him to stay or the tournament fans' ova-
tion. Clearly, this is a reference to the audience's tendency to do the
same. And, might we not extend this willing seduction to the notion
of family? Are we seduced by the notion of a safe haven, an ideal
family that will love us no matter what, which is somehow always
a future homecoming or a paradise lost, precisely because it is a
form of centralizing the self, particularly the male self, who can
project himself as patriarch (who is surely more centralized in our
contemporary myths of family than is the female)? But, of course,
the paradox is that what seduces us is the naturalistic sign itself,
and as I have argued, in this play Cossa presents that naturalistic
sign as ambiguous, open to more than one interpretation, not limited to just the *either/or* but including the *and/also*. Thus, the figure
of family seduces because it is ambiguous, flexible enough to provide something for everyone at any given moment. Like the ambiguous cousin Rodolfo, who, according to Marucha, does wonderful
things and horrible things (you never know if he loves you or hates
you), the figure of family is both positive and negative; it all depends on one's position and the moment. While Saludador wanders
the world and remembers (mythicizes) family, it is the safe haven
to which he would return; while he is at home and remembers
(mythicizes) the elsewhere, those metaphoric walls are viewed as
an entrapping, devouring structure that would clip his idealist's
wings. Yet, family, as Cossa dramatizes, is both and neither. I
would argue that the same is also true of naturalistic theater.

That said, let me return to the wall, this time to the theatrical
fourth wall at the front of the stage. I have discussed at length the
patio wall that runs along the back of the stage, but the fourth (invisible) wall of this home/patio is definitely the theatrical fourth
wall at the front of the stage. Like all theatrical fourth walls, this
one provides us access into the theatrical fiction even as it maintains

us firmly entrenched on the other side, in our comfortable seats. And, that fourth wall definitely attains added significance in this play. First, it reminds us of the complicity of theater in promulgating our image (myth) of family and maintaining us within the assigned family gender roles, as I have argued in earlier chapters. Gender begins at home, and indeed, the metaphor of the four walls imprisoning family members in gender roles that are controlled from both the outside and the inside is literalized here. Surely, theater has long provided the models for our familial performances at home even as it has presumed to reflect them, providing what Butler has labeled "the reiterative and citational practice by which discourse produces the effects that it names."[36] As a result, as Butler also argues, "the norm . . . takes hold to the extent that it is 'cited' as such a norm, but it also derives its power through the citations that it compels."[37] As the circularity of this mutual reinforcement suggests, again the inside is not so easily divided from the outside, the original from the reproduction, in spite of what the icon of the wall might suggest.

At the same time, this fourth wall at the front of the stage is both transgressed and sustained, as is the more literal wall at the back of the stage. I would argue that Saludador's repeated traversing of the literal wall as well as the metaphoric wall of difference is repeated by Marucha in her conversations with the audience. Saludador may pass through the concrete wall at the back of the stage, but Marucha continually crosses the fourth (invisible) wall at the front of the stage as she talks to the audience and brings us into the play, refusing to acknowledge our difference. On one level her monologues serve to mark the passage of time; when she concludes, the action continues, but at a later point in time. Her monologues simultaneously create a pause, a break from action to narrative, and mark a separation of doing and saying. What is particularly interesting about these monologues (and unlike monologues in much theater) is that they do not break the fiction but in fact expand it, extend its realm by including the audience and casting us in the role of the neighbor (or perhaps even family member) with whom one might chat over coffee or over the back fence, a neighbor who would share and corroborate one's values and beliefs.[38] Or, on the contrary, we might view Marucha's monologue not so much as bringing the audience into the play as taking the play/fiction into the audience; again it all depends on one's perspective and positionality. Indeed, Cossa himself refers in the program to the breech of the spectator's space insofar as the horseshoe-shaped stage on which the play was first performed (and on which it in fact was developed, visualized, and worked out) was extended into the space of the audience where it was squared off and seats were removed.[39] Nonetheless, until the audience is directly addressed, we believe ourselves to be safely outside the play and the represented world. Once we are addressed, we become a part of the play, traversing the wall like Saludador and in some sense erasing differences, within and between.

In this way and in an original twist, Cossa subtly reminds us not only that the fourth wall provides the audience with the mirror of ourselves as we have long expected theater (at least naturalistic theater) to do, but also that the mirror works in both directions insofar as, inversely, the audience reflected here (or engulfed by the fiction) is patently a fiction, a creation designed (indeed forced) to reflect and corroborate what is dramatized onstage. In other words, while the audience expects the play to reflect us and our lives to some degree, the inverse also occurs in this play: the audience is placed in the position of passively accepting and then reflecting back (perpetuating) the beliefs and values of the character—in a gesture that again tends to erase difference and emphasize sameness (family). Marucha's conversations with the audience (which like so much else in this play are not really conversations but monologues that pass as conversations) presuppose (or construct) a certain uniformity within the audience and between herself and that audience. In some sense it is as if she were talking to herself as she casts the audience as her mirror reflection, as neighbors or family members who would unquestionably endorse her ideological position. What we witness in the play is a literalization of the power of theater to seduce us, to make us a part of its family and collective memories, as it casts us in certain roles and shapes our beliefs. Indeed, as Marucha answers questions that are not asked, responds to comments that are not made, she is creating the audience she would like to have (in much the same way as Saludador at the beginning of the play tries to create the ideal audience in Marucha, one that would share his joys of embracing the undifferentiated multitudes). In both cases, the goal seems to be the erasure of otherness and difference, the casting of the other so that s/he would mirror the self. Again, the metaphoric walls that would separate inside from outside, homogeneity from other, familial similarity from the different other, are destabilized, and we are unable to discern unambiguously which is in and which is out, which is private and which public.[40] Thus, we find ourselves in a position that evokes Saludador's on the occasion of his third rejection. That time, he was seduced by the audience (represented by son and wife) applauding his success at the card tournament. Like the protagonist of the story that provided

Cossa the seminal image for the play, Saludador reads their naturalistic performance (theater) and applause literally but to his detriment, for the apparent applause masks rejection. Similarly, we as audience may have all too often been seduced by the naturalistic performances (signs) and read them too literally, applauding perhaps what challenges our assumptions and/or vice versa. The problem then is that like the wall, signs can often be read in more than one way and can point to both sameness and difference, closure and opening.

Similarly, *El saludador* ends with both closure and nonclosure as it again destabilizes traditional icons of beginnings and endings to remind us that endings are beginnings and vice versa. The play opens in early morning (Vicente has just gotten up) in what marks a literal and metaphoric new day, the return of Saludador and the eventual establishment of the cooperative, as well as the end of family life as Marucha and Vicente have come to know it—Vicente is about to get a job and they are eventually to reincorporate Saludador into the framework of the cooperative. Significantly, the play closes as darkness falls. Again, we are presented with an icon from naturalistic theater that functions bidirectionally insofar as nightfall can be associated with negative connotations (end, danger) or with positive connotations (return to the family fold, safety and security at the end of a workday). The play provides the closure we expect from naturalistic theater: the issues seem resolved; all will apparently live "happily ever after." Yet, at the same time, the play refuses that closure, underscoring the temporal indebtedness of closure, of having selected this moment for the end rather than some other. Depending on where one places the words *The End,* one can emphasize connotations of closure (which could be positive or negative—they could live happily or unhappily ever after) or connotations of openness (which similarly could be positive or negative—like Sisyphus one could struggle forever against unsurpassable obstacles or one could face new experiences in a positive sense). The same is true with our figuring of family as positive or negative, safe haven or devouring entrapment. It all depends on when and where one is positioned.

Epilogue: Final Words on the Playwright's Final Words

The action of the play ostensibly ends on a note of tranquillity, of having returned to safe haven (if indeed a somewhat different safe haven than that implied by the traditional figure of family).

Marucha is about to prepare the mate, Vicente settles in, and Saludador greets the neighbors as darkness falls—a relatively unevent-
ful conclusion to an exceptionally funny comedy. All seems well in
the world as the audience prepares to depart the theater. Revealingly, however, the play text adds two more sentences. The first one
proffers stage directions that state, "*Las sombras van encerrando
el patio, el muro y el extramuro*" (*The shadows are enclosing, locking in the patio, the wall, and the area beyond the wall*) (*ES,* 117),
stage directions that might seem merely to provide a logic for dim-
ming the stage lights and signaling the audience that it is time to go
home. But, as the theater audience watched the darkness slowly engulf, in some sense devour the stage and its setting, there was a
distinct sense of dis-ease, of things not being right with the world.
I personally was reminded of the ending of *One Hundred Years of
Solitude,* where we read that "it was foreseen that the city of mirrors (or mirages) [a qualification that seems particularly apropos for
naturalistic theater] would be wiped out by the wind and exiled
from the memory of men."[41] What happened to the comedy here?
Why this sense of doom at the end? In addition, and particularly in
light of my discussion up to this point, one is struck by the term
encerrando (enclosing, locking in, entrapping). What metaphoric
darkness is entrapping this family, the patio, the stage, the world
beyond it, and perhaps even us? Could it be naturalistic theater itself? Even more chilling, to this critic at least, and in view of the
ostensibly lighthearted nature of the play, is the final sentence of
the published play text, a sentence to which the theater audience
would not have access since it provides neither dialogue nor didascalia, but a sentence that would impart a certain tone to the director
and the actors, and most likely motivated the effects that created
the sense of dis-ease at the end of the production. Specifically, that
sentence reads, "*Y ya no queda más tiempo para nada*" (*And
there's no more time left for anything*)—old images of family or
naturalistic theater.

Thus, we return to the beginning. Although at the start of the play
spectators may have felt as if we were settling in at home as we
viewed the open stage, at the end that sense of familiarity is turned
on end as everything disappears (engulfed, devoured by the darkness). Our imagined homecoming, our desire to return to a safe
haven, a secure, crystallized past, proves to be limited to its shell,
the hollow and ambiguous place/space of the theater building itself.
In this way Cossa has successfully employed the conventions of
naturalism not only to seduce his audience but also and paradoxically to disrupt our complacency as he subverts both the conventions of naturalistic theater and the old discourse of family.

5

¿Homo sapiens? by Marcela del Río:
Who Framed the Family?

¿HOMO SAPIENS?, SUBTITLED, *"SUSPENSO FAMILIAR EN DOS ACTOS"* (Family Thriller in Two Acts), is one of the more recent works by Mexican Marcela del Río (b. 1932), written between 1988 and 1991.[1] Unlike many of the other plays analyzed in the course of this study in which the question of family might be overlooked, as indeed it has been by those critics who have chosen to look elsewhere, del Río tackles the question of family head-on and places it at center stage, literally and figuratively, in order to challenge the perceived naturalness of that institution. Although we generally understand the family as a given in nature, she links it directly to economic and political interests as well as to all theatrical forms, but especially to television, tool of those interests, in order to demonstrate the dependence of our sociopolitical structures on the perpetuation of a very specific image of family.[2] Thus, del Río proposes that the institution is not natural but rather a social creation motivated by vested interests, hidden though they may be.

The interrelation of the family and various sociopolitical institutions is underscored from the first moments of the play in an invisible parade. Although at first glance this parade might seem completely unrelated to the play that follows, it will become clear that it in fact provides an excellent, if indeed paradoxically invisible, mirror of and frame for the themes and motifs of the rest of the play. Nonetheless, since the opening moments of the play attain significance only in retrospect, I will discuss them at the end of the chapter, in retrospect as it were, thus modeling my discussion of it on the play itself (which in turn models itself on our perceptions of our sociopolitical world, where motives generally become apparent only after the fact, if ever).

¿Homo sapiens? is a fascinating, humorous play, which is on some level a parody of soap operas. Briefly summarized, the play spotlights a family of two actors, Pericles Infante and Gloria Rey,

who, along with their son Shakespeare Infante Rey, have just
moved into their new home in the Institución de la Familia Planetaria (Institution of the Planetary Family), under contract to J.C., a
wealthy government employee/politician married to the young, innocent Inés.[3] In the course of the play we learn that J.C. has contracted this particular family because of his grudge against Pericles,
who, he believes, killed his father years earlier. The play ends as
J.C. accidentally kills Inés while trying to shoot Shakespeare. The
cast of characters is rounded out with two others, designated merely
as Hombre (Man/Husband) and Mujer (Woman/Wife), who assume
a number of different roles during the course of the play. On the
surface, the plot revolves around spousal infidelity, abuses of
power, thefts, murders to be solved, and old grudges—all the elements of a "good" soap opera. And, to highlight its similarities to
those popular melodramas, the work begins with what Pericles calls
the mania of television, its central position in contemporary homes,
and the obsession with having it turned on continually.[4] Nevertheless, del Río uses this soap opera background to address very serious contemporary social, political, and economic issues. Indeed, I
would argue that the work revolves around two principal axes, thematic focal points, both ultimately linked to the subject of family.

The first focal point is overtly sociopolitical and dramatizes several aspects of contemporary society: the hypocrisy that structures
the bourgeois family at the end of the twentieth century; the political situation in Mexico at that time; the marginalization of women,
who are not necessarily considered full "card-carrying" members
of the group labeled Homo sapiens; and, as noted, television, which
gives us ideals to live by but ideals that prove to be vested, at the
service of a patriarchal, commercialized society. The second thematic axis, which is implicitly linked to the first, deals with theater
per se, the theater that is the world, and especially the theater that
marks both politics and family life, theater that again is already
evoked in the opening parade as we shall see. Del Río suggests that
often commercial theater, like television, is at the service of these
other metaphoric theaters—the political and the familial. At the
same time she reminds us that all representations, observations, or
studies of people, whether artistic, sociological, scientific, and so
on, depend on the criteria, values, and ideology of the artist or scientist, who structures and controls the picture, the spectacle, the ex-
periment, according to specific ideological goals, hidden though
they may be.[5] Although the scientist or artist may appear dispas-
sionate and objective, he or she inevitably mediates and frames
what we see: including some details, excluding others; focusing

here rather than there. As a result of this framing, we perceive and interpret the object of study, and ultimately the world, in one way rather than another and draw "appropriate" conclusions, conclusions again at the service of a certain ideology, a certain hegemony, or certain personal, egocentric goals, none of which is necessarily visible. In this way the play undermines our pragmatic, scientific credence in the possibility of perceiving objectively—we believe that what we see is true, valid, without mediation, but as this play demonstrates, such is rarely, if ever, the case, for in both art and science that truth is always someone's truth and subject to being interpreted differently when viewed from a different perspective.[6] Thus, we should take quite literally the words of J.C. when he says that he cannot believe what he is seeing (*HS*, II), because, as we shall discover, we, the audience, cannot believe what our eyes see either. As a result, the questions that we do not ask until the end but that, as del Río demonstrates, we should be asking all along are: Who is controlling the spectacle/performance (whether the family, politics, or television/theater), what we see or think we see, and for what ends, for whose benefit? And, more specifically, who framed the family?

Perhaps the most original aspect of the play is the fact that the action takes place in a cage. That cage is located in what was a zoo and has now been converted into the Institution of the Planetary Family. Or, perhaps better expressed, that zoo has been renamed (reframed) by politicians so that we perceive it differently, see it as something other than what it is. The stage is dominated by that large cage, which serves as a visual reference to the limitations of sociopolitical and socioeconomic life and the family in particular. Described as similar to a birdcage, with a big cupola from which a chandelier hangs, this cage is outfitted with the furnishings of an upper-middle-class household (in which the television maintains a central position) and is the residence of Pericles, Gloria, and their son, Shakespeare, who have recently moved in. Significantly, this cage is surrounded by the trees of the park in a paradoxical metaphor that brings to mind a certain freedom even as it simultaneously negates it. Although the trees here evoke nature, this nature is limited at its outer boundaries by the city (sign of the society or culture) that surrounds it. In addition, as a park/zoo, it is a pocket of nature created and controlled by man. Thus, although the surroundings appear natural (like our perception of the family), they are in fact man-made, an indicator of the conquest of nature by culture, and reflect the manipulation and exploitation of that nature in the service of culture.[7] And, like any zoo cage, this one is open to the observation and inspection of the public, a public that is embodied onstage by actors, the characters (citizens) who go to the Institution to observe the animals. Significantly, however, this cage is also open to the observation of the theater audience, who in some sense watches themselves doubly mirrored on the stage, as both the family in the cage and as the public (characters) who go to look at them. As we shall see, this double mirror is repeated in many other aspects of the play.

At the start of the play the family's presence in the Institution and its inclusion in the "planetary family" are so recent that the cage's plaque has yet to be unveiled. The honor of unveiling it falls to J.C., a *funcionario* (government employee, civil servant, later called an influential member of the Party), since it is at his doing (if indeed with the encouragement of his *mujercita* [dear or little wife]) that this final branch of the planetary family, the "family of Man," has been included in the Institution.[8] As he rehearses his unveiling speech for Gloria early in the play, we learn that the goal of including the family of Man in the Institution is to unite the family and raise families "hasta la altura de aquélla que es la elegida para guiar a la familia planetaria. Así pues, es la elevación de los habitantes de este planeta y no la degradación del Hombre, lo que estamos develando" (to the height of the one that is the chosen one to guide the planetary family. That is, it is the exaltation of the inhabitants of this planet and not the degradation of Man that we are unveiling) (*HS,* I). Clearly, the fact that he has to state and even insist that Man is not being degraded here merely signals that on the contrary such is precisely what is happening. Obviously, his rhetoric serves a double function. First, it distracts from the fact that the plaque he is unveiling clearly places the human family on the same level as the other animals: like other plaques for animals in a zoo, this one indicates only the biological name, order, suborder, superfamily, class, species, and genus. Thus, the Institution's ostensibly egalitarian gesture, by means of which in one fell swoop it would unite not only Man with the animals but also the various groups of Man that are divided by race, socioeconomic standing, and so on, effectively reduces all in status, rhetoric to the contrary. Paradoxically, as J.C. acknowledges in his speech, Man (and the reference is clearly to the white male) does not want to be included in a family with other races of men or with animals. That the Institution (guided by political, social, economic, and even personal interests, as we will learn) would impose family ties on those who would reject them, clearly suggests that our image of family might well be similarly imposed, an artificial construct put in place by those who would profit the most by it, and that it is thus a product of culture in the guise of nature. Second, his speech assures us of the superiority of the family "elected" to guide the rest of the planetary family, a family that at first glance seems to be that of human beings in general. Nonetheless, as is the case with many other examples of the duplicitous rhetoric that del Río unveils throughout this play, it soon becomes apparent that J.C. is intentionally communicating two contradictory messages at the same time. While that "elected family" might well be interpreted as the human family (a family that is superior to the other animals), he surreptitiously refers to only certain members of that group, elected because of their even greater superiority, the family of Man, which in a clever slight of hand subtly excludes women. Significantly, at the same time, the term *elected* surely denotes elected politicians and moneyed classes like himself.[9] Thus, while his rhetoric celebrates those selected few and tries to convince the others that they are not excluded, it ultimately creates an even greater divide between the two groups. Like so much sociopolitical rhetoric, this too uses the same words to convey different messages to different audiences. Indeed, the title of the play, ¿*Homo sapiens?* evokes a similar sleight of hand or double entendre, saying different things to different audiences. Referring to the plaque, Inés asks Shakespeare what *Homo sapiens* means. He translates, "man who knows," and she concludes that the plaque must be referring to him since he is so smart. When he assures her that it refers to the entire species, she wonders, with all the innocence her name evokes, what the name of the species of women is. Although he informs her that women too are part of the species, he is not quite sure what to answer when she asks him if he would feel included if the species were named "woman who knows." Thus, while the language assures women that we are included, it also assures us (and the rest of humanity) that we are not. Throughout the play del Río similarly depicts political rhetoric that falls apart and reveals its hollowness at the slightest inspection or challenge.

The power of language to communicate two contradictory messages at the same time is also apparent in the name of this government employee. Self-baptized J.C., initials based on his name, Julio César (Julius Caesar), which in turn alludes to his goal to become the conquering chief, he who holds the power, those letters also encourage one to think of Jesus Christ (as Shakespeare does at one point) and the image that J.C. would like to project of himself as the savior. Paradoxically, however, but in keeping with this redoubled message of the work, he does not die for humanity, but rather kills for Man at the end when he shoots Inés, but more of this below. It is significant, too, that J.C. is not the name given him by his parents but one he adopts for a very specific reason. After a traumatic experience in his youth, when he felt powerless and promised to become strong to avenge his father's death, he renamed himself, changing Julito to J.C., because, as he notes, on television the important people use their initials as names (*HS,* II). As his words suggest, the word is used here as an instrument to convince us that things are as someone would have them be. It is not irrelevant either that although J.C. also lives in the park, he lives in the only house in the park, in what separates him from others, underscores his superiority to the rest of the family of Man, and functions as what I understand as a reference to los Pinos, the presidential home in Chapultepec Park in Mexico City.[10] His connection with the controlling political group is reinforced by Gloria's reference to his name: "¿Con las iniciales, como a los presidentes?" (With initials, like the presidents?) (*HS,* I). Thus, again, his position as a man of political and socioeconomic power and representative of the government should lead one to wonder about his vested interest in this Institution of the Planetary Family, with its goal of elevating the family. To what extent does it serve his personal goals? As we will see, it definitely does on a number of levels.

Clearly, the cage that is the home metaphorically evokes bourgeois family life at the end of the twentieth century in several senses, but, as we will see, it also evokes theater insofar as here the cage is the theatrical space and vice versa. Obviously, the cage is a space that is physically limited and limiting, but it is also psychologically limiting, as is the structure of the family in Western society and the rules of behavior within that family, rules that the Institution would shore up, although perhaps unnecessarily since, as Shakespeare observes in response to Inés's request that he change the plaque so that it reads *Humanus sapiens* instead of *Homo sapiens* and includes her in the group, it is not so easy to change the rules of the world (*HS,* I). Furthermore, it is not clear that the Mexican family has ever ceased being united nor should one have to raise Man and civilization, which, according to J.C., are already at the peak of progress. One might conclude then that what needs to be shored up is the political structure per se. It cannot be irrelevant that the years during which this play was being written (1988–91) were precisely the years in which the controlling political party in Mexico was beginning to lose some of its sway: the PRI, Partido Revolucionario Institucional (whose oxymoronic name perhaps reflects its character, *Institutional* Revolutionary

Party), product of the Mexican Revolution of 1910 and, for all practical purposes, sole controller of Mexican politics from the late 1930s (although its name was not changed to PRI until 1946) until the year 2000, and this in spite of its blatant corruption and frequent disregard for any interests other than its own.[11] Still, as the play will demonstrate, it is precisely the family on which the sociopolitical structure is based and which shores up that structure.

Within the play, surely, the Institution and the supposed elevation of the family serve two goals not unveiled by either the plaque or the speech of the government official. On the contrary, those goals are definitely obscured by the speech, as they so often are by political rhetoric. In the first place, the emphasis and insistence, by the politicians, on the values of the bourgeois family and the achievements of Man, manage to distract the public and direct its attention away from the crisis—and one presumes that the reference here is to the economic crisis Mexico suffered in the 1980s into the 1990s—a crisis that J.C. assures his audiences, with more hollow rhetoric, affects us all but is only a transition that will lead us to a better future (*HS*, I). He does not, as might be expected, address the question of who might or might not benefit from that "better future." In response to the rhetorical question planted by J.C., why now? (ibid.), one might argue that the Institution's unspoken goal is to provide its visitors with something else to think about, something other than the social, political, economic problems that are plaguing the country, or at least afflicting those who are not politicians during this transition period. Indeed, in answer to his own question, J.C. reveals just how implicated politics and the Party are in the creation of the Institution (and in turn in its goal of elevating the family), for he notes that the Institution was created in response to the imperative from the Candidate and the President to unite the family (ibid.).[12] In this way, del Río underscores the political motives behind the exhibition of and insistence on this artificially created, theatrically united family or on any specific limited and limiting image of family.

At the same time, the Institution serves another veiled interest insofar as, like television, it allows other people to observe close up this (ostensibly) economically comfortable family. As a result of their exposure to this carefully orchestrated portrait/experiment (it is presented in many ways as both art and science), the populace will come to desire the lifestyle and material goods that the members of this class possess (or in this case seem to possess). They too will want to climb the social ladder of material possessions and reach its summit (like the mountain climbers of the parade float discussed below). Although J.C. assures his imagined audience that the Institution plans to raise (note the insistence on the spatial metaphor) even the most humble families, the truth is that it, again like television, will raise only its aspirations, its materialistic desires, its dedication to consumerism. In other words, not unlike commercial advertising, it will create a market that in the end will make the wealthy even wealthier. Insofar as the cage provides a model that imposes a certain norm on others, it (and by implication the family structure presented there) ends up imprisoning everyone, metaphorically at least—those inside as well as those ostensibly outside.[13]

Del Río dramatizes this at the beginning of the first act when a man and a woman, seated in the audience, get up and go onto the stage to observe the cage from a closer vantage point. Designated Lavandera (Washerwoman) and Albañil (Bricklayer), that is from a lower socioeconomic class than the caged family, they comment on what they see. He says, "Mira, así exactamente, es cómo yo te decía ayer, aunque sea una casita chiquita, puede tener todo, bien puestecito . . . todo es cosa de voluntad" (Look, it's just like I told you yesterday, even though it is a very small house, it can have everything, nicely done . . . it's all a matter of willpower). To her response, "Y de pesos" (And money), he retorts, "No tanto, si trabajaras más duro . . ." (Not so much, if you would work harder . . .) (*HS,* I). What follows is a series of mutual recriminations in which each blames the other for their material lack— recriminations that will be repeated later in the play by various characters. Thus, del Río not only underlines the distance that exists between the norm promulgated by the Institution and the capacity of the public/observer to achieve it, but she also signals the trick, the sleight of hand, by means of which politicians have managed to divert attention so that those lacking material goods lose sight of the sources of their economic problems and blame each other (or others in the same situation) rather than the system itself and those who have become skilled at taking advantage of that system—the corrupt politicians and businesspeople who profit from the consumerism and the labor of the lower classes and who, via stratagems such as the Institution and the "family of Man," have sold them an ideology that supports their own personal, vested interests, both economic and political. Similarly, one might well question, as Donzelot does in *The Policing of Families,* to what extent the perceived problems of the family at the end of the twentieth century are a product of sociopolitical interests and institutions.[14]

It is important to recognize also that this particular couple, which approaches to observe the cage, has come from the audience. After going up onto the stage, they sit down on the park bench, which invites one to sit and observe just as a sofa in front of a television or a seat in a theater might. In a visual redoubling, these two actors reflect the audience itself and lead us to ask, to what extent are our image of family and our desire to embody that image equally a product of the various media and arts? To what degree do we desire what we desire (including the perfect family) precisely because television, theater, or cinema has presented it as desirable? To what point is desire a creation, a sociopolitical, socioeconomic product, created and manipulated by those who would profit most from it? Later in the first act, the man and the woman who earlier played the roles of the washerwoman and the bricklayer enter again. This time they play the parts of two thieves who plan to rob the home/cage, take by force what they have been unable to obtain in any other way. But, as he observes in response to her question to him about whether it is worth the bother, "No sé. Pero si se encierran, es porque guardan algo de valor . . . Todo el que echa llave, es que teme que le roben algo" (I don't know. But if they lock things up, it's because they have something of value . . . Anyone who locks things up is afraid something will be stolen) (*HS,* I). Nevertheless, as she pertinently observes, the question is what that something is. And, as is later suggested, that something is not only the material but also the entire ideological system of images that supports the sociopolitical structure, the patriarchy (and by implication the PRI), which finds itself about to lose some of its authority and thus needs to *echar llave* (lock things up) to safeguard the above from other hands, use the keys that, like the pistol, will later be presented as symbols of power.[15]

Significantly, within the fictional world of the play, the adults of our so-called model family are actors and have accepted their new job precisely because the crisis (transitional though it may be for people like J.C.) has prevented them from finding work in the theater.[16] The fact that J.C. acknowledges that he contracted the family *because* they are actors highlights the fact that he is paying them to play a role, perform his script, with its very specific (and vested) image of family. Thus, the question of economics is directly linked to that of the projection (creation) of an appropriate (profitable) image of family. Later, of course, we shall discover that we cannot rely on everything (or perhaps anything) J.C. says, but nonetheless it is clear that Gloria and Pericles' new job is not very different from one in the theater, since here too their primary responsibility is to allow themselves to be watched, indeed, as if they were onstage (which they are, both literally and figuratively). Nevertheless, the irony is that their own lack of economic resources has led them to this job where they are perceived as those who do indeed have economic means, again reminding us how seldom things are as they are presented. We are faced here with a family that is a theatrical product and one that is doubly commercialized and at the service of the sociopolitical, socioeconomic system. In what can only be viewed as a vicious circle, those who control the Institution/theater profit from those without material means, using them to project an image of material means, which will in turn engender desire for material goods, which will profit the small group in control and further raise their status in the eyes of the nonelite. As Gloria emphasizes in reference to her career in television commercials, "¡Qué triunfo! Y si no, dime Jota Ce: ¿no compraste tu coche porque yo te lo vendí, con la belleza de mi cuerpo?" (What a triumph! If not, tell me Jay Cee: didn't you buy your car because I sold it to you, with the beauty of my body?) (*HS*, I), thus reminding us how often we buy (and buy into) X believing we are buying Y. I would add that what the actors are selling now, with their performance in the Institution, albeit unwittingly, are the false values of the bourgeois family, the authority of the patriarchy (and/or the PRI), and the consumerism of a society obsessed with materialism.

The fact that the family itself does not have a key to the cage suggests that they are indeed imprisoned, unable to escape or change either the rules or the roles; they are metaphorically locked within and into the system. And, they cannot change anything because, as in theater or television, this cage is a space framed and controlled by entities who are not always visible and who prove to have hidden motives and sociopolitical agendas. The difficulty of escaping from the roles that we play in life and the influence of the familial roles promulgated by the various media, roles to which we have been exposed since childhood, are also among the primary themes of the play. For example, throughout the work Pericles and Gloria recite various speeches borrowed from theatrical works in which they have performed, not always distinguishing clearly between role and reality.[17]

In addition, del Río dramatizes the fact that the roles we assume in life are often mere repetitions or imitations of the roles we have seen our own parents perform, but they are roles that are several times removed from their originals. For example, in the first act, we witness two simultaneous situations in which the males, heads of family, imitate their own fathers and impose their will, primarily because they can (they have the power to do so) and because they have been taught that such is expected of fathers (it is how fathers

act, in both senses of the word) although in both cases their arrogant, overbearing attitude is clearly gratuitous. J.C. says to his wife,
Inés, "No me obligues a darte explicaciones de cada cosa . . .
cuando te ordeno algo . . ." (Don't make me explain everything to
you . . . when I give you an order . . .) (*HS,* I). At the same time,
Pericles commands Shakespeare to come here and begins to scold
him for not being quick enough in obeying him. Shortly thereafter,
we witness a retrospective scene from J.C.'s youth. By taking us
back to his past, the scene underlines not only the frustrations of
that past but also the image of the father that the son carries with
him, an image that is not fully valid insofar as it is fictionalized and
subjected to the limited comprehension of the then child, but it is
one that will nonetheless serve as his model. Emphasizing the distance between the original and the reenactment, the retrospective
scene is introduced by Gloria's asking J.C. if he remembers his
father and his response, "Cómo no me voy a acordar, era tan
bueno" (How would I not remember, he was so good) (ibid.). Significantly, the fictional quality (or wishful thinking) of those words
is highlighted in the scene that follows, when Hombre (Man), now
in the role of the voice of J.C.'s past (or perhaps that of "Truth,"
which, as the play proposes, is inevitably a personal creation),
speaks to him: "No puedes deshacerte de mí. Tal vez si perdieras
definitivamente la memoria . . . pero entonces dejarías de ser tú, y
finalmente . . . volverías a recrearme" (You can't get rid of me. Perhaps if you permanently lost your memory . . . but then you would
stop being you and finally . . . you would reinvent me) (ibid.). Thus,
the voice suggests that J.C. has already re-created his past and/or
that all pasts are re-creations, including that of the family of Man.
Thus, while we generally acknowledge that children are products of
their parents (literally and figuratively), the play suggests that the
inverse is equally true: parents are the products (fanciful imagina-
tions, re-creations) of their children. That voice continues by urging
J.C. to answer Gloria's question about whether he remembers his
father (ibid.).[18] This question finds its answer in the retrospective
scene. There we find a father who is considerably less than "so
good." In this scene from his past, J.C. is with his father as the latter
threatens to beat him if he tells his mother about the infidelity he
has just witnessed. With words more literal than he might imagine,
his father threatens him, "¡Hijo de tu puto padre ¿qué chingados
estás espiando?" (Son of your whoring father, what the hell are you
spying on?) (*HS,* I).[19] He continues echoing (or providing the model
for—it is a question of chronological perspective, whether we look
forward or backward) what J.C. had earlier snarled at Inés, "Aquí

no hay más palabra que valga que la mía, y oígala bien: *yo soy muy vengativo,* y 'onde usté hable, le rompo la madre" (Here the only word that matters is mine, and listen carefully: *I am very vindictive, and if you tell, I'll break your neck) (HS,* I, emphasis added). The fact that J.C., as we will discover, has devised the idea of including the family of Man in the Institution and has carefully set up this particular show as well as the coming theater of Inés's death with the specific goal of getting revenge, surely underscores the extent to which he has indeed taken his vengeful father as his example.

Perhaps the most significant aspect of this retrospective scene is that in it a simple change of lighting allows the same actors to play new roles: J.C. plays the role of his father while Shakespeare plays the role of the young J.C., thereby signaling the similarities between the two historical moments and the fact that the past is still with us, psychologically at least (both in terms of the individual and in terms of the family of Man). This technique also underscores the difficulty of freeing oneself from familial roles and highlights once again the fact that we are all actors playing our learned parts. J.C. can play the part of his father because, in so many ways, he has become him in the present. That is, his father has functioned as his model just as the bourgeois family in the Institution is meant to function as a prototype for other families, and this in spite of the fact that neither paradigm can be considered ideal in any way.[20] Nevertheless, in the case of J.C., he has appropriated the abusive patriarchal language and values and has accepted them as the only truth. It would appear then that the primary patrimony bequeathed J.C. is precisely this language that frames and influences perception, the rhetoric that he has used to impose his values on others in order to have them see things his way and allow him to exercise the power that he believes his father possessed. The irony, of course, is that J.C.'s father, a soft-drink deliveryman, with little economic or political power, like Pericles, was effectively powerless outside of the family unit. But, as the scene emphasizes, the child's desire for power leads to his complicity with the powerful by means of which he hopes to partake in that supremacy. More specifically, that complicity is predicated on silence, on not telling, on the child's guarding the masculine secret, and, under the threat of severe punishment or violence, not exposing the paternal infidelity and violation of the very rules (marital fidelity, among others) the patriarchy has established. It cannot be irrelevant either that as dramatized in the play the complicity is predicated on a double gesture of silencing: not only does J.C. keep the secret from his mother in the past; he also keeps the secret from Gloria (and perhaps himself) in the present, erasing the facts and insisting that his father was "so good." Thus, even those who may not gain directly or immediately (but who nevertheless hope for some future gain) are forced into complicitous silence, a silence "como tumba" (like a tomb) (*HS,* I), a tomb that perhaps evokes a metaphoric death for us all.

It is noteworthy that at one point in the first act it appears that this vicious circle of paternal imitation is going to be broken and that Shakespeare is going to opt for another way of life, one that would reject the model (the cage) of the fathers. It is his birthday, and his father gives him a pistol so that he can go hunting like men do (*HS,* I).[21] Revealingly, the patrimony Pericles gives him is the phallic symbol of manhood, the instrument of power (as it is called in the second act) with which one can impose one's word, one's truth. But unlike J.C., Shakespeare refuses the legacy, the world as it is, and casts doubt on the civilization that destroys rather than constructing and corrupts rather than teaching (*HS,* I). It is here too where del Río includes the most direct criticism of the family unit: "¿Y qué es para ti la familia, papá? ¿Un hombre y una mujer que duermen juntos?" (And what is the family to you, papa? A man/husband and a woman/wife that sleep together?) (ibid.). In the absence of a convincing response, he insists that he will not remain a prisoner in the cage of their decisions (ibid.). He will leave this literal and figurative zoo, this city of humans who act like beasts as they wait to devour each other. Thus, he returns the gun in what would appear to signal his rejection not only of civilization as he knows it but also and by implication, the father, the fatherland, and the patriarchal system. But, once again, as we will see, things may not be as they appear.

Nonetheless, although he rejects that symbol of the patriarchy and power, someone else will certainly use it. In fact, the first act concludes, like many soap opera episodes, with a blackout during which a shot is heard. As the lights come back up and the music rises in intensity like in soap operas (*HS,* I), we discover that Inés, the innocent who wanted to learn, has been killed. The curtain falls.

The second act begins where the first one ended, with the death of Inés. After several minutes of playing detectives as in television shows and investigating in an attempt to discover the criminal and a motive, minutes fraught with mutual recriminations, it is discovered that Inés is not dead after all. The crime is not a crime. Everything has been a sham, another play within the play, this one machinated by J.C. But, for me what is most significant is the fact that we, the audience, have failed to recognize the death as make-believe; we have been as deluded as the characters. Earlier in the first act we recognized the metatheater (the retrospective scenes) as such. But, at the beginning of the second act, we are kept as unaware of what is happening as are the characters, a fact that again leads us to ask to what extent can we believe what our eyes seem to see, to what extent are we ourselves those whom J.C. labels people who do not even know what they are seeing (*HS*, II). In this way del Río exposes the double game/trick since not only have we been fooled by the death of Inés (the play within the play), but, as we are about to discover, we have also been fooled by the play that frames that inner play, by that which has not been presented quite so obviously as theater. The confusion here functions as an index to the world outside of the theater where, as the play suggests, we may have also been duped by the image of family that we have accepted and the way it has been framed. In other words, up until this point we believed we understood (such as I have been explaining it) what was going on in the Institution as well as J.C.'s sociopolitical, socioeconomic motivations in hiring the actors. But, as it turns out, J.C.'s motivations have been strictly personal and even more concealed than we have imagined. Here in the second act we learn that he contracted the family of actors to avenge the death of his father, a death provoked, unconsciously to be sure, by Pericles as a child. Thus, paradoxically, the family (this individual family as well as the institution in general) functions as both the instrument of revenge and its target. By blaming Pericles for the death of Inés, J.C. would finally make him feel the same impotence that he (J.C.) felt earlier. As he states, "No hay nada peor en la vida que la impotencia" (There is nothing worse in life than impotence/powerlessness) (ibid.).[22] In other words, all has been motivated by his desires to do violence to others and not to feel impotent, violated, as he felt as a child, an impotence that is in some degree at least, a product of the socioeconomic system and his class position within it, but that is also, and let us not miss the irony here, experienced at another moment in time precisely *because* of his father. In other words, his motivating desire here is to be, in Mexican slang, the *chingón* or *jodón* rather than the *chingada* or *jodida:* he who violates (rapes, abuses) rather than the one who is violated.[23] For this reason, J.C. has worked so hard to become what he is: the one with power, he who possesses the keys, the word, the weapons (the "phallic" pistol among others) with which to impose/enforce his word.

In this way we return to the theme of the old hostilities and grudges that determine our present demeanor, whether personal or political. Del Río's point here is particularly original, for, inverting the feminist slogan "the personal is political," she demonstrates that the inverse is equally true: the political is personal. At the same time, the dramatist emphasizes the fact that no matter how much we would prefer to ignore the past, it is precisely that past that has occasioned the current problems, again, whether personal or political. Although Pericles shouts, "El pasado está enterrado y no hay para qué estarlo removiendo, sólo nos intoxicará" (The past is buried and there's no reason to be stirring it up, it will only poison us) (*HS*, II), Shakespeare wisely responds, "Y mientras más tierra tenga encima, mejor ¿no es así? Nadie olerá la putrefacción. Es la historia de siempre, caminamos sobre nuestros propios gusanos" (And the more dirt on top of it the better, isn't that it? No one will smell the putrification. It's the same old story, we walk on top of our own worms) (ibid.). Indeed, one might interpret Shakespeare's comment here specifically in light of the family, the continuing concept of family, which has been something of a sacred cow in twentieth-century Western society, something we are not supposed to challenge (and generally do not). For example, after Shakespeare has rejected the pistol and announced that he is going away, to live differently, it occurs to no one to question Pericles' repeated assertion (in what might be understood to be the voice of society or the patriarch) that Shakespeare's place is with/in the family (*HS*, I). As other plays discussed in the course of this study demonstrate, we have been allowed, perhaps even encouraged, to look at individual families, the metaphoric illnesses or dysfunctions within them, as individual failures to live up to the model, but rarely is the image itself challenged, nor do we question where it came from, whose vested interests it serves. Still, as Donzelot has argued, an entire "science" (psychoanalysis) has grown up around the family, to police it, and in some sense to coerce its members into fulfilling their assigned roles.[24] Thus, one of the most original aspects of the del Río play is that while it does not deny that the families portrayed are all dysfunctional, it does propose that the source of the "illness" is the structure itself, not only because the roles proffered are unrealizable as we have seen in other works, but because of the vested interests that structure those roles. Obviously, if we do not examine the past (including both the individual's family history and the history of the notion of family), we will not understand the present nor unravel that question of culpability, the personal guilt as well as the sociopolitical and socioeconomic. As we will see in the question of Pericles' guilt or lack thereof, sometimes in fact there is no guilt that is not, to some extent, shared by all of society. What's more, and in what I interpret as a reference to the negligence and corruption of the Mexican government and the PRI during decades in

Mexico, J.C. implicitly queries, when does negligence become crime? But here, the situation is even more complicated because we would also have to ask to what extent J.C.'s vengeance and his emphasis on the crime of the other function to divert attention from his own crimes. As the thief notes, suggesting that politicians in general and J.C. in specific are as thieving as he is,

¿Qué fácil es quitarle a uno el trabajo o quedarse con el fruto de él, legalmente, apoyado por las leyes? . . . ¿Y las comisiones que recibes por cada compra que haces . . .? ¿No es dinero del pueblo? Una tajadita por aquí, una tajadita por allá y a comprar diamantes.

[Isn't it easy to take someone's job away or keep the fruits of it, legally, backed by the laws? . . . And the commissions you get for each purchase you make . . .? Isn't that the people's money? A little slice here, a little slice there and it's off to buy diamonds.] (*HS*, II)

At any rate, according to J.C., his father died as a result of an accident that occurred when the young Pericles was riding his new bike, a gift from his own father and one that marks the socioeconomic difference between him and J.C.—the latter did not have a bike; he was too poor.[25] Although Pericles maintains that it was an accident, J.C. insists, "Siempre hay detrás de [los accidentes] un maldito asesino que se escuda en su irresponsabilidad, . . . el 'asesino de las manos limpias,' que ni siquiera se inclinó a ver la sangre que derramó" (Behind [accidents] there is always a damn murderer who hides behind his irresponsibility, . . . the "murderer with clean hands," who didn't even bend over to see the blood he shed) (ibid.). The irony, of course, is not only that his words reflect the misdeeds of government employees, businessmen, and politicians like himself, as I have already indicated, but also that at the end of the work, he himself repeats the accident, killing Inés as he attempts to kill Shakespeare. Although this time the "criminal" stops to see the spilt blood, the final words of the play, articulated by Pericles, suggest that no one is going to take his crime very much to heart and little is going to change: "Vamos, Julio César, la función debe continuar" (Come on, Julio César, the show must go on) (ibid.).

Doubtlessly, del Río mocks melodramatic soap operas here, but she also criticizes the influence of television in our lives with the questionable values and examples it offers us. In effect, according to what we learn in another retrospective scene in the second act, a scene that takes place shortly after the death of his father, J.C. gave his word to his father that he was going to become strong in order to be able to avenge his death, that he was going to become rich and powerful in order to have enough money to pay a *television* detective to find the person responsible for his death (*HS,* II). Apparently, as a child he did not distinguish between real life and what he saw on television, but what is certain is that he wanted to have what he saw on television and live like the people he saw there. In this respect, the Institution is promulgating the same goals as television and theater, encouraging the public to accept the models proffered and turn a "blind eye" as it were to the political or ideological motivations. One must wonder too to what extent a "blind eye" is being turned here with regard to the family. As noted, based on J.C.'s recollections as presented in the retrospective scene, his father was "so good" that he threatened the child with violence, coerced him into silence to cover for his crimes (thereby making him an accomplice in crime), and taught him the importance of being unfaithful and treacherous along with the necessity of over-looking, silencing both. Yet, because the image of the family that society has imposed posits that the child will and indeed should follow the model of the father, it occurs to no one (and especially not to J.C.) to contest either the imperative or the paradigm. In a curious example of double thinking, society seems to tell the child, this is who you should take as your model; by implication, therefore, it is a positive model.[26] Paradoxically, however, in yet another retrospective scene, this time between Pericles and his mother, del Río underscores a further aspect of this double thinking. In that scene, Pericles assures his mother that sons follow the paternal models, but as she responds, "Cuando te conviene entras en el molde, cuando no, lo rompes. Linda práctica" (When it suits your convenience you go along with the norm, when it doesn't, you break it. Nice practice) (*HS,* I).

But the theater functions on yet another level here since at several moments in the second act it is suggested that everything we watch may be part of a work that Shakespeare has been writing, in what provides a spiraling mise en abyme from which there seems to be no escape. For example, toward the end of the second act, he says that he is writing the conclusion of his work.[27] A little later, after he offers the gun to the three arguing adults so that they can finish the "cacería" (hunt), he turns to Inés and invites her to the theater/show (*HS,* II), later assuring her, when J.C. announces that he is going to kill him, that this is just theater (ibid.), words that place in doubt everything we have seen so far.[28] At this point, we would do well to remember Shakespeare's words to his father in act 1 as he rejected his gift/inheritance: "Tal vez tú necesites una pistola, yo no" (Maybe you need a pistol, I don't) (*HS,* I). If he is a writer, and if the pistol serves to impose one's word/truth as it does in this play, then perhaps we should understand that Shakespeare does not need the pistol because he has the pen; he can impose his word via litera- ture, theater, or television. As he has noted, each instrument of power can be outpowered by another except for the word, which is the most powerful of all (*HS*, II). As a writer he is *authorized* to impose his word in other ways. Indeed, the fact that Shakespeare's primary activities alternate among writing, playing the flute, and sketching positions him as the artist par excellence. That his musi- cal instrument is specifically a flute evokes the Pied Piper and his "magical" ability to persuade all to follow him. But, let us not for- get that the Pied Piper used his artistic ability for both good and evil. He rid the city of the rats, but then, in revenge/retaliation for not being paid, he also led all the children away.[29] So, the question that remains is how Shakespeare will use his artistic authority. While he at one point refers to his divine chromosomes, suggesting that he too partakes of his mother's divine ability, her ability to cre- ate, to give life (*HS*, I), he also acknowledges that he has inherited other divine chromosomes from his father. Thus, one might well surmise that he will follow the models of J.C., his father, and their fathers (all of whom are ultimately interchangeable, with little dif- ference among them) and use that power, as all the others have, to create structures, artistic images, and models that will enhance his own position and achieve his own hidden goals.[30] Although he is a writer, we do not know that what he is writing is not a play for commercial theater or a television script, a work that would again provide a show to support the status quo.

This question of how Shakespeare might use his artistic power is accentuated at the conclusion of the play when J.C. shoots at Shake- speare and accidentally kills Inés. This time the death appears real (within the representational economy of the play, of course), but it seemed real the first time too. And, if it is real, then we find our- selves facing yet another irony insofar as Shakespeare's reaction to this death is to state, "No te vas a morir, Inés . . . Tú me salvaste y yo . . . escribiré sobre ti" (You're not going to die, Inés . . . You saved me and I . . . I'll write about you) (*HS*, II). Once again, the word, this time written rather than transmitted by television, seems to be more valuable than life. It does not matter that Inés dies sav- ing his life; Shakespeare will recreate her in language. But with what validity? With whose truth? Whose Inés? As a female in the world we have inherited, can she ever be anything but the (re)cre- ation of a male? Thus, Inés, desired by all three males and in so many ways a symbol of innocence, is killed by them, victim of their aggression, quest for power and control, their desire to be the *chingón* (aggressor) and not the *chingado* (recipient of aggression). Indeed, Shakespeare specifically uses the words, "escribiré *sobre* ti" (I will write about, on/over you), in what takes us back to the question of throwing dirt (words?) on top of the past to bury it, to make it seem other than what it was.

Revealingly, the play ends as it began: Gloria turns on the television. Again she answers Pericles' question of why by stating that there might be important news (*HS,* II) thus proposing that what we see on television must be more important than the life, and in this case death, that form part of our immediate (if not unmediated) surroundings. Indeed, the fact that the principal action of the play begins and ends with the television being turned on suggests that the entire play, like our perception of the theater of the world outside the play, is mediated by television and various art forms. A man with a microphone arrives, and Pericles articulates the final words of the play: "Vamos, Julio César, la función debe continuar" (Come on, Julio César, the show must go on)—the plaque must be unveiled; his speech must be delivered. Nothing has changed. Early in the play, Gloria distinguished (perhaps erroneously) between politics and theater by noting that in the latter the audience just sits there, silently looking and listening (*HS,* I).[31] In other words, there is no participation, no change (although surely the same might well be said for politics Mexican-style, until, as Pericles notes, those in power become too abusive [*HS,* II]). The cycle (vicious circle) will be repeated; more misleading, distracting rhetoric will be uttered, and although arbitrary, Western society's image of family, an image promulgated for the economic and political gain of a few, will continue. Thus, we necessarily return to the questions I posed before, who has controlled the show/spectacle, what we see, and for what ends, for whose benefit? Who framed the family, in both the artistic sense and the criminal sense? And, more important, how can we know?

At least a partial answer to these questions can be found in the parade with which the play opens. As promised, I would now like to return to the opening moments of the play and consider that parade, whose motifs can now be shown to have been carefully selected for their bearing on the issues addressed in the rest of the play.

At the start of the play, but before the lights go up, the audience is bombarded with the celebratory sounds of a parade that we do not see (as we tend not to see the interconnectedness of the numerous sociopolitical institutions depicted there) but that is itself another form of theater and one with definitive goals: to celebrate what those in power would have the populace celebrate (e.g., national holidays, heroes, and so on) and to distract that populace from and encourage it to forget, temporarily at least, other problems and issues (e.g., the crisis) that those in power would prefer to downplay or erase (make invisible).[32] The fact that del Río has chosen specifically a parade, which metaphorically links the various institutions visually and spatially in a chain of images (if we could see it, that is), is particularly effective in evoking the associations among the institutions. Significantly, this invisible parade is described to us by a disembodied voice whose reliability we have no choice but to accept. While we have no reason to suspect that this voice is anything other than impartial, its positioning (interests), loyalties, and motives must remain a mystery, as they do in the play and so often do in life, as hidden as the voice's body. The first float mentioned by that voice represents the Mexican family. It is followed by the float of a mountain climbers' club, on which two Boy Scouts "climb a mountain," in what underlines the theatricality of it all since obviously whatever they scale is not a mountain but merely simulates one in some minor degree, just as on a number of levels the families portrayed in this play only simulate in some small degree the ideal of what families should be. A band that plays the Zacatecas march and carries placards supporting the Candidate follows this float. After the band comes the Military School float, followed by the float of the Official Delegation of Coyoacán, decorated with trees and signs about saving the environment.[33]

In this invisible way (we only hear, we do not see), del Río uses the first moments of the play to introduce most of the motifs on which the play will focus and subtly underline the interconnections among them. Specifically, the parade links the family, as an institution, with Boy Scouts and mountain climbers. Although the connection may not be immediately apparent, we must remember that the Boy Scouts are a bourgeois group, imitating foreign models, not unlike the ideal of the Mexican family, based as it is on the Catholic model imported from Europe in the sixteenth century and imposed on the native population. The float's focus on mountain climbing imparts a sociopolitical message insofar as the members of this bourgeoisie have sufficient leisure to dedicate themselves to something as unproductive as mountain climbing, an activity that accomplishes little except to prove that Man can conquer/colonize nature. Surely, members of the lower socioeconomic classes would be too busy trying to meet basic needs to have time to worry about conquering literal mountains. But, they will have to conquer metaphoric mountains, and thus the parade's mountain climbers also evoke social climbers, those whose materialistic desires are shaped by television and theater, theater in this case embodied by the parade. As noted earlier, the status of the family may not be raised by the Institution but its materialistic aspirations certainly will be. In addition, the mountain climbers (or better, and more revealingly expressed, the actors [Boy Scouts] who perform the role of mountain climbers) function as a reference to those who would tame or conquer nature, not only to demonstrate the superiority of Man, but also to convert that nature into a commodity, either in the form of a controlled nature to be sold to tourists (tourism) or in that of zoos and *viveros* (open green spaces in the city), which would, like the parade, help distract the populace from other problems. The paradox, of course, is that these same groups who would tame nature ultimately destroy that natural commodity by their very presence, their hobby, and their economic interests. And, as the play demonstrates, this taming and re-creation or re-invention of nature by culture is directly linked to the notion of family, for in spite of the fact that the sociopolitical institutions would have us perceive the family as a natural entity, it is ultimately a product of those institutions, merely painted over with the aura of the natural.

The next float, that of the Military School, signals the importance of proper education (enculturation) in achieving the greater political goals, of educating (or brainwashing) youth so that their ideals reflect those of government or social leaders and so that they support or fit into the various sociopolitical institutions as perpetuated by those leaders. Significantly, however, this is a military school, thus evoking the force or coercion (the gun by means of which one imposes one's will and version of Truth) lying just beneath the surface of the educational apparatus, while the cadets that accompany this float are dressed in turn-of-the-century outfits, reminding us how old this particular institution is and that, as the play demonstrates, the past is still very much with us if indeed buried and concealed (e.g., J.C.'s childhood). It is relevant too that the Military School, although linked to the family (structured as it is on the patriarchal norm and the principle of patriarchal supremacy), is in many ways a replacement for it: boys are removed from their homes and families (often perceived as a world of women) and placed in all-male institutions where they are taught to behave like "men" and fight for their *patria* (*father*land), both literally (war) and figuratively (as defenders of the patriarchal sociopolitical system).[34] It is here too where the young men often form the alliances on which their future economic and political successes depend. Although not removed from their families for the sake of military school, both J.C. and Pericles, as has been noted, have adopted similar masculinist, aggressive models, in the form of their fathers, and have allied themselves with other males.

Lest there be any doubt about the interconnection between these two floats, they are bridged by a band playing a patriotic song and campaigning for the Candidate, which again highlights the connection between all these institutions and government or politics itself while reminding us that even such innocuous amusements as parades have a political agenda.[35] As described to us, the campaign for the Candidate is at the very center of the parade, flanked by two floats on either side. And, of course, the campaign for the Candidate (whom one would suppose is a member of the PRI) would be a campaign for the status quo, for ensuring that the power remains in the same (patriarchal) hands. Although later J.C., who is called an influential member of the Party, will acknowledge that the campaign is in full swing (HS, I), the opening parade of images and the play itself suggest that the metaphoric campaign to maintain the power in the hands of a few and shore up the patriarchal sociopolitical system is always in full swing as is the related campaign to perpetuate a singular, unified, profitable image of family.

Last but not least, we find the float of the local government, in some sense metaphoric child of, modeled after, the larger national government, and one that paradoxically seeks to save the environment even while it is one of the entities that helps to destroy it.[36] And, let us not forget, this parade or chain of sociopolitical institutions has at its head (linguistically at least since it is the first mentioned) the float of the Mexican family, a float not described except to say that it is sponsored by the Voluntariado Nacional (National Volunteer Group), a group made up of the wives of public officials who "voluntarily" assist in various social programs, and a group that has a significant investment in both politics and family. Thus, the intricate position of the institution of the family within the sociopolitical structure is underscored right from the very first (dark) minute or two of the play.

By employing her own frame, one that proffers a different perspective on family and society, del Río makes visible the institutions that have long framed and controlled the image of family. While theater and art are often used to shore up the status quo and social institutions, they can also be used to challenge them. Again in many ways, it is all a question of frame, where the artist places the frame, what she or he makes visible or conceals. Depending on the motives, the ideology, the vested interests of the artist, the frame can function as a cage or as a tool of disclosure. Nonetheless, the use of the parade as a framing device is even more complex, for—in what provides a commentary on the sociopolitical institutions criticized throughout (including theater)—the parade is not only the frame, but it is also framed in what provides a dizzying mise en abyme. Clearly, we are presented with only a part of the parade, a part chosen for what it shows us about the interconnectedness of the parading institutions, but that part in turn forms part of a larger show that we cannot perceive, just as we cannot always perceive how sociopolitical situations fit together, that is, just as we cannot always perceive the larger picture of which our object of study is only a small portion. In this manner, del Río draws attention to the very frame, which is not only unavoidable, but also already framed itself.

Thus, if Donzelot is correct that the family is a "moving resultant, an uncertain form whose intelligibility can only come from studying the system of relations it maintains with the sociopolitical level," then del Río certainly provides an eye-opening dramatization of those relations insofar as she demonstrates that the image we have of family is a product of sociopolitical institutions with their individual vested (personal) interests by means of which culture is not merely imposed on what we would like to label natural (the family), but in fact creates that product and labels it natural to distract attention from the same institutions and their vested interests.[37] As a result, the question of blame (which surfaces a number of times in the course of the play) is more diffuse. As depicted here, individuals are neither guilty nor guiltless, since they are caught up in the system, in many ways as victimized by it as are those whom they would personally victimize. It is not irrelevant that early in the play, Inés, who wants to learn, asks Pericles what certain words mean. Although he represents the patriarch who insists that rules be followed, even he is not always sure of the meanings. In fact, the play proposes that we are all like Pericles, who as a child unwittingly caused the death of J.C.'s father, too busy thinking about other things to see what surrounded him, unaware of the consequences of his acts, since his vision was framed to focus elsewhere. Busy thinking about other things, we too accept the model imposed and perpetuate it in our own children. We buy into the family image we have been sold, perhaps in part like all colonized peoples, and as Donzelot has argued, because of our craving for betterment and private pursuit of well-being—a desire that as I argued earlier is a product of our sociopolitical institutions.[38] Thus, the child unaware of the consequences of his acts grows up to be an adult who either does not know or does not want to know those consequences. Although like J.C. we would all like to find the responsible party, find someone to blame, perhaps it is not that easy. Still, it is that same character who notes, "Todos los irresponsables tienen una disculpa . . . : 'no lo vi', 'no me di cuenta'" (All you irresponsible people have an excuse . . . : "I didn't see," "I didn't realize") (*HS,* II), suggesting then that it is time to "see." If our civilization is, as Pericles declares it, "conocimientos acumulados de todas las generaciones que nos han precedido" (knowledge accumulated from all the generations that have preceded us) (*HS,* I), then perhaps framing the family differently while recognizing, indeed insisting on the existence of the frame, as del Río has done, will help future generations to view the family differently and recognize it as a cultural construct that responds to vested, ideological ends. It is all a question of who places the frame, where, and why.

2
After the Great Divide

6
Fathering the Nation in Sabina Berman's
Entre Villa y una mujer desnuda

THE SHADOWS OF HISTORY AND NATIONAL AGENDAS LOOM LARGE
over the stage of Sabina Berman's 1993 *Entre Villa y una mujer
desnuda (Between Pancho Villa and a Naked Woman)*, most
overtly, but certainly not exclusively, in the figure of Pancho Villa.[1]
As noted in the introduction, the family unit no longer occupies
center stage here. Indeed, the family romance, as I have been using
the term in the non-Freudian sense, is elided or inverted, and the
figure or model of the patriarch, in the form of Villa, proves insuf-
ficient.[2] At the same time, both gender and generational models are
challenged as generation and genealogy are inverted. In this play,
the traditional family unit, as a tangible entity, has become post-
modernized: it has been fragmented and multiplied. Nonetheless, as
the Berman play demonstrates, issues of family are intricately
linked to history and national agendas. Furthermore, if we accept
the argument promulgated by Donzelot and other contemporary political scientists (as Berman apparently does) that family functions
as a means to channel and police sexuality (and I would add, desire
in general), then myths of family are intricately related to myths
of nation.[3] As Berman dramatizes, both have been instrumental in
channeling desire in a way that maintains the status quo. Ultimately, however, like the master narratives of nation in which the
metaphor of family is a significant element, the notion and representation of family are denaturalized and challenged here and
shown to be constructions that serve various, often contradictory,
sociopolitical, socioeconomic goals.[4]

Like several other plays analyzed in the course of this study,
Entre Villa y una mujer desnuda comprises both a frame play (set
in contemporary Mexico) and an embedded play (set at the time of
the Mexican Revolution). Briefly stated, the frame play focuses on
the interpersonal (primarily erotic) relations among Gina, Adrián,
Andrea, and Ismael, while the embedded play is protagonized by

Pancho Villa, the fictitious-historical character from Adrián's monograph, and presents scenes of his encounters with both his mother and a potential lover as well as his advice to Adrián. In two previous articles, I examined the Berman play in terms of desire, the performance of gender, and historiography and/as narrativity.[5] In this chapter I would like to consider how the myth/metaphor of family mediates those three aspects of the play and show how they are all linked to narratives of nation—hence my title, "fathering the nation."

It cannot be irrelevant that political leaders frequently turn to the rhetoric of family values at moments of national crisis, although it might well be argued that what those same leaders label national crisis is, more often than not, a crisis of the power and position of the individual leader or the interests he represents more than one of the nation or its people. Nonetheless, as I argued in chapter 5, that rhetoric helps to distract from other sociopolitical or socioeconomic problems and perhaps even misdeeds or irresponsibility on the part of political leaders. It cannot be irrelevant either that since its inception the nation-state is often imaged as a family, as was/are monarchies whose fathers/kings derive their power directly from god-the-father. To be sure, the trope of the patriarchal family has long served political interests well by invoking a natural state and superimposing it on what is definitively a political construction—whether the family or the nation. By conflating the individual family and its desires with the national family and its desires, political leaders shore up the status quo. In this way family functions as a metaphor, or myth in the sense in which Barthes employs the term, one that is carried over to other, ultimately unrelated areas.[6] At the same time, that trope helps establish a (pseudo) homogeneity that clearly defines inside and outside, us and them, while maintaining power in a leader (or group of leaders) whose supremacy, like that of the father, is unchallengeable, in part because (as the rhetoric goes—circularly to be sure) it is natural and thus naturally good for the family—father knows best, which translates father has a long-term vision and goals, which will benefit us all but which the rest of us, as mere mortals (not fathers), cannot fathom, focused as we are on immediate needs and day-to-day issues. This paternalistic attitude maintains the power in the hands of a few and reminds the rest of us, marked as we are by gender, ethnicity, class, and so on, of our inferiority and our good fortune to have a superior being watching out for us. In the case of Mexico in specific, historian Ilene O'Malley has noted, "in the 1920s and 1930s the Mexican government assumed a paternal posture vis-à-vis the citizenry, in whom a filial identification with the government was encouraged."[7]

In the Berman play, that father figure, along with the *patria (father*land) itself, are demythologized and shown in all their impotence; like Villa in the third act, the (for some) father of modern Mexico, both figures are metaphorically riddled with holes as the myth and discourse are brushed aside to reveal all their emptiness, insufficiency, and duplicity. In metaphoric terms, they simply do not hold water, but that certainly does not mean that they are dead. Pancho Villa may ostensibly die at the end of act 3, but he is right back there again, center stage, in act 4, suggesting that myths do not die easily.[8] Similarly, the family may have been relegated to the wings as a tangible presence in this and other recent plays, but as a myth, trope, or image, it has certainly not disappeared—and this in spite of the incompatibility of that imagery with contemporary experience (many, perhaps the majority of Mexicans today—like the protagonists of the play—do not participate in the nuclear family of myth). Yet, despite the characters' protests that the traditional family is not what they desire, that trope proves to be as omnipresent and controlling as that of Pancho Villa himself. Thus, it would seem that the image of family has a function very similar to that of revolution as discussed by Octavio Paz: "Every revolution tries to bring back a Golden Age."[9] According to him, revolution would recuperate a paradise lost or violated, even as it simultaneously searches for a future paradise. I would argue that narratives of family do the same, with their quests both forward and backward, for genealogy (in the past) and continuity (in the future). In this play, Berman demonstrates how the notion of family both penetrates and is penetrated by the other grand Mexican myth, that of the Revolution, with its parallel quests.[10]

The action of both the frame drama of *Villa,* with its scenes from contemporary Mexico, and that of the embedded drama, with its scenes from the time of the Revolution, take place in the same setting—Gina's living room. The fact that Berman has brought Pancho Villa and the Mexican Revolution (or their myths) into the living room in this play underscores the effects of history (even if mythologized) on the present as well as the connections between that Revolution (with its role in the formation of national identity) and family (with its parallel/complementary role in the formation of identity, both gender and national). I will argue that the contemporary myths within which each are enveloped serve to disguise the founding violence(s) upon which each depends. If we turn to Roland Barthes's definition of myth as a type of speech and system of communication whose function is to empty reality, representations of revolution, family, and nation show significant parallels.[11] As Barthes asserts, "Myth does not deny things, on the contrary, its function is to talk about them; simply, it purifies them, it makes them innocent, it gives them a natural and eternal justification, it gives them a clarity which is not that of an explanation but that of a statement of fact . . . In passing from history to nature, myth acts economically: . . . it organizes a world which is without contradictions because it is without depth, . . . it establishes a blissful clarity."[12]

Many scholars have viewed the Mexican Revolution of 1910 as the founding moment of modern Mexico; Berman's protagonist, historian and scholar of the Revolution, Adrián Pineda, is no exception. Nonetheless, by establishing (arbitrarily to some degree) the Revolution as the founding moment of the nation and national identity (as Adrián and others do), scholars effectively elide the other two moments that might equally be viewed as the origin of the nation: the Conquest and Independence. Berman's focus on the Revolution and Villa as father of the Mexican people underscores the perception, on the part of Adrián as well as that of a significant portion of the Mexican people, of a certain masculinity characterizing both the Revolution and Villa, a masculinity that, I would argue, is lacking or at least compromised in the other two possible founding moments—the Conquest and Independence. Indeed, Adrián repeatedly focuses on the machismo of Villa and his campaign, attempting to instill in his own writing that same virility: he wants to be "mounted" on the topic, galloping with the Centaur.[13] He would write his monograph without "delicadezas, mariconerías lingüísticas" (*EV,* 30) (linguistic finesse. My book won't be written with a limp wrist) (*PV,* 94); he wants "hacer sentir toda la violencia del asunto" (people to feel the violence of the situation) and "que [su] libro huela a caballo, a sudores, a pólvora" (*EV,* 30) ([his] book to smell of horses, of sweat, of gunpowder) (*PV,* 94). The paradox, of course, is that as expressed here his desires are diametrically opposed to the experiences of his everyday life. In contrast to Pancho Villa, who was often perceived as one with his horse (thus the Centaur) and who apparently walked with some awkwardness as a result of so much time on his horse, Adrián, middle-class academic that he is, would probably never have ridden a horse and would be unlikely to find it a particularly pleasant or comfortable experience. Similarly, his *"elegancia calculadamente descuidada"* (*EV,* 19) (*calculated unkempt stylishness*) (*PV,* 91) would surely contrast sharply with that smell of horse, sweat, and gunpowder. Revealingly, Adrián's admiration for Villa, which functions as a synecdoche of that of the larger population, is based on a certain romanticization of the "noble savage" and an implicit experiential distance from him, a veneration of and yearning for experiences that are unfamiliar and exotic to him as a middle-class resident of Mexico City (and desirable perhaps precisely because they are alien to his own lived experiences).

Furthermore, it is interesting that as (re)told by Adrián, women are absent from the narrative of the Revolution (except as the erotic playthings of heroes like Villa, but more of this below). While such is not the case historically, the virility of the Revolution has certainly become a part of its mythology and what O'Malley refers to as the exploitation of patriarchal attitudes in politically convenient ways.[14] Significantly, narratives of both the Revolution and the Conquest tend to conflate erotic desire with desire for power and wealth. What is more, they both tend to elide class and gender issues, overlooking the very real oppression of women and the lower classes perpetuated by those narratives, even as they rely on gender for their metaphors. Cypess has noted (in relation to another Mexican play) that the Revolution has been converted into an icon of the patriarchy to maintain a hierarchical and unjust society whose minimal success affects women's lives.[15] Even more important, perhaps, to my discussion here, O'Malley has further argued that "the glorification of machismo is an especially effective deterrent to political consciousness because it functions as a safety valve, giving politically innocuous (though personally destructive) expression to what are, in the final analysis, political discontents caused by domestic and international socioeconomic inequities."[16] As we will see, Berman subtly dramatizes that Mexican-style virility, machismo that has been authorized as part of the national identity (cf. Paz), in many ways functions to elide or cover over issues of class.

But first, let us return to the other two potential founding moments that are relegated to the background in the aggrandizement of the Revolution as the founding moment, as dramatized in *Entre Villa y una mujer desnuda*. Unlike the (perceived) predominance of the virile in the Revolution, the Conquest surely compromises that clear-cut masculinity, dependent as it is on the image of the female. Today, in part as a result of Paz's imagery, the Conquest is generally depicted as the violent rape of the native (whether the concrete human being or the "penetrated," feminized land) by the conqueror (implicitly masculine, macho, and definitively foreign).[17] Although this is considered to be the moment that produced the Mexican culture and mestizo people, it fails to provide the neat borders and distinctions, perhaps, that the Revolution can provide (or has been made to provide). The Malinche of the Conquest, "mother" of Mexico and the mestizo population (but of course not all the population is mestizo, as none of the major contemporary characters of the Berman play are), is the native victim who is raped, but at the same time and paradoxically she is implicated in the Conquest as the betrayer, the collaborator who opened the door as it were to the foreign invasion.[18] Similarly, the Independence of 1810 was led by Hidalgo, a priest and thus a figure that is perhaps not masculine enough for Adrián's tastes. At the same time, he was perhaps also not distinct enough insofar as the Church itself was a significant colonial power, often linked with the Spanish royalty. Furthermore, although the struggle for independence theoretically freed Mexico from the yoke of the Spanish Crown, foreign invasions did not end there: the United States invaded in the 1840s, France in the 1860s. Once again, borders, national and otherwise, are not as impervious as one might like. And, specifically, in neither of these historical narratives (Conquest and Independence) are gender divisions as neatly polarized as they might be and as they have been made to be in the narratives surrounding the Revolution, particularly in those surrounding national heroes such as Villa.

It would appear that just as Western society has selected one representation, one possibility for family (the Holy Trinity), Adrián, like other veritable (not fictitious) historians, has selected one founding moment over another, eliding the ideology involved in the choice. Indeed, Berman's Adrián provides a synecdoche of the process by which the Revolution and the metanarratives of that Revolution are created (remember that Adrián is a historian/writer, creator of historical narrative). Perhaps equally revealing, and a choice highlighted by Berman, is the fact that even once the Revolution is chosen as the mythic founding moment, the historian then must choose a mythic father for the nation. Adrián, as I have noted, has chosen Villa, but he might equally well have chosen any number of other founding fathers, among them, Plutarco Elías Calles (who is mentioned several times in the course of the play) since under his administration the PRI, the political party that has effectively controlled Mexican politics until recently (2000), was organized in its initial form (then called the PNR). Furthermore, once Adrián's monograph is written, once his choice is made, he refuses to modify that choice in any way, blaming Calles for all that is wrong with Mexico, calling him the "máximo traidor de la Revolución" (*EV*, 31) (supreme traitor of the revolution) (*PV*, 94)—in what evokes the inversion or projection of desire and blame that I will discuss below. When his granddaughter and Gina's partner, Andrea Elías Calles, offers to give Adrián access to all his papers, suggesting that he might find information that would contradict his dogmatic stance and lead him to a different narrative, he adamantly refuses, in what might be read as an acknowledgment that his negative label/judgment of Calles may be as mythic as his heroic label of Villa and that neither could be supported by historical evidence. His refusal signals an unwillingness to learn anything that might challenge his fixed notions, the authorized (by him, in part) mythology. Although Adrián has learned to view things in terms of black and white, good and bad, desiring (indeed creating) the "blissful clarity" that myth provides, the suggestion here is that those neat borders between polar opposites cannot hold up to close scrutiny: surely neither political figure was all good or all bad.[19]

In this respect Octavio Paz again offers some interesting insight into the Mexican Revolution in specific and revolutions in general. As he notes, "The Revolution was going to invent a Mexico that would be faithful to itself."[20] The language here is revealing, for it suggests that the Revolution will invent a true nation, one faithful to itself, even as it suggests that, like family, the nation and national identity both precede the Revolution and are produced by it, as is the case in Adrián's creation of Villa. In the Revolutionary imaginary the nation is singular (*a* Mexico), and its "true" essence is simultaneously, if indeed oxymoronically, rediscovered and invented—reminding us that the discovery is an invention, a re-creation, as indeed are both Adrián's monograph and the figures/narratives/myths of the Revolution and Villa. Although Paz has accurately captured the rhetoric of the Revolution, it is important to note that the rhetoric itself already implies a certain blurring of differences, a certain homogeneity and a return to origins, all of which may never have existed apart from myth and representation (wishful thinking and narrative invention). And, if Mexico had to invent a new self, there is certainly the suggestion that something was wrong with the previous self. In fact, Paz earlier argues, "most revolutions, although they are presented as an invitation to realize certain ideas in the near or not so near future, are founded on an attempt to restore a legal or social order that has been violated by the oppressor."[21] He is more specific later, "Por la Revolución el pueblo mexicano se adentra en sí mismo, en su pasado y en su sustancia, para extraer de su intimidad, de su entraña, su filiación" (literally, by means of the Revolution the Mexican people go into themselves, into their past and their substance, in order to pull from their intimacy [or private parts], from their entrails, their filiation).[22]

And as Berman dramatizes in Adrián's perpetuation of the myth/cult/narrative of Villa and the Revolution, the Mexican people, whoever that might be, will engender itself: in a circular gesture it will provide its own mythic family. As we see in the play, Villa provides something of a father figure for Adrián as he does for much of the populace of Mexico (much of the lower-class populace, that is). But, by the same token, metaphorically, Adrián (re)creates, metaphorically gives birth or new life to Villa by writing about him and citing him in the sense in which Butler uses the term.[23] The fathering of the nation is not only circular but also self-sufficient, not of woman born. In this founding narrative (and unlike that of the Conquest) women (real or mythic) have no role in this engendering, in spite of the fact that it is the very metaphor of the patriarchal family that is used to describe the founding and perpetuation of the national identity. As Paz notes, the Mexican people go into themselves (a metaphor that clearly evokes the erotic) and pull from their *intimidad* (intimacy or private parts), *entraña* (entrails, insides), their *filiación* (their filiation, particulars, and details, as in characteristics). Not irrelevantly, however, *filiación* is etymologically derived from *filius* (son). The nation born of the Revolution and as depicted by Adrián is simultaneously its own father and son, not of woman born.

But, let us continue with Paz's notion of the Revolution that would invent a Mexico faithful to itself. By "faithful to itself," we must presume he refers to a return to its origins, its previous Eden. Again, as Paz's phraseology indicates, that perceived return is an invention—it is faithful to itself because it invents itself. Indeed, when imaged as the birth of modern Mexico, the Mexican Revolution provides a founding moment that would effectively erase the earlier birth of the mestizo people, which in turn would erase the even earlier birth of the Mexica/Aztec nation.[24] While Paz's rendition of popular ideology is probably correct, it is important to underscore the ideological sleights of hand here and the utilization of the image of family to accomplish them. First, as noted, the birth of the mestizo people, which resulted from the Conquest, is perceived as the product of a rape (literal and figurative); Malinche (Indian woman) like the land (inevitably feminized) is violated by the European conqueror (male).[25] Paradoxically, the return to an earlier Eden, while desired, is thwarted insofar as that Eden is anything but Edenic. On the contrary, it was fraught with violence and violation at the founding moment. Nonetheless, the Revolution simultaneously evokes and erases this founding moment by replacing it with a newer founding moment—the Revolution itself—and, in replacing that earlier moment, it relegates it to an even more distant past and thus violates the even earlier people and their founding myth: that of the Mexica/Aztec nation. But, in another sleight of hand, the violence of this second founding moment (the Revolution) is also elided. Just as the violence of the Conquest—the rape, murders, and exploitation of the native peoples—was justified in the name of God, the violence of the Revolution was justified in its search for equality and better conditions for the peasants.[26] The rhetoric of the Revolution and the hero worship or cult of Villa, Adrián's included, praise the lost paradise (in this case the time of the Revolution) when men were men and ideals reigned while it elides (erases?) the violence of the moment and the fact that thousands of Mexicans died, unknown numbers of women were raped, many of them the same campesinos for whom the Revolution was presumably being waged, and the exploitation continued—all in the name of the Revolution. Add to this the fact that the Revolution, imaged in familial terms as the birth of the nation, in fact like all wars, actually divided or destroyed families. In the end, tragically, those country peasants, who proportionately suffered the most, gained the least. As Adrián recognizes in the final act of the play, "¿De qué sirvió la Revolución, la lucha del general Villa, si sus nietos están igual de chingados que él de escuincle? A otros les hizo justicia la Revolución, . . . a los burgueses" (*EV*, 83) (What was the Revolution for, what did General Pancho Villa fight for, if his grandchildren don't have any more hope than he did as a kid? The Revolution gave justice to [the bourgeoisie]) (*PV*, 106).

The irony, of course, is that he himself is one of the bourgeoisie who has personally done nothing to benefit Villa's descendants or others in the same socioeconomic situation and one who in fact has exploited the myth of the Revolution for his own personal and professional gain (in the form of lecture tours and his monograph). His rhetoric here seems to ring as hollow as what Day has labeled "his feigned desire to marry Gina."[27] Clearly, his socioeconomic position has allowed him to dedicate himself not to producing something new or bettering society but to reproducing the past, rewriting, perpetuating the status quo. His monograph on Villa contributes to the hero worship or the mythmaking process but produces nothing new, changes nothing. The literal and figurative insignificance of Adrián's book is highlighted by the fact that it can be bought at VIPS (a popular chain in Mexico that has a restaurant and sells sundries), suggesting that it is directed not to an academic audience but to a popular one, and by the fact that it is, in the words of Andrea, a novel and "very small" at that. Furthermore, if we take Villa as a model, and particularly the Villa portrayed by Berman, men of the Revolution were perhaps not so macho as it has been wont to believe—to some degree at least such representation seems to be more mythmaking, but mythmaking perpetuated by middle-class academics like Adrián. Villa is specifically characterized (here and elsewhere) as alternating between hypermasculinity and sentimentalism or emotionalism. And, while probably none of the revolutionary leaders became famous for their ideals, Villa's ideals were perhaps among the most narrow—help the campesinos and return their land—laudable goals to be sure but vague enough to be virtually unrealizable. Furthermore, Villa, like many other revolutionary leaders and charismatic though he may have been, surely had little idea of how to accomplish those ends on or off the battlefield.

I would argue that Berman has chosen precisely this historical moment to underscore the ironies and paradoxes of the founding moment of the Mexican family. She has clearly chosen this historical moment and this national hero to emphasize the mythology and the fact that, in spite of their accompanying myths, neither embodied the Golden Age lost, in terms of nation or in terms of family. In this work, which in many ways is a play about representation per se, and thus about family, history, and gender as representation, and about how choices are made as to what to represent and what not to represent, Adrián chooses one representation of the birth of Mexico over other alternatives. But just as the audience is ever aware of alternative accounts of family, alternative histories and births are often evoked. In this regard the Berman play evinces numerous parallelisms with the theories of postcolonial critics and theoreticians such as Bhabha and Mulhern. As the former notes, "the nation emerges as a powerful historical idea in the west . . . whose cultural compulsion lies in the impossible unity of the nation as a symbolic force."[28] The same can surely be said of family as depicted by Berman. Similarly, Mulhern has observed, "Tradition [might we not read family?], usually said to be received, is in reality made, in an unceasing activity of selection, revision, and outright invention, whose function is to defend identity against the threat of heterogeneity, discontinuity and contradiction. Its purpose is to *bind*."[29] I would add that its purpose is equally to blind: to blind the citizen or family member to other possible, less patriarchal and less paternalistic forms of organization, to other, diverse scripts in which they might perform, possibilities that Berman allows her audience to glimpse if not always to grasp completely.

Surely, the figure of Villa, noted as he was for the number of children he fathered, functions to underscore the inconsistencies and rhetorical gaps in perceptions of nation, patriarchy, and paternalism. Indeed, Berman's (and in turn Adrián's) Villa, when asked by his mother how many children he has, answers that he is not sure, because "andamos haciendo patria" (*EV,* 45) (we're forging [literally, making] a nation) (*PV,* 97), in a play on words that links the notion of creating a nation with that of siring children. The irony, of course, is that although he fathered them biologically, Villa rarely stayed around long enough to be sure that his offspring were educated or properly cared for (properly, that is, according to the reigning ideology, whatever that might be at any given historical moment). That task fell to the miscellaneous women that passed through his life, or perhaps better expressed, through whose lives he passed, since they were more stationary than the Centaur, tied to home and (his) children as they were. In his words, "Huyendo o atacando. Es el destino del macho" (*EV,* 37) (Attacking or running away. That's a man's lot) (*PV,* 96)—but again that destiny is clearly a construction, a performance, not necessarily a personal, willful choice, but certainly a citation in Butler's terms.[30] It cannot be irrelevant either that Adrián is portrayed as similarly neglectful of his paternal duties. As Gina notes in the first act, Marta, his second wife and the woman he refers to as the mother of his daughter, has called her (Gina) because Adrián has not sent the monthly child support (*EV,* 30). Similarly, while the contemporary Mexican government would have its people view themselves as part of the family, its leaders often seem to have equally abandoned their sons preoccupied as they are *haciendo patria* (making a nation). Indeed, in many ways, it might be argued that Villa accomplished little other than reproduction. As noted, little has changed for the lower classes of Mexico in spite of official recognition of his status as hero.

Nonetheless, as O'Malley has cogently argued, the glorification of masculinity, which was codified as part of the myth of the Revolution (and perhaps particularly in Villa), has provided a psychological compensatory potential that allows (indeed encourages) reactions against a socially based inferiority to be redirected and take a sexual outlet rather than a political one and thus divert attention from those class issues.[31] Berman underscores this channeling of desire (this time economic rather than erotic) in the final act in a very brief scene between Andrea, Adrián, and doña Micaela, the servant. This is the act in which Adrián has returned to Gina's apartment after having attended a ceremony in the cemetery commemorating the death of Villa. Having seen the some seven hundred children and grandchildren of the hero, he recognizes how little has changed for the lower classes, a situation that he blames on the "perjumados. Los leídos. Los licenciados" (EV, 83) (The educated ones. The ones with degrees. Those fucking bourgeois bastards) (PV, 106), among whom, as I have noted, he should count himself. Andrea, somewhat less idealistic, but, of course, also granddaughter of one of those "educated ones," suggests that the problem is that all Villa left to those children and grandchildren was his "memoria. Ni educación ni oficios. Sólo su sombra inalcanzable" (EV, 83) (memory. No education, no jobs. Only his unattainable shadow) (PV, 106). A short time later, as the two are still conversing in the living room, the servant appears to announce that she is finished. Claiming not to have any small bills, Andrea promises to pay her on Tuesday, overlooking the fact that the servant probably does not have surplus money (as Adrián and Andrea do) to tide her over until Tuesday. And, in spite of his recent harangue about the poverty and the implicit exploitation of Villa's progeny—in his twice-repeated words, "Era como para llorar" (EV, 82) (It was enough to make you cry) (PV, 105–6)—Adrián fails to pay the woman himself or offer Andrea change for her larger bills. Instead, he gives the servant only his permission to leave, without the money due her in return for her labor. The myth of the national family works only in words, on paper, not in practice. His compassion is purely verbal and (as usual) stops short of action. Lest there be any doubt about the connection between this scene and the implied failure of Villa's revolution, the servant is specifically named doña Micaela—the same as Villa's mother—and played by the same actress who plays that mother in act 2.

Significantly, Villa's presence in Gina's living room underscores the influence of the metanarratives of nation and of the Revolution that inform gender performance in contemporary Mexico. Perhaps more than any of the plays discussed up to this point, Entre Villa y una mujer desnuda overtly dramatizes role playing and citational performance as discussed by Butler.[32] In particular it stages gender role playing and the performativity of our desires, as it also highlights familial role playing, reminding us that familial roles are ultimately, and by definition, gender roles and that both have a history.[33] Gender begins at home and in specific historical circumstances. And, even though main characters, Adrián and Gina, have ostensibly eschewed the traditional family unit and the attendant roles in their modern relationship, those roles are continually juxtaposed to and viewed in contrast with alternate possibilities, as characters waver and/or negotiate between competing options, contradictory discourses, and the internal contradictions that arise and cannot be reconciled easily. In this way, Berman provides her audience the opportunity to reconsider traditional familial roles as she draws attention to the problematics of those roles via the characters' endeavors to discover (invent) other possibilities—new citational performances that might result from their negotiations. This vacillation is dramatized as Adrián alternates between sensitive modern man and supermacho (under the tutelage of Villa), but it is also apparent in Villa's fluctuation between supermacho and sentimentalist. Similarly, when Gina's citational performance as modern woman fails to prove rewarding in act 2, she resorts to her earlier role as mother, calling her son in Boston, only to discover that there will be no satisfaction in that role either for he has grown into a man, as capable as Adrián of seducing a woman, and thus no longer wishes to play the role of son necessary for her performance as mother. Similarly, Adrián in act 1 adopts the role of patriarch who believes he knows what is best for her even as he refuses to discuss his wife and daughter and by implication his role(s) within that family unit, while in the final act he resorts to the role of son/child when he returns seeking solace in Gina.[34] Although the play offers no definitive solutions, we watch the characters continually try on different subject positions, cite alternative (often contradictory) possibilities. By thus juxtaposing the personal and gendered with the public and political, Berman links family and gender to questions of history and nation and in turn to notions of borders, perceived peripheries, and metropolises with their ever-shifting terms of engagement. Just as nation depends on neat divisions between "them" and "us," so too does gender, and these are precisely the borders that prove to be tenuous and permeable in this play. And, since they are permeable and tenuous, they are ever renegotiable. As depicted by Berman, neither gender nor the sociopolitical are destiny. Change may not be easy, but it is a possibility if indeed remote. Throughout the play we are presented with characters at the point at which they must make choices, and we are allowed to glimpse both the path taken and that rejected. At other moments it seems clear that Berman is suggesting that neither option is viable: the characters opt for neither this nor that path. At those moments, they and the audience must try to imagine some other alternatives/ desires that have yet to be scripted or perhaps even thought—in both the personal and the political arenas.

Although the frame play focuses on the interpersonal relations among the characters, Berman demonstrates the by now well-known feminist adage that the personal is political, for it would not be difficult to view the middle-aged history professor, Adrián, as something of an analogy or synecdoche of the (then) ruling Mexican political party, the PRI (Partido Revolucionario Institucional [Institutional Revolutionary Party]), the party that ruled Mexico since the Revolution (1929 to be exact), under various names, that owes its existence to the Revolution, and that is intricately implicated and caught up in the mythmaking I have been discussing. Specifically, the political group has been instrumental in mythologizing that Revolution in order to shore up its own position of relatively unchallenged power during much of this time (until recently, of course).[35] Indeed, Adrián's relationship with the almost middle-aged Gina in many ways metaphorically evokes the relationship between the party and the Mexican people. Although Gina and Adrián are involved in a "modern" relationship predicated on its lack of commitment (read, refusal to form a family unit), their modern liaison proves to be highly conventional, however, limited as it is to a series of erotic trysts, contingent upon Adrián's "urges." Specifically, those desires periodically bring him and his rhetoric to her door, where, not unlike politicians in an election year, he assures her that "me muero si un día me dices: no, ya no, ya nada" (*EV,* 26) (I'd die if one day you said: no, no more, it's over) (*PV,* 93) and then proceeds to (re)seduce and (re)conquer her—admittedly with only limited resistance on her part. It cannot be irrelevant either that Gina tends to perceive his visits and his implicit need/desire for her as occurring with more frequency than they actually do, as is suggested in her opening dialogue with Andrea, where she also acknowledges the ritualistic aspect of those visits (i.e., nothing changes):

Gina. Cada dos o tres semanas.
Andrea. ¿Dos o tres semanas?
Gina. O cuatro días. (*EV,* 23)

[*Gina.* Every two or three weeks.
Paulina. Two or three weeks?
Gina. Or four or five days.] (*PV,* 92)

We soon learn, however, that in fact it has been a month since his last visit. Like a politician, he woos/seduces her when it serves his purposes, assuring her, however, that he thinks about her constantly and that everything reminds him of her. What is surely revealing, however, and what recalls my earlier discussion of the Revolution, is the misperception involved here, the mystification and belief (or willing suspension of disbelief) that allows her—like many of the Mexican people—to believe and perceive things as other than they are, as other than experience indicates. Thus, again we find a certain conflation of erotic desire and other desires.

In the first act this conflation of desires is directly related to the tea ritual, which might well be viewed as a metonym of other social rituals designed, like the family, to postpone and channel desire. When Adrián periodically appears at her door, Gina refuses to go directly to bed with him, in spite of her own desire to do so, but rather acquiesces to a certain social pattern and insists that they have tea first and converse, in what both postpones and heightens his desire. Interestingly, however, that same ritual effectively denies her desire, charged as she is, with policing and enforcing the delay. The institution of the family, particularly perhaps as it is construed in Mexico, similarly functions to deny female desire in several ways. First, in keeping with the mythologized narrative of the Virgin of Guadalupe (another significant figure in Mexican history and national mythology, and one specifically mentioned in the Berman play), the perfect Mexican woman must be virginal (read, sexually undesiring).[36] The only desire permitted her, it would seem, is the desire to be a mother (but preferably a virginal one), and specifically a mother whose desire is centered exclusively on her child (preferably a son), as I discuss in more detail in the next chapter on performing motherhood. Obviously this virginal ideal has little relation to the experiences of real women in Mexico, but it is the model that is held up to them, just as that of Villa is to men—two models that provide, in the words of Andrea, a "sombra inalcanzable" (*EV,* 83) (unattainable shadow) (*PV,* 106)—and one that in its very inaccessibility functions to channel desire in certain directions and not others, and thus maintains women in positions/citations that deny them subjectivity as well as the role/status of desiring subjects. They should be desired, but not desire. Hence, Gina and Adrián's pact: he comes to her apartment when he desires, when he gets the urge, but she is not supposed to go to his (read, she is not supposed to desire unless it originates in him, is projected from him onto her). Similarly, and returning more specifically to the issue of family, within a more formal family unit (i.e., married couples) in Mexico, female desire is either denied or more severely policed than male desire insofar as marital infidelity is tolerated (perhaps even encouraged) on the part of the male but severely chastised on the part of the female. He must be the source of all desire, in what might also provide a metaphor of politicians' relationship to their constituency ("big daddy" will tell you what you desire).

Continuing the focus on desire, in act 2 Gina is encouraged by her son's friend, Ismael, into believing that she desires a different (more traditional and more dependent) relationship. Note that in both cases a male tells her what she desires and/or converts her desire into a reflection of his own. As a result, Gina decides to force Adrián to make a commitment, but when she breaks their pact and appears at his apartment, she discovers he is seeing another woman. Apparently, and contrary to his insistence in the first act that he thinks about her all the time, there are moments when, like politicians, he and his thoughts are not totally dedicated to her—when his desires might not include her and her best interests. Ismael consoles her, but he is soon outmaneuvered by the more mature and more experienced Adrián with his *labia hipnótica* (mesmerizing way of speaking) (again, cf. politicians) and (pseudo) promise of marriage and a son—a family. It is at the end of this act (which also marks the center point of the play) where the pervasiveness of the familial trope and its channeling of desire is perhaps most obvious. (And, let us not forget that the question of desire, along with that of choosing between alternatives and competing desires, is already evoked in the title of the work—between Villa and a naked, thus eroticized, woman.)[37] Although earlier Gina insists to Andrea that she does not want to marry Adrián, the litany of desires she articulates here evokes the difficulty of escaping from socially authorized desires (family among them) as well as the difficulty of even glimpsing alternatives, much less of keeping them steadily in view or in fact enacting them—difficulties Berman has at least partially overcome in this play. Indeed, as Berman seems to remind us here, the family has long served to control individuals, particularly their sexuality, and by implication their desires, erotic or otherwise.[38] One can only suppose that Gina's desires are shaped and authorized by the family and culture (i.e., what has been imaged as the meta-family) in which she grew up. Interestingly, and as Berman implicitly posits in this play, one might well argue that the desire most perpetuated by that family is self-perpetuation—another family. When asked by Adrián, "¿Qué quieres? ¿Qué es exactamente lo que quieres?" (*EV,* 58) (What do you want? What exactly is it that you want?) (*PV,* 101)—in a gesture that simultaneously evokes the politicians' feigned interest in the desires of the people and/or Freud's in the desires of women ("What does a woman want?")—she responds with a very domestic and domesticated list that comprises daily activities to be done together (activities that she can and does do just as well alone), possessions that she could acquire by herself and that for the most part are superfluous (e.g., a house in the country and another house by the sea), self-discipline (to stop smoking, to exercise every day—which only she can give herself), and so on. It seems unclear why she would desire these things except that they are what she has been taught she should desire. The list evokes the tautological reasoning that I have discussed elsewhere: "I want it because I want it, because I am supposed to want it."[39] Significantly, however, all the desires she expresses here are directly or indirectly related to the icons of home and family, conformity and normality (normality as scripted, again tautologically, by the patriarchy). Again, the personal parallels the political, insofar as her desires are directly comparable to many political desires—those with money and power seem eternally to seek more, again, just because, because I want it. More important, perhaps, with the exception of a companion for the daily, domestic activities, her desires either cannot be fulfilled by him (e.g., self-discipline) or conversely can readily be fulfilled without him (a gold necklace with her name). I would further propose, however, that paradoxically, given Adrián's characterization, he could ultimately not fulfill the role of companion for the daily activities. He would have to desire differently and perform very different citations to content himself with having breakfast together, talk to her son on the phone, and so on. Let us not forget that he has two failed marriages, and in his words, "Abandono lo que más amo . . . Quieres cambiarme. Pero más fácil sería que me cambiaras por otro hombre" (*EV,* 31) (I abandon what I love the most . . . You want to change me . . . It would be easier to just trade me in for another man) (*PV,* 94)— another man who would cite a different masculinity, less à la Villa. Still, and again linking the personal with the political, I would argue that the desires that Gina articulates here reflect the desires that have been authorized by society precisely because they change nothing and offer no serious threat to the status quo. Society will not be altered if she does or does not exercise every day or have a gold necklace with her name.

What is perhaps most revealing in Gina's list of desires here is that at no point does she mention a child—the desire most encouraged or authorized in women, again because it is one that perpetuates family and in turn the sociopolitical status quo. Although earlier, when she confronts Adrián, she demands, "hazme un hijo" (*EV,* 52) (let's make a baby [literally, make me a baby]) (*PV,* 99), here there is no mention on her part of that child.[40] Adrián, on the other hand, after listening to (but apparently not hearing) her list, states simply, "Y quería un hijo mío" (*EV,* 58) (And you wanted a son of mine) (my translation), ignoring all else except what suits his own agenda, a son that would be tangible proof of his virility and whose siring would provide an outlet for his erotic desire. In this way he ignores her unauthorized (read, erotic) desire, translating it into an authorized desire (the maternal). When she points this fact out to him (that he has focused only on the earlier desire for a child), he, like a good politician, avoids the issue, stating only "está bien" (all right) in what his interlocutor can interpret anyway she would like and in what encourages the misperception that may well lead to mystification. The act concludes with Adrián returning to the issue of a son (and there never seems to be any doubt that it will be a son, not a daughter) with the words, "Va a ser un niño de ojos grandes y despabilados" (*EV,* 59) (It will be a boy with big round eyes) (my translation)—the eyes of Pancho Villa.

Again we are faced with a tautology that parallels that of the Revolution and the perceived founding of modern Mexico. Adrián's model, father figure, Villa, will also be his son. He will, in some sense, give birth to his own father, as he does insofar as he writes his biography. In addition to making a statement about family and nation, *Entre Villa y una mujer desnuda* also functions to comment on representation and to mock the mirror of art, suggesting that it mirrors only itself. Adrián represents/mirrors Villa in writing him, but as we have noted that mirroring is a creation that to a large degree mirrors or projects the world as Adrián would have it. That tautology is doubly underscored in the scenes where Villa gives advice to Adrián in what might be understood as an effort to (re)create Adrián in a mirror reflection of himself (Villa), who, in a continuing spiral, by this point is merely a projection of Adrián. Add to this the complication of the fact that the Villa created/mirrored by Adrián is already a creation of myth and film.[41] With this sort of eternal mirroring (echoing) back of the same, Berman seems to suggest that it is little wonder new roles, new performances, new representations and citations are so difficult to find or invent.

When Adrián and Gina meet again in the third act, for the first time after his unexplained absence of three months, she rejects him because she is now in love with Ismael. In a typical move (and one that parallels Villa's military maneuvers) Adrián, the politician and seducer, attempts to distract her from the real issues, now employing his mesmerizing way of speaking to focus on cosmetics as it were and dispute Gina's vocabulary—suggesting that she is the one misusing rhetoric and language, not him. Although his rhetoric is seldom challenged onstage (although it is certainly contested mentally by members of the audience), he repeatedly questions the terminology of the two women onstage. In this case, he assures Gina that *love* is a complex term that signals a state of illusion with a long bibliography. Given that family in the Western world in the twentieth century is predicated on love (marriages are no longer arranged but the result of love between the man and woman), Adrián's lecture serves to underscore the fact that family, like love, is a historically specific illusion. Failing to convince her of her illusion in regard to Ismael, he reacts by throwing himself out the window, which happens to be on the ground floor, a detail that effectively underscores the hollowness or even disingenuousness of his melodramatic gesture and rhetoric. Let us note too that in this act, when Gina concretely cites the lines of act 1, "Ya-no. Ya-no" (*EV*, 66) (It's over. OVER) (*PV*, 102), he definitively does not die as promised in act 1—more melodramatic, empty (political) rhetoric, designed to seduce the listener.

Interestingly, however, in this act Berman highlights the fact that the desires authorized by society vary by gender—perhaps not so much because of any innate differences of desires, as because, and again tautologically, society has authorized different desires for each gender. More important for our focus is that those variations also find resonance in the family and in the desires that are authorized and thus cited within that institution. Adrián, like Villa, is not supposed to desire a stable family unit while Gina is. The paradox in which Adrián is caught, in which many men are caught, is that while he is not supposed to desire that stable unit, the country depends on it, and, furthermore, as that unit has traditionally been structured, he personally benefits from it—his domestic day-to-day needs are taken care of so he has time to devote himself to other, more public activities; he has a stable outlet for his erotic desires and so on. As a result, and just as Villa's desire for Mujer (who, not irrelevantly, happens to be the daughter of a Callista general) in act 1 is displaced onto her and perceived as proceeding from her—"Ya me ve amaneciendo arrepechadito a usté, ¿no es verdá?" (*EV*, 36) (You already imagine me waking up in your arms, don't you?) (*PV*, 96)—Adrián's unauthorized and thus not socially acceptable or citable desire for stability (which does not become apparent until the final act) must also be displaced onto the female, Gina, so that she is blamed for wanting to tie him down. As he complains, "tenías que dejarte arrastrar por ese instinto de las hembras de hacer nido . . . Tenías que atraparme aquí en tu casa, tenías que comportarte como 'toda una mujer'" (*EV*, 78) (you had to let yourself get carried away by the female urge to nest . . . You had to trap me here in your home, you had to conduct your self like a "woman") (*PV*, 105), in a linguistic sleight of hand that not only projects the blame onto her but also suggests that her desire is natural (an instinct) rather than socially scripted. Thus, he blames her for the failure of their relationship, conveniently overlooking the fact that it is she who is ending their relationship, not him. Paradoxically, and in what underlines the twisted rhetoric often employed by politicians and other guardians of cultural mores, he objects to her implicitly depriving him of his freedom at exactly the moment she is giving him his freedom—she does not want to make a "nest" with him. At numerous moments throughout the play (act 2 in the scene between Villa and his mother, act 4 in the scene of Adrián's return to the "womb," as it were, to seek solace in Gina), the males are shown as seeking maternal support and blessing but simultaneously rejecting it and fleeing from it, focusing instead on properly masculine activities (including inventing a father) and casting the blame for their need or desire (lack) back onto the female, thus absolving themselves and giving birth metaphorically to the man they believe they are or should be.

Some time later, in the final act, Adrián returns to Gina's apartment one last time and is seduced by its new owner, Andrea, Gina's former business partner, to whom Gina has sold the apartment and its contents (and by implication Adrián) in a gesture that flies in the face of patriarchal notions of propriety and property (and further, suggests that the two are linked in ways other than the etymological). The play concludes when, after a dramatic buildup, Adrián's erotic performance proves to be less than award-winning, and he exits, shoes and socks in hand, muttering that he does not think he is going to be able to ". . . olvidarla" (*EV,* 94, ellipsis in original) (. . . forget her) (*PV,* 108). The referent of the direct object pronoun is purposefully ambiguous. It might refer to Gina, to his monograph, to the way life used to be, and so on. The possibilities are multiple. Nonetheless, what seems apparent once again is the analogy between Adrián and government officials or politicians. Like them, he metaphorically hops in and out of bed, from one alliance to another, in what can only be viewed as self-serving, as he embraces what are clearly contradictory positions. For example, Adrián derides Andrea for being the granddaughter of Calles, who like Mujer, whom Villa kills in act 1, belongs to the socioeconomic class of the privileged bourgeoisie, who in the case of Calles are often viewed as having ignored or betrayed the promises of the Revolution as well as having sold out to the United States by allowing the oil companies to remain after the Constitution of 1917 had declared all subsoil resources were national patrimony. In spite of all those criticisms, however, he still wants to have sex with her.

Similarly, he accuses Gina of exploiting her employees in her *maquilladora* (a small assembly plant that receives materials or parts from the United States and then ships the assembled products back to the United States) and embraces the cult of Villa with his ostensibly anti-U.S. stance (which seems to be part of his objection to Gina's *maquilladora*), but he travels to North America and is presumably paid to lecture on Villa.[42] His principles, it would seem, never get in the way of his desires, and his alliances, like those of the Revolutionary leaders, change readily.

Meanwhile, in a gesture that historicizes gender identity as well as notions of family and nation while underscoring the mythic quality of both and the role of the Revolution in that mystification, Berman juxtaposes these scenes of contemporary life with the embedded drama protagonized by Pancho Villa, the fictitious-historical character from Adrián's monograph. Significantly, however, the borders between the two plays and the two temporal moments are repeatedly traversed in both directions, demonstrating the porousness and instability of all borders and neat divisions into inside and outside, in spite of the fact that political alliances, like narratives of family, would pretend to make them impervious to any slippage. Like the frame drama, the embedded Villa drama comprises four acts. In each of them, Villa's actions are related to those of the frame play and/or he offers Adrián advice on how to handle Gina and conduct himself like a "real" man. Interestingly, as we shall see, his advice frequently mirrors national agendas (and Adrián as a synecdoche of the politician)—seduce the enemy with your rhetoric and mesmerizing way of speaking where possible and without regard for the validity of your words (that is, convince her and/or the people that your desire is their desire and then promise them whatever they want); if that fails, eradicate the threat by eliminating the enemy with violence.

In act 1, after Gina and Adrián disappear into the bedroom, we witness a parallel scene of seduction as Mujer serves Villa tea. In each case, by focusing on the erotic and thus (potential) procreation, the scenes signal what might develop into the beginning of a new family—a beginning that is thwarted and that, like the new beginning and new family promised by the Revolution (or any other founding moment), is marked by violence. In Adrián's case, his abrupt exit and abandonment of Gina after he has satisfied his erotic desire (a departure that mirrors Villa's abandonment of any number of women and children) borders on violence if indeed not in the physical sense certainly in the etymological sense. Unlike Adrián, the more primitive Villa acts more directly and kills his desire not by sleeping with the woman but by killing her, violently eliminating what he (mis)perceives as the source of his desire. This redirection of desire anticipates Adrián's in act 3 when he blames Gina for her nesting instinct and which in turn evokes the tendency of society to blame the female for wanting the family on which the nation depends and which national agendas have taught her she is supposed to want (again because, according to the rhetoric, it is natural, instinctual).[43] In act 2 Villa visits his mother to bestow upon her the gifts he has stolen from other women. He seeks but is denied her blessing. Perhaps what is most interesting in this scene is its overt dramatization of the use of language and rhetoric to redirect perception and create myths as I have been discussing in terms of the Revolution and narratives of family. At various moments in this scene, Villa corrects his mother's language or terminology (much as Adrián frequently corrects the women's in the frame play). What she calls "canica de agua" (some pieces of yellow glass), he renames "ópalo" (*EV,* 41) (topaz) (*PV,* 97), thereby assigning more value to his gifts (and implicitly himself) than she does. She does not value what he values, including, but not limited to, his political ideas, while he, perhaps, overvalues them. And, let us not forget that to rename and thus assign value, as Villa (like Adrián, or is it vice versa?) does here, is ultimately a gesture that creates desire: I am or the object is valuable; therefore it is desirable. In both cases, the male would mold the female's desire to conform to his own, so that she values what he values.

In both act 1 and act 2, Berman literalizes but chronologically inverts the notion of citationality by having Villa perform Adrián's and/or Gina's words rather than vice versa, in what serves to remind us of the circularity of our gender and, by implication, familial and national citations and performances. In act 1 it initially appears that Villa is acting independently, but when the bed in which Adrián and Gina are resting is rolled out onto the stage, we find that they are narrating his story—his actions, in fact, (re)enact their words. In act 2 the citationality of Villa's performance is more overt insofar as Gina is typing Adrián's manuscript as the characters from it appear onstage. As she stops typing, they freeze in place. In this manner Berman dramatizes that the citations (regulatory practices, as Butler labels them) chronologically function both forward and backward, producing not only the citational performance *but also* what we understand as its source.[44] At the same time she dramatizes the effects of history (as representation) and narrative on national identity, which eventually to some degree becomes internalized, personal identity. To wit, as a result, at least in part, of historical representation and manipulation of language, both Villa and Adrián perceive the former as a revolutionary rather than as the bandit his mother perceives. By rewriting (inventing, in Paz's words) the past and national identity, politicians and historians impose a myth and image that serves their needs.[45] In this respect, the Mexican playwright provides an insightful analysis of the power of discursive practices and dramatizes how narrative (in the form of history, popular culture, or even the stories told us by others) author(ize)s the gender/familial roles we cite and perform. Although the myth or rhetoric have depicted the family and gender roles as natural, that is predating contemporary political structures, they are, on the contrary, constructs at the service of the political structures. Again, they are historically specific.

Revealingly, in act 3 and in what is simultaneously the most humorous and the most tragic act of the play, Villa speaks directly to Adrián, advising him on how to conquer the recalcitrant Gina. As a result of Adrián's work on his story, Villa has come to life as it were and now speaks to him, literally and figuratively. His advice and macho model have been internalized, but in what acknowledges some degree of agency on the part of the characters, the fact is that while historical representation has tended to limit our perceived options, there might be a way out. Thus, the stage provides a site of negotiation, and what we witness here might be read as a dramatization of alternatives, different citations, different masculinities as Adrián tries on, indeed negotiates between, two possibilities: macho à la Villa and sensitive modern man (although the latter role seems to be played in bad faith for the most part and is perhaps merely another manifestation of his mesmerizing way of speaking). Similarly, both Gina and Andrea assume more than one subject position. Even if the alternatives are never fully attained by the characters, the audience glimpses those other possibilities.

Finally, at the end of act 4, as Adrián and Andrea disappear into the bedroom, Villa rolls out a huge cannon and extends its telescopic barrel until it literally fills the stage. When he finally fires it, presumably in analogy to what is happening (or not happening) offstage in the bedroom, the cannon barrel goes limp and all that comes out is a tiny ball. While the erotic innuendo and its reference to machismo are obvious here, the scene might also be read in the context of the Revolution and the national agendas produced there: much ado about nothing; lots of buildup but little consequence for the contemporary Mexican. (Although, of course, the death, rape, and deprivation for those who lived through the war are all too consequential.)

Gone, then, in *Entre Villa y una mujer desnuda* is the single, more or less coherent, contained (and constrained), limited (or at least definable) family unit that provided the core of the plays studied up to this point. Not irrelevantly, the "families" in this play are in many ways nonfamilies, families that do not exist in the traditional sense but only in multiple fragments, families that by their very multiplicity and fragmentation deny notions of telos, progress, and closure—concepts fundamental to national agendas. These are families that have broken through or defied the containment, borders, and limits between inside and outside, them and us, by which family has traditionally been defined. Gina, divorced, lives alone and has only sporadic contact with her grown son who is studying in the United States and involved in his own amorous relationships. Adrián, separated from his second wife, apparently also lives alone, although he seems to have more frequent contact with his wife than Gina with her ex-husband. Similarly, the relationship between Adrián and Gina traverses family borders and definitions: this is neither marriage (an implicitly authorized and legal family) nor adultery. The fact that there is no long-term commitment flies in the face of the telos (family [re]production and continuity) implicit in notions of family and nation. Ismael and Andrea come and go from the apartment/stage with little reference to any existence apart from their relationships with Gina. The familial ties mentioned in the frame play are distant: Gina and her son in the United States, Adrián and his daughter (whom he apparently fails to support regularly), Andrea and her grandfather Plutarco Elías Calles. Within the embedded drama, the notion of family is similarly elided in the traditional sense: Villa fathers numerous children biologically, with numerous women, but never forms anything that might be called a family unit, and, although he meets with his mother in act 2, the infrequency of their encounters is stressed, and no father figure is included (or even mentioned, for that matter) in that family reunion. The result is that Berman unravels the myth of the traditional nuclear family, demonstrating its status as wishful thinking, always located in an Edenic past or imagined future—just as national identities are (à la Paz). But, and perhaps even more important, at the same time she unravels the myth of the national family. In spite of repeated governmental, political attempts, at least since the times of the Mexican Revolution, to present the Mexican people (to themselves and to the outside world) as a unified, homogeneous group (mestizo), the fact is that like most nations Mexico is thoroughly heterogeneous, comprising multiple ethnic groups—mestizo, certainly, but also Jewish, Arab, African, European, indigenous, and so on, groups whose existence (with the obvious exception of the mestizo) has often been elided, perhaps not so much marginalized as simply not acknowledged, wished away, made invisible.[46] By emphasizing multiple, fragmented families (or family fragments) on the stage, Berman reminds us that the national family offstage is equally multiple and fragmented.

I have already mentioned the fact that the Revolution was a moment of rapidly shifting alliances along with the implicit tenuousness of "us" as opposed to "them," ally as opposed to enemy. Yet, it is that founding moment that provides the myth of unity. Indeed, the Revolution, perhaps like any war effort, was dependent upon the notion of an impervious border between us and them, good guys (us, of course) and bad guys, allies and foes. Surely the family unit is dependent on similar borders, particularly when inheritance is involved. Paradoxically, however, one might well view the insistence on national unity as an unwilling recognition that those borders are not nearly so well defined. To what extent can an insistence on similarity be construed as a recognition (with its attendant denial) of irresolvable differences?[47]

That breakdown of the mythic family (national and personal) is nowhere more apparent than in the final act. Not only does Villa's cannon sputter, but also, significantly, Gina is gone, absent from the stage, in what I read as a comment on the sociopolitical system and its institutions. Gina has metaphorically left the stage where the family might potentially be (re)formed in what is surely the recognition on the part of the feminist dramatist of the oppressive and detrimental effect of family on women. Within the representational economy of the play, Gina has effectively written herself out of the script, choosing to perform differently (or at least, elsewhere). While, as I have argued elsewhere, I find Ismael not to be significantly different from Adrián, Gina has at least said, "it's over," exited the oppressive stage, and abandoned the male script. She has rejected the narrative frame into which she and women have been written and has set out on an independent journey, with a young man her son's age, seeking a different, alternative script or narrative. Whether that relationship will be a success or not remains unclear and is perhaps irrelevant, for Gina apparently has embraced the role of businesswoman, independent and self-sufficient, in a relationship (most likely tenuous, but certainly tender) with the very young Ismael in what again renders borders in terms of gender or family and genealogy ephemeral and/or porous. And, lest we conclude that rejecting the authorized script is easy (for either gender), the pain is all too apparent in act 3.

In conclusion, Berman's focus on the myths of Villa and the Revolution in juxtaposition with myths of family serves to remind us
of the implicit violence in the myth/origin of family, which assigns
the female a place and position of inferiority in relation to the male.
Like narratives of Malinche and the Virgin of Guadalupe, the narrative of family serves to keep woman in her place (the home, under
the tutelage of a male, destined to maternity, which is simultaneously exalted and debased), a space (the private, the domestic) and
a position (of inferiority) that are essential to the functioning of the
nation and the patriarchy. By exalting virility, the narratives of the
Mexican nation and Revolution serve to assure even the lowest
class, most socioeconomically oppressed men that they are still better off than women—hence the "compensatory potential" that
changes nothing in the words of O'Malley—and thus assures their
complicity in maintaining the status quo that oppresses them.[48]

Gina's absence in the final act signals a movement out of the living room, bedroom, kitchen, the private, domestic space of the early
acts, into a public realm. Revealingly, however, the public realm is
beyond the view, out of the sight of the theater audience in what
might well be a comment on the traditional role of theater (especially melodramatic and commercial theater), which can (is able
and is allowed to) deal with issues of sex and family, the domestic,
in regard to women, but not with larger feminist issues that might
challenge the status quo by suggesting new possibilities for our citational performances outside the theater.

7
Performing Motherhood: Griselda Gambaro's *De profesión maternal* and Hugo Argüelles's *La esfinge de las maravillas*

THROUGHOUT THE YEARS, MOTHERHOOD HAS BEEN ALTERNATELY idealized or reviled, at times the pinnacle of perfection to which a woman might aspire, at others, an unpleasant necessity, and this in spite of the fact that it has long been assumed that the maternal instinct is natural, innate in all female bodies except for the most aberrant.[1] Thus, mother has often been viewed as a synonym of woman; she who was not a mother was somehow unnatural, less womanly. Only in recent years have feminist scholarship and postmodern theory begun to question much of what we have traditionally understood to be natural. As Judith Butler has convincingly argued, even presumably basic and unchangeable biological characteristics, such as sex, are dependent on sociohistorical context as well as on the master narratives that we have inherited (and internalized) and thus are anything but natural.[2] As a result, we are beginning to recognize that "motherhood," like our concept of family, which dates from the Industrial Revolution of the seventeenth and eighteenth centuries, is a relatively modern development.[3] In the words of Ann Dally, "There have always been mothers but motherhood was invented."[4]

Using Judith Butler's theories of performativity, this chapter will discuss two plays that examine the unnaturalness of the so-called "maternal instinct": *De profesión maternal* (Of the Maternal Profession) by Argentine Griselda Gambaro (b. 1928), written in 1997 and staged in 1999 in Buenos Aires at the Teatro del Pueblo, under the direction of Laura Yusem, and *La esfinge de las maravillas* (The Sphinx of Marvels) by Mexican Hugo Argüelles (1932–2003), written in 1994 and staged in 1995 in Mexico City at the Foro de la Conchita, under the direction of José Antonio Alcaraz.[5]

171

Clearly the two plays are separated by formidable divides on a number of levels. They are distanced by the continent of physical space between Argentina and Mexico, by the very different cultures and master narratives of the two countries, by the gender of the playwrights, and so on. Furthermore, one deals with assorted family relationships while the other limits itself to the mother-daughter relation. Nonetheless, both address the question of motherhood and suggest that the maternal instinct is a product of sociopolitical, cultural scripts, a role performed unconsciously as well as consciously, and one severely policed by other members of society. As Judith Butler defines it, performativity should be understood "not as a singular or deliberate 'act,' but rather, as the reiterative and citational practice by which discourse produces the effects that it names"; she later adds that "it is always a reiteration of a norm or set of norms."[6] Let me note here that I am talking about theatricality and performance on two levels: (1) the conscious level whereby, as in theater or life, we knowingly assume a role, a role that often eventually becomes (perhaps unconsciously) a part of the self, and (2) the explicitly unconscious level that concerns Butler, whereby the performance or citation is the matrix through which the self comes to be perceived as a member of the body politic, which is to say, human.[7] But, it is also important to recognize that these two types of performance frequently overlap or become a palimpsest, as they do in the performance of motherhood in these two plays, so much so that it often becomes difficult to separate or distinguish one clearly from the other.

The protagonist of the three-character Gambaro play, Matilde, is a retired professional woman, who forty-five years earlier, when her daughter was born, had neither time for nor interest in her and allowed the father to raise her. At the start of the play, Matilde and her daughter, Leticia (who is now a mother herself), are about to meet for the first time since her infancy. Although Matilde understands the socially scripted role well, knows how the scene of her meeting with the daughter should be performed (and indeed rehearses it while she awaits her arrival), she soon realizes that she cannot play the role now anymore than she could forty-five years earlier, and this in spite of the fact that, as a former professional performer, she theoretically has stage presence. After a series of painful, antagonistic scenes between the two, with the daughter leaving and returning several times, she finally decides to stay and have tea with the mother and her female companion "como unas damas" (like ladies) (*PM*, 59), words that overtly evoke a role to be performed in the most conscious sense. Although the play is inconclusive, and, in spite of what might be interpreted as a reversion to infancy as Leticia utters the final word of the play, "Mamá" (*PM*, 80) (which in the stage production was accompanied by tears and perhaps an overly dramatic, infantile, "Mamaaaaaaaaaaá"), its open ending encourages us to imagine a future in which the two women might begin to construct new subject positions and accept each other as neither mothers nor daughters but as adult women, on an equal (if indeed unsure) footing. In short, even if the naturalness of motherhood is severely contested in the Gambaro play, there seems to be hope for the female characters; they can at least continue in some other roles—perhaps less compulsory and less rigorously policed.

Such is not the case in the Argüelles play, which ends with the destruction of the woman. Here the mother, Lucía, knows what her role is and how to perform it. Indeed, she plays it all too well. Although at the start of the play her focus on her adopted son is being eclipsed by her obsession with screen idol Pedro Infante and his films of the 1940s and 1950s (an obsession, which, as we will see, proves to be related to the question of motherhood), in the prehistory of the play she had apparently centered her entire life on that son (raising him to be the incarnation of Infante), nearly suffocating him, and leaving little space in her life for any subject position or existence apart from motherhood.[8] But, of course, that is precisely how many cultural scripts have said it should be (perhaps particularly the script of the eternally self-sacrificing mother propagated by Catholicism and as understood and practiced in Mexico with its focus on the Virgin of Guadalupe). Unfortunately, however, the script Lucía has embraced is in direct conflict with the script the father, Leonardo, would have her perform. In his script, borrowed from opera, her entire existence should be devoted to him rather than to the son, for, as opera has taught him, the only good female is one who has sacrificed herself for the man she loves. As he notes, to their daughter Isolda, whom he wants to accompany him to the opera as part of the education he would give her, "¿ya has descubierto cómo invariablemente las heroínas operísticas, todas, al final dan su vida por el hombre amado?" (have you discovered yet how the heroines of opera, all of them, inevitably give their lives for the man they love at the end?) (*EM*, 282). But, as Catherine Clément has cogently argued, opera effectively works the "undoing of women."[9] And in this play, the woman is undone in a particularly horrific way. Since Lucía will not give her life for, devote her every thought and emotion to Leonardo voluntarily, his operatic script is forcibly and literally inscribed on her when he coerces Alfonso, his friend and her therapist, into performing a lobotomy, a lobotomy that would excise other scripts and conflicting roles (both Oedipal motherhood and her newer but related obsession with Pedro Infante). As a result, in the end she is converted into a type of Sphinx, unmoving, always smiling, effectively rendered genderless and unthreatening. Thus, her reward for performing her maternal role to perfection is that she is forcibly written into another script of feminine perfection—that of complete passivity, eternal ornament—forfeiting her life for the man she loves, or from his perspective, should love.

Argüelles highlights the incompatibility of the roles of ideal mother and wife insofar as one role demands exclusive focus on the husband's needs, the other equally exclusive focus on the child's needs—a paradox from which there may be no escape until we reconceptualize our expectations—and this in spite of the fact that society has traditionally insisted that a woman be a wife in order to be a good mother.[10] In this play, the mutual exclusiveness of the roles and the resulting failure on the part of the mother to centralize the father sufficiently and provide the reflection of his supremacy that he needs to shore up his own festering insecurities produces two effects. First, in response to his anxiety and sense of marginality, Leonardo assumes an overly domineering attitude, trying to control Lucía in every way, making an already suffocating situation more so. As he admits, "Necesito todo el tiempo saber que yo solo, y yo sobre todo, y únicamente yo, soy lo que más le debe importar a tu madre" (I need to know all the time that I alone, and I above all, and only I, am what must matter most to your mother) (*EM*, 260). Second, her lack of focus on him leads to a conflict between him and the son, to what is often labeled an Oedipal conflict, although in this case, since the son is adopted rather than biological, Argüelles seems to be positing that the Oedipal conflict itself is another cultural script, neither innate nor inevitable.

While neither Argüelles nor Gambaro underestimates the complexities of the dramatized situations nor offers facile solutions, Argüelles does seem to suggest that the adult's need to be the exclusive center of attention may be the result of excessive nurturing as a child. For example, when Juan Carlos, the adopted son whom Lucía had nurtured obsessively, becomes an adult, he is a womanizer who exploits and mistreats women, just as Leonardo is. It would appear then that, having become accustomed to being the focus of the mother's attention as a child, the adult male cannot tolerate any situation in which he is not central to the (m)other and thus continually surrounds himself with women so that at any given moment one will be available to focus exclusively on him.[11]

Nonetheless, even after Lucía's lobotomy, which turns her into even more of a smiling Sphinx than she had been, Leonardo is still not satisfied, for as he recognizes, even in that state, a part of her mind may still escape his control. She may still be replacing him (mentally, psychologically) with another man, still not centralizing him enough and suitably confirming his dominance. In fact, from his perspective (encouraged by the daughter to be sure) her lobotomy may in fact have freed her from his control altogether, allowing her to exist exclusively in her world of fantasy with her ideal lover, Infante. Mythology's smiling Sphinx needs no man and perhaps for that reason is absent from the Freudian developmental paradigm (family romance), even though her myth is indeed (and not irrelevantly) populated by the other actors from the Oedipus myth.[12] Although the mystery (riddle) of Argüelles's Sphinx (Lucía) is never solved, the final moments of the play do parallel what we find in the classic myth insofar as when the classical Sphinx's riddle is finally solved, it merely reveals the ultimate impotence of the male in the face of his brief life, from dependence (as an infant) to dependence (as an old man), with only a short-lived and possibly illusory interlude of glory and authority. In the final moments of the Argüelles play, although Leonardo has exercised his patriarchal power and privilege to undo the woman who would not perform his script, his own dominance is shattered; in our final glimpse of him, he is bent and metaphorically beaten. In this respect, Argüelles evokes not only the performative nature of all our familial roles but also their contingency. At the very moment when the power and control seem to have been exercised to their fullest (in this case with notable exaggeration) and the other has been destroyed, the self has still not been sufficiently centralized nor empowered with a sense of invulnerability. The power and control exercised not only prove to be deficient but also simulacra to the extent that they are still subject to other and greater, if indeed less visible, power and control (in this case that of the daughter, as we will see). This is not to suggest that significant damage has not been done but rather to posit the slippage to which power seems so often subject. Leonardo's abuse of patriarchal power and undoing of Lucía still do not forestall his own undoing.

It is interesting too that in the Argüelles play issues of gender, race, and class intersect, reminding us that motherhood, as we conceive of it today, is very much a product of a white (European), bourgeois, capitalistic culture—and one that, let us not forget, was

imposed on the Native American people by the Spanish imperial-
ists. Leonardo's concern about his role in society is directly related
to his concerns with racial purity and class and parallels the concerns of colonial Mexico (then, New Spain).[13] He worries that his
daughter's darker complexion (inherited from her mother, of
course, who is from Veracruz) will lower her, and by implication
his, social status "en este país de perdedores, prietos y feos" (in
this country of losers, dark-skinned and ugly people) (*EM*, 287),
and this in spite of the fact that she has been exposed to "otra
formación . . . más a la europea" (a different education . . . more
European-style) (*EM*, 287), one that includes specifically European
scripts such as opera. Similarly, he worries about how his upper-
middle-class neighbors in Coyoacán will react to his family's failure to embody the social ideal. As he insists, his wife's fantasies
about Pedro Infante "me resultan cada vez más humillantes" (are
increasingly more humiliating to me) (*EM*, 287–88), and her behavior "pone en peligro mi prestigio social" (endangers my social
prestige) (*EM*, 288); "¡En Coyoacán se cuida mucho el vivir en paz
y en orden! ¡Por eso lo elegí . . . !" (In Coyoacán one is very careful
to live in peace and order! That's why I chose it . . . !) (*EM*, 285).
As quickly becomes apparent, Lucía's "proper" performance as a
"proper" woman (in terms of class, race, and gender), that is,
mother and wife, is necessary to shore up the male's socioeconomic, racial, and gender identity.

The Gambaro play approaches the topic from quite a different
perspective. With males completely absent, the focus is strictly on
the conflict between mother and daughter.[14] Yet, Gambaro still presents the maternal role as overtly performative. At the start of the
play, as Matilde and Eugenia await the arrival of the daughter, the
former acknowledges, as any actress about to go onstage might,
that she is nervous. What's more, she envisions the scene to come:
"Tocaré su pelo, miraré sus ojos. Un vendaval de caricias, de besos,
abrazos" (I'll touch her hair, look into her eyes. A rush of caresses,
kisses, hugs) (*PM*, 52). As she later notes in what evokes a theatrical imaginary, perhaps borrowed from music (Matilde was a singer)
or melodrama, "Yo creía . . . yo creía . . . que abriría la puerta y se
arrojaría en mis brazos. Que lloraría en mis brazos" (I thought . . .
I thought . . . that she would open the door and throw herself into
my arms. That she would cry in my arms) (*PM*, 61). When the
daughter does arrive and refuses to play the necessary supporting
role for the imagined scene, Matilde is left literally not knowing
how to act (in both senses of the word) and finally exclaims, again
highlighting the fact that their roles are part of a set script, "¡Reac-

cioná como es debido entonces!" (React appropriately then!) (*PM,* 56). Significantly, her imaging of how the daughter should act is as idealized as the daughter's image of how the mother should perform. As Leticia says, imagining a past in which the mother's focus (like Lucía's in the Argüelles play) would have been exclusive and unconditional, "Estoy enferma y no te apartás ni para beber un vaso de agua. Cada día estás conmigo, cada mañana despierto y te veo" (I'm sick and you don't move from my side even to drink a glass of water. Each day you are with me, each morning I wake up and see you) (*PM,* 79). Although Gambaro is not specific as to what the source of this imaginary might be, it certainly bears at least some relationship with popular children's stories or family television of the 1950s and 1960s. As in the Argüelles play, here both mother and daughter roles come with very specific rules of performance; yet again those roles are unrealizable because they are so absolute, demanding total dedication from the other. Just as Matilde's role is empty and pointless without the supporting role of the daughter, the daughter's earlier role (as daughter) had been rendered hollow by the lack of a mother.[15]

Revealingly, throughout the play Matilde's companion, Eugenia, functions as something of a stage director, suggesting to both mother and daughter what they should do or say. For example, as the play begins in medias res, Eugenia's opening statement to Matilde is "Yo se lo diría" (I would tell her it) (*PM,* 49), instructions to which Matilde vigorously responds, "Yo no" (Not me). Then, after the daughter has departed, Eugenia explains to Matilde what was wrong with her performance: "No fuiste tierna. Debías . . . haberle hablado de otra manera. Más . . . maternalmente" (You weren't affectionate. You should . . . have spoken to her another way. More . . . maternally) (*PM,* 67), to which the mother responds, again underlining the conscious performance of it all, "¿Maternalmente? ¿Cómo? No sé. Nunca supe. Ni cuando ella nació" (Maternally? How? I don't know how. I never knew how. Not even when she was born) (*PM,* 67). When Eugenia queries, "¿Y el instinto?" (And your instinct?), Matilde replies, "Estaba dormido, muerto" (It was asleep, dead) (*PM,* 67). And to the question of whether or not she knew at the time of the daughter's birth that to be a mother implies responsibility, she retorts, "¡Lo supe siempre! Pero no podía" (I always knew it! But I couldn't) (*PM,* 67). Paradoxically, however, the stage director here, Eugenia, who would give advice to Matilde as to how to perform her maternal role, is not a mother herself. Gambaro seems to suggest that part of what is wrong with motherhood as scripted by society is that the normativizing directives often come from those who are not mothers themselves (i.e., political, religious leaders, often male, whose imperatives are motivated by their own vested interests).

In this way, Gambaro proposes that the maternal is not instinctual; on the contrary, it is performative and must be learned. It is, in the words of the title, a profession, a term *Webster's New World Dictionary* defines as "a vocation or occupation requiring advanced *education* and *training,* and involving *intellectual skills*" (emphasis added).[16] And, etymologically, *profession* is related to the verb *to profess* (<L *profiteri,* to avow publicly), a link that underlines the performative nature of the role as it highlights the problem with the maternal scripts as prescribed by society—they are often dictated rather than adopted by choice, a freedom of "religion" evoked in the term *to profess* that is often absent in our cultural scripts. Not irrelevantly, the dialogue throughout the Gambaro play is dry, stilted, clipped, a series of short sentences or single word responses, in what again reflects the forced nature of the conversation, the relationships, and the roles. It is also noteworthy that the conversations between the two oscillate between what each knows she should say and feel (according to the social script promulgated by the media and other cultural mandates) and what each apparently does feel. For example, when Leticia accuses Matilde of not having tried to find her when the father took her away as a baby, the latter's response reflects the duality of the imposed role and the chosen role. She begins, "Sí, sí. ¡Lo hice! [looked for her] Moví cielo y tierra. Todo es cierto" (Yes, yes. I did [looked for her]! I moved heaven and earth. It's all true) (*PM,* 75). According to the stage directions, however, she interrupts herself and diametrically changes her tack, "¡Te busqué poco! . . . Un simulacro de búsqueda, un simulacro de inquietud" (I looked little for you! . . . A pretense of searching, a pretense of worry) (*PM,* 75–76). The repetition of the word *simulacro* (pretense, sham) here surely underscores the conscious role playing involved. In a parallel fashion, and as I discuss below, Argüelles also highlights the fact that what we call natural is merely performance perfected.

The reputed naturalness of the maternal instinct is not only overtly undermined by the Gambaro play's explicit focus, but it is also subtly called into question via numerous other codes. For example, Eugenia, who, as I have noted acts as something of a stage director and in many ways the voice, if you will, of society, repeatedly resorts to metaphors of nature to describe how the relationship between mother and daughter should be, but because those metaphors are frequently clichés or completely gratuitous, they tend to ring hollow. For example, she advises Leticia, "Vuelve atrás. Si agarró hacia los árboles, agarra para los yuyos" (Go back. If she headed for the trees, head for the weeds) (*PM,* 70) and labels Matilde's desire to find her daughter after all these years, "Un sentimiento natural" (A natural emotion) (*PM,* 77). Similarly, Matilde falls back on a metaphor from nature when she asserts, "Los sentimientos no brotan como agua de manantial" (Emotions don't well up like water from a spring) (*PM,* 60). I find it interesting, however, that the stage production directed by Laura Yusem (who took significant liberties with the written text, adding elements that were not in the play text, deleting others that were) was punctuated with the sounds of dripping water, an oblique reference perhaps to that fountain of emotions, or, more likely, to the fact that something here is in dire need of repair. Those sounds of dripping water perhaps also function as an ironic reference to the naturalness of the maternal inasmuch as they were without apparent source or motivation and had no relation to the action onstage, action that takes place in a living room when it is not raining. Since Western culture has taught us to associate water with fertility and in turn the feminine or the maternal, any so-called naturalness is clearly undermined here and shown to be supplementary, that which is not inherent to the thing but added later, as indeed is our association of naturalness with the maternal, added long after the historical fact of mothers, for reasons that are surely more political and ideological than natural. This naturalness is further undermined by the fact that Leticia does not recognize Matilde as her mother when she first arrives; initially, she assumes that her companion, Eugenia, is her mother. As she comments, "En realidad . . . ella calza mejor" (Actually . . . she's more the type) (*PM,* 55), to which Eugenia responds with another cliché borrowed from nature: "A veces la voz de la sangre está muda" (Sometimes the voice of blood is silent) (*PM,* 55). To be sure, Eugenia appears to be the more nurturing individual of the couple, but again the association of nurturing with mothers and the notion of motherhood as lifework are relatively recent developments according to Hirsch, products of the "institutionalization of childhood during the eighteenth and nineteenth centuries," which resulted from "representations of the child's vulnerability and need for nurturing."[17] At the same time, and not unlike Isolda in the Argüelles play (or Dolores in Gambaro's *La malasangre* [*Bitter Blood*], as I discussed in chapter 2), Leticia would disassociate with the maternal role: when she first arrives she lies, saying that she is separated (she is not) and has no children (she has two). In *De profesión maternal,* both mother and daughter

would prefer not to see themselves in the other. Still one must wonder if the daughter's image or fantasy of the mother, what she
should have done and said when she was a child, reflects the mother
that she (Leticia) is or is merely more wishful thinking, projection
of the socially promulgated role. Similarly, Argüelles too undermines the naturalness of the maternal instinct by depicting a mother
who is obsessed with her adopted son, but totally indifferent, when
not antagonistic, to her birth daughter.

What is perhaps particularly interesting about both these plays is
that the two mothers, one who seeks out the previously unwanted
daughter and one who obsesses with Pedro Infante via the corporeal
presence of his/her son, more than anything seek to return to an
earlier time, a time when they believed that role-playing options
were still open to them and when they could still believe in the
myth of happily ever after.[18] But, I would also argue that the same
is true of the males in the Argüelles play, who resort specifically to
the world of opera to return to the years of their youth. In this play,
the opera additionally becomes an instrument in male bonding. As
noted, while Leonardo, the father/husband, and Alfonso, his friend
from youth, remember their happy bachelor days and plot the lobotomy of Lucía, they frequently recall opera scenes, in specific *The
Barber of Seville*, intoning lines such as "*Zitti, zitti, piano, piano*"
(*Softly, softly, silently, silently*) (*EM*, 287) and noting that the words
have always been a secret way to "ponernos de acuerdo sólo los
dos" (reach an understanding just the two of us) (*EM*, 287). As Alfonso recalls, "yo entendía y buscaba el modo de realizar tu peti-
ción" (I would understand and look for a way to carry out your
request) (*EM*, 287), which is precisely what he does when he performs the lobotomy and perpetuates a simulacrum of the status quo,
as each tries to hang on to the "good old days."

So, if these cultural roles are not natural, where do they come
from? As I have indicated, the Gambaro play obliquely evokes song
lyrics, melodrama, children's stories, and perhaps even family television as possible sources. The Argüelles play, with its epigraph
from Agatha Christie, "La vida debe imitar a la ficción, siempre
que sea posible" (Life should imitate fiction, whenever possible)
(*EM*, 251), suggests at least three distinct sources: popular culture
and the media, opera, and science/psychoanalysis. The setting itself
highlights these sources insofar as the stage is divided into two
areas. One area, Lucía's, is specifically labeled a multimedia room.
Here she watches old movies, fantasizes about her hero, and even
sets up an altar "de diseño popular casi tipo taxi" (with a folk de-
sign, almost taxi style) (*EM*, 251) in his honor. The second space,

Leonardo's, is labeled a study. It is here that Leonardo listens to opera and discusses medicine and psychoanalysis with his friend, Alfonso. But, let us examine these three sources more carefully.

The first is popular culture and media, in this case cinema. I have mentioned Lucía's obsessive relationship with her son and fascination with Pedro Infante. The Mexican movie star is in fact a catalyst in her relationship with her adopted son, Juan Carlos, since he may or may not be his father. Adopted precisely because of that hoped-for father-son link, Juan Carlos has been raised to be the replica of Infante—the idealized lover who stands in sharp contrast to her husband—(although, paradoxically, as I have noted, Juan Carlos is in many ways a mirror image of Leonardo). Furthermore, Lucía demands that Juan Carlos act out scenes from Infante's movies with her, rehearsing them over and over again, trying to perfect their performances so that they appear natural, because, as she recalls oxymoronically, "Pedro era tan *natural* al actuar, tan . . . creíble" (Pedro was so *natural* when he acted, so . . . believable) (*EM,* 285, emphasis added).[19] In this way, Argüelles again highlights the fact that what we call natural is merely performance perfected: repeated and cited (consciously or not) until, in Butler's words, the "discourse produces the effects that it names."[20]

At the same time, the play juxtaposes these movie scripts of the populace with the operatic scripts of the elite to demonstrate that in spite of the class distinctions, both are equally insidious in their proffering of unrealistic, unrealizable roles for women (and, perhaps also for men).[21] In the words of Isolda, the daughter, "El amor que se promueve a través de la ópera es el mismo de las telenovelas y fue el de los folletines para criadas y señoras ilusas" (The love that is endorsed by means of opera is the same as that of soap operas and was that of cheap magazines for servants and naive ladies) (*EM,* 283), because, as she noted in her previous speech, "¡Si ésos son los ejemplos que se ponen, y por siglos, ante las mujeres, es lógico que entonces piensen que así debe ser el amor! ¿Pero quién pone esos ejemplos? ¡Puros compositores varones, si no es que machistas!" (If those are the examples that are presented to women, and for centuries, it's logical then that they think that's how love should be! But who provides those examples? Strictly male composers, if not sexist ones!) (*EM,* 283).

Indeed, Argüelles's Leonardo provides an excellent example of the influence of art in general and opera in specific. As he acknowledges, he listens to opera (a particularly unnaturalistic theatrical genre) because it relaxes him (*EM,* 263). I would posit that it relaxes him precisely because it presents a world that is organized according to the desires of his gender and class, with few unpleasant surprises. When order is momentarily broken in opera's rendition of the world, it is soon reestablished according to traditional (read, patriarchal) rules. As John Berger has reminded us, art is often used "to bolster the illusion that nothing has changed . . . With its unique undiminished authority, [art] justifies most other forms of authority . . . [and] makes inequality seem noble and hierarchies seem thrilling."[22] As Leonardo listens to opera, he can feel confident (momentarily at least) that his race, class, and gender are eternally authorized (in the feigned natural order of things) to reign supreme. Yet, Argüelles undermines this imaginary in the final image of a weak, dependent Leonardo (as I discuss below) and in the subtle emphasis in the play on the shifting quality of all roles. One aspect of the play that might easily be overlooked, but one that recalls Argüelles's use of the Medea role in *Escarabajos* (Dung Beetles), is the playwright's dramatization of how our borrowings from the "mirror" of art are distorted as they are re-mirrored, re-performed so that with time they are distanced from their source and evolve into something quite different from the presumed original. Hopefully, one brief example from this play will suffice to illustrate my point. The line borrowed from Rossini's opera, *"Zitti, zitti, piano, piano"* (*Softly, softly, silently, silently*), that, as I noted, becomes an indicator of the males' friendship and complicity has quite a different function in its original context. In *The Barber of Seville,* these words follow a duet between the heterosexual lovers Almaviva and Rosina, which is sung by the couple along with their friend and accomplice, Figaro, as they try to free her from the oppressed life she is living in the house of her guardian, who would marry her to control her fortune.[23] Although in the opera the line is an indicator of heterosexual complicity, love, and a woman's freedom from oppressive male rule, in the Argüelles play it becomes an indicator of male bonding, of what feminist critics, borrowing from Irigaray, have called hom(m)osociality, as well as, as we shall see, latent homosexuality, and the oppression of women.[24]

Nonetheless, to my mind at least, *La esfinge de las maravillas* proposes that the most pernicious scripts come from psychoanalysis. The reference to the Sphinx in the title evokes the subtext of the Oedipus myth, and throughout, the play is punctuated with references to Freud's family romance—Oedipus complex, Electra complex, and so on. At first glance the references may appear to be at least partially valid insofar as the relationship between father and daughter and that between mother and adopted son do seem potentially incestuous. Nonetheless, I would suggest that, more carefully considered, those relationships prove to be other than incestuous—their erotic overtones merely screen other motives, ones that we are less likely to perceive immediately perhaps precisely because we have been taught to view familial relationships in terms of the Freudian scripts rather than as the complex power plays they often are. In contrast to psychoanalysis's scripts, the play subtly proposes that Lucía desires not Juan Carlos, but an idealized (and controllable?) Pedro Infante. At the same time, her obsession with Infante is clearly motivated by a desire to return to an earlier time, the era of her brief meeting with the screen star, when she was still a young girl and believed (erroneously, as it turns out) that life might hold a starring role for her, before her marriage to Leonardo, a womanizer, who married her because she was the most submissive, and, in his own words, "Porque vi que la podía educar a mi manera, porque era la más dispuesta a eso: a que la formara" (Because I saw that I would be able to educate/train her my way, because she was the one most willing/ready for that: to be shaped) (*EM,* 277). It is to evade this compulsory female role of submissiveness that she escapes into her fantasy of and with Infante, which involves Juan Carlos to be sure, but primarily as a tool or medium.[25] In this way, the role of Infante is thrust on Juan Carlos much as the roles of ideal wife and mother are imposed on her, in what again underscores the perniciousness and the wide-ranging effects of society's policing of performative family roles. Let us note, however, that just as the roles imposed on her are distanced from their source and a palimpsest (operatic, psychoanalytical, and popular media scripts), so, too, is the Infante role as scripted for Juan Carlos insofar as Infante the man plays the role of or projects his star image (and thus for Butler would already be a citational performance), and then in turn assumes a series of roles in his various movies—a series of roles and role playing that would render any innate (were such to exist) or original "Infante" invisible and a series of roles that might well not be understood as such or distinguished one from the other by his fans (e.g., Lucía).[26] Similarly, the eroticism of the father-daughter relationship also proves to be a screen, more specifically, a tool on the part of the daughter to control the father and in turn the mother. Indeed, the fact that at one point father and daughter consciously act out an incestuous script under the direction of the daughter and for the benefit of the mother underscores Argüelles's perception of what I shall call the potential misfocus or misreading of psychoanalysis. In each case, the mask of eroticism thinly disguises the will to power and the desire to control the other. Like Dolores of *La malasangre (Bitter Blood)* and Cecilia of *Los huéspedes reales*

(The Royal Guests) as I discussed in earlier chapters, the daughter here desires not the father himself but his privileged position.

Furthermore, insofar as the psychoanalytical pronouncements in the Argüelles play are articulated primarily by Isolda and Alfonso, two sources that we are encouraged to view as unreliable, those pronouncements are rendered suspect. Isolda has taken a few courses in popular psychology such as "psychological appreciation" and "extrasensory perception" and tosses psychoanalytical terms around but with very little depth of understanding. Still, her pedestrian psychoanalytical theories allow her (perhaps have encouraged her?) to blame the mother for everything wrong in the household and by implication, in society, as much popular Freudian theory has been wont to do.[27] And, while the psychoanalyst, Alfonso, should be a reliable source, his authority is undermined on several levels. First, he is an alcoholic and a drug addict. Because his license to prescribe drugs has been revoked, he is dependent on Leonardo for prescriptions to support his habit—thus his complicity in the lobotomy. Second, he is a closet homosexual, enamored of Leonardo since their medical school days. Now, lest there be any doubt, I am not suggesting that Alfonso is unreliable because he is homosexual, nor is Argüelles. On the contrary, he is unreliable because his obsession with Leonardo has made him the latter's pawn, and because, in spite of all his psychoanalytical rhetoric, he has not come to terms with his own sexuality but rather lives the life and plays the role of a heterosexual, bourgeois husband and father. Yet it is he (as a therapist) who would offer advice to others on how to live their lives. In many ways psychoanalysis itself is challenged here. Or perhaps better expressed, the potential misuse or even abuses of psychoanalysis are brought into question. As a result of what psychoanalysis and Freud have taught us (or perhaps as a result of the popular, superficial deployment of many of the theories of psychoanalysis), we tend to find what we expect to find, often misreading, as we superimpose that psychoanalytical model (the Oedipal family romance).[28] In some sense the psychoanalytical model, not unlike opera or cinema, proffers a fantasy projection that influences how we perceive the other and perhaps ourselves.

I would suggest that what appears at first glance to be an Electra complex on the part of Isolda proves to be more of a power play (and definitely one that neither we nor the patriarch want to see), whereby she uses a certain eroticism to control her father rather than being controlled by him, as he would have it. Like Hernández's Cecilia as discussed in chapter 1, Isolda disassociates with and rejects the maternal role and with it the mother herself, not necessarily because she desires the father (as the Freudian scripts would have it), but because she wants to be the one in control and avoid the submissive role into which the mother has been forced and for which the father would similarly educate the daughter. In other words, while psychoanalysis may well have some basis in fact, Argüelles seems to suggest that the situation is always far more complex than psychoanalysis would present it for (a) it is always subject to misuse, and (b) appearances are seldom to be trusted; there is all too frequently another manipulator behind the scenes, orchestrating the moves for reasons that are not immediately apparently (e.g., Leonardo's manipulation of Alfonso and Isolda's manipulation of Leonardo).[29] Nevertheless, and more important to my reading of the play, Isolda's manipulation of both mother and father demonstrates, among other things, that Lucía's violence, aggressiveness, and hysteria are not natural but rather creations, convenient inventions that serve other political or personal ends.

Argüelles indirectly suggests that, like the insistence on the naturalness of the maternal, psychoanalysis is often used to shore up the dictates of the patriarch. Clearly, Leonardo utilizes psychoanalytical principles as well as the psychoanalyst himself to destroy Lucía. The implicit paradox, however, as I have suggested, is that Alfonso is manipulated so that he champions the same patriarchal society, with its mandatory heterosexuality, that is as detrimental to him as a homosexual as it is to women. In what can be read as a metaphor of larger patterns of society, the patriarch here controls or tries to control all, including males such as Alfonso. Paradoxically, however, as these patriarchs set themselves up as the voices of authority—scientists, religious leaders, lawyers, politicians—they recruit men like Alfonso to be on their team and work with them to help naturalize a structure that oppresses all those perceived as deviant from the patriarchal (masculinist, heterosexual) model (including homosexuals like Alfonso). As Leonardo insists in reference to the social arrangements and the fact that "¡. . . en la especie humana el que triunfa es el macho porque él tiene los redaños, la casta y la fuerza para sacar adelante su familia y su especie! . . . ¡Así lo hizo *la naturaleza* y por eso es quien manda!" (in the human species he who triumphs is the male because he has the guts, the breeding and the strength to advance his family and his species! . . . That's how *nature* made him and that's why he is the one who rules!) (*EM*, 279, emphasis added).[30] Thus, the play demonstrates that, in the words of Judith Butler, "To the extent that a specific use of psychoanalysis works to foreclose certain social and sexual positions from the domain of intelligibility . . . psychoanalysis appears to work in the service of the normativizing law that it interrogates."[31]

And surely what we witness here is psychoanalysis at the service of the hegemony. First, throughout the play, Alfonso encourages Lucía to modify her behavior to conform to societal norms (acquiesce to the role patriarchal society demands), ignoring her personal happiness and fulfillment as well as the inequities and injustices in that status quo. Second, by performing the lobotomy, Alfonso, Lucía's friend and confidant, as well as therapist, betrays her in the name of a greater love and a greater addiction, Leonardo and narcotic drugs (or are they one and the same?).[32] At the conclusion of the play Lucía is converted into a Sphinx, but paradoxically it was her earlier Sphinx-like smile that so irritated Leonardo and in part at least motivated his destruction of her: "esta expresión como de ausencia . . . De esfinge, según papá" (this expression almost of absence . . . Sphinx-like, according to papa) (*EM*, 253). Still, as the son notes, her reaction is a result of the father's treatment of her: "porque trata de tenerla siempre sometida y ella se le escapa así interiormente" (because he tries to keep her under control all the time and she slips away from him inwardly that way) (*EM*, 253). Again, as noted earlier, the father has to be central. In other words, her Sphinx-like smile must be created by him (as it is in the end, after the lobotomy), not in defiance of him. Yet, one might well argue that her catatonic state at the end is really not very different from what he had demanded of her earlier. Tragically, for both him and her, Leonardo fails both times. She may be catatonic at the end, but he still cannot be assured of her complete devotion, a devotion made necessary by the gender roles that are compulsory in contemporary society. In the final moments of the play, after Isolda suggests that he has somehow freed her to live in her fantasy world and he recognizes that there is still something he cannot control, he doubles over and explodes in screams, venting his rage on various objects in the room until he ends up crying "*como un niño aterrado*" (*like a terrified child*) while Isolda "*le acaricia la cabeza*" (*strokes his head*) and embraces him, "*pegándolo a su vientre*" (*pressing him to her abdomen*) (*EM*, 321). In a direct antithesis to his earlier statement about the natural triumph of the macho, Leonardo is anything but triumphant here, and Argüelles seems to be suggesting that the natural triumph of the macho has always been an invention, a script imposed and policed by society. Meanwhile, and again paradoxically, "*En Isolda hay una absoluta expresión de triunfo*" (*In Isolda there is an absolute expression of triumph*), and she states, "Y ahora vamos a poner esto en orden" (And now we are going to put this in order) (*EM,* 321). Part of putting things in order (perhaps not unlike what happens in opera and cinema as well as in politics as presented in the play) consists of, in Leonardo's words, which in many ways echo Isolda's and return us to Berger's words (cited earlier) in regard to art, "Cuidado y orden . . . eso . . . y sobre todo, saber maquillar la realidad para sostener las apariencias, ajá: las formas del orden" (Carefulness and order . . . that's it . . . and above all, knowing how to cover up reality in order to maintain appearances, aha: the forms of order) (*EM,* 321). At this point Isolda interrupts to add, "y del 'aquí no pasa nada'" (and of the "nothing's happening here") to which he quickly adds, "porque no pasa" (because it's not happening). Nothing has happened here; order is restored; Leonardo can relax and continue to listen to opera. Everything continues, on the surface at least, according to the age-old script.

Revealingly, both plays are about performing motherhood, but by implication they are also about performing all societal roles, as both proffer somber critiques of the societies they portray. The Argüelles play is particularly overt in linking familial, gender-role problems with problems of state, and the larger Mexican society. In fact, Isolda refers to Tlatelolco and the suppression of the student uprisings in 1968 twice in the first scene.[33] In this way, Argüelles links the "aquí no pasa nada" (nothing's happening here) of the family with that of the Mexican government, both with their *dictablandas* rather than *dictaduras.*[34] As a result, one must wonder to what extent the state, as something of a metonymy of the patriarch and patriarchal rule, is responsible for (and benefits from) various constructs of identity (gender, race, class).

It is perhaps as part of this general questioning of gender roles that both plays incorporate homosexual desires or relationships. As depicted in the Argüelles play, those desires have been hidden because of the dictates of "proper" society. In the Gambaro play the lesbian relationship is understated, both in the stage production and in the recognition on the part of the characters that their relationship could not and should not be completely open. In the text the stage directions are specific that Matilde and Eugenia should be seated on the sofa at the start of the play, holding hands, a kinesic gesture that would bring their lesbian relationship into immediate focus. Because this opening image was omitted in the stage production, the relationship between the women did not become apparent until about halfway through the play, and even then it might well have been overlooked. Indeed, the opening statement of the Gambaro play, "Yo se lo diría" (I would tell her it) (*PM,* 49), attains signifi-

cance only when we identify that relationship. Although that brief
comment is vague and obscure when we first hear or read it and
quickly forgotten until we hear or read it again, the referent of the
lo (it) is ultimately the fact of their lesbian relationship; if the
daughter is coming to live with them, she will have to know because in the words of Eugenia, "Si no se lo decimos, será difícil
convivir. No hay convivencia que aguante un secreto" (If we don't
tell her, it will be difficult to live together. There's no coexistence
that can tolerate a secret) (*PM,* 49): In this way, both works highlight the fact that the performance of motherhood is but one aspect
of the larger issue, what Butler has labeled, the "regulatory apparatus of heterosexuality" with its attendant "compulsory appropriation and identification with those normative demands."[35]

So, why does it matter that these two playwrights have presented
the maternal role as a performative? If Victor Burgin is correct that
what we see and the way we see it is a product of representation
whose effects come to be seen as natural, and Butler is right that
"the production of texts can be one way of reconfiguring what will
count as the world," then theater and the other arts have long been
complicitous in convincing us that motherhood as it is understood
in the late twentieth and early twenty-first century is inborn rather
than a social construct.[36] The plays discussed here surely challenge
that allegation. Furthermore, if, as Butler has argued, "the ideal that
is mirrored depends on that very mirroring to be sustained as an
ideal," then our mirror of theater has long helped sustain the norm
of motherhood as it constructs and convinces us of its naturalness.[37]
The stage production of *De profesión maternal* underscored this
mirroring via the ever-present looking glass that occupied a prominent position throughout the performance, a mirror that does not
appear in the play text and was presumably added by the director. I
would argue that the presence of that mirror highlighted the traditional complicity of theater (like opera and popular movies) in perpetuating the norm of motherhood (as well as other gender roles).
Thus, in the stage production, when Leticia flips the mirror over, it
seems at first that she is refusing to look in the mirror, to see herself
as the mother she is, and to stop seeing herself only as the victimized daughter. Later, however, it appears that, via that tangible mirror, the production encourages us all to reject those externally
imposed idealizations, to stop looking to the mirrors of art to find
ourselves, or vice versa to demand that the mirrors of art reflect us,
not what someone else would like us to be. The mirror here seems
not only to undermine the "mirror" of theater but also to emphasize
the play as a moment for mothers and daughters to take a different

look at ourselves and challenge the roles we often assume without question. Insofar as, in Butler's words "the norm . . . takes hold to the extent that it is 'cited' as such a norm, but it also derives its power through the citations that it compels," portraying mothers in theater or any art form necessarily authorizes and perpetuates that portrayal as a (the) norm, running the risk of another metaphorical lobotomy that will produce yet another smiling, passive Sphinx.[38]

By daring to portray mothers differently, challenging the norm, and showing it to be a performative, a product of representation and systems of normativization, both Gambaro and Argüelles begin to open the door to other possibilities. When they depict mothers who deviate from traditional citations and who are simultaneously victims of society and victimizers within it, both playwrights underscore the violence and perniciousness of the either/or polarities with which we have tended to perceive mothers and within which we have expected them to perform: good mother vs. bad; the Judeo-Christian tradition's self-sacrificing, eternally suffering (preferably virgin) mother vs. the devouring or castrating mother of psychoanalysis.

Replacing Butler's term, *heterosexuality,* with *motherhood,* we might summarize the message of the two plays: "[motherhood] offers normative . . . positions that are intrinsically impossible to embody, and the persistent failure to identify fully and without incoherence with these positions reveals [motherhood] itself not only as a compulsory law, but as an inevitable comedy."[39] Earlier in the same book, Butler's words seem even more pertinent to these plays: "what passes as 'maternal instinct' may well be a culturally constructed desire which is interpreted through a naturalistic vocabulary."[40] As she goes on to argue, that naturalistic vocabulary "effectively renders that 'paternal law' invisible."[41]

A FINAL OBSERVATION

Since my focus here has been on the question of theatricality and theater's role in perpetuating gender roles that are (mis)construed as natural, a final comment in regard to audience response to these two plays seems to be in order. Interestingly, for the most part theater audiences have apparently failed to recognize themselves in either play. Mexican audiences typically perceive Argüelles's plays as bizarre plays that deal with dysfunctional families that are totally unlike any Mexican family, and this one was no exception. Along similar lines, the night I saw the Gambaro play, in an audience that was nearly 100 percent female, one of the comments I heard as I was leaving the theater was, "ninguna madre podría ser así de mala" (no mother could be that bad). Although both Argüelles's work and opera as analyzed by Clément offer ostensibly facile "undoings" of women, it is far more difficult to undo the normativizing, naturalizing mirrors of art, if we are to judge by these reactions.[42]

8

Of Mothers, Gauchos, Knishes, and Desire: Transculturation in Eduardo Rovner's *Volvió una noche*

> I fear the encounter with the past that again confronts my life.
> —"Returning" (a tango)

THIS CHAPTER BEGAN IN AN EFFORT TO ADDRESS THE QUESTION OF what there is about Eduardo Rovner's play, *Volvió una noche* (*She Returned One Night*) (1993), that allows it to be successfully produced around the world in spite of its obvious "Argentine" character.[1] The play has been staged in such diverse countries as Uruguay, Argentina, Israel, United States, Mexico, Czech Republic, Costa Rica, Cuba, Finland, Chile, and Brazil, and this, again, in spite of its "Argentineness," as epitomized in the language of the play, the tango music that informs the title and is scattered throughout the work, as well as in the repeated appearances onstage of the gaucho, Sargento Chirino, an "escapee from the Gutiérrez novel" and romantic figure of Argentina's past.[2] Added to this almost folkloric Argentine flavor are the ethnically specific references embodied by its Jewish protagonists. How and why, then, can the play be successfully "translated" in disparate cultures and delight audiences throughout the Western world?

I believe the answers to this intriguing question lie not simply in the play's comic nature but rather in the serious issues addressed within that cloak of comedy.[3] I have proposed elsewhere that the play's international success is due at least in part to Rovner's skill at underscoring similarities, the points of contact we find among various groups, while not erasing differences, thus allowing us to identify to some degree with all the various characters, living ones as well as dead ones, historical figures as well as contemporary ones.[4] Here I will propose that it is also, and perhaps principally, the figure of the mother, common denominator in the experience of most of us in the Western world, that renders the play culturally translatable. In other words, although the histories and cultures of our diverse nations and even of various groups within the same country are multiple, we do have many elements in common, not the least of which are the very notions of culture/society and the mother who imparts those social/cultural norms, different though they may be.[5] In this play that mother specifically comes to embody the concept of transculturation, which, although we may not always recognize it as we cling tenaciously to our particular cultural differences and perceived uniqueness, is also part of the cultural baggage and experiences of most members of Western societies today. In *Volvió una noche,* Rovner allows us to witness (and perhaps even reconcile ourselves to) our own inevitable transculturation in our rapidly changing world of globalization and diaspora, a transculturation that is dramatized not only in the union of Manuel (Argentine Jew) and Dolly (Argentine Catholic) but also in Manuel's mother, Fanny or Fannushka as her friends call her (an Argentine Jewish mother and Russian immigrant), ostensible antagonist but one who paradoxically is already a product of transculturation herself. I will argue that the mother here becomes an index and perpetuator of culture, but culture (like the mother herself) is never monolithic (etymologically, made of one stone, one building block) but inevitably comprises contradictory characteristics (a mixture of self and other as well as of past, present, and imagined future), always already a palimpsest, a transculture in the process of yet another transculturation.[6]

The plot of *Volvió una noche* is relatively simple. When Manuel, a young Jewish man, announces to Fanny, his deceased mother (with whom he "chats" every Sunday when he visits her grave), that he is getting married, she returns from the dead to meet his fiancée, Dolly, to punish him for having made her suffer by not mentioning this startling news earlier (and this in spite of the fact that he never failed to share neighborhood gossip and the plots of countless movies with her), and to verify that he has become all that she had dreamed he would be and all that he has told her he is: a surgeon and a classical musician. After settling herself into his home, Fanny soon discovers that he has been lying to her, for he is not a surgeon but a pedicurist and not a classical musician but a violinist in a tango group. To make matters worse, he is planning to marry not a good Jewish girl but a Catholic one and, worse yet from Fanny's perspective, a single mother. Much of the humor of the play is produced by Manuel's efforts to keep his mother from discovering the truth of his life and by the many misunderstandings on the part of Dolly and his friends who can neither see nor hear Fanny. After a series of very funny scenes, Fanny finally reconciles herself to the fact that Manuel is not going to live the life she has chosen for him, but rather the one he has chosen for himself (or, perhaps better expressed, the one that his sociohistorical circumstances have permitted), a life, which, as we shall see, is a product of his transculturation and one that in many ways reflects Fanny's own earlier process of transculturation.

Interestingly, although Manuel responds to his mother's disappointment about the realities of his life with the words "¡Ya sé que eso era lo que vos querías! ¡Pero yo elegí otra cosa!" (*VN*, 66) (I know that was what you wanted! But, I chose something else!) (*SR*, 37), he seems not to recognize that his "something else," what he has chosen (a) was not freely chosen but rather already constrained by his sociohistorical possibilities (just as Fanny's life was), and (b) is a cultural and temporal palimpsest, one that is "overwritten" by Manuel to be sure but that still manifests traces of Fanny. In many ways, his life is perhaps not as different from hers as he would believe. At the very least both lives are products of transculturation and evince traces of previous (trans)cultures.[7] As the play suggests, those traces of an "other" way of life, of other(s') desires, are perhaps not noticed unless and until one starts searching for them. In this play, however, those "others" are foregrounded and made discernible in the appearances on the stage of characters who are already dead—in a technique by which the past is made visible and physical, embodied in these characters, and becomes a tangible presence, evocative of the less-tangible presence of earlier (trans)-cultures. Those traces—the residue of former mores—are also physically, if indeed more subtly, underscored insofar as Manuel not only lives in what was Fanny's house but also sleeps on what was her pillow.[8] And this in spite of the fact that he perceives his life as dramatically different from hers and what she wanted for him. But then Fanny too perceives it as diametrically opposed to what she, and she presumes, he, wanted: "¡¡No sos nada de lo que ibas a ser!!" (*VN*, 78) (You aren't anything that you were going to be!!) (*SR*, 46). Paradoxically, however, those words might equally apply to her and indeed to all of us to the extent that we are probably all, to a greater or lesser degree, consciously or not, the consequence and product of our desires, which would overwrite (and erase?) the desires of the other but which are concurrently (alternately?) overwritten by those of yet an "other"—individual, culture, and so on. This is poignantly dramatized in scene 16 when Manuel tries to give the pillow, index of Fanny, her culture, and her

desires, back to her and do the impossible: start with a clean slate
or in this case a new pillow, one not marked, inscribed by previous
(trans)cultures and/or desires of the other. In the end, Fanny decides
to let Manuel live his life and to return with her friends to her "life"
in the world of the dead (which very much resembles our own lives
in the world of the living and is similarly presented as a series of
negotiations among conflicting desires). In a gesture of reconciliation, which I read as an attempt not to forsake his past completely
while not eschewing his future either—that is, as an indication of
the very transculturation, palimpsest of desires, I am analyzing
here—Manuel proposes that he and Fanny meet once a month in
the *confitería* (tearoom) of his childhood. In some sense his future
will overtly comprise an overlap of past, present, and future or what
we might again label a palimpsest created from memory, wishful
thinking, projection, imagination, and/or perspective.

Transculturation is a term that "refers to the reciprocal influences
of modes of representation and cultural practices of various kinds
in colonies and metropoles."[9] As Mary Louise Pratt has maintained
in her seminal study *Imperial Eyes: Travel Writing and Transculturation*, "Transculturation is a phenomenon of the contact zone,"
and, while relations of domination and subordination between the
periphery and the metropolis are often asymmetrical, that transculturation does work in both directions.[10] The metropolis/colonizer
not only influences the periphery/colonized but is in turn influenced
by it, often in subtle and unexpected ways. Pratt defines *contact
zone* as "the space of colonial encounters, the space in which peoples geographically and historically separated come into contact
with each other and establish ongoing relations, usually involving
conditions of coercion, radical inequality, and intractable conflict."[11] For her the term *contact* foregrounds "the interactive, improvisational dimensions of colonial encounters so easily ignored
or suppressed by diffusionist accounts of conquest and domination."[12] As the Rovner play reveals, the terms Pratt uses to describe
the colonial encounter also effectively describe the contact zones
produced when an immigrant (such as Fanny) comes to the perceived metropolis (in this case, Buenos Aires). At the same time,
however, Rovner underscores the perhaps inevitable slippage in the
distinctions between metropolis and periphery and emphasizes the
self-serving impetus of a culture's definition of itself as center/me-
tropolis insofar as this particular immigrant has moved from the
perceived center (Europe, if indeed Eastern Europe, already understood as somewhat off center) to the periphery (Argentina, former
colony), but specifically to Buenos Aires, which is perceived as the

metropolis/center of this particular periphery. Thus, as the Rovner play dramatizes, neither centers nor peripheries are quite as pure, clearly delineated, and uncontaminated by the other, as we are wont to perceive them. Although each is defined by the other and indeed does not exist except in relation to the other, the demarcations are necessarily relative and continually shifting, as are family relations as depicted in this play. What is perceived as the metropolis/center by one group of people is often the periphery to another. Furthermore, a group's very insistence on its centrality may well belie a certain anxiety about the precariousness of that definition. To define oneself as center, as dominant, may signal the desire (wishful thinking) as much as, if not more than, the experience. As we will see, *Volvió una noche* also suggests that our personal desires are similarly defined, delimited, by those of the other(s), but again the demarcations among them blur and shift, producing the perhaps inevitable transculturation that is my focus here. Indeed, throughout this chapter I will argue that although the question of desire has generally been omitted from postcolonial theory, in fact, colonialism, as it is defined today, is, among many other things, a process through which desire is manipulated, negotiated, (re)acquired, and adapted in relation to the other.

At the same time, *Volvió una noche* underscores how *contact zone* might equally well refer to the space of the home, where one generation encounters the other; where members of the various generations spar and negotiate for centrality and dominance (temporary though that dominance may be); where culture, social mores, and desires (socially acceptable desires, to be sure) are (re)-produced, accepted, rejected, and adapted; where the parent (metaphoric center of power, colonizer) not only shapes the child (metaphoric colonized, subordinated other) but is simultaneously, if indeed inadvertently, shaped by that child as well; where the desires of one are continually bent, defined, delineated by those of the other because of, but also in spite of, their asymmetrical power relations.[13] It is surely not irrelevant to my argument that the very term *metropolis* derives etymologically from the Greek *polis,* state, and *meter,* mother. Specifically, in *Volvió una noche, contact zone* certainly describes the space in which Fanny, former center of maternal power but now metaphoric immigrant from another place (death) and earlier time frame, encounters Manuel, formerly subjugated (as child and son) but now empowered as an adult. Even more significant, that encounter takes place in the home that was hers but is now his, in a gesture that signals the inevitable passing of power, the slippage of the very terms colonizer and colonized, as well as the relative, provisional, and, to borrow a term from Pratt, improvisational makeup of those roles: today's colonized is tomorrow's colonizer while even today some individuals of the colonized group surely colonize others within that ostensibly homogeneous group.[14] In many ways, as Pratt indirectly suggests in her title and introduction, it may depend on whose eyes are seeing.[15] I would add that this slippage between colonizer and colonized also signals each individual's capacity to occupy more than one subject position, alternately colonizer and colonized. What makes *Volvió una noche* such a successful play is its skill at negotiating (and indeed intertwining) these two levels of colonization and transculturation: the personal/family level and the public/(inter)national(ist) level. We have seen in earlier chapters that the apparently personal space/place of the family is the site of politics, policing, and training for life in the patriarchy.[16] *Volvió una noche* also presents it as the basic site of the colonial paradigm.[17]

The play is in fact punctuated with assorted indicators of transculturation and contact zones, which, subtle though they may be, serve as constant reminders of what I read as one of the play's deep structures. Several of these indicators are relatively readily identifiable as signs of transculturation (e.g., tango, gaucho) while others are less obvious (e.g., Fanny, Manuel's opening lines). Perhaps the most overt trope of transculturation is the figure of the gaucho, embodied here in the character of Sargento Chirino. Lest there be any doubt as to the Argentine gaucho's status as a product of transculturation, I would like to cite just two descriptions of this colorful, folkloric figure: "a sort of in-between type who lived in a no-man's land between urban civilization and the complete savagery of the Indian territory," and the Andalusian horseman adapted to the savage life of the pampa and mixed with the Indian.[18] As these two quotations indicate, the gaucho epitomizes a palimpsest of two or more different worlds/cultures, one superimposed on the other, and lives on the border where they overlap (Pratt's contact zone). As a further indication of their transculturation, the poetry and songs for which the gauchos were known blended Spanish melodies with local indigenous products. And, not unlike the tango as we will see below, the lyrics of those songs were often about a love lost or a way of life either already past or in the process of disappearing.

Revealingly, most popular knowledge about gauchos comes from the poetry written about them by city writers. That is, most gaucho literature was written not by gauchos themselves but by educated, cultured, urban poets. Furthermore, that literature became fashionable only when the real gauchos were already well on the way to extinction and thus no longer viewed as a significant threat to urban populations. Although originally viewed as vagabonds, idlers, and smugglers, gauchos eventually came to be perceived as romantic symbols of individualism, independence, and self-sufficiency, perhaps, in part at least, because of the literature written about them.[19] In other words, via literary renditions the figure of the gaucho was "tamed," romanticized, and resemanticized to make him palatable to urban readers of the dominant culture, to make him an unthreatening reflection of their desires for freedom and individualism. Further emphasizing the transcultural in our contemporary image of the gaucho, Anderson Imbert and Florit have noted that what is considered the most important (and best known) gaucho poem, *Martín Fierro* (1872), by José Hernández was a muffled polemic against a pro-European group, a statement that again signals the extent to which the literary gaucho is an emblem of as well as a response to transculturation.[20]

Significantly, Rovner's gaucho, Sargento Chirino, hired by Fanny to enforce her "law," is a distinctly literary, theatrical gaucho, one who is often associated with the origins of Argentine theater and one who, like the historical gaucho, also underwent significant modification as he was tailored to meet the needs (desires) of his authors and audiences. As I earlier indicated, Sargento Chirino is a character in the Gutiérrez serial novel, *Juan Moreira,* published in 1879.[21] The title character, Moreira, was a real-life gaucho who had been killed by the police in 1874.[22] In 1884, José J. Podestá staged the novel in pantomime form. Later, in 1886, dialogue was added. As Pellettieri notes in his study, during the play's tour through the provinces, the audience gradually added and deleted characters, lengthening some scenes and leaving out others.[23] As a result, it became the very emblem not only of transculturation, but also of giving audiences what they want, a mirror of their own desires. Interestingly, however, the edition of the play published in 1944, bearing the authorship of Gutiérrez-Podestá, includes no character named Sargento Chirino. Instead, there is a Sargento Navarro who tries, unsuccessfully, to capture Moreira. At the end of the play, Moreira wounds Navarro, but then bandages those wounds and buys him a drink, thereby gaining Navarro's admiration and devotion. The play ends not with a dead Moreira, but with a very live one who rides off, leaving Navarro behind, not threatening to kill him but to beat the eyes out of anyone who calls him a bandit. Clearly, both the figure of the gaucho as well as this particular character have been handed down to us in a romanticized and resemanticized form, a hybrid or synergy that has evolved over time, and

again one that gives the audience a reflection of its own values and
desires, much as traditional images of the family have long done in
theater.[24]

It is important to note the extent to which Rovner's Chirino also
evokes the colonial paradigm. As I have indicated, the gaucho in
general was a marginalized type that the Argentine society felt it
had to civilize (read, colonize), dominate, and bring around to a
specific, superior way of life (theirs). Significantly, and in what I
read as an emphasis on the provisional status of the colonizer and
the colonized (that today's colonized is tomorrow's colonizer, as
we will see below in the mother and son), Rovner's Chirino offers
Fanny his assistance in dominating and civilizing Manuel, in bringing him around to her way of thinking. Indeed, in nearly every
speech, Chirino reflects on the question of domination and refers to
Manuel as a gaucho. In his first speech he begins by stating that no
one should ignore the pleas of "una madre que al fruto de sus entra-
ñas no ha podido dominar" (*VN*, 18) (a Mom who has not been able
to control the fruit of her womb) (*SR*, 5) and then refers to "la doma
del gaucho" (*VN*, 19), the domination or taming of the "gaucho"
Manuel. In this way, he explicitly links the maternal to domination
(acculturation) and implicitly to colonialism. Later, in a confrontation with Manuel, Chirino is more specific that Manuel give in to
the will or domination of his mother and/or the dominant culture:

> Que ansí como la tranquera
> es pa' cuidar del ganado,
> los mandatos están dados
> para obediencia del gaucho. (*VN*, 79)

> [Just as the staff controls the sheep,
> we have commandments we must keep
> To force a gaucho to obey.] (*SR*, 47)

Like the staff (gate, in the original) that controls or restricts the cattle, the rules of culture are in place and need only to be obeyed
without question. As is probably typical of colonial discourse, Chirino implies that neither the gate nor the rules are in place to oppress, but rather to take care of, to look after (*cuidar*, as a mother
does with a child). But, of course, as the play will demonstrate,
sometimes those rules can be adapted, desires (re)negotiated. The
gate of culture may be strong, but some cattle may well escape,
temporarily at least, as is the case here where the gaucho, Chirino,
formerly the colonized, becomes the enforcer for Fanny, the colonizer, at least until the tables turn again.

It cannot be irrelevant either that Fanny specifically links the figure of Moreira and the tango: "¿Así que te gusta el tango? ¡¿Pero quién te creés que sos, Juan Moreira?!" (*VN*, 78) (So you like the tango. Who do you think you are, Juan Moreira?) (*SR*, 46). To be sure, the genre of the tango from which the play takes its title and with which the play opens and closes should also be read as a paradigm of transculturation and precisely the contact zone phenomenon to which Pratt refers.[25] With its origins in the fringe areas, brothels, and tenements of Buenos Aires and among lower-class immigrants, the tango began in the late 1880s. In many ways the epitome of transculturation, it adapted and blended gaucho tradition (already a [trans]culture as we have seen), African rhythms (imported via Cuba), and Spanish-Arabic melodies, among other elements.[26] Aided by the aura of French immigrant Carlos Gardel in the early decades of the 1900s, the musical form moved from the periphery to the metropolis as it was eventually accepted by the Argentine elite, who initially may have despised it for what it represented—the rise of the middle class with its threat to their hegemony (although this aspect was usually disguised in moral condemnations of the musical form). Revealingly, however, before the Argentine elite semiaccepted the tango, it had already been accepted by another metropolis, the inhabitants of the capitals of Europe. As Simon Collier, et al. have argued, the "sub-metropolis" (my term) of the Argentine elite may have finally accepted their native product only because it had been accepted (if indeed modified and tamed) in the salons of Paris and London that they so admired—that is, their desires were occasioned by and perhaps even scripted in response to those of the other, in this case the metropolis.[27] Returned to Argentina, now Europeanized, the tango embodies a palimpsest of periphery and metropolis, the powered and the disempowered, present and past, competing desires. Furthermore, the lyrics of many tangos evoke the very process of transculturation precisely in their nostalgia for a disappearing way of life as the first generations of inhabitants of Buenos Aires (formerly immigrants of the peripheries) adapted to their new urban experiences and learned to embrace new desires, to desire differently. Thus, the tango provides a vivid example of transculturation in which "subjugated peoples cannot readily control what emanates from the dominant culture, [but] they do determine to varying extents what they absorb into their own, and what they use it for."[28] Yet perhaps even more important, it provides a dramatic example of the (often overlooked) bidirectional nature of transculturation and the fact that peripheral or colonized groups may well permeate and influence the perceived center and then, in turn, be the recipients of their own products, which have been altered and now boomerang back to them.[29] It also underscores the duality implied in colonialism as well as any construction of self insofar as the self may desire what the other desires precisely because the other desires it (triangular desire à la Girard) or conversely may reject what the other desires, again precisely because the other desires it and the self would distance itself from that other (what we might well call negative triangular desire)—both of which are at work, and perhaps simultaneously, in any process of transculturation and, specifically, in the power plays we witness between Manuel and Fanny.[30]

It cannot be irrelevant that early in the play, Rovner proffers a very subtle indicator of a metaphoric contact zone, one that might not initially be recognized as such, for in this case it is not a meeting of peoples historically separated but of levels of fiction generally alienated and deemed mutually exclusive. I refer to Manuel's early conversation with his mother at the gravesite—indeed the opening words of the play—words that at first glance seem trite or border on meaninglessness: "¡No se puede creer! Primero, él la mira desde la pantalla a ella que está comiendo pochoclo en la platea. ¿Te das cuenta? ¡Desde la pantalla!" (*VN*, 15) (You won't believe it! First he looks at her from the screen where she's eating popcorn in the front seats. Do you realize? From the screen!) (*SR*, 2). The point of reference is a movie he has seen, but in these few words perceived hierarchies, "normal" contacts are destabilized; demarcations between fictional levels are blurred. First, in an inversion of Mulvey's theory of the cinematic gaze, in which the female character or actress is the object of the gaze (and of the implied desire) of the male spectator, imaged and framed to produce his pleasure (a gaze that in the terms of my analysis of the Rovner work is a play of power that colonizes the female actress), here the spectator is female and the actor, male.[31] She is looking at him. But, second, and taking the challenge one step further, Rovner presents a mixture of levels of fiction: the male actor/character looks out (down) from the screen at the female spectator in what disrupts the theoretical unilateral power of the gaze with its encoded hierarchy, leaving in doubt the object of the gaze. Who is colonizing whom, but more important, how can he (a character in a movie and implicitly the colonized, powerless) look back at the spectator? Are we meant to interpret this as an example of the boomerang effect I mentioned above, by which both colonizer and colonized are defined by and exhibit traces of the other; where the perceived traces of one (real or not) are projected onto the other and then bounce back again to their source? This disruption of levels of productivity carries directly over to the perception and characterization of the mother, as I will discuss below, and will once again lead us later to the question of the mirror of theater—wherein lies the source and wherein the mirror. Whose eyes are seeing? Furthermore, the fact that Manuel is performing, mirroring onstage, exactly the actions he describes (looking down from the stage at his mother and the audience) also destabilizes the encoded hierarchies.[32] What is more, Rovner's cinematic hero is dressed expressly as an explorer, in shorts and a hat, in an image that evokes the European imperialist discussed by Pratt, ready to invade new lands, see, describe, colonize, impose his (trans)culture on the other.[33] Yet, another, similar inversion of power and blurring of levels of fiction continues later in this same scene when characters that are already dead appear onstage. Expressing all the desires and petty conflicts of the living, reflecting them and being reflected by them, these same dead characters will soon mingle with the living characters, again defying our notions of the separation of the worlds of the living and the dead, and/or the fictionality of the latter. I would argue that the admixture onstage of living characters and dead ones evokes (a) the very palimpsest that is (trans)culture (old mingled with the present) and (b) the constructed nature of any (trans)culture—(trans)culture not only as an admixture but also as a series of subjective projections, desires, and power plays.

I have dwelt at some length upon these assorted signs of transculturation in the play because without them we might well overlook the importance of the mother's position here as yet another trope of transculturation. Yet, by utilizing the figure of the mother as an image of transculturation, Rovner ultimately sheds light on and provides insights into both family relations and transculturation, as a consideration of the characteristics they share will demonstrate. First, culture (which is probably never original but always a [trans]culture that may not recognize itself as such), like the maternal, is (re)productive; it (re)produces a version of itself that is never quite itself. Both are sites of (re)productivity where disparate elements merge to produce a new hybrid or synergetic entity. At the same time, like the mother in *Volvió una noche,* (trans)culture is always, already internalized (if indeed not immune to modification); we already know what its mandates to us and expectations of us will be. Like the gate that restricts Chirino's cattle, its presence and limitations are no surprise. Remember that in the Rovner play, Fanny is already dead, part of the past, not unlike those other past (trans)cultures we carry with us (perhaps particularly those of us with immigrant ancestors); but the traces remain, and she "lives" in some sense in Manuel, as does her cultural heritage, even though this cultural heritage itself is already plural, a hybrid (Russian, Jewish, Argentine, etc.). As Fanny's friend Salo (also dead) suggests, if Manuel forgets her, she will cease to exist even in the world of the dead.[34] Indeed, it cannot be irrelevant that in scene 2, as Manuel visits her grave and chats with her, his monologue appears to be a dialogue insofar as he speaks for her, in or from her place: he addresses himself as he believes she would. Similarly, Rovner's technique of having dead characters appear on the stage with living characters surely underscores the traces of the past that exist in our present. The dead characters move among the living, and, as depicted in this play, their "lives" in the world of the dead are merely an inverted mirror image of our own lives. At one point they gossip about people in the neighboring graves; at another Jeremías tells Fanny not to get upset because "te va a hacer mal" (*VN*, 17) (It will hurt you) (my translation), as if she were not already dead (a condition that, from the perspective of the living, is as bad as it can be).

Once again, the perspective of the dead underscores the question of whose imperial, colonizing eyes are seeing. For example, to celebrate *el día de los muertos* (day of the dead) Fanny and her friends perform a play that underscores this question of perspective, from which side of the mirror one is viewing and desiring, for they stage not *Death of a Salesman,* but *Arrival of a Salesman.*[35] Let us not forget either that in the southern hemisphere the day of the dead (November 2) falls in the spring, season of renewal and rebirth. And, significantly, at the end of *Volvió una noche,* Fanny's friends come to take her with them back to the world of the dead, not for any morbid or negative reason, but rather to celebrate (in the most positive sense of the term) the tenth anniversary of her death. As part of that celebration, tellingly, if indeed humorously, they sing "Happy Birthday" to her. In this way Rovner underscores the issues of perspective, desire, and subject position that underlie colonial/imperial discourse, emphasizing that it all depends on (a) who is observing, desiring, judging, and from where, as well as (b) each individual's ability to occupy more than one subject position, simultaneously or sequentially.

In this respect, Manuel's conversation with his mother at her gravesite, where he speaks for her, in or from her place, not only reveals the degree to which he has internalized her, traces of her former being, but also (and inversely) the degree to which she is now a product of him as much as vice versa. Fanny, former colonizer, center of power, is reproduced or projected here by Manuel, the formerly colonized, and thus she, in turn, is metaphorically colonized anew. Within the fictional world of the play, Manuel engenders (has engendered) her as much as she, him.[36] Like numerous other aspects of the play, their relations of power continually slip and/or reverse, only to slip and/or reverse again in what might be viewed as the very basis of ongoing transculturation. As Rovner dramatizes, that transculturation inevitably works in both directions insofar as Fanny, like the gaucho or the tango, like history or the past, is rewritten, reconceived, and reperceived in light of the present. Similarly, old values are replaced by new, and then reconceived and replaced anew. Indeed, the very staging of this scene, as suggested by the play text, visually underscores this concept. The scene begins with a dark stage, and only the upper half of Manuel's body is illuminated. At first, we do not know where he is or to whom he is speaking, although he is alone, and the visual focus on the upper half of his body clearly emphasizes the mental, spiritual, psychological elements that we associate with the upper body. As his monologue continues, his level of anxiety rises until he finally lashes out at Fanny with the words, "¡No me pongas nervioso! . . . ¡Es que no se puede hablar con vos, mamá! ¡No escuchás nada!" (*VN*, 15) (Don't make me nervous! . . . I just can't speak to you, Mama! You don't listen to anything!) (*SR*, 2), words that are most literal in the nonfictional world, and words that in some sense also implicitly invert their previous parent/child roles since, one might well imagine, they echo words that she had at some point addressed to him.[37] In addition, those words evoke the basic colonial paradigm to the extent that he is shown to be hesitant to express a desire (to marry Dolly) to a colonial power whose desire may be (and in this case, is) other.

At the same time, part of the experiences of leaving either childhood (and by implication, the mother) or our immigrant origins (which as a result of the process of colonization are, like the mother, often undervalued if not openly scorned by the new [trans] culture/society to which we would adapt ourselves) includes learning to desire differently. Specifically, desiring differently frequently involves a certain repudiation of that "inferior" culture and/or of our childish, dependent relationship with the mother, both of which we often try to deny or forget. And that renunciation produces anxiety, as we have seen in the "conversation" between Manuel and his mother at the cemetery. Indeed, since Fanny is primarily a projection of Manuel in that scene, it is difficult to determine the extent to which what the audience perceives as *her* anxiety over his pending marriage is not in fact his own (projected onto

her). I would further argue that although much current use of Freudian and Lacanian psychoanalytical principles focuses on the name
and/or the "law of the father," both of which implicitly gender cul-
ture(s) as masculine, for a child at least that "law," that (trans)cul-
ture, is often communicated and enforced largely by the mother. As
depicted in this play, it is not "big daddy" who is watching (on
either the personal or the political level), but "big mommy." [38] This
is highlighted by the fact that, as Fanny acknowledges, she raised
Manuel alone, without the presence of a father figure, a factor that
for me leaves little doubt about the primacy of the role of the
mother (at the very least, of this particular mother) in the process
of transculturation and socialization. [39]

Nonetheless, *Volvió una noche* also recognizes the fictionality,
the invention (and perhaps desire, wishful thinking) that engulfs
one's perception of the (m)other insofar as that perception (whether
that other is the center as perceived from the periphery or vice
versa) is always a product of earlier encounters or experiences, now
internalized and fictionalized (distorted, adapted, adjusted to the individual's or society's current circumstances, desires, and/or expectations) as part of the memory process. This element of fiction/
projection/adaptation is also apparent in the cemetery scene I have
already discussed and is underscored by the fact that Manuel's
"conversations" with Fanny there center, for the most part, on
other fictional constructs: he repeats the neighborhood gossip
(surely not noted for its strict adherence to truth or reality); he describes the plots of movies and plays; he shares his professional
"successes" as a surgeon and a musician (inventions, roles/facades
donned to placate the powers that be, to convince the colonizer that
one has accepted the imposed [trans]culture, that one's desires reflect those authorized by the colonizer). Once again he gives his
audience the show he believes she desires. But, surely, the question
is, how accurate, indeed, is his perception of her and her desires?
To what extent is what he perceives as her desire in fact shaped by
his own? Like the tango returned to Argentina but now Europeanized, how distant and different is his reproduction of her from any
possible original? In Pratt's terms, what use have the colonized people made of what emanates from the dominant culture? [40] And, I
would add, how do they adapt, modify those borrowings or traces,
rescript them for their own purposes?

In so many ways, then, the return of the mother here personifies
the return of the repressed, the return of the other (trans)culture that
we have internalized and would, perhaps, repudiate. At the same
time, that return signals the presence of both the colonizer and the

colonized that we carry within.[41] It is not irrelevant that throughout much of the play, Fanny is presented, and indeed within the dramatic fiction presents herself, as impervious to external influences and change, fixed and closed to adaptation or assimilation. Ironically, however, it soon becomes clear that she, like Manuel, is in fact already a product of transculturation, having already assimilated what was other—the Spanish language, the New World way of life, and so on. And it seems clear that the recognition or acknowledgment of transculturation in and of itself reflects a certain acknowledgment of the existence of this difference within, this internal coexistence of both colonizer and colonized with the implicit slippage between positions of power and conflicting desires.[42] This slippage between the performance of empowerment and that of disfranchisement is repeatedly enacted in the Rovner play, as we will see.

More important for my focus here, as portrayed in *Volvió una noche,* the figures of the mother in general and Fanny in specific function not only as products of this bidirectional transculturation, as temporal and colonial palimpsests, but also as emblems of the very contact zone itself, where colonizer (alleged power) encounters the colonized (presumed disfranchised). As she moves back and forth between apparent positions of power and disempowerment, Fanny becomes an index of that difference within. But, let us not forget that in Western tradition the mother already occupies an intermediary position, simultaneously both the colonizer and the colonized insofar as she lives in a patriarchal society that often undervalues her and the rest of her gender, yet she is still in a position of power vis-à-vis her children. Her power on the one hand seems limitless, on the other, contingent and fragile. Indeed, one might well argue that she is the paradigm of Foucault's notion of power as multilateral and multidirectional.[43] Specifically, in her hilariously funny character as the stereotypical Jewish mother, Fanny enacts this oscillation of power: at one moment domineering despot, at the next, misunderstood victim, even though ultimately both postures must be recognized for what they are—culturally authorized performances or citations à la Butler—which, like all performances or subject positions, carry with them certain perceived rewards and/or penalties.[44] For example, she berates Manuel because he has become a pedicurist instead of a surgeon: "¿Sabés lo qué necesitarías? ¡Una buena lección! ¡¡Eso es lo que te merecés!!" (*VN,* 67) (Do you know what you need? A good lesson! That's what you deserve!!) (*SR,* 38). And then she immediately assumes the role of victim: "¡Pedicuro! . . . ¡Un Stern pedicuro! ¿Por qué? . . . ¿Qué hice yo mal? . . . ¿Por qué este castigo?" (*VN*, 67) (Pedicurist! . . . A Stern . . . a pedicurist! Why? . . . What did I do wrong? . . . Why this punishment?) (*SR*, 38). Not getting the reaction she expected or desired, she begins to complain about the terrible shape her feet are in after ten years in the grave, as if this too were somehow his responsibility.[45] Later in the play, she insults Manuel and screams "Renegado" (*VN*, 89) (Traitor) (*SR*, 55) at him after learning that Dolly is Catholic. But, again, this is immediately followed by a diametrically different performance as she feigns to be dying: "Ay . . . ay! ¡No puedo respirar! . . . ¡Ay . . . me muero!" (*VN*, 90–91) (Oh . . . oh! I can't breathe! . . . Oh . . . I'm dying!) (*SR*, 56). After initially demonstrating concern for her, Manuel finally realizes what is happening and retorts, "¿Otra vez? . . . Decime . . . ¿Cuántas veces te vas a morir?" (*VN*, 91) (Again? . . . Tell me . . . How many times are you going to die?) (*SR*, 56). To this she counters, still assuming the role of long-suffering mother and victim, "Con hijos como vos . . . Una se puede morir mil veces" (*VN*, 91) (With children like you . . . You can die a thousand deaths) (*SR*, 56).[46] Surely Fanny's stance and words here, humorous as they are, are equally applicable to culture with its constant tug at our lives and with its seemingly monolithic power and inescapability, which is, nevertheless, overpowered time and again: old forms die repeatedly as we continually modify them to form new synergies in our ongoing processes of transculturation. Nonetheless, the fact that such disparate roles, identities, and positionalities are enacted by the same character signals the inherent contradictory identities with which (and within which) we all exist, as individuals, (trans)cultures, or societies—the differences within.[47]

At the same time, it is certainly important to recognize that like the mother depicted in the Rovner play, culture/society also sends us contradictory messages in its oscillation between seeming power and seeming disfranchisement, and inversely, we react to its messages or mandates inconsistently, sometimes accepting, sometimes rejecting. This internal oscillation between acceptance and rejection, past and present, fantasy and reality, is staged in the Rovner play via an overcoat, which links scene 4 to scene 5, and to some degree epitomizes Manuel's position as colonizer and colonized, torn between two historical moments, two (trans)cultures, two (or more) conflicting desires, and in some sense two mothers: one from the past, Fanny, and one for the future, Dolly, who, already a mother herself, will also be the mother of their future children. In scene 4, which opens with a power struggle over whether they will do things (in this case, shower and have breakfast) her way or his,

Fanny is adamant that Manuel wear his overcoat, in spite of the fact that it is spring and warm outside. Like a mother with a young child, she not only insists that he wear it (and he seems to have no choice but to obey) but helps him put it on. That coat, however, as the stage directions specify, *"Es notoriamente chico"* (*VN,* 28) (*It is noticeably small*) (*SR,* 12), signaling the extent to which the former identity, desires, and way of life (exemplified by the clothing) are no longer appropriate: the coat is too small, and it is the wrong season for it. Thus, the coat becomes an index of the past, former subject position that he has outgrown and that no longer quite fits. The fact that in this scene the focus is specifically on an overcoat associated with the cold of winter and by analogy, death, further signals its current status as a "dead" custom, culture. Even though it is still a tangible presence, current conditions have obviated its usefulness. Scene 4 ends as Fanny exits with the words, "¡No salgas sin el sobretodo!" (*VN,* 30) (Don't go out without an overcoat!) (*SR,* 14), in what might be read as an admonishment (a) to acquiesce to her maternal powers and (b) to continue in the old way of life, maintain things (desires) as they have always been (another fantasy to be sure; as we have seen, things have not always been the same but are rather in a constant state of transculturation with its multiple reversals and palimpsests). Revealingly, then, the overcoat functions as an index of identity, something we put on at certain times, take off at others, and sometimes outgrow, evoking the continual flux of identity and by inference (trans)cultures, which are not inherent but always subject to change, modification, hybridization.[48]

Significantly, and in a parallel gesture, a few scenes later (at the end of scene 7), Fanny too tries on old clothes and old identities. Here, however, the old clothes are more overtly linked to desire, and indeed erotic desire, for, as she removes them from an old trunk and tries them on, Fanny walks coquettishly and eventually dances, ever more passionately, to sensuous music *"ante el asombro y éxtasis de Manuel"* (*VN,* 47) (*with Manuel's astonishment and delight*) (*SR,* 26), astonishment that reflects the fact that, as scripted by most Western cultures, erotic desire and the maternal are presumed to be incompatible desires. Nonetheless, here Rovner dramatizes that they too can coexist, like other differences within, like other conflicting desires, for as soon as Fanny stops dancing, she immediately reassumes an exaggeratedly maternal role, lulling Manuel (an adult) to sleep with a lullaby.

At the start of scene 5, Dolly enters, comments on the fact that the coat is too small, and suggests that he not wear it. In a reversal of the previous scene, where Manuel struggled against wearing the coat, and in what we might read as an acceptance of what he had previously resisted if not openly rejected (that is, of desiring differently), now he is the one who insists on wearing it, noting that it might get cold (in spite of Dolly's assurance that it is hot outside). Eventually he overreacts: in the words of the stage directions, "*Reacciona enérgico*" (*VN*, 32) (*He reacts forcefully*) (*SR*, 15), as he reveals his anxiety about his liminal position between two cultural frameworks, two temporal moments, two (m)others and conflicting desires: "¡Lo quiero llevar! ¿Qué hay? ¿Qué te importa si yo quiero ir con sobretodo?" (*VN*, 32) (I want to wear it! So what? What do you care if I want to go out in an overcoat?) (*SR*, 15). He knows that the old identity no longer fits, but he is still not quite ready or able to let go of it. That internalized mother/culture is not easily shaken. Anachronistic as it might be to our current situation, and like the gaucho, it is something that may have been rejected, but its traces have not been totally eradicated. We still cling to it if indeed only in mediated, fictionalized forms, but those forms conspicuously oscillate between glorifying that mother/culture at times and demeaning it at others.

Or is it merely a question of empowerment? Throughout the play we are witness to any number of interchanges and situations where the desires of one character seem predicated on a contradiction of the desires of the other. When Fanny wants to fix Manuel breakfast the first morning of her return, he objects. On the following morning, when she does not want to fix him breakfast, he insists that she do so. Along similar lines, when one character does accede to the will or power of another, that character, like Manuel in the scene with the overcoat, is quick to insist that s/he is doing it because s/he wants to, not because s/he is succumbing to the desires or authority of the other, in what may again signal the contradictions or anxieties that transculturation provokes in all of us. This is most dramatically illustrated near the end of the play when Fanny fires Sargento Chirino, the gaucho she had enlisted to punish Manuel: "¡Dije que no sigas! ¡No me discutas y andate!" (*VN*, 101) (I'm telling you not to keep this up. Don't argue with me. Leave!) (*SR*, 64). After his response of "¡Está bien, no se ponga así!" (*VN*, 101) (Okay, don't get like that!) (*SR*, 64), he starts to exit but then turns back "decidedly" and begins to recite poetry to an imaginary audience. His verses tell us that he does not want to leave his audience (whoever that might be) with a false impression; he is not going because he is a coward, and he does not want his true motivation forgotten. He continues, "Se los digo . . . sin rodeos ["sin rodeos" (without beating around the bush) but after twenty-four lines of verse]: / Lo hago . . . ¡¡Porque yo quiero!!" (*VN*, 102) (I'll tell you straight, so that you know: / I go because . . . I want to go!) (*SR*, 65). But, then, of course, this is part and parcel of the discourse of colonialism: the colonizers would like to flatter themselves and believe in the superiority of their culture, their way of life, and thus convince themselves (and the colonial subjects as well) that the latter have adapted the former's mores (that is, that the colonial subjects desire as and what the colonizers desire) because they (colonial subjects) want to, because they too recognize the superiority of the colonizers' (trans)culture. But, whose desire is this anyway? This adaptation is dramatized in Manuel's role playing and lies to his mother, as he pretends to be something he is not in the presence of the colonizer/powerful, feigns to conform to the colonizer's norms even though, as he insists, he has chosen something else. One of the aspects of transculturation frequently overlooked by postcolonial theory is precisely the question of desire and the fact that part of the process of colonization is learning to desire differently and to reflect (mimic) the desire of the colonizer. Indeed, this construction of desire is apparent in the family paradigm where the parent's primary role in preparing the child for future life in society may well be precisely an acculturation by means of which the child is taught (coerced, compelled) to desire (on the surface at least) what the master society would have him/her desire. As we have seen, however, that acculturation is seldom completely successful, and the result is a palimpsest of desires, often contradictory (ostensibly or in fact).

At the same time, the play also suggests that transculturation is not only an inevitable fact of life, it is necessary for continued life, renewal. As Fanny recognizes early in the play, "¡Renovarse es vivir!" (*VN*, 23) (Renewing yourself is living) (*SR*, 9), paradoxical words given her stance on the changes that Manuel has made in his life. Yet, the importance of renewal is underscored in scene 17 when Fanny's dead friends arrive to take her back to their world. They try to talk Manuel into returning with them and almost convince him. The scene seems to suggest that just as the mother/colonizer must eventually let go of the child/colonized, so too must that child let go of the mother, the former (trans)culture, along with the fiction of permanence and stability implied in the term culture. It is at this very moment that Manuel does indeed choose something else; he chooses to renew himself, to live rather than to die and specifically to live with the cultural hybrid his life has become. Thus, suggests Rovner, a refusal of transculturation is the equivalent of death, stasis.

This duality of the old and the new, empowerment and marginalization, is also personified and dramatized onstage in the figure of the gaucho who, as something of a spoof on the genie who appears from the lantern when called upon, is invoked by Fanny to punish Manuel for his transgressions of her law if you will, for marrying without her permission. The fact that what is at issue initially is the question of permission reinforces Fanny's role as a colonial power—Manuel should desire only when and what her authority permits. At any rate, the paradox of Chirino's position here is that the gaucho, who was once the colonized (indeed to the point of extinction for all practical purposes), is now the enforcer of the colonial powers and desires in what once again represents not only the other within but also the tenuous and ever-shifting nature of power in general. At the same time, Rovner's gaucho becomes an index of the extent to which the colonized internalizes the colonizer's mores in the process of transculturation, producing that ambivalence of which Bhabha has written.[49] It is significant too that the gaucho first appears in Manuel's world (as opposed to Fanny's) just after the conversation between Manuel and Dolly about their future together and just as they are about to make love and perhaps (re)produce that future concretely in the form of a child.[50] What seems particularly pertinent to our topic here is the fact that the gaucho's gesture in this scene is a visual reflection of Manuel's: just as the latter is about to "thrust," penetrate Dolly, the gaucho thrusts his bayonet into Manuel's back.

Rovner debunks the notion of unilateral and unidirectional power (in terms similar to those of Foucault and recent postcolonial theorists) as well as that of a single, coherent, consistent subject position for the individual while staging the dynamic, contestatory, and dialogic nature of transculturation. Perhaps this is nowhere more poignantly dramatized than in the knishes Dolly prepares for Manuel. To be sure, Dolly's knishes are anything but kosher. Feeling that they were lacking something and on the advice of her own mother (presumably not Jewish), she has added paprika, much to the dismay of Fanny: "¿Pimentón? . . . ¿Knishes con pimentón? ¿Dónde se ha visto? ¡Hizo knishes a la gallega!" (*VN,* 84) (Paprika? . . . Knishes with paprika? Whoever heard of that? She made Galiziner knishes!) (*SR,* 51). Those knishes may not be kosher, but they are nevertheless an emblem of transculturation, indicative of the hybrid or synergy produced by the meeting of disparate peoples in the contact zone and, significantly, motivated by both mothers. Indeed, Fanny might well ask of the knishes the same question she asks of Manuel on more than one occasion: Who do you think you are? The answer, an answer that applies equally well to Manuel, is of course a palimpsest, a hybrid, a synergy, whichever term one prefers. While, like Manuel, those knishes do retain something of Fanny, representative of the (trans)culture that was, they are unquestionably different, indicators of yet another (trans)culture. And, yet, if we are to judge by all else in this play, they too will undergo still more transformations in the future—ever returning if indeed in contradictory senses.

It seems to me, too, that the final moments of the play and its closing gesture, which shape the mental image with which we leave the theater, highlight precisely this notion of transculturation, reversal, and return, as I have been discussing them. Dolly, who leaves Manuel's apartment upset at the end of scene 15, returns at the end of the final scene, just as Fanny has prophesied with the words, "Va a volver" (*VN*, 100) (She's going to come back) (*SR*, 63). In this respect the play highlights the double referent of its title. Up until this point in the play, we assume that the grammatical subject of the verb *volvió* (she returned) in the title is Fanny. Now we realize that Dolly is also the subject of the verb, for like all else in the world portrayed, she too returns (although, like so many other aspects of [trans]cultures, the term *volver* [to return] may not always have exactly the same meaning). Now that Dolly has returned to him and Fanny is about to return to the other world, Manuel takes Dolly by the hand and heads for the door (another signifier of the liminality that is inherent in my sense of [trans]culture always in the process of another transculturation). At this point, and in an image evocative of 1940s and 1950s cinema, he stops, looks back, and raises his hand "*para saludar a Fanny, quien también levanta su mano*" (*VN*, 103) (*and waves to Fanny, who also waves*) (*SR*, 66). When Dolly asks him what he is doing, he replies simply, "Saludá . . . a la vieja" (*VN*, 103) (Wave . . . to my mother) (*SR*, 66). The final stage directions state, "*Dolly, entre sorprendida y complaciente, levanta la mano. Manuel, también saludando, mira a Fanny, quien mantiene su saludo. Sobre esta imagen, música y apagón*" (*VN*, 103–4) (*Dolly, surprised and compliant, raises her hand. Manuel, also waving, looks at Fanny, who keeps waving. With this image, there is music and a blackout*) (*SR*, 66). Surely, at first glance this might appear to be a rather unspectacular way to end a play. Nonetheless, I would suggest that this deceptively simple ending (which recalls the ending of *El saludador* as discussed in chapter 4) captures the essence of this deceptively simple play. In fact, insofar as the verb *saludar* (to wave or to greet) indicates a gesture whose meaning changes according to context, it signals the very notion of transculturation. A sign of both hello and good-bye, it evokes what is entering and what is leaving, what will be and what was. In some sense it recalls the overcoat, with its gesture toward the past, and links it to the knish, with its gesture toward the future transculturation, which initially tastes strange and does not seem to be what one desires. But, at the same time and perhaps even more important, it is a gesture that acknowledges the existence of the other (the not same, not self) and the other's desires, and thus implies a recognition or even acceptance of difference, the differences between and the differences within. Nonetheless, and this may be the most revealing element, although Manuel and Fanny can see each other and know why and to whom they are waving, Dolly does not. Dolly is obeying an external mandate while being unaware of the liminality of her position and probably only partially aware of the transculturation she is about to undergo as a result of her marriage to Manuel.

In many ways then the play returns us to the beginning. In the first scene a tango group plays; although it is not clear where they are or why they are playing, they are happy. But, and meaningfully, that happiness is juxtaposed, intermeshed with, the melancholy of the tango they play—"Volver" (Returning)—a tango (cited at the start of this chapter) that recognizes not only the juxtaposition of the past and the present, but also the fear of facing one's past in the light of one's present, the knowledge that one cannot really go back; to return is inevitably to continue forward even though one may not know where or what that forward or that past really are. In the second scene, as noted, the stage is dark, only Manuel's upper body is illuminated, and the audience, as in the first scene, is metaphorically in the dark as to where we are. Rovner's point seems to be that like Dolly, we seldom really understand where we are in the process of transculturation. We can only understand after the fact, when we are already at yet a different point in the ongoing process, and even at that only understand the previous point/location, the previous (m)other, in terms of its difference from the present, from the perspective of the present, from the perspective of what we did or did not want that (m)other to be.

In conclusion, then, if we agree that, as Gay McAuley has cogently posited, "theater . . . exists at the interface between residual and emergent culture and necessarily activates both," then it would appear that theater is the logical instrument not only to illustrate this transculturation, but also to effect it, as I think *Volvió una noche* does in so many ways as it teaches us to laugh at and empathize with the anxiety and discomfort that transculturation and finding ourselves in liminal positions so often cause us (inside the home or out), whether we try to cling to past traditions and ignore assimilation and new mores or vice versa, embrace the new and reject the old.[51] In fact, as this play so dramatically demonstrates, theater itself functions as a contact zone. By offering us a Fanny who is ultimately an emblem of *trans*culture, Rovner underscores the fact that culture itself is a contradictory invention that is internalized by each of us in distinct ways, never singular but always and already multiple, diverse, and varied, different even within itself, and clearly already in the process of yet another transculturation.

9

More Mothers and Daughters in Performance: Simulacra and Commodification in Diana Raznovich's *Casa Matriz*

AN ANALYSIS OF *CASA MATRIZ* (*MATRIX, INC.*) (1989) BY ARGENTINE Diana Raznovich perhaps provides a fitting conclusion to this book since in many ways it returns us to the beginning and the notion of the Freudian family romance in which "through fantasy, the developing individual liberates himself from the constraints of family . . . [in] the imaginative act of replacing the parent . . . with another, superior figure."[1] In this play, which comprises a number of scenes but which is not divided into acts, the protagonist Bárbara treats herself to a birthday gift and rents a substitute mother from Casa Matriz Inc. Agency, a "mother" who will perform various maternal roles, although one imagines that in this case the invented parent(s) are not necessarily superior to the real one(s). Still, via Madre Sustituta (Substitute Mother), Bárbara can in some sense preview the various "mothers" or try them on, as it were, to see if they fit. Furthermore, in this play, as we will see, Raznovich makes it clear that the daughter does not in effect invent the "mother" but merely rents her (pays to use her temporarily) from a group of finite and preprogrammed possibilities. Freud's "imaginative act" here proves to be little more than assembly-line (re)production. At the same time, and in what might also be read as a deviation from the Freudian paradigm of the family romance, the play implicitly questions whether the fantasy parent imagined here (or in Freudian theory either, for that matter) liberates Bárbara from the constraints of family or merely enmeshes her more deeply in them. I will argue that the latter is indeed the case, although surely the play underscores those constraints and makes them visible to the audience in a way that may ultimately contribute to liberating the audience (if not the character) from those very "constraints of family" as they have been packaged and "sold" by the various media, among them theater itself.

My analysis of *Casa Matriz* might well have been included in my earlier chapter on performing motherhood, since Raznovich also overtly dramatizes the role playing inherent to our notions of mothers and the maternal.[2] Indeed, the play evinces a number of similarities with *De profesión maternal* (Of the Maternal Profession) and *La esfinge de las maravillas* (The Sphinx of Marvels). Like the former, *Casa Matriz* rejects the notion of the patriarchal family and writes the father out of the script. Bárbara's fixation is exclusively on the mother, and the play ends (like the Gambaro play) with another ambiguous, prolonged cry, "¡Mamá!" a cry that might be interpreted as a plea for a specific mother role or for the (fantasy, substitute) mother who has just abandoned her. On the other hand, it might well be interpreted not as a plea at all but rather as a demand for the mother's presence, support, attention, and (exclusive) focus on the "child." Nevertheless and paradoxically, in spite of the emphasis on the maternal, the real mother is ultimately written out of the Raznovich script as much as the father. No reference is made to Bárbara's real mother (or to real mothers in general—flesh-and-blood human beings), as the play posits that our images of real mothers are as fictitious (substitute) as the inventions, commodities, and preprogrammed roles, products of commercialism, which are embodied and reproduced here by Madre Sustituta. Even more overtly than several of the plays analyzed previously, this one proposes that the maternal (at least our preconceived, unacknowledged, and probably unchallenged notions of the maternal) is based on role playing and theatrical performances not necessarily recognized as such, and, specifically, on the theatrical performances that we have been "sold" and that we have "bought into," both literally and figuratively. As a result, and like the Argüelles play, *Casa Matriz* highlights the influence of the arts and various media on our concepts of familial roles by including several references to opera (another form of theater and commercialized role playing if indeed often patently unrealistic) and the typical opera endings with their victimization of women. In fact, the influence of various styles of music in the shaping of women's roles is underscored throughout the play, for the playwright frames each maternal role within a specific musical form.[3] Also, reminiscent of *La esfinge de las maravillas,* where Lucía and Juan Carlos rehearse and act out scenes from Pedro Infante's movies, in the Raznovich play the same mother-daughter scenes are repeatedly started, stopped, and played again until the two characters "get it right," generate a product that fulfills the needs or desires (demands?) of the customer, Bárbara. In this way, *Casa Matriz* continually foregrounds the artificial (in the sense of pre-scripted, constructed) nature of the familial roles as well as the difficulty of maintaining those roles. As Castellví de-Moor has observed, the work is conditioned by its character of total performance.[4]

I have chosen to dedicate a separate chapter to the Raznovich play because unlike the works analyzed up to this point, this one performs something of a mise en abyme of metatheatricality that continually reminds us that what we are viewing is theater, not reality, and specifically not a mirror of nature as some of the more naturalistic works I have examined might seem to suggest. Thus, even more than the other plays, this one posits that familial roles (specifically mother and daughter) are imitations (reproductions) of imitations (in theater or other media) of imitations ad infinitum with no original model (à la Butler) and that the product (the familial role) already exaggerated to improve sales in the theater or the media in turn produces even more exaggerated reproductions on the home front in an endless spiral of production and reproduction.[5] At the same time, the work toys with the notions of consumerism, in literal and figurative terms, in ways the other plays did not. In this respect, Raznovich carries the question of the performance of the maternal one step further, for she highlights not only the role playing involved in motherhood, this time completely conscious, but also mothers and the maternal as commodities, theatrical products bought and paid for, and ones that, like any theatrical performance, are required to meet the desires (demands) of the paying audience. Nonetheless, at the same time, Raznovich proposes that the "commodity syndrome" works in both directions, for the customer (in this case the thirty-year-old Bárbara) is also required to perform the appropriate role, one that corresponds to the chosen mother's role. We might well question to what extent Bárbara, presumed consumer, is ultimately being shaped and trained by the commodity. Although we generally assume that the products we choose to buy reflect our desires, Raznovich suggests that perhaps our desires are in fact shaped by the products we purchase—we desire what we have been trained to desire, the desires we have been "sold." At the same time, the text is specific that Bárbara's "contradicciones personales" (*CM,* 263) (personal contradictions) (my translation) allow her to adapt quickly to the various daughters that she should play, words that underscore the instability, ambiguity, and ambivalence underlying all the roles we internalize and embody. Thus, once again matters of family and theatricality are shown to be intricately intertwined.

The play is set in one of the studios of Casa Matriz Inc. Agency, a setting that emphasizes the theatrical, repetitive, preprogrammed character of all we are to see, even as it links our perception of familial roles to a certain commodification effected by the various media. As noted, it is Bárbara's thirtieth birthday, and she has treated herself to a substitute mother who will play the various roles that Bárbara has chosen ahead of time, roles selected from a group of finite, preprogrammed possibilities. Not irrelevantly, and in what emphasizes the similarities between this seemingly private, family matter (the relations between mother and daughter) and theater itself (particularly commercial theater), the same actress will play all the chosen roles. Thus Raznovich proposes, there is nothing natural or innate about the maternal role if there are so many possibilities to choose from and one actress can embody them all. In this respect, Raznovich debunks the essentialism so frequently associated with women and the maternal. In fact, the "Aclaración" (Clarification) clearly states that Madre Sustituta is a consummate actress, "perfectamente entrenada para satisfacer los 1,200 roles" (perfectly trained to fulfill the 1,200 roles).[6] Translate, she knows how to and will give the audience (Bárbara and at the same time us, the extratextual audience that Bárbara reflects in so many ways) the show it has paid to see, even though, on yet another level, the play continually destabilizes and undermines that very show and our complicity with it. The fact that the "Aclaración" also specifies, "El compromiso del cliente será adecuarse a las distintas madres que eligió" (The client's obligation will be to adapt herself to the chosen mothers), reminds us that it is not just the mother who is cast or programmed into a role in society, but that the other members of the family are similarly pigeonholed into corresponding roles. The performance of one effects, elicits, shapes, and delimits the performances of the others. When one steps out of or misplays her role, the show falters and the other must readjust her role in what effectively dramatizes the distancing from any original that is brought about by mass production as discussed by Baudrillard.[7]

The play opens as Bárbara is led into the studio by employees of the agency. Once alone she puts on a recording of Bach's *Magnificat* and proceeds to direct an imaginary orchestra with a baton.[8] Her "direction" is interrupted by the "reality" of the persistent ringing of the doorbell announcing the arrival of Madre Sustituta (a "reality" that, let us not forget, is strictly theatrical, part of the play). The insistence of the bell triggers an attack of fury on Bárbara's part; she breaks the baton, the music stops, and she answers the door. For me, this brief scene, which, revealingly, is repeated in two other variations during the course of the play, serves as a synecdoche of the play itself. Here, as throughout the play, Bárbara would seem to be in control, to be the director as it were of this mise en abyme of theater that she has paid to experience (and paid dearly, a grand total of $1,000). Nonetheless, her direction here, like all else, is a simulacrum. The orchestra that she seems to be directing is nonexistent. In many ways it is a memory or a phantom captured by means of the recording (another commodity available for purchase and consumption). At the same time and perhaps even more important, all appearances to the contrary, the music is in fact directing her: her movements (which simulate those of an orchestra director) are controlled by and in response to the already recorded music. She ultimately does not and cannot direct or control anything since that music (like the roles available to mothers and daughters) is already recorded, preprogrammed, a past moment or memory, commodified and in some sense imposed on the present.[9] In this way, Raznovich underscores the illusion of agency, power, and control and posits that, while it may appear that we are making choices when we opt for one role (or one commodity) over another, in fact, we are merely choosing one of the already preprogrammed possibilities. As Taylor has noted in her discussion of another Raznovich play, "dominant systems of representation . . . not only reproduce scenes of desire . . . but demarcate their limits."[10]

Similarly, throughout the play, Bárbara assumes that she, as the consumer, controls and directs the maternal performances for which she has paid, but in fact, as noted in the "Aclaración," she is continually required to adjust her role to that of Madre Sustituta. Just as the musical recording controls her direction, Madre Sustituta's roles control the "daughter's" in what appears to be an endless circle of production and reproduction (mass production) without origin. On the most obvious level, Bárbara is also repeatedly manipulated by that Madre Sustituta. For example, at the start of the play, as the actress enters, she begins her performance of the mother who has been abandoned by her Indian lover and returns to her daughter in search of solace (rather than the other way around as a more traditional mother-daughter narrative might be emplotted). As Bárbara protests that this is not the mother she selected, that she ordered a cold mother, recently returned from Paris, who makes her feel rejected, Madre Sustituta steps out of her role, reminding us that what we observe here is theater, not reality. She feigns to recognize that she has made a mistake and that the mother returning from India is for tomorrow's client but rebukes Bárbara for not appreciating her acting ability. When she goes on to tell Bárbara that, as one of the most sought-after actresses in the agency, she has too much work and too many other clients, she effectively manages to generate in Bárbara the very emotions the latter had paid to experience. In what seems to be a comment on theater itself, Madre Sustituta notes that the actress's job is to produce emotions, even if they are the wrong ones (*CM*, 265). Although Bárbara had specifically requested a mother who would make her feel unloved, and although the first role assumed by the actress *seems* to be an error, by stepping out of her role and talking about her other clients, the actress produces in Bárbara precisely that sense of not being loved, of having a mother who has her own life and is indifferent to her, which Bárbara had ordered.

Still, the plot thickens, for as the audience (both the external one and Bárbara) later discovers, this is more acting within the acting. Madre Sustituta's references to her other children have apparently been a conscious choice rather than an error. As both Madre Sustituta and Bárbara step out of their roles and discuss the commodity Bárbara has bought (or at least rented—a financial transaction that Bárbara repeatedly emphasizes lest Madre Sustituta or the audience forget the basis of this interaction), we are once more confronted with an apparent inversion of power and control: the actress imposes her will on Bárbara and orders her not to reveal why she has contracted her. This inversion of power is underscored in Bárbara's words, "¿Me está dando órdenes? . . . Yo soy quién tiene que dar las órdenes" (*CM*, 266) (Now you're telling me what to do? . . . I'm the one who gives the orders around here!) (*MT*, 103). But, as Madre Sustituta later notes, the wrong entrance coupled with talking about other clients always produces the desired jealousy (*CM*, 268). Thus, Raznovich dramatizes the fine line between acknowledged or conscious performance and that which is unacknowledged, unconscious. Where does reality end and the show begin? Are we capable of discerning the difference(s)? I would argue that the point here is that all being is performance (whether conscious or not) insofar as we necessarily imitate and are limited to what we have seen, read, heard, and so on—that is, what is already in the catalog of possibilities. And, surely, theater, media, and mass production have been instrumental in orchestrating those imitative performances and in creating the desires that make those performances mandatory, what Butler had called, "the compulsory appropriation and identification with those normative demands."[11] Let us not forget that even as Bárbara and Madre Sustituta step out of their roles of the inner plays and revert to their "real" selves, those "real" selves are still part of a performance, the one we are watching. By highlighting the theatrical and even metatheatrical, Raznovich underscores Butler's notion of performativity as "a reiteration of a norm or set of norms . . . [that] conceals or dissimulates the conventions of which it is a repetition," while she simultaneously exposes those very conventions that remain hidden in daily life and in most theater.[12] As Castellví deMoor has noted, it is precisely by the separation among role/actor/person that Raznovich underscores the effects of the codification of roles.[13] Surely, here, the codification of roles has led to or been conflated with commodification.

More important to my point, however, is that Bárbara's reaction to the question of multiple clients is an overt parody of a child's reaction to multiple siblings. She insists that Madre Sustituta belongs to her, becomes jealous of the other clients with whom she will implicitly vie for Madre Sustituta's attention, and eventually implies that the latter is a prostitute. All are elements that point to several interesting subtexts in the Raznovich play: (a) the question of possession, (b) the relation between substitute and prostitute with the commodification implied in the latter and in the maternal as Raznovich presents it, and (c) the image of the devoured (rather than devouring) mother.

Let us begin with the question of possession. The result of Bárbara's jealousy about the other clients is her insistence that Madre Sustituta belongs to her: "Usted me pertenece" (CM, 266) (You belong to me) (MT, 103). On one level this evokes the child's demand for the exclusive attention of the mother and that child's reluctance to accept that the mother's attention and dedication cannot be total and undivided insofar as mother (and specifically the role of my mother as opposed to the mother of my siblings) is only one of the many roles a woman is required to assume at any given moment. As I have discussed in earlier chapters, the notion that motherhood is a full-time job and that the child needs the complete dedication of the mother is a relatively recent invention.[14] Nonetheless, it has come to have the same effect as any preprogrammed memory or phantom. Like the recording of Bach's Magnificat, no one wonders why it is the way it is or what the source of this preprogrammed, phantom memory might be, least of all the child. Raznovich's insistence on the studio setting suggests that the source may well be the various media and arts.

In this way Raznovich evokes what may be the core of the problem: who belongs to whom? Although we regularly use the terms my mother and my daughter (and perhaps even more so in Spanish—mi mamá [my mama] and m'hijita [my dear daughter]), the terms themselves suggest (or create) an exclusivity that is a fiction, and one that effectively masks the nonexclusive nature of the relationship and the possession as well as the anxieties provoked by that very nonexclusivity (implicitly, if we do not name it, it does not exist). In other words, by using the expression *mi mamá,* the child, consciously or not, denies the possibility that she is anyone else's mother or has any other role. In Western society, where the valorization of the individual has been raised to a cult and where individualization often seems to be bought by surrounding oneself with possessions that are nonessential and consumable, it has become intolerable to think of the self as anything other than unique and irreplaceable. Yet, *my mother* is also the mother of others, and *my daughter* is also the daughter of someone else (biologically, at least). What repeatedly surfaces in the Raznovich play is the nonuniqueness of the individual, of the various roles that the individual performs, and of the commodities with which one surrounds oneself in a paradoxical effort to assure oneself that one is indeed unique. It is not irrelevant that Casa Matriz Inc. has a catalog of some 1,200 maternal roles, a large number to be sure, but still finite. The roles acted out for each client must necessarily be repeated. Since the "Aclaración" informs us that Casa Matriz has a branch in every major city in the world, we must presume that the agency has far more than 1,200 clients and that the roles and "mothers" (like the actresses themselves) must be shared. Furthermore, as Madre Sustituta declares to Bárbara, the clients tend to ask for the same roles over and over.[15] Thus, here, as even the maternal has been converted into a commodity that can be bought (or at least rented), the paradox is that the commodity does not stay possessed. Because of its mass-produced character, it does not ultimately belong solely to the buyer or provide any stable sense of uniqueness. On the contrary, it continually slips from the buyer's grasp and control (a slippage that reminds us that this is all temporary, theatrical simulacrum). What has been bought is in fact art for consumption (as is literalized in the breast-feeding scene late in the play, to which I will return), and its nonuniqueness reflects the buyer's own. Indeed, Bárbara's nonuniqueness is underscored early in the play when she responds to Madre Sustituta's comments on her other clients with, "¡No me compare con todos esos pervertidos! Soy diferente" (*CM,* 267) (Don't compare me to those perverts. I'm different) (*MT,* 105), and Madre Sustituta retorts by asking how she is different, a rhetorical question that says it all. It is surely in compensation for this anxiety of nonuniqueness that part of one of the mother-daughter scenes enacted here includes the mother's assurance (if indeed only after Bárbara in her role as theatrical director insists that the former be more explicit and play her role better) that Bárbara is "absolutamente insustituible" (*CM,* 279) (absolutely irreplaceable) (*MT,* 118). Paradoxically, the facts that Bárbara has purchased a commodity to reassure herself of her uniqueness and that she has had to remind the commodity of her function/job merely point to her nonuniqueness and the selling of an image involved in any commodity exchange. Ironically, the customer/consumer needs to feel original even while playing (reproducing) a role. One of the other paradoxes that might be missed in this play, which I find particularly poignant, is the fact that although Madre Sustituta is easily recognized as a substitute, a replacement, a nonoriginal commodity, Bárbara is ultimately equally so. Although she never seems to comprehend this (and the audience may not either), she is in fact an Hija Sustituta (Substitute Daughter).

As Bárbara recognizes that she does not have exclusive rights to Madre Sustituta, Raznovich employs a play on words in which Bárbara implies that the substitute is a prostitute. Although she does not actually articulate the word, the stage directions specify, "*Esta* [*sic*] *a punto de decir 'prostituta'*" (*CM,* 267) (*She's at the point of saying, "prostitute"*) (*MT,* 104). Significantly, the two words are similar in sound and are etymologically related: *substitute* derives from placed under, put in the place of, whereas *prostitute* derives from placed forward, exposed, and, by implication, for sale, associated with an exchange of money. One could, of course, argue that the prostitute is also a substitute, rented (read, commodified) to provide services in the place of another. But, perhaps even more important, as Susanne Kappeler has argued, the prostitute is not only commodified, but her commodification represents the power of the client—a power play that becomes quite evident in the Raznovich play.[16] Having "bought" the prostitute, the client exercises and reassures himself of his power (real or imagined). But, as Kappeler has argued and as Raznovich dramatizes, that power (simulacrum though it is in this play) leads to violence. It cannot be irrelevant that shortly after Bárbara almost calls Madre Sustituta a prostitute, Bárbara attacks her (and not vice versa in response for the insult); she lets go of her throat only after Madre Sustituta threatens her that she will have to indemnify Casa Matriz if she harms her (*CM,* 268). By suggesting that Madre Sustituta is the prostitute, the guilty one, the collaborator (as Kappeler defines our perception of prostitute), Bárbara erases her role in the commodification process and disregards the fact that without clients there would be no prostitutes. In the words of Kappeler, "Responsibility has been hidden in favour of blame."[17] In a metaphoric sense Bárbara echoes much of contemporary society's response to the maternal as she resorts to blaming the mother. What is wrong with the individual is the fault of the mother, a theory that has long been supported by readings of Freudian theory and popular psychology. Significantly, this casting of blame on the (m)other not only cleanses the individual of any responsibility for his or her actions and being in the world, but it also erases the role and responsibility of patriarchal society. In this sense, Raznovich points to the double elision. If it is the mother's fault, then we need to look no further for the source of the problem (it is not a "social" or societal problem but an individual one), and thus both the individual and the patriarchal society are exonerated from all blame or guilt.

What I find particularly noteworthy in this scene, however, is the fact that Bárbara never actually articulates the word *prostitute*. Implied but not spoken, the word functions on two different levels. On one level it evokes the unspoken, unwritten, patriarchal structures or "rules of the game" that, because they remain unarticulated, are difficult to resist or alter. We cannot challenge what we cannot name. By having Bárbara almost call Madre Sustituta a prostitute, Raznovich tacitly names our internalized images so that we can challenge, question, and reconceive them. But, at the same time, by not actually articulating the word, Raznovich manages to negotiate a very fine line: she makes the negative perception visible but does not promulgate that perception. In this way, she successfully shows the violence (and naming, particularly this name, is violence/violation) without condoning or perpetuating it. The spectator leaves the play blaming neither Bárbara nor Madre Sustituta, while empathizing with both.

In an original twist to this portrait of the child who demands the complete and exclusive devotion of the mother and then blames that mother when she or he does not get it, however, Raznovich allows the mother to respond. Indeed, I would argue that one of the characteristics that makes *Casa Matriz* unique is the polyvocal quality of the work, the fact that this is neither the mother's story nor the daughter's, but rather simultaneously both. Marianne Hirsch has noted that until very recently mother-daughter tales have been told predominantly by the daughter, with the daughter either telling only her own story or speaking for (in place of) the mother.[18] Here, however, the "mother" speaks for herself to present a perspective that is neither more nor less valid than that of the "daughter." After Bárbara's display of jealousy about the other clients, followed by her insistence that they do not exist as far as she is concerned, Madre Sustituta assures her that they do exist for her—her livelihood depends on them. Then, in a hyperbolization of the "normal" maternal position, she asks, "¿Usted se imagina satisfacer las demandas de doscientos cuarenta hijos al mes? . . . ¿Se imagina la cantidad de exigencias y demandas delirantes que tengo que satisfacer?" (*CM*, 267) (Can you imagine satisfying the whims of two hundred and forty children per month? . . . Can you imagine all the crazy stipulations and obligations I need to fulfill?) (*MT*, 104). This image of the mother overwhelmed by the demands of the children is expanded in the same dialogue as Madre Sustituta refers to the "voracity" of her clients/children. In this way, the clichéd image of the devouring mother (as perceived from the stance of the son or daughter) is inverted, and here it is the mother who is potentially devoured by her children and their demands. This voracity is literalized and highlighted at the end of the play in a brief scene where Bárbara breast-feeds, if indeed from an artificial, replaceable, and (one imagines) rechargeable "breast" that Madre Sustituta slips on—another commodity designed for consumption. In this way Raznovich posits a fine line between the classic image of the maternal as a nurturing mother and the devoured mother, who is consumed precisely as a result of her role as nurturer. But, of course, the question soon arises as to who is the devoured and who is the devourer in this society of consumerism. Revealingly, at the end of the play Madre Sustituta does not remain devoured but steps out of the inner play, out of the role and walks off this stage (if indeed onto another stage and the next customer), and away from this "daughter" who is very "demandante" (*CM*, 286) (demanding) (*MT*, 127). Significantly, Raznovich draws attention to this curious choice of words by having Madre Sustituta continue, "¿Esa es la palabra?" (Is that the word?) (my translation). Although in context, the word would certainly be understood as the equivalent of demanding, technically the word means plaintiff, one who brings a suit into a court of law and demands redress (often economic) because one's legal rights have somehow been violated, one has not received what one has the *right* to receive.

At the same time, and as I have already submitted, the insistence on possession evokes one of the principal concerns of the play, the question of commercialism and commodification. Bárbara presumes that, because she has rented Madre Sustituta, she is hers, if indeed only for a finite quantity of time, but Raznovich underscores the illusory character of this possession and implicit control. Bárbara obviously does not possess Madre Sustituta anymore than she possesses or directs the *Magnificat*. She may have spent money for each, but the possession is only an illusion that would distract attention from the fact that many others have bought and possess the same products. In our late twentieth- and early twenty-first-century Western culture, materialism has become a way of life, and we have been deluded into a notion of some sort of personal relationship to the objects we have bought or rented, with which we have surrounded ourselves, and which we readily consume. Let us not forget that Madre Sustituta plays the same roles for all her clients. Although it would appear that the client can buy or rent the ideal that she or he does not have or experience, in fact, the mother just returned from India belongs to Bárbara no more than to tomorrow's client. But perhaps even more important is that the consumable goods (in this case Madre Sustituta) are merely instruments. It is not her that the client is buying but rather something much more abstract: the emotions or experiences that the interactions (theatrical simulacra) can produce. Indeed, the fact that the various maternal roles are based on stereotypes, commodities perpetuated and sold (to continue the metaphor) by various media (television, music, literature, and the arts, including theater) merely reminds us of their commonality, of their distance from personal possession, all appearances to the contrary.

It is particularly significant, however, that the "mothers" performed here are anything but perfect (with one possible exception, which I will discuss below). Surely, the question that one is led to pose is why, within the representational economy and the logic of the play, would one buy or rent an imperfect commodity? If one were going to spend that much money, why not rent the ideal, the perfect mother one dreams of, a mother who would meet all of one's needs? Doubtlessly, the question can be answered in several ways. One answer, implied by Foster, is the perhaps common conviction that mothers can never be perfect: "These deficiencies are as much brutal evidence of the impossibility of attaining the ideal prescribed by the patriarchy as they are signs of the way in which the clients of the service personnel perceive that mothers can never be . . . anything other than failed human beings," a response that again signals the double bind in which real mothers must inevitably find themselves.[19] Another answer might relate to the question of casting the blame on (m)others as discussed above. If mother were perfect, then, as her progeny, logically the individual would have to be perfect also. Since the individual is not, then the mother must not be either. At the same time, if mother were perfect, she could not be responsible for one's inadequacies. Then, one would have to find someone else to blame. In both cases, this negative imaging of the mother provides a convenient scapegoat for the wrongs of society. Indeed, the play makes explicit the major attraction of Casa

Matriz: by paying the high fee the client can "salir ganadora en algunos juegos . . . Estas son alguna [sic] de las satisfacciones que Casa Matriz ofrece a su clientela" (CM, 285) (win some of the games . . . This is part of the satisfaction that MaTRIX offers our clients) (MT, 126). As Madre Sustituta observes just a few pages earlier, all the clients want to be rebellious children, and it is easy to rebel against certain types of mothers: "Todos buscan la cosa facilona, denigrable. Les gusta verme llorar, porque se sienten libres, rebeldes, jóvenes" (CM, 282) (Everyone wants the easy route, denigrating. Everyone enjoys seeing me cry, because they feel free, rebellious, young) (MT, 122). But, finally, and in more immediate and practical terms, if mother (or family in general) were perfect, she would not be very interesting or provide the basis for attention-grabbing theater; she would not meet the requirements of Bárbara or us. She would not provide food for theatrical consumption; she could not be artistically, metaphorically, devoured anew in the theater.

As I noted, the one possible exception to the series of imperfect mothers can be found in the final scene in which Bárbara is given the breast on demand. In many ways, dar la teta (literally, to give the breast; implicitly, to allow the child to breast-feed) provides an apropos metaphor for the services of Casa Matriz. Bárbara's demand for the breast immediately follows Madre Sustituta's breaking of the baton (symbol of the power or control that Bárbara would like to wield but does not) and the former's comment on the satisfactions the agency offers (cited above). Dar la teta evokes the way in which the agency (and by implication, art and the media in general) nourishes the fantasies of the audience as it provides the imagined lost plenitude of the breast even while on yet another level it serves to remind the extratextual audience that such a plenitude is another simulacrum, as imaginary as the perfection of the mother. Interestingly and surely revealingly, after happily feeding for a few minutes (like an infant), Bárbara observes, "Es un final operístico" (CM, 285) (This is a finale worthy of an opera) (MT, 126), words that serve to underscore the illusory character of the scene, the fact that it is more simulacrum/theater than reality.[20] Thus, once again, Raznovich negotiates that fine line between naming/showing and condoning/promulgating that I discussed above.

Surely, one of the primary themes of this play is the role of art, here specifically theater, in this buying and selling, in this commodification and consumption and how our consumer/commodity mentality carries over into our family relationships. Not irrelevantly within the representational economy of the play, Bárbara's real mother is an absence, used up, consumed as it were. We know nothing about her; she is a nonexistence (devoured, to continue the metaphor). Indeed, this absence is in some sense rehearsed in one of the scenes with Madre Sustituta, the one in which the mother is dead. Here, because she does not exist, the mother quite literally is, can be, only what Bárbara would make of her; she is exclusively and revealingly Bárbara's creation. Only in death or absence can the mother indeed belong to Bárbara, since it is she who (re)creates and (re)invents her. And, because she is dead, she cannot step out of the role(s) Bárbara would impose on her as Madre Sustituta can. Still, like all else in this play, this possession/invention also turns in on itself and negates itself.

Significantly, this death scene underscores the contradictions involved in the familial relations even as it simultaneously undermines itself. At the start, Bárbara comments on how much more beautiful the mother is in death than she was in life, thus highlighting the notion that beauty, perfection, and the ideal depend on death, absence, nonexistence, and the violation implicit in that absence. Revealingly, Bárbara begins by recalling (inventing) the positive aspects of their relationship. That soon takes a turn, however, and in what emphasizes the fictive nature of it all, she quickly begins to lament her lack of a positive relationship with the mother and wants an opportunity to be different, which of course is precisely what Casa Matriz provides: a chance (artificial to be sure) to be different, another commodity to be consumed. What Raznovich underscores here is contemporary society's (erroneous) perception that commodities are unlimited. With sufficient funds another one can be purchased to replace the one we have wastefully consumed. Mass production provides another product, essentially undifferentiated from the first (which was still not original in the true sense of the word and as the play continually emphasizes). The paradox is that the opportunity to be different is merely another illusion, repetition of the same. Indeed, when Madre Sustituta "resurrects" from the dead, sits up and talks to Bárbara, in some sense giving her that very chance to be different that she has pleaded (and paid) for, the latter is furious and commands, "Vuélvase a morir si es tan amable" (*CM*, 278) (Die again if you would be so kind) (my translation). Unlike real deceased mothers, Madre Sustituta will not stay dead and thus cannot and will not fail to slip from the assigned role. Clearly, even in the play within the play, and lip service to the contrary, Bárbara is not prepared to deal with that which is different. She can deal only with more of the same, more of the clichéd roles that we have all been sold by the media. This notion is underscored by the repetition of the expression *volver a* in this dialogue and its stage directions (*volver a* plus an infinitive translates "to do something again"). On this same page, after Madre Sustituta is asked to die again, we find four more uses of the term *volver a* in just eight lines, in what again emphasizes the repetition, the playacting, and the inescapability of repeating the same old (pre)scripted roles.

Nonetheless, at the same time, and as this scene highlights, the needs or desires of the consumer are still not fully met; the consumer, Bárbara, will always desire yet one more commodity or yearn nostalgically for one that has already been relegated to the past. In a chilling commentary on contemporary society, although Bárbara has had to save for a year to finance this gift to herself, at the end she is prepared to take out a loan to finance more time with Madre Sustituta. Real mother just will not do; the theatrical substitute, which the spectator thinks he or she can control, is far more desirable. Again, in this sense we return to the image of the devoured mother I discussed earlier. Bárbara just cannot get, possess, feel, or feed enough. But, of course, this is precisely the result that advertising and our consumer society have worked so hard to achieve. Remember, the goal of Casa Matriz is to produce strong emotions, the pathos, perhaps, that Aristotle deemed essential to good tragedy. In what appears to be another commentary on theater in general, Raznovich highlights the commodification of that emotion. Bárbara hires Madre Sustituta in some sense to provide the emotional experiences one must presume are lacking (or undesirable) in her real life. Similarly, one might also argue that theatergoers attend plays for the same reason: to experience emotions they may not experience or would prefer not to experience in their lives outside the theater. The mediated emotions provided by theater or any other art form (like mediated travel with its proper tour guides who speak our language and hotels that model those we have at home) are much more manageable and far less threatening. Indeed, at one point when Bárbara complains that Madre Sustituta does everything in excess and makes it asphyxiating (*CM,* 279), Madre Sustituta retorts that such is her job, "Si no nadie contrataría una Madre Sustituta. El cliente se quedaría con su madre naturalista real" (*CM,* 280) (Otherwise no one would contract a Substitute Mother. The client would stick to her own mother) (*MT,* 119).

Again we return to the role of theater in the shaping and perpetuation of familial roles. As I have suggested more than once, although Bárbara is the consumer, she is in fact shaped, trained, by the theater in which she participates and (into) which she has bought, literally and figuratively. She is being trained as she watches and as we watch her watch. The purchased commodity (theater) is definitively not without influence. We may think we are buying, exercising choice, but in fact we are being shaped, and desire is being created for more of the same. Furthermore, Raznovich posits that all theatrical productions partake of this commodification and salesmanship.[21] Indeed this is literalized in the play by the fact that the "Aclaración" states that the client has to "adecuarse" (become adequate to, adapt to, adjust to, fit in with) the represented roles, and in the play Madre Sustituta checks to see that Bárbara knows the "rules of the game" (*CM,* 266). But, as noted, the play also underscores the difficulty of performing, consistently and without slippage, those roles the audience has demanded and paid for. One must question to what extent, when we go to the theater, are we being fed or sold the role, the performance someone thinks we want, or vice versa, are we getting the performance we desired, bought—seeing what we paid to see? To what extent does theater create its own market and convince us that what we see is what we want to see? And, in either case, how do we break this circle of commodification? Perhaps even more important, Raznovich proffers an anti-Aristotelian (and anti-Hamlet) view of theater, suggesting that theater is not a mirror of life. In Taylor's words, "the show does not 'represent' the real—as in Aristotelian logic. Rather, 'the real' is produced through these constant enactments."[22] Madre Sustituta is explicit that her clients contract her to play roles that are not those of their real-life mothers. But surely, those "not real-life" mothers portrayed onstage become the models for our expectations of real-life mothers offstage. Again, as I argued in chapter 3, life mirrors theater and not vice versa, while "desire is created and constrained through the scopic and economic systems that supposedly only represent it."[23]

By calling attention to its status as theater and to the dangers of theater, *Casa Matriz* mitigates those dangers. Surely the Raznovich play performs what Griselda Pollock has labeled "dis-identificatory practices."[24] By that she refers to "the strategies for displacing the spectator from identifying with the illusory fictional worlds offered in art, literature and film disrupting the 'dance of ideology' which engages us on behalf of oppressive regimes."[25] Unquestionably, this play precludes spectator identification. There is definitely recognition here but little identification, in part, because of the insistence on the metatheatrical. At the same time, the play's repeated emphasis on theater itself disrupts and challenges "dominant modes of realist representation which naturalize bourgeois hierarchies."[26] As Pollock further argues, "Denying the fact of being a construction, being produced, the realist text offers itself as merely a picture of the world which does not depend for its sense on any other texts, references or information."[27] By exposing the constructedness of both theater and the familial roles and spotlighting the strings that are being manipulated (and specifically for money), the Raznovich play undermines our notions of theater as a mirror (rather than a construct) and as a "pure art form" rather than a commodity.

It cannot be irrelevant either that the death scene discussed above is followed by a birthday scene, in which the inner play overtly reflects the frame play insofar as it is also Bárbara's thirtieth birthday in this inner play and her mother (played by Madre Sustituta, of course) arrives with a gift. Although this time the gift is not her (the mother) as it is in the frame play, it is still a telling gift, for it is a dress identical to the one the mother is wearing. In an artistic choice that reflects the brilliant crafting of this play as a result of its repeated rewritings and the linguistic economy that Raznovich has achieved here, where every word, every gesture is charged with multiple meanings and connotations, the dress that Bárbara is given is specifically one with *lunares* (polka dots). Revealingly, in Spanish *lunar* is related to *luna* (moon) presumably for the round shape. But, of course, moon is also traditionally associated with the female and the feminine (and some would argue in essentialist terms that the maternal is intrinsically feminine). Even more significant, *luna* is a word that also means mirror. In this respect, the dress becomes one of female mirrors, reflections and evokes the daughter who will become (mirror) a (the) mother. Interestingly too, Bárbara puts the dress on over the one she is already wearing, thus metaphorically juxtaposing mother and daughter, creating a palimpsest that evokes the play as a whole and our perceptions of mothers and daughters, as Raznovich draws attention to both the circularity of replacement that is at the heart of a commodity culture and the imagined mirror that is art itself. In this case, the play within the play highlights its own capacity for (re)producing more of the same. Indeed, once Bárbara has donned the dress, she notes that they look like twins (*CM,* 279). Since the gift merely (re)produces more of the same (as indeed does the gift to herself of Madre Sustituta in the frame play), Raznovich evokes another metaphor of theater that often (re)produces just more of the same, severely limiting rather than expanding possibilities.

The positioning of this birthday scene immediately after the death scene draws our attention to the cycles of both life and commodity replacement. What is lost (dies) can be replaced by another commodity (birth, substitution), a notion that is subtly dramatized in the fact that although Bárbara breaks the baton with which she directs the *Magnificat* at the start of the play (*CM,* 264), another one has miraculously appeared when she is ready to "direct" again (*CM,* 270). What has been broken and consumed is produced anew, replaced by a substitute that is indistinguishable from the previous commodity.[28] At the same time, this is also a scene that center-stages each member of the family's expectations of the other members, the degree to which our relationships are reproductions, framed (in both senses of the word) by prior training, expectations, and creation of desire. Evoking a mother's expectation (perhaps better expressed unfulfilled desire or hope) that she will be pivotal to her daughter's happiness, that her own existence and happiness are fulfillment enough for the daughter, Madre Sustituta responds, "Me imagino" (*CM,* 279) (I can just imagine) (*MT,* 118) when Bárbara gushes that it makes her so happy to hear her sing. The expression, *me imagino,* is extremely effective in evoking the mother's expectation/wish—that's how I want and expect it to be (expect it to be perhaps because I want it to be)—even as it also subtly underscores the element of fantasy implicit in that very expectation: *me imagino,* from the Latin *imaginare,* to form an image, to fantasize and to create, that is, (re)produce an image of the same. In this case the "mother" would (re)produce the self via the daughter. This motif is repeated and inverted just a few lines later, in the same scene, in what skillfully reflects the fact that the imag(in)ing works both from mother to daughter and vice versa. Here Bárbara employs exactly the same words to respond to Madre Sustituta's assurance that having her (*darte vida* [giving you life]) gave meaning to her existence (the mother's). Again, this is what the child expects, desires, demands, imag(in)es for the maternal role. As a result, we are caught in a dizzying mise en abyme of both theater and reproduction, as well as mirrors and reflections, as Raznovich cleverly moves us from the notion of birthday as the celebration of one's existence to birthday as the moment the mother gives birth and is simultaneously reborn herself (as a mother), adding another role and all its baggage to her sense of self. These two moments are, as Raznovich dramatizes, intricately interlinked even though we have often come to isolate them, viewing the birthday only from the perspective of the child. At the same time, the playwright highlights the question of gift versus commodity. Were we to re-image this day in terms of its simultaneous significance for both mother and daughter, our perception of the gift-giving involved would surely be muddled. Who is the giver; who or what is the gift; and who is the recipient? Is the daughter a gift to the mother or is the mother's gift to the daughter life? That the daughter Bárbara inverts this process and gives herself various, alternative "mothers" for her birthday marks the complexity of the issue even as it once again signals the reproduction or metaphoric rebirth: by means of the theater enacted by Madre Sustituta, Bárbara is (imaginatively) reborn as the various, alternative daughters of those substitute mothers.[29] Furthermore, if, as Madre Sustituta underscores in the scene of wishful thinking, giving you life gave my existence meaning, then my gift to you is ultimately a gift to myself. Thus, the inherent egocentricity of most human beings, including the mother, is made patent. Paradoxically, of course, it is only to the mother that this very human characteristic has traditionally been denied. Only she, in patriarchal religion's and society's idealization of her, is expected to devote her entire existence to the other(s) with no thought for herself. When she exhibits this human quality, her unwillingness and/or inability to meet the ideal, she is disparaged and demoted to the level of bad mother (and often imaged as devouring).

Significantly, there are several birthday scenes in the play as well as several scenes in which the daughter is pregnant, about to become a mother herself, all of which function as indicators of the metatheatricality of the play as well as repetition and substitution, absence of an original role or commodity. I have argued throughout this chapter that Bárbara's gift to herself allows her to "try on" the various mothers and rehearse the various daughter roles required by those mothers. I have also argued that in this respect Bárbara is in training much as theatergoers are when we attend the theater. Raznovich carries this notion yet one step further by signaling Bárbara's (potential) status as a future mother herself. She is pregnant in the scene of the Italian immigrant mother and again as the rebellious rock fan. In both cases, and paradoxically, the mothers reproach the daughters for the pregnancies, for becoming mothers, as it were. In the case of the Italian immigrant mother, the daughter's pregnancy is treated as a reflection of her weakness and her inability to say no to her husband. In the case of the rock fan, the pregnancy is a disgrace, a rebellion against the mother, designed perhaps to hurt the mother, especially insofar as the daughter defies the mother (who is denigrated and demeaned) by insisting that she does not even know who the father is.

In what marks yet one more oscillation between the literal and the figurative, this potential to reproduce is literalized in one of the final scenes. There, Bárbara is presented as a playwright composing a play in which her mother is the protagonist in what is an obvious reference to the play we are watching, reminding us again that the daughter creates or shapes the mother as much as vice versa. In this respect Raznovich links writing to (re)production and carries the notion one step further by having the daughter (re)produce (give birth to in metaphoric terms) the mother. Again echoing the frame play, the mother here is determined to teach the theatrical "mother" how to play her role but still insists, "No quiero sugerirle que tome el modelo real . . . Es mejor que me *reinvente*" (*CM,* 283, emphasis added) (I'm not suggesting that she try to recreate me exactly . . . I think she should *reinvent* me) (*MT,* 123, emphasis added). The mother, already theatrical (re)production, will teach the actress tricks to be more theatrical, more convincing, but implicitly also more distanced from any being in the world outside of theater and art. It cannot be irrelevant either that within this inner play, the daughter writes in order to forestall violence, to avert herself from killing Lourdes, her current lesbian lover and the mother's former lover. As Madre Sustituta states, "Si la matás en la ficción te va a aliviar la furia" (*CM,* 284–85) (If you kill her in your fiction it will alleviate all your anger) (*MT,* 126), evoking theater's potential for averting violence rather than perpetuating it. It all depends on the placement of the mirror.

Once again we return to the beginning of this book. In my analysis of *Los huéspedes reales,* I argued that while Hernández was certainly dramatizing conflict and perhaps even competition between mother and daughter, that conflict was not occasioned by desire for the father's phallus as Freudian theory would have it. Raznovich seems to support this perception of mother-daughter relations by completely eliding the father's phallus here and presenting the third party in this triangular desire (à la Girard) as definitively female.[30] Unlike real-life reproduction (children), Bárbara's play can be written without the intervention of the male or the phallus. Thus, the terms of this reproduction in writing have changed.

In this way Raznovich underscores the framing of the mirror and the positioning of the subject within that mirror of art, which are the focus of the works of theorists as different as Griselda Pollock and Susanne Kappeler.[31] But, as noted earlier, here the pretended mirror is continually undermined as the play performs a mise en abyme of metatheatricality. Like several other plays in this study, this one unquestionably comments on theater and theater's role in selling certain images. Specifically, the naturalistic or realistic theater found in early chapters can delude one into believing that what is seen there is a possibility, a reality, a reflection of something outside of theater itself. And we as the audience tend to buy the image projected. By continually calling attention to the theater, the role playing, Raznovich denies us the comfort of buying into the images and thus evades the dangers of more realistic art as discussed by Pollock. By emphasizing the metatheatrical Raznovich proposes that mother and daughter roles (and by implication family roles in general) are not innate, fixed, eternal, nor inalterable. To quote Butler again, the norm, the role, is merely a citation that "takes hold to the extent that it is 'cited' as such a norm, but it also derives its power through the citations that it compels."[32] Nevertheless, Raznovich also posits that the interdependence of the two roles (mother and daughter) renders altering them an arduous task since "it takes two to tango" as it were.

As we have seen throughout this study, art (but specifically theater) and family might also be imaged as that tightly woven couple of the tango, each moving to the rhythm of the other and in response to the other. The two dancers of the tango may not execute identical steps and gestures, indeed at times they move apart and execute quite different moves, but each responds to and triggers the other. Indeed, we might view the relationship between the two as Griselda Pollock views representation in all its forms: "Representation can also be understood as 'articulating' in a visible or socially palpable form social processes which determine the representation but then are actually affected and altered by the forms, practices and effects of the representation."[33] As I argued in the introduction, theater is always and necessarily complicitous in shaping social relationships (either by resisting the status quo or by perpetuating it) and is less an imitation of reality than an interpretation of it. As a result, theater necessarily contributes to the formation of both our past memories and our future perceptions of those collective communities we call theater and family. But, like dancers, neither art nor family is frozen, but rather constantly in motion. Just as theater has changed significantly in the last fifty years, so too have both the image of family and its daily reenactment in the world. There is every reason to expect that both will continue to mutate in the future. Undoubtedly, those changes will be painful and find resistance, as was the case in Rovner's *Volvió una noche* studied in chapter 8. We can only hope, however, that those transformations will allow both theater and the family to continue to move beyond the limitations of Freudian formulas for discontent.

Notes

INTRODUCTION

1. It is important to bear in mind throughout this study that the family we are talking about is a distinctly bourgeois, Western image. It would not be difficult to argue either that the theater is also a bourgeois institution, catering to middle-class tastes.

2. Roberto Cossa, *El saludador, Teatro XXI* 5, no. 9 (Spring 1999): 107–17; also published in Felipe Galván, ed., *Diálogos dramatúrgicos México-Argentina* (Puebla, Mexico: Tablado IberoAmericano, 2000), 37–61. Significantly, *El saludador* [The Greeter or The Waver] premiered in June 1999 at a moment when street crime was increasing in Buenos Aires and people were ever more reluctant to venture out to go to the theater. At that time, the country was in the early stages of the growing political and economic unrest that would eventually lead to the downfall of the government and the nation's default on much of its national debt in late 2001 and early 2002.

3. As Jacques Donzelot has argued, the image of the family is just that, an image promulgated by various institutions of the state as part of a system of regulatory practices. Donzelot, *The Policing of Families,* trans. Robert Hurley (Baltimore: Johns Hopkins University Press, 1997). I have insisted on the term *pseudomirror* here because I concur with Jill Dolan's argument that theater "is not really a mirror of reality" insofar as a mirror "implies passivity and noninvolvement, an object used but never changed by the variety of people who hold it up and look into it. The theatre has in fact been much more active as an ideological force." Dolan, *The Feminist Spectator as Critic* (Ann Arbor: University of Michigan Press, 1988), 16.

4. See Diana Taylor, *Disappearing Acts: Spectacles of Gender and Nationalism in Argentina's "Dirty War"* (Durham, NC: Duke University Press, 1997) and Jean Franco, "Death Camp Confessions and Resistance to Violence in Latin America," *Socialism and Democracy* 2 (1986): 5–17, for discussions of the deployment of the trope of family by political regimes. Amalia Gladhart, *The Leper in Blue: Coercive Performance in the Contemporary Latin American Theater* (Chapel Hill: University of North Carolina Press, 2000) and Jean Graham-Jones, *Exorcising History: Argentine Theatre under Dictatorship* (Lewisburg, PA: Bucknell University Press, 2000) also discuss governmental oppression hidden under the guise of the family in specific plays.

5. Donzelot, *The Policing of Families.*

6. Let us not forget that one of the characteristics that theoretically defines theater is the communal nature of the experience. Unlike poetry or the novel, it is not an art form that one experiences in solitude.

7. Argüelles, *Escarabajos* (Guadalajara, Mexico: Agata, 1992).

8. Hugo Argüelles, *La esfinge de las maravillas,* in *Teatro vario II* (Mexico: Fondo de Cultura Económica, 1995), 251–321.

9. Berman, *Entre Villa y una mujer desnuda* (Mexico: Milagro, 1994). Translated by Shelley Tepperman as *Between Pancho Villa and a Naked Woman, Theatre Forum* 14 (1999): 91–108.

10. Del Río, *¿Homo sapiens? Suspenso familiar en dos acto,* in *Cien años de teatro mexicano* (Mexico: Sogem, 2002), CD-ROM.

11. Hernández, *Los huéspedes reales,* in *Teatro mexicano del siglo XX,* ed. Antonio Magaña-Esquivel (Mexico: Fondo de Cultura Económica, 1970), 84–140. Although technically Cecilia does marry and leave the home of her parents for that of the husband, she returns shortly thereafter in a gesture that negates the potential outward journey.

12. Rovner, *Volvió una noche,* in *Eduardo Rovner Teatro I* (Buenos Aires: Ediciones de la Flor, 1994), 9–104. Translated by Charles Philip Thomas as *She Returned One Night / Volvió una noche* (Chula Vista, CA: Avetine, 2003), 1–66.

13. Raznovich, *Casa Matriz,* in *Defiant Acts / Actos Desafiantes: Four Plays by Diana Raznovich,* ed. Diana Taylor and Victoria Martinez (Lewisburg, PA: Bucknell University Press, 2002), 263–86. Translated by Victoria Martinez as *MaTrix, Inc.,* in *Defiant Acts,* 99–127. Gambaro, *La malasangre,* in *Teatro I* (Buenos Aires: Ediciones de la Flor, 1984), 57–110. Translated by Evelyn Picon Garfield as *Bitter Blood,* in *Women's Fiction from Latin America,* ed. Evelyn Picon Garfield (Detroit: Wayne State University Press, 1988), 111–57. Gambaro, *De profesión maternal,* in *Teatro* (Buenos Aires: Norma, 2002), 45–80.

14. Hirsch, *The Mother/Daughter Plot: Narrative, Psychoanalysis, Feminism* (Bloomington: University of Indiana Press, 1989).

15. Ibid., 9.

16. Ibid.

17. Ibid.

18. Sommer, *Foundational Fictions: The National Romances of Latin America* (Berkeley: University of California Press, 1991), and "Irresistible Romance: The Foundational Fictions of Latin America," in *Nation and Narration,* ed. Homi K. Bhabha (New York: Routledge, 1990), 71–98.

19. I have discussed at length this notion of desiring differently in relation to the Berman play in "Tea for Two: Performing Desire in Sabina Berman's *Entre Villa y una mujer desnuda," Latin American Theatre Review* 30, no. 1 (Fall 1996): 55–74.

20. Jean-François Lyotard, *The Postmodern Condition: A Report on Knowledge,* trans. Geoff Bennington and Brian Massumi (Minneapolis: University of Minnesota Press, 1984).

21. I employ the term *implied performance* much as Wayne Booth has used the term *implied author* to refer to the performance/production that the written text seems to propose. Obviously some written texts attempt to control that production more than others, and surely some productions strive more than others to comply with the stage production outlined or implied in the text. Booth, *The Rhetoric of Fiction* (Chicago: University of Chicago Press, 1961), 71–76.

22. My notions of performance and citationality are based on the theories of Judith Butler as developed in *Gender Trouble: Feminism and the Subversion of Identity* (New York: Routledge, 1990) and *Bodies That Matter: On the Discursive Limits of "Sex"* (New York: Routledge, 1993).

23. Blau, *The Audience* (Baltimore: Johns Hopkins University Press, 1990), 25; emphasis in original.

24. Amalia Gladhart, *The Leper in Blue,* 189.

25. Butler, *Bodies,* xi.

26. Jacques Donzelot, *The Policing of Families;* Butler, *Bodies,* x.

27. Donzelot, *The Policing of Families;* Elisabeth Badinter, *Mother Love: Myth and Reality* (New York: Macmillan, 1981); Ann Dally, *Inventing Motherhood: The Consequences of an Ideal* (New York: Schocken, 1983).

28. Andreas Huyssen, *After the Great Divide: Modernism, Mass Culture, Post-modernism* (Bloomington: University of Indiana Press, 1986).

29. The exception is Mexican Hugo Argüelles's *La esfinge de las maravillas,* which I discuss in chapter 7. Because of its challenge to psychoanalysis and some of its terms, it might well have been discussed in chapter 1 with *Los huéspedes reales.* Because it treats many of the same issues that Argüelles addresses in *Escarabajos,* it would have fit nicely into that discussion also. At the same time, because of its penetrating examination of how popular media (specifically film) and elite art forms (particularly opera) affect gender and familial roles, it might have merited its own chapter. I have chosen to discuss it in chapter 7, in terms of the performance of motherhood, because I think it offers interesting parallels to the other play, authored by an Argentine woman, discussed there.

30. Maurice Halbwachs, *On Collective Memory,* ed. and trans. Lewis A. Coser (Chicago: University of Chicago Press, 1992), 38.

31. Judith Butler, *Bodies,* xi–xii.

32. Jean Graham-Jones, *Exorcising History,* 21.

33. Ibid., 28.

34. Laura Mulvey, "Melodrama In and Out of the Home," *High Theory / Low Culture: Analysing Popular Television and Film,* ed. Colin MacCabe (New York: St. Martin's Press, 1986), 82.

35. Ibid., 95.

36. Jacques Donzelot is less direct than my words may suggest here. After a lengthy analysis in which he theorizes "the emergence of the modern family and the expansion of the 'psy' organizations [is] a single process, and one that is not politically innocent in the least," he goes on to question, "This crisis of the family, *together with* this proliferation of 'psy' activities, are themselves the solution to what problem?" *The Policing of Families,* 220 (italics in the original). He ultimately concludes that "the 'psy' specialist furnishes a neutral terrain for the resolution of differences of regime between the management of bodies and the management of populations." Ibid., 229.

37. Camilla Stevens, *Family and Identity in Contemporary Cuban and Puerto Rican Drama* (Gainesville: University of Florida Press, 2004).

38. Catherine Larson, *Games and Play in the Theater of Spanish American Women* (Lewisburg, PA: Bucknell University Press, 2004); Margo Milleret, *Latin American Women on/in Stages* (Albany: State University of New York Press, 2004); Gladhart, *The Leper in Blue.* Two other very useful studies of recent years include Diana Taylor and Roselyn Costantino, eds., *Holy Terrors: Latin American Women Perform* (Durham, NC: Duke University Press, 2003), which combines translations of theatrical and performance pieces by female artists from several countries with critical analyses of their works and/or historical, autobiographical essays, and Catherine Larson and Margarita Vargas, eds., *Latin American Women Dramatists: Theater, Texts, and Theories* (Bloomington: Indiana University Press, 1998), which includes critical essays on various playwrights.

39. Sandra M. Gilbert and Susan Gubar, *The Madwoman in the Attic: The*

Woman Writer and the Nineteenth-Century Literary Imagination (New Haven: Yale University Press, 1979).

40. Judith Butler, *Gender Trouble,* 91.

CHAPTER 1. *LOS HUÉSPEDES REALES*

1. Luisa Josefina Hernández, *Los huéspedes reales,* in *Teatro mexicano del siglo XX,* ed. Antonio Magaña-Esquivel (Mexico: Fondo de Cultura Económica, 1970), 84–140 (hereafter referred to as *HR* and cited parenthetically in the text). All translations from the Spanish are my own. Born in 1928, Hernández has written over thirty plays and numerous novels. A student of the famed Rodolfo Usigli, she assumed his position in dramatic composition at the Universidad Nacional Autónoma de México. She found success in theater from an early age. Her first play, *Los frutos caídos* [The Fallen Fruits], was her master's thesis, written in 1955 and staged in 1957. Staging details about *Los huéspedes reales* are sparse and often contradictory. In his introduction to the play, Antonio Magaña-Esquivel lists 1956 as the date of the play and says it premiered in 1957 at the Festival Dramático del INBA (Instituto Nacional de Bellas Artes) in Monterrey. *Teatro mexicano,* 82. According to him, it was first published in *La Palabra y el Hombre* in 1957. Valdés, on the other hand, gives 1959 as the premiere date. María Elena de Valdés, "Luisa Josefina Hernández," in *Escritoras de Hispanoamérica,* ed. Diane E. Marting (Bogota: Siglo Veintiuno, 1990), 247. More recent publications, as well as information on the Internet, set the premiere in 1968. She has won numerous prizes for her theater.

2. The back cover of the 1958 Universidad Veracruzana edition notes that under the simple face of a Mexican girl Hernández managed to find the pathetic mask of Electra. John Kenneth Knowles states that in *Los huéspedes reales,* Luisa Josefina Hernández presents the classic theme of Electra in a contemporary Mexican family. Knowles, *Luisa Josefina Hernández: Teoría y práctica del drama* (Mexico: Universidad Nacional Autónoma de México, 1980), 41. Frank Dauster labels the work a version of the Electra myth, although admittedly his interest is more in the tragic form than in the specific myth itself. Dauster, "La forma ritual en *Los huéspedes reales,*" in *Ensayos sobre teatro hispanoamericano* (Mexico: SepSetentas, 1975), 60. Joan Boorman recognizes the psychological rather than mythic foundation of the readings and declares that in this play "Hernández' interest shifts to a study of prototypical behavior based primarily on Freudian models. The play considers the consequences of a contemporary Electra complex and thoroughly analyzes the psychological motivations of the characters." Boorman, "Contemporary Latin American Woman Dramatists," *Rice University Studies* 64 (1978): 76–77. Gloria Feiman Waldman, however, centers more on female relationships and "the anguish of mother-daughter relationships," although she too notes "the powerful dilemma of a father and daughter caught in an Electra situation." Waldman, "Three Female Playwrights Explore Contemporary Latin American Reality: Myrna Casas, Griselda Gambaro, Luisa Josefina Hernández," in *Latin American Women Writers: Yesterday and Today,* ed. Yvette E. Miller and Charles M. Tatum (Pittsburgh: Latin American Literary Review, 1977), 75 and 78.

3. Derrida, *Of Grammatology,* trans. Gayatri Chakravorty Spivak (Baltimore: Johns Hopkins University Press, 1974).

4. Fetterley, *The Resisting Reader: A Feminist Approach to American Fiction* (Bloomington: Indiana University Press, 1978).

5. It is not irrelevant that this "analytical" emphasis subtends psychoanalysis as well as literary analysis since both are influenced by cultural codes, and literary analysis is particularly susceptible to the metaphoric figures of psychoanalysis.

6. Indeed, Luce Irigaray has devoted two volumes to demonstrating how the valorization of the masculine and the phallic subtends all our cultural constructs. Irigaray, *Speculum of the Other Woman,* trans. Gillian G. Gill (Ithaca: Cornell University Press, 1985); and *This Sex Which Is Not One,* trans. Catherine Porter (Ithaca: Cornell University Press, 1985).

7. Irigaray analyzes our cultural "oculocentrism," which privileges the visual over the other senses, as one of the conditions of this phallic fixation in *Speculum of the Other Woman* and *This Sex Which Is Not One.*

8. Most contemporary theory (borrowing from Michel Foucault) recognizes that our cognizance of our world is based on a series of contradictory discursive fields, which Chris Weedon defines as "competing ways of giving meaning to the world and of organizing social institutions and processes." Weedon, *Feminist Practice and Poststructuralist Theory* (New York: Basil Blackwell, 1987), 35.

9. Although I use the term *reading* here, I use it in its broadest and most metaphoric sense. The spectators of a play metaphorically read the work as they watch the performance. The use of the word *read* is not intended to distract from the representational nature of the performance or from the play as staging rather than literature.

10. In recent years, numerous critics have refuted the notion of theater as a mirror of reality. For example, Jill Dolan posits, "The theatre . . . is not really a mirror of reality. A mirror implies passivity and noninvolvement, an object used but never changed by the variety of people who hold it up and look into it." Dolan, *The Feminist Spectator as Critic* (Ann Arbor: University of Michigan Press, 1988), 16. Similarly, Rozsika Parker and Griselda Pollock have noted, "Art is not a mirror. It mediates and re-presents social relations in a schema of signs which require a receptive and preconditioned reader in order to be meaningful." Quoted in Dolan, *The Feminist Spectator,* 16.

11. In the Sophocles play, Electra hates her mother, Clytemnestra, and wishes to see her dead for having orchestrated the death of her father, Agamemnon, and having married his usurper, none of which occurs in *Los huéspedes reales.* Even the psychoanalytical reading of the Sophocles play—a reading that engenders the Electra complex—is founded on some questionable premises. As employed by psychoanalysis the Electra complex describes the daughter's incestuous desires for the father; she desires his phallus. But, in the classic Electra myth (not the rewriting of the myth proposed by psychoanalysis) it would be as difficult to speak of an incestuous relationship between the father and the daughter as it would be to speak of an incestuous relationship between Hamlet and his father. In both cases the child's antagonism toward the mother is based on the mother's sexuality (that the child would deny) or the mother's failure to comply with the stereotypical, generic maternal role, as well as the possibility that the father's power will now pass not into the hands of the child but into the hands of others. Let us note too that throughout this study my objections to psychoanalytical constructs, Freudian and Lacanian particularly, are based as much on interpretations and reductionary applications of those theories as on the theories themselves.

12. Editors Juliet Mitchell and Jacqueline Rose note that Freud himself never accepted the term. Mitchell and Rose, eds., *Feminine Sexuality: Jacques Lacan and the école freudienne,* trans. Jacqueline Rose (New York: Norton, 1985), 12–13. Others have labeled the same phenomenon the "female Oedipus complex."

13. To the extent that the Electra complex is merely a reformulation and renaming of the Oedipus complex, an explanation of the same phenomenon in females that Freud proclaimed to observe in males, the Electra complex also privileges the phallic in spite of its feminine nomenclature. Both Jane Gallop and Luce Irigaray have argued that although Freudians and Lacanians insist that the phallus is merely a symbol and not to be confused with the virtual penis, it often is. Irigaray says of the female as perceived by Western culture, "Her lot is that of 'lack,' 'atrophy' (of the sexual organ), and 'penis envy,' the penis being the only sexual organ of recognized value." Luce Irigaray, *This Sex,* 23. Gallop notes, "Yet 'phallus,' the signifier in its specificity . . . is always a reference to 'penis'. 'Phallus' cannot function as signifier in ignorance of 'penis'. 'Phallus' is not the originary, proper name of some referent that may get contingently translated as 'penis'." Jane Gallop, *The Daughter's Seduction* (Ithaca: Cornell University Press, 1982), 98. She also argues, "The penis is what men have and women do not; the phallus is the attribute of power which neither men nor women have. But as long as the attribute of power is a phallus which refers to and can be confused . . . with a penis, this confusion will support a structure in which it seems reasonable that men have power and women do not." *Daughter's Seduction,* 97.

14. I use the adjective *pseudo* here because although we generally view the home as a center of matriarchal influence and power, in fact, as Luce Irigaray demonstrates, it is a limited, permitted power within a society organized by men for men to (over)value the masculine, the phallic. *This Sex,* 142–43.

15. Although it is certainly true that scene 5 is also the only scene that might be viewed as positing any degree of hope for Cecilia's future, since it offers the possibility of escape from the course of events preplanned even before her birth, this potential is negated kinesically in that the stage, the park, remains empty, devoid of all human presence, at the close of that scene. All other scenes conclude with one or more characters still present onstage, if indeed static. Also, although scene 3 does take place outside, since its locale is the front steps of the house, the presence of that house is still very much felt.

16. The critical insistence on perceiving the Electra complex at the heart of the play leads one to wonder if this too is not a diversionary technique necessary to disguise the fact that Cecilia is essentially disinterested in the phallic. Such a reading parallels the gesture of the Father who, according to Irigaray, covers, subverts, and diverts his desire with his Law. Luce Irigaray, *Speculum.*

17. Both Luce Irigaray and Roland Barthes have suggested that the principal pleasure of love is talking about it: Irigaray, *This Sex,* 103; Barthes, *A Lover's Discourse,* trans. Richard Howard (New York: Hill and Wang, 1978). Also, there can be little doubt that critical analyses of the play have tended to accept these words too literally and have failed to recognize that their veracity (from Cecilia's perspective at least) is undermined by the rhetorical and kinesic indicators: the overt playacting (signaled by quotation marks) and her physical gestures (dancing a waltz, laughing). Still it is important to recognize that, as presented, although Cecilia recognizes the theatricality and absurdity of the situation, Ernesto perhaps does not, for in reaction to her laughter and verbal emphasis on the playacting, his response is one of confusion and shame: "*El padre se desconcierta, se avergüenza*" (*The father is disconcerted, he becomes embarrassed*) (100).

18. Knowles, *Teoría y práctica del drama,* 41.

19. Cecilia's relationship to her mother would necessarily be misinterpreted in a traditional reading since, according to Luce Irigaray's theory, the relationship between mother and daughter cannot be articulated without a new (other) syntax and grammar. Irigaray, *This Sex,* 143.

20. Luce Irigaray and Jane Gallop have argued that the entire Oedipal systematics (myth) is necessary to disguise, divert, and invert the father's desire for the daughter, which is hidden in his Law and must be kept invisible. Luce Irigaray, *Speculum of the Other Woman;* and Gallop, *Daughter's Seduction.* Perhaps readers of Hernández's play, like readers of Freud, would also invert this desire and view it as originating in the daughter rather than the father.

21. Knowles, *Teoría,* 57.

22. Hirsch, *The Mother/Daughter Plot: Narrative, Psychoanalysis, Feminism* (Bloomington: University of Indiana Press, 1989), 10–11.

23. Luce Irigaray has expressed it succinctly: "Why should a woman have to leave—and 'hate' . . . —her own mother, leave her own house, abandon her own family, renounce the name of her own mother and father, in order to take a man's genealogical desires upon herself?" Irigaray, *This Sex,* 65.

24. Marianne Hirsch has discussed the "daughter's anger at the mother who has accepted her powerlessness, who is unable to protect her from a submission to society's gender arrangements." *The Mother/Daughter Plot,* 165.

25. Although Elena would also like to halt the flow of time, she seems to recognize that as an Edenic impossibility. In fact, Cecilia's desire to remain young and stop the flow of time is mirrored in her mother, Elena, who also wishes to return to what, from her point of view, was an Edenic state—the time when she and Ernesto were young and presumably in love, the time before Cecilia's birth (although this paradise probably never existed except as a mythic chimera of her own making). At one point, however, Elena complains that since the daughter's birth, their lives have centered on her to the exclusion of their own desires (doubtlessly, in both senses of the word) (*HR,* 102) and that she wants more from life than this stasis and emptiness (the banquet without food evoked in the title), which resembles death more than life (*HR,* 95). This sensation of inertia and fixation, which foreshadows what awaits Cecilia as future wife and mother, is physically manifest at the conclusion of each scene as the characters remain motionless and stare into space. Throughout the play, the underlying conflict may be that between being and becoming, which again may be the specularization of the visible and the invisible. While all characters would like time to stand still, to remain in or return to one fixed role (which unfortunately can only be valid for one stage of life), Ernesto's inability to tolerate the fact that being is a continuous process of becoming leads him to commit suicide and halt the process violently: "no sé cuál es mi lugar en el mundo" (I don't know what my place in the world is) (*HR,* 137). Ultimately, Ernesto himself will provide the barrier to Elena's wishes just as he does to Cecilia's, for even before his suicide he rejects the former physically and emotionally as he accuses her, "En este momento quieres ser Cecilia y le tienes envidia . . . Has vivido con celos y con rabia de que ella era joven y bonita" (At this moment you want to be Cecilia and you are envious of her . . . You have lived with jealousy and anger that she was young and pretty) (*HR,* 130). Ernesto patently seeks stasis, identities that are fixed, clearly differentiated (mother and daughter), and reduced to a label.

26. While I recognize the discordance between Elena's speech and praxis, I cannot view her as totally evil as John Kenneth Knowles does in *Teoría.* When Ernesto declares that she has never loved Cecilia, she does not deny it but merely states that she was not able to (*HR,* 132), and yet the first scene ends in a gesture of love on her part when she requests permission to embrace Cecilia, who, both parents admit, is incapable of loving anyone (ibid.). Similarly, her relationship with Ernesto is fraught with apparent contradiction as she seeks the future with him yet

refers to unarticulated past problems (*HR*, 103). From his perspective, however, she has merely emasculated him, wanting to weave a web around him like a spider until he has been immobilized (*HR*, 114–15). Perhaps they are both right. The validity of the Hernández play rests in her refusal (unlike that of critics) to reduce the complexity of the problem and place the responsibility on the shoulders of any one character. More accurately we must recognize that the problem has its roots in the sociopolitical gender arrangements.

27. See the first chapter of Sharon Magnarelli, *The Lost Rib: Female Characters in the Spanish American Novel* (Lewiston, PA: Bucknell University Press, 1985).

28. Along the same lines, Freud posited that both male and female children experience an initial attachment to the mother, which must be overcome at a later age.

29. We generally consider the creation and maintenance of the home along with the bearing and raising of children to be feminine tasks, if indeed assigned by patriarchal society. Ironically, however, although Juan Manuel will assign Cecilia the task of educating the children (which in Spanish refers to both raising and instructing), their marriage will effectuate the end of her education since, from his perspective, it no longer matters if she misses class (*HR*, 106).

30. There is an interesting parallel here between Hernández and her character, for by means of the stage directions Hernández also makes visible what might not be visible or apparent on the stage. It would surely not be easy to convey this contradiction by means of gestures or actions onstage.

31. Were there any doubt as to the role playing and falseness that will be implicit in this metaphoric banquet, Hernández reminds us that Cecilia has to be dressed in a special manner and made-up (i.e., disguised, masked, theatrical) in order to attend the ritual: "Ya vino una mujer a peinarme y a pintarme. Me dejó como . . . como debo estar" (A woman already came to arrange my hair and do my makeup. She left me as . . . as I should be) (*HR*, 118). Luce Irigaray posits that the only path historically assigned to women is that of mimicry as they must deliberately assume the feminine role. Irigaray, *This Sex*, 76.

32. The irony, of course, is that she is already possessed by the father as Elena's speech acknowledges in her use of the verb *tener* (to have).

33. Frank Dauster, "The Ritual Feast: A Study in Dramatic Form," *Latin American Theatre Review* 9, no. 1 (Fall 1975): 5–9; and Dauster, "La forma ritual."

34. I base my analysis of the story of Iphigenia on that found in Rex Warner, *The Stories of the Greeks* (New York: Farrar, Straus, and Giroux, 1967), 352–63.

35. John Kenneth Knowles, *Teoría*, 45.

CHAPTER 2. *LA MALASANGRE*

1. Gambaro (b. 1928) is one of Argentina's most prolific playwrights and continues writing today. She has received an impressive number of prizes and has been honored in international conferences around the world. A few of her recent works include *Lo que va dictando el sueño* [What the Dream Announces] (written 1999/2000, staged 2002), *Mi querida* [My Dear] (written 2001, staged 2003), *Pedir demasiado* [Asking Too Much] (written 2001, staged 2004). *La malasangre* was restaged as recently as 2005 in a fairly lavish production at the Teatro Regina in Buenos Aires; directed by Laura Yusem (who is well known and respected and has directed a number of Gambaro works), it starred Lorenzo Quinteros. Griselda Gambaro, *La malasangre*, in *Teatro I: Real envido, La malasangre, Del sol naci-*

ente (Buenos Aires: Ediciones de la Flor, 1984), 57–110, hereafter referred to as *LM* and cited parenthetically in the text. It has been translated by Evelyn Picon Garfield as *Bitter Blood*, in *Women's Fiction from Latin America*, ed. Evelyn Picon Garfield (Detroit: Wayne State University Press, 1988), 111–57, hereafter referred to as *BB* and cited parenthetically in the text. Except where otherwise noted, all translations are from Picon Garfield.

2. Sharon Magnarelli, "Interview with Griselda Gambaro," *Hispania* 68, no. 4 (1985): 821.

3. Griselda Gambaro, "¿Es posible y deseable una dramaturgia específicamente femenina?" *Latin American Theatre Review* 13, no. 3 (Summer 1980): 21. The dramatist continued by observing that women's situation is evident in a transparent omission; in the questioned works, the world of men was a world marked by incomprehension, selfishness, and injustice, but it is the world in which women live.

4. Gambaro herself has noted that women appear more and more in her dramatic work as her own awareness of the situation of women in the world grows. Magnarelli, "Interview," 820. In that same interview she declared that she believes that the problems of women are the same as those of men; women suffer the same way, but with the added obstacle of their historic situation of dependency and submission. Ibid. She also talks about her growing awareness in another interview with me. Sharon Magnarelli, "Giselda Gambaro habla de su obra más reciente y la crítica," *Revista de Estudios Hispánicos* 20, no. 1 (1986): 130.

5. The late 1970s and early 1980s was a period marked by political abuses in an Argentina at the height of the military dictatorship, the Proceso, and what has come to be known as Argentina's "dirty war," during which thousands of citizens "disappeared." Nonetheless, ever conscious of the possibility of censorship or political reprisal, Gambaro used frameworks that temporally or spatially distance each play from 1970s Argentina. *La malasangre* is set during the time of the Rosas dictatorship in the 1840s. *Real envido* assumes a fictional, fairy-tale ambiance, as I have discussed in detail in my article on that play. Sharon Magnarelli, "El espejo en el espejo: El discurso reflejado/reflexivo en *Real envido* de Griselda Gambaro," in *En busca de una imagen*, ed. Diana Taylor (Ottawa: Girol, 1989), 89–102. *Antígona furiosa*, as the title suggests, returns us to the classical period, and *El despojamiento* focuses on the private drama of an actress.

6. Gambaro has assigned the role of actress to these female characters, albeit in varying degrees, for she sees women as continually cast in this role by our social institutions. From her perspective women are much more oppressed than men and forced to play a role for the most part. She adds that even those of us who think we have reached a certain level of freedom exercise our freedom within a society that imposes other rules on us. Magnarelli, "Interview," 820.

7. As Ann Dally has argued, "There have always been mothers but motherhood was invented." Dally, *Inventing Motherhood: The Consequences of an Ideal* (New York: Schocken, 1983), 17. For an analysis of other theories of the origins of motherhood, see Marianne Hirsch's enlightening study (particularly pages 13–14). Hirsch, *The Mother/Daughter Plot: Narrative, Psychoanalysis, Feminism* (Bloomington: University of Indiana Press, 1989).

8. For example, Othello may have been a Moor (biologically marked as to his race), but his problem was universal rather than a "Moorish" problem.

9. There can be little doubt that the roles of mother and daughter are not only socially determined but also politically, to the extent that in a patriarchal society in which females are defined in relation to males, mothers' and daughters' rights, privileges, and duties are also defined by laws.

10. Red was the official color of the Rosas regime, and those who refused to wear the color were terrorized.

11. For an analysis of the female as actress in *El despojamiento* see Sharon Magnarelli, "Acting Women / Seeing Women / Seeing Nude: Griselda Gambaro's *El despojamiento*," in *Latin American Women's Writing: Feminist Readings in Theory and Crisis,* ed. Anny Brooksbank Jones and Catherine Davies, (Oxford: Oxford University Press, 1996), 10–29.

12. In Spanish the verb *violar,* from the same etymological root as *violencia* (violence), translates *to rape.*

13. Bergson has noted that laughter implies an absence of feeling in that we cannot laugh at that to which we are emotionally tied. He has also noted that it involves a sense of superiority and that "we laugh every time a person gives us the impression of being a thing." Henri Bergson, "Laughter," in *Comedy,* ed. Wylie Sypher (New York: Doubleday Anchor, 1956), 97.

14. We might understand the verb *ausentarse* metaphorically and conclude that he is giving her permission to absent herself in the sense of let her mind wander; in other words, no need for her to pay attention and/or she is not bright enough to understand what is going on.

15. Hayden White discusses at length the notion of the savage or wild man as one whose human status is questioned. White, "The Forms of Wildness: Archaeology of an Idea," in *Tropics of Discourse: Essays in Cultural Criticism* (Baltimore: Johns Hopkins University Press, 1978), 150–82.

16. Indeed Michel Foucault studies this division in the ancients, where the love of the soul is viewed as superior to the love of the body. See vol. 2 of *The History of Sexuality,* especially pp. 233–34. Foucault, *The Use of Pleasure,* vol. 2 of *The History of Sexuality,* trans. Robert Hurley (New York: Vintage, 1986). In other parts of the same study, he implies that it is precisely this division that problematizes sexuality.

17. Of course, earlier Dolores too had figured the father as "bondadoso . . . Una bondad desbordante como un río . . . que ahoga" (*LM,* 67) (good-hearted . . . Overflowing with goodness like a river . . . that drowns) (*BB,* 119). The fact that she says it with a twisted smile signals the irony involved.

18. Revealingly, Benigno is motionless at both the opening and closing of the play in a kinesic gesture that suggests that the powerful need only to set the events in motion, not to act themselves, and leads the spectator to view the events as not motivated by him.

19. This kinesic motif of ritualistic drinking is repeated when the father does offer wine to Rafael after having forced him to undress, when Dolores drinks the wine alone, when Fermín serves hot chocolate with only one cup to Rafael and Dolores, when Rafael is asked to serve liquors to Juan Pedro and the father and then is served boiling tea by Fermín, and finally when in the last moment the father suggests that the family drink hot chocolate and not talk about Rafael's death. And, while the servants in Benigno's house eat the same food as the masters do, they are not served wine. It is probably not irrelevant either that we employ the term *heads* (in both Spanish and English) to refer to the leaders, chiefs, or superiors of a group.

20. Significantly, the allusion to Christian symbolism as well as the reduction of the woman to the status of animal are repeated at the end of the play when Benigno images Dolores as a snake ("víbora"), symbol of evil associated with the female challenger of the status quo in the Garden of Eden and with original sin (carnality).

21. For a more complete discussion of the king's control in *Real envido,* see Sharon Magnarelli, "El espejo en el espejo: El discurso reflejado/reflexivo en *Real envido.*"

22. It cannot be irrelevant in the context of this play that the term *ley* (law) comes from the Latin *lex,* law, originally religious. But let us not forget that *lexis* is the Greek term for *word,* and without the word there can be no law.

23. Susanne Kappeler, *The Pornography of Representation* (Minneapolis: University of Minnesota Press, 1986), 155.

24. See my "El espejo en el espejo," especially pages 94–95.

25. Kappeler, *The Pornography of Representation,* 152.

26. Diana Taylor also examines the question of the eroticization of violence in Gambaro's works. Taylor, *Theatre of Crisis* (Lexington: University of Kentucky Press, 1991).

27. This scene is poignantly reminiscent of Freud's description of the crucial scene in the development of the little boy's sense of self: the moment when the little boy perceives the mother's (female's) "lack."

28. I think specifically here of the post-Freudian Electra complex and of Lacan's privileging of the paternal phallus as the object of desire par excellence.

29. Here, too, we find a reference to Argentina's "dirty war" and the manipulation of perceptions in order to enlist the aid of ordinary citizens in the perpetuation of the oppression on the part of a controlling few.

30. Susanne Kappeler's book, *The Pornography of Representation,* offers an interesting analysis on the willing victim/collaborator as opposed to the unwilling. Positing that the choice of posture and attitude (willing or unwilling) is not a choice of action (willing or not the victim will be victimized), she demonstrates how this notion of willingness carries over into our perception of sexuality and the virgin/whore dichotomy. "The woman-object consists of body alone, without the dimension of a human will. When it is new, unused, intact, it bears the seal of its 'unwillingness' in its virginity . . . Once the seal is broken, however, the woman-machine gets going, responding to its use. The presumed unwillingness was only a state of inexperience." Kappeler, *The Pornography of Representation,* 157–58.

31. It is probably not irrelevant that Dolores has employed a plural verb here, *mandaron* (they ordered), for our perception of power leads us either to believe that it is shared by many (but not us) or to perceive the powerful figure as multiple in his power.

32. Marianne Hirsch reads the plots of conventional nineteenth-century novels of family romance as controlled by a fantasy, the "desire for the heroine's singularity based on a disidentification from the fate of other women, especially mothers." Hirsch, *The Mother/Daughter Plot,* 10. She also understands the heroines' allegiance to fathers and brothers as protecting them from marriage and maternity. See page 34 of the same work.

33. Dolores's earlier use of the term *papito* (little daddy or daddy dear) signaled her playing the role of the pampered child.

34. The reader will note that my reading of the play is far more pessimistic than are other fine analyses of the play: Peter Roster, "Griselda Gambaro: De la voz pasiva al verbo activo," in *En busca de una imagen,* ed. Diana Taylor (Ottawa: Girol, 1989), 43–52; Sandra M. Cypess, "La imagen del monstruo y su víctima en las obras de Griselda Gambaro," in *En busca de una imagen,* 53–64; Becky Boling, "Reyes y princesas: La subversión del signo," in *En busca de una imagen,* 75–88; and, more recently, Enrique A. Giordano, "*La malasangre* de Griselda Gambaro: Un proceso de reconstrucción y recodificación," in *Teatro argentino du-*

rante el Proceso (1976–1983), ed. Juana A. Arancibia and Zulema Mirkin (Buenos Aires: Vinciguerra, 1992), 57–74; and Gail A. Bulman, "El grito infinito: Ecos coloniales en *La malasangre* de Griselda Gambaro," *Symposium* 48, no. 4 (1995): 271–76.

35. Gambaro, *Teatro I.*

36. In the introduction to their anthology of plays by female dramatists, including Gambaro's *La malasangre* (which came into my hands after the completion of this essay), Andrade and Cramsie also recognize that little changes when they observe that the subverted order does not change substantially. Elba Andrade and Hilde F. Cramsie, "Estudio preliminar," in *Dramaturgas latinoamericanas contemporáneas: Antología crítica,* ed. Elba Andrade and Hilde F. Cramsie (Madrid: Verbum, 1991), 44.

37. Peggy Kamuf, *Fictions of Feminine Desire* (Lincoln: University of Nebraska Press, 1982), 22–23.

38. Griselda Gambaro, "Entrevista," in *Teatro: Nada que ver, Sucede lo que pasa,* ed. Miguel Angel Giella et al. (Ottawa: Girol, 1983), 28.

CHAPTER 3. *ESCARABAJOS*

Epigraph is from Jean Anouilh, *Medea,* in *Jean Anouilh,* vol. 3, trans. Luce and Arthur Klein (New York: Hill and Wang, 1967), 86. In the original French, we read, "C'est moi! C'est l'horrible Médée. Et essaie maintenant de l'oublier!" Jean Anouilh, *Médée* (Paris: Table Ronde, 1953), 88.

1. Hugo Argüelles, *Escarabajos* (Guadalajara, Mexico: Agata, 1992) (hereafter referred to as *E*). Subsequent quotations are cited parenthetically in the text; all translations from the Spanish are my own. Argüelles had a long, prolific career in theater. Born in Veracruz in 1932, he began his career as a playwright in 1957, with his one-act "Velorio en turno" [Wake in Shift], which won him the first of many prizes for his drama. That play was expanded to a three-act play titled *Los cuervos están de luto* [The Ravens Are in Mourning] that also won prizes. His most recent play, *Los coyotes secretos de Coyoacán* [The Secret Coyotes of Coyoacán], premiered in 1999. A student of Luisa Josefina Hernández, he was known for his work in theater, cinema, and television. He also taught seminars and workshops in creative writing and playwriting in various institutions and trained several of today's successful Mexican playwrights (Sabina Berman among them). His plays frequently deal with abuses of power. *Escarabajos* won the Sor Juana Inés de la Cruz prize for best play of the year in 1991.

2. See Sandra M. Gilbert and Susan Gubar as well as Shuli Barzilai's discussion of their work. Gilbert and Gubar, *The Madwoman in the Attic: The Woman Writer and the Nineteenth-Century Literary Imagination* (New Haven: Yale University Press, 1979); Barzilai, "Reading 'Snow White': The Mother's Story," in *Ties That Bind: Essays on Mothering and Patriarchy,* ed. Jean F. O'Barr, Deborah Pope, and Mary Wyer (Chicago: University of Chicago Press, 1990), 253–72.

3. See the introduction for a discussion of my use of the term *family romance.*

4. For example, in his prologue to Argüelles's *Obras* [Works], Mario Saavedra refers to his theater as a faithful reflection of Mexico's rather troubled and painful national identity. Saavedra, "La visión trágico-burlesca en el teatro de Hugo Argüelles," prologue to *Obras* by Hugo Argüelles, vol. 8 (Mexico: Gaceta, 1994), 9–10. He later categorizes it as a faithful mirror of the Mexican condition—of the people's authentic reality and idiosyncrasy. Ibid., 11–12. To my knowledge, only one

scholar, Domingo Adame, has seen his works otherwise and proposed that the world we view on the Argüellean stage is a theatrical world in every sense of the word, a creation complete unto itself and not necessarily nor merely a reflection of life and society offstage. Adame notes that theatricality is a fundamental characteristic of most of his work, adding that in Argüelles's work theatricality is intimately tied to a solid construction of plot and characters. Domingo Adame, "La teatralidad en la dramaturgia de Hugo Argüelles" (paper read at Las Cuartas Jornadas Internacionales de Teatro Iberoamericana in Puebla, Mexico, July 8–12, 1996). He also notes that what emerges is a totally unusual world, where the most direct and immediate references are to theater itself. Admittedly, *Escarabajos* is, on the surface at least, more realistic than most of the plays Adame discusses in his paper. As I will argue, the Argüellean world is both theatrical and a reflection of life offstage. (Adame does not discuss *Escarabajos*.)

5. Judith Butler, *Bodies That Matter: On the Discursive Limits of "Sex"* (New York: Routledge, 1993), 12.

6. Linda Kintz, *The Subject's Tragedy: Political Poetics, Feminist Theory, and Drama* (Ann Arbor: University of Michigan Press, 1992), 29.

7. *Bodies That Matter,* 12.

8. Ibid., 13.

9. Ibid., 12.

10. Timothy Murray, *Drama Trauma: Specters of Race and Sexuality in Performance, Video, and Art* (New York: Routledge, 1997), 10. Although this chapter was written before the publication of Marvin Carlson, *The Haunted Stage: The Theatre as Memory Machine* (Ann Arbor: University of Michigan Press, 2001), there are numerous points of contact, including my focus on specters and memory.

11. Directed by Enrique Rentería, *Escarabajos* premiered October 10, 1991, in the Foro de la Conchita in Mexico City. I saw the performance in January 1992. It received the Sor Juana Inés de la Cruz prize from the Unión de Críticos y Cronistas de Teatro as the best Mexican play of 1991.

12. Although written in 1959 this inner play was first produced in combination with the frame play added in 1991.

13. In the stage directions of the published version, there is no indication that the dressing room should be on a higher level; they only state, "puede estar en un ángulo del proscenio, juega aparte de la escenografía descrita" (it can be in an angle of the proscenium, it is separate from the described setting) (*E,* 28). I base my comments here on the production I saw in 1992.

14. The *casa chica* (literally, small house) is the other home frequently maintained (in the past at least) by the Mexican male. It is usually the home of his illegitimate children and their mother. What is interesting about the *casa chica* in this case is Mauro's insistence that it mirror a legitimate family. In a revealing play on words, at the end of the play, when the children decide to leave, Mauro states, "Venderé esta casa. Resultó demasiado grande" (I will sell this house. It ended up being too big) (*E,* 142).

15. Jaime's dual positionality is further underscored by the fact that he is a gay living in a world of mandatory heterosexuality. At the same time, he is implicitly racially mixed—his mother is from Veracruz, his father from the capital, Mexico City. While there are no overt references to race in this particular play, it is an implicit subtext; in *La esfinge de las maravillas* (1994), the female protagonist, like Jaime's mother, is also from Veracruz, and her husband expresses his sense of superiority for being more European in appearance than her, as well as his distaste for his daughter's darker skin (inherited from her mother from Veracruz, of course).

16. The fact that it is Anouilh's Medea and not the "original" from Euripides also underscores the theatrical repetition, the performativity and citation of previously authorized roles.

17. Basing himself on C. S. Pierce, Elam distinguishes between three sign-functions: icon, index, and symbol. Keir Elam, *The Semiotics of Theatre and Drama* (New York: Methuen, 1980). The icon represents by similarity (here Pierce includes the image, the diagram, and the metaphor). The index is causally connected with its object, but here Pierce includes "the pointing ('index') finger." Elam, 22. In the symbol "the relationship between sign-vehicle and signified is conventional and unmotivated" (ibid.). In my discussion of the theatricality of Argüelles's play, I shall focus on the icon and the index, but I shall blur the distinctions between them, suggesting instead that each functions by pointing, by evoking something else, whether by metaphoricity or contiguity (metonymy). However, I would argue that Argüelles's repeated evocation of Greek tragedy functions at the level of symbol.

18. In fact, were we to try to view both at the same time, one of the stages would take on the character of a convex mirror in the style of anamorphosis.

19. I am intentionally altering the spelling of *remember* to evoke both the standard meaning of the word and the fact that memory re-members, puts things together, re-joins elements, but not necessarily in quite the same way. To re-member is always an act of creation.

20. The stage directions themselves are not specific. My description here is based again on what I saw in the 1991–92 production directed by Rentería.

21. Quoted in Kintz, *The Subject's Tragedy*, 108.

22. Of course, Freudian psychoanalysis with its implicit mandatory heterosexuality would probably attribute Jaime's identification with the mother to his homosexuality or vice versa.

23. In the stage directions of the published text, there is no indication of how Jaime should look once he has completed his makeup at the end of the play. The text only specifies, "*Se levanta ya totalmente caracterizado de 'Medea'*" *(He stands up totally in the role of "Medea")* (E, 149). Nonetheless, in the 1991–92 production, the Medea that Jaime embodies at the end of the play is completely exaggerated, grotesque, and surely unrecognizable as Medea. The fact that the published text includes a photograph of that image leads me to conclude that Argüelles viewed the effect as a valid one.

24. Linda Kintz has insightfully argued that the tragic Oedipal discourse of the family "is founded on a 'correct' reading of the *desire of the mother*" and then asks, "What if the desire of the mother is not for Dad?" *The Subject's Tragedy,* 110, emphasis in original.

25. It is also relevant that what I am calling Elvira's performance, because it is designed to please her primary external audience, Mauro, definitively displeases the secondary external audience, her children, Leticia and Jaime. In part it displeases them precisely because it is intended to please him. But, at the same time, it displeases them because, according to Western societal norms, a mother's sexuality should remain invisible to her children. Her visible desire should be strictly maternal and should focus on the child as it makes him the center of her universe.

26. I find it significant that no critic has questioned Jaime's interpretation. Since very little has been written about the play, I base my statement on the short critical analyses found in the program and those included in the published version.

27. Susan Carlson, "Revisionary Endings: Pam Gem's *Aunt Mary* and *Camille*," in *Making a Spectacle: Feminist Essays on Contemporary Women's Theatre,* ed. Lynda Hart (Ann Arbor: University of Michigan Press, 1989), 112.

28. Cypess, "Myth and Metatheatre: Magaña's Malinche and Medea," in *Perspectives on Contemporary Spanish American Theatre,* ed. Frank Dauster (Lewisburg, PA: Bucknell University Press, 1996), 37–52.

29. Although at the end of the inner play it appears that Mauro's wife is going to divorce him and not reconcile with him, Jaime indicates at the end of the frame play that they did reconcile and that he (Mauro) "se había vendido caro" (had sold out for a high price) (*E,* 148).

30. *Bodies That Matter,* 2.

31. When he insists to Jaime that what interests him most is "dirigirte hacia lo que debía [*sic*] ser" (to direct/guide you toward what you should be) (*E,* 135), he acknowledges that the same had been done to him—that is, he too had been forced into a role that he did not choose.

32. As Elvira's cousin and something of a family servant, Candelaria occupies an interesting position as observer of the family, for she is simultaneously an outsider and part of the family. It is from this perspective that she also emphasizes that Mauro does not need Elvira, only the children. When Elvira states that Mauro "nos necesita" (needs us), Candelaria responds, "A sus hijos, quizás . . . ¿pero a ti?" (His children perhaps . . . but you?) (*E,* 63). Later, as Mauro announces that he is leaving her, he declares not only that he does not love her but also "¡Eran mis hijos los que me importaban, no tú!" (It was my children that mattered to me, not you!) (*E,* 145).

33. Sharon Magnarelli, "Masculine Acts / Anxious Encounters: Sabina Berman's *Entre Villa y una mujer desnuda,*" *Intertexts* 1, no. 1 (Spring 1997): 45–46.

34. I would propose that the same might be true of the "original" Greek Medea. What has been read as her passion by male interpreters may also pertain more to the realm of ambition. Indeed, in both Anouilh's and Euripides' versions, if we were to swap Medea's skirts for male attire, her actions would no doubt be attributed to ambition rather than to passion, to a desire to maintain her status both for herself and for her children, which, of course, is precisely what Jason claims he is doing as he abandons her for a younger woman who is also more highly positioned socially and economically.

35. Judith Butler, *Bodies That Matter,* 14.

36. Euripides, *Medea,* in *Ten Plays by Euripides,* trans. Moses Hadas and John McLean (New York: Bantam, 1960), 31–63.

37. Ibid., 62–63.

38. Ibid., 62. Jason's self-serving perspective is apparent a little earlier when he calls her the "most loathsomest [*sic*] woman, to the gods and me and all mankind." He continues, "You had the heart to take the sword to your children, you their mother, *leaving me childless.*" Ibid., 61, emphasis added.

39. Ibid., 59.

40. Ibid., 62.

41. That longer tale can be found in *Bulfinch's Mythology* (New York: Avenel, 1978).

42. Jean Anouilh, *Medea,* 62. The original reads, O ma haine! Comme tu es neuve. Jean Anouilh, *Médée,* 20.

43. *Medea,* 62–63. In the original: J'ecoute ma haine . . . O douceur! O force perdue! . . . Je me retrouve . . . c'est moi. C'est Médée! Ce n'est plus cette femme attachée à l'odeur d'un homme, cette chienne couchée qui attend" (*Médée,* 21).

44. *Medea,* 64. In the original: Jason, tu l'avais endormie et voilà que Médée s'éveille! Haine! Haine! . . . je renais (*Médée,* 24–25).

45. *Medea,* 86. In the original: Je suis Médée, en fin, pour toujours! . . . C'est l'horrible Médée. Et essaie maintenant de l'oublier! (*Médée,* 88).

46. Jason recognizes the inevitability of the role he must play: "I cannot prevent anything. I must simply go on playing the part which has fallen to me since the beginning of time." *Medea,* 76–77. In the original: Je ne peux rien empêcher. Tout juste jouer le rôle qui m'est dévolu, depuis toujours (*Médée,* 62).

47. *Medea,* 65. In the original: Tu ne l'aimes plus, Médée. Tu ne le désires plus depuis longtemps (*Médée,* 30).

48. *Medea,* 68. In the original: Qu'il ne reste de Médée qu'une grande tache noire sur cette herbe et un conte pour faire peur aux enfants de Corinthe le soir (*Médée,* 36).

49. *Medea,* 80.

50. Ibid.

51. Daniel Peri Lucid has argued that *Oedipus* has "the capacity literally to mold or 'model' the world in its own image, shaping the minds of society's members to fit its structure." Quoted in Linda Kintz, *The Subject's Tragedy,* 13–14.

52. See Gilbert and Gubar as well as Barzilai's discussion of their work. Sandra M. Gilbert and Susan Gubar, *The Madwoman in the Attic;* Shuli Barzilai, "Reading 'Snow White': The Mother's Story," in *Ties That Bind* (both cited in note 2).

53. Moses Hadas, Introduction to *Ten Plays by Euripides,* trans. Moses Hadas and John McLean (New York: Bantam, 1960), ix–x.

54. Susanne Kappeler, *The Pornography of Representation* (Minneapolis: University of Minnesota Press, 1986), 2.

55. In fact, Jaime refers to Euripides' *Medea* in his opening monologue, when he states that the Medea he would have preferred to play is the Greek one, the one that made Guilmaín famous (although he cannot remember if it was written by Euripides or Sophocles). His statement is also an oblique reference to Argüelles's earlier Medea play, whose dedication states, "Este 'collage' es un homenaje a la magia interpretativa de Ofelia Guilmaín (This collage is a tribute to the interpretive magic of Ofelia Guilmaín). Hugo Argüelles, *Medea y los visitantes del sueño,* in *Obras,* vol. 8 (Mexico: Gaceta, 1994), 225. Guilmaín, considered one of the great actresses of Mexico, played the lead role (which included famous monologues from great female characters) when the play was performed in Havana in 1968. The Medea whose monologues form a significant part of that play is Euripides'.

CHAPTER 4. *EL SALUDADOR*

1. Roberto Cossa, *El saludador, Teatro XXI* 5, no. 9 (Spring 1999): 107–17 (hereafter referred to as *ES*). Subsequent quotations are cited parenthetically in the text; all translations from the Spanish are my own. Born in 1934, Cossa began his career as a dramatist in 1964 with the staging of *Nuestro fin de semana* [Our Weekend]. His early works were generally considered realistic, and he was initially classified among the so-called new realist generation. Later his works exhibited characteristics of theater of the grotesque and theater of the absurd only to return eventually to naturalism or realism. He participated in the Teatro Abierto (Open Theater) movement of the 1980s, in which Argentine dramatists came together to present annual cycles of plays that subtly or not so subtly criticized the political climate of the time, including the "dirty war" and the Proceso (process, the military dictatorship of the late 1970s and early 1980s). Having won numerous prizes, he is considered a major interpreter of the middle class of Buenos Aires. He won the Premio Konex in 1984 and 1994, and several of his plays have been made into films. In addition to his career as a dramatist, he has also worked as a journalist.

He is frequently called upon to act as a spokesperson for the world of theater in Argentina.

2. Osvaldo Pellettieri, "Roberto Cossa y el teatro dominante (1985–1999)," in *Teatro argentino del 2000,* ed. Osvaldo Pellettieri (Buenos Aires: Galerna, 2000), 27–35. For Pellettieri and the GETEA group, *reflexive realism* both reflects reality and reflects on it, functioning as a tool for the eventual betterment of society. Sikora, a member of GETEA, also situates Cossa and specifically *El saludador* within the category of reflexive realism, which has passed through various stages, but always tends to a present harsh criticism of the middle class. Marina Sikora, "*El saludador* o la persistencia del realismo," *Gestos* 15, no. 29 (April 2000): 185. Pellettieri has also employed the term *modern realist position* to refer to Cossa's works. Osvaldo Pellettieri, "El teatro argentino del año 2000 y el teatro del futuro," *Latin American Theatre Review* 34, no. 1 (Fall 2000): 13; Pellettieri, "Roberto Cossa y el teatro dominante," 29. In his dialogue with Pellettieri, Cossa himself acknowledges his view of theater as an instrument for change and says that he believes that theater continues to be a direct reference to reality. Roberto Cossa and Osvaldo Pellettieri, "Diálogo de apertura," in *Tradición, modernidad y posmodernidad (Teatro iberoamericano y argentino),* ed. Osvaldo Pellettieri (Buenos Aires: Galerna, 1999), 18 and 22. My discussion of the play is based on the Teatro San Martín (Buenos Aires) production, directed by Daniel Marcove, which debuted in June 1999 and which I saw in August of the same year.

3. George Woodyard, "The Theatre of Roberto Cossa: A World of Broken Dreams," in *Perspectives on Contemporary Spanish American Theatre,* ed. Frank Dauster (Lewisburg, PA: Bucknell University Press, 1996), 94.

4. Pellettieri notes that Cossa recognizes that it is necessary to make his message even more transparent. Osvaldo Pellettieri, "Roberto Cossa y el teatro dominante," 31. Sikora states that the play is a text that reaffirms the conviction of the necessity of presenting a clear message to the spectator, a message in which a critical perspective prevails. Marina Sikora, "*El saludador* o la persistencia del realismo," 187. Mogliani asserts that all the sign systems of the production have harmonized in pursuit of demonstrating the social thesis proposed by the text. Laura Mogliani, "*El saludador:* Del fracaso de las utopías comunitarias," *Teatro XXI* 5, no. 9 (Spring 1999): 37. At the same time she recognizes that the text parodies both idealistic tendencies and skepticism. In fact, her comments on Cossa's works prior to *El saludador* are most applicable to this play as well since she proposes that the texts unfold a *complex look* at the characters, who appreciate and yearn for that youthful, revolutionary fervor; but, by presenting those characters as ineffective and contradictory beings, the play reveals the inadequacies of the orthodox left. "*El saludador:* Del fracaso de las utopías comunitarias," 35, emphasis added.

5. Mogliani refers to the presence of family in Cossa's previous plays, while Sikora too has seen the family as a primary issue in this play, arguing that the four main themes of the play, themes that are not discussed on the Argentine stage of recent years, are the loss of ideals, the disintegration of the family, liberalism, and the problems of globalization. Laura Mogliani, "*El saludador:* Del fracaso de las utopías comunitarias," 35; and Marina Sikora, "*El saludador* o la persistencia del realismo," 186. The dramatist himself, as early as 1984, recognized the centrality of the middle class and the family in his works. Sharon Magnarelli, "Roberto Cossa habla del teatro," *Latin American Theatre Review* 20, no. 2 (Spring 1987): 133–38. More recently Graham-Jones has studied some of his plays from the early 1980s in terms of their use of the metaphor of the family to depict Argentina's

situation under the military dictatorship. Jean Graham-Jones, *Exorcising History: Argentine Theater Under Dictatorship* (Lewisburg, PA: Bucknell University Press, 2000).

6. For an overview of Cossa's plays prior to *El saludador,* see George Woodyard, "The Theatre of Roberto Cossa: A World of Broken Dreams."

7. Vicente is described as around twenty years old, but the gift his father has brought for him is a toy for a five-year-old, reflecting not only Saludador's oblivion to the passage of time, but perhaps also an indicator of the passage of time itself.

8. While this maiming does not sound at all amusing, it is a source of laughter, in large degree, I believe, due to its hyperbolic nature as well as to the fact that it is clearly not real, but merely symbolic. There is no blood, no pain; Saludador makes a joke of it; and we in the audience can discern the "missing" limbs. In many ways, again, it is like the cartoon character that is beaten up and bounces right back.

9. Interestingly, my search for the etymological roots of *ambiguous* (*ambiguo* in Spanish) turned up less unambiguous results than I would have liked. According to Moliner, *ambiguo* comes from the Latin *ambiguus,* derived from *ambígere,* to discuss, to doubt, from *ágere,* to conduct, with the prefix *amb-.* María Moliner, *Diccionario de uso del español,* 2 vols. (Madrid: Gredos, 1966), s.v. "ambiguo." Corominas says that it is taken from the Latin *ambiguus* itself, derived from *ambigere* "to be in discussion," and this from *agere* "to conduct" with prefix *amb-* "around." J. Corominas, *Diccionario crítico etimológico de la lengua castellana,* 4 vols. (Madrid: Gredos, 1954), s.v. "ambiguo." *Webster's New World Dictionary* provides the following etymology of *ambiguous:* "L *ambiguus* < *ambigere,* to wander < *ambi-,* about, around + *agere,* to do, ACT." *Webster's New World Dictionary,* 3rd college ed. (New York: Simon and Schuster, 1989), s.v. "ambiguous." Partridge traces *ambiguity* back through the same path as the above to *ambigere,* from *agere,* to drive, to go, to lead, plus *ambo,* on both sides. Eric Partridge, *Origins: A Short Etymological Dictionary of Modern English* (New York: Greenwich House, 1983), s.v. "ambiguity, ambiguous." While all these etymologies are relevant to the play, it is interesting that what is left up in the air is the question of agency. For a somewhat different interpretation of the question of ambiguity in the play, see Miguel Angel Giella, "La metamorfosis individual de las utopías: *El Saludador* de Roberto Cossa," in *Itinerarios del teatro latinoamericano,* ed. Osvaldo Pellettieri (Buenos Aires: Galerna, 2000), 121–25.

10. In the comments he wrote for the program of the Teatro San Martín (Buenos Aires) as well as in his interview with Martínez Landa and Mogliani, Cossa reports that the play began with a mental image of a man being thrown over a wall and that he worked with the space (especially the wall) and the actors during the course of three months in order to develop the play. Lidia Martínez Landa and Laura Mogliani, "Entrevista a Roberto Cossa," *Teatro XXI* 5, no. 9 (Spring 1999): 105–6.

11. Since the play text does not specify what type of housework she should perform, but merely states, "realiza alguna tarea doméstica" (she performs some household task) (*ES,* 107), the focus on laundry was presumably added as part of the stage production at the Teatro San Martín. Clearly, the clothes being hung on the line might function as an index of the ultimate emptiness (shapes without bodies) of our images of family and theater, which, in my reading, the play stages.

12. Mogliani notes the effort that went into changing the scenic space (which is semicircular) to make it conform to a more traditional theatrical stage (à la italiana). Laura Mogliani, "*El saludador:* Del fracaso de las utopías comunitarias." I

will argue that the goal was precisely the sense of familiarity, of being "among family," in a traditional theater space. Sikora refers to the setting as a naturalistic universe in which mimesis is apparent in even the most minor details, adding that the scenic signs allude to an impoverished middle class. Marina Sikora, "*El saludador* o la persistencia del realismo," 187.

13. The diminutives here function as both indicators of affection and of perceived age.

14. I refer to the prodigal son parable as related in Luke 15:11–32.

15. Cossa tells us in the program that the play's original title was *El muro* [The Wall] and developed from an image in a story told him by a friend. In that story, filled with nostalgia, a young singer requested permission to sing in a club. The audience listened politely to his less than professional performance and applauded politely. Misunderstanding the applause as a license to continue, he sang another song. The audience then applauded enthusiastically (if indeed insincerely), cheered him, carried him through the crowd like a hero (cf. Saludador's third ejection), and finally threw him over the wall.

16. For a discussion of humor in the play, see Gail A. Bulman, "Humor and National Catharsis in Roberto Cossa's *El saludador*," *Latin American Theatre Review* 36, no. 1 (Fall 2002): 5–18.

17. Interestingly, yet another metaphor is literalized upon Saludador's final return. Now limbless, he announces, "Yo ya no doy más" (I'm done in, literally, I don't have anything more to give) (*ES,* 115), an expression that refers to the fact that he is old and tired and wants someone else to take over the cause. In literal terms, it might be understood, however, as his unwillingness (and inability) to give or donate any more body parts.

18. To be sure, although I have referred to expressions in English that use the term *wall,* the idiomatic expressions in Spanish that employ the term *pared* (wall) are similar but not identical. Still, there are several expressions in Spanish that might well evoke Saludador and his endeavors: "darse (con la cabeza) contra la(s) pared(es)" (to beat one's head against the wall[s], to encounter insurmountable obstacles); "dejar a alguien (or quedarse) pegado a la pared" (to leave someone [or be left] hanging, confused, without resolution); "entre la espada y la pared" (between a rock and a hard place); "hablarle a la pared" (talk to a brick wall); "subirse o treparse por las paredes" (to climb the walls, to reach an extreme point in terms of anger, boredom, or anguish). The exaggeration implied in the last idiomatic expression certainly applies to Saludador even though he is neither angry, bored, nor in anguish.

19. The irony of his continual fascination with the ex-centric, the foreign, is underscored in the fact that as he reflects that the world organization to preserve the Wichi community would be a good place for Vicente, he also notes that he would have to go live in Oslo. Apparently, this project could not be undertaken from within Argentina; one must go elsewhere and doubly distance oneself.

20. This tendency toward not being able to differentiate is reflected by his own report that while in Kiev he "saw" Marucha in the form of a Ukrainian peasant. That peasant, however, unlike Saludador, tries to insist on the difference, that she is Pavlova, not Marucha. Let us recall, too, that he assures Marucha that he thought about his family all the time and repeatedly yearned for her *milanesas* (breaded cutlets), requesting them in the jungle of Ecuador where he lived with an Indian community—a gesture that again reflects his failure to comprehend the vast differences between the Ecuadoran jungle and Buenos Aires. In so many ways, Saludador might (must?) be viewed as a tourist, roaming the world in search of exotic views, always observing from the sidelines. He *does* very little.

21. The play is filled with subtle, humorous innuendos such as this one, which probably escape the spectator. After Saludador has been evicted for the third time, he keeps reappearing above the wall, as mother and son talk about strategies for getting a raise. She tells him that he has to convince his boss that he can improve his profits. In one of Saludador's catapults, he shouts, "¡Eso se llama plusvalía" (That is called capital gain or added value) (*ES,* 114), and she notes that this is the word that brought them to poverty. The opposite of *plusvalía* is *minusvalía,* which means a drop in value, but it also means handicap or disability, as he clearly is in the end.

22. The fact is that in spite of his idealism he has changed nothing in the larger world. Similarly, Cossa frequently refers to the inevitable failure of revolutions and theories designed to change the world, attributing that failure to practical errors, or even their impracticality. See his interview with Lidia Martínez Landa and Laura Mogliani, "Entrevista a Roberto Cossa." Similarly, Woodyard has noted, "Cossa's concerns about life, society, and politics led to plays that express the inability of the people to create and sustain a government that serves its needs because of the character flaws within the people themselves." George Woodyard, "The Theatre of Roberto Cossa: A World of Broken Dreams," 94. Onstage, this unproductive activity is highlighted in his entrances and exits. As noted, he exits as he is thrown over the wall. Even more significant, perhaps, is the fact that he always enters over (or in the last case, through) the wall. It seems not to have occurred to him simply to use the door, just as it apparently never occurs to him to communicate with his family while on his journeys or give any thought to the complexities of the issues and peoples he has embraced.

23. Judith Butler, *Bodies That Matter: On the Discursive Limits of "Sex"* (New York: Routledge, 1993).

24. There are any number of studies on the development of the family in the United States and Europe. Stone traces some of the causes for these changes as does Dally. Although the latter's focus is on mothers and motherhood, many of her conclusions are equally applicable to the notion of family since, as imaged, the mother's role is essential to the family. As she notes, "Other trends have further increased the separation and isolation of motherhood [and, I would add, family] in our time. The decline of community life and the increase in the sense of privacy have tended to shut each family into its four walls, which means, during the day, mothers with their children. Television has taken over from outside activities as the main source of amusement" (and, I would add, more recently, computers). Ann Dally, *Inventing Motherhood: The Consequences of an Ideal* (New York: Schocken, 1983), 106; Lawrence Stone, "The Rise of the Nuclear Family in Early Modern England," in *The Family in History,* ed. Charles E. Rosenberg (Philadelphia: University of Pennsylvania Press, 1975), 13–57. I would note too that while it is important to recognize that the patterns of change in Spanish America are not identical to their North American and European counterparts, there are significant parallels, a product to large degree of the fact that the conquering Europeans imposed their mores and customs on Latin America in the sixteenth century, and Western culture continues conquering and imposing our cultural norms via mass media and technology today.

25. This has also been the general trend in Spanish American countries, although the changes may have postdated these developments in the United States, and those modifications of family life have perhaps still not reached the extreme of isolation that we find in the United States. In Argentina, as in the United States, there are often significant differences between life in the large cities and life elsewhere.

26. Again, as Ann Dally has noted, "The decline of community life and the increase in the sense of privacy have tended to shut each family into its four walls." Dally, *Inventing Motherhood*, 106.

27. J. Corominas, *Diccionario crítico etimológico de la lengua castellana*, s.v. "muro."

28. Along these lines, the image of family in this play might be read in terms of Graham-Jones's readings of Cossa's earlier plays. Jean Graham-Jones, *Exorcising History: Argentine Theater under Dictatorship*. That is, one might interpret the family as a symbol of the nation. In this sociopolitical reading, the message would be that the country's political leaders, like Saludador, are maimed, useless, and incapable of anything other than pursuing unrealistic goals via rhetoric, memory, and seduction. Marucha might be read as the country's citizens, who have to face the practical day-to-day realities and in whose hands incompetent leaders have left the survival of the nation.

29. J. Corominas, *Diccionario crítico etimológico de la lengua castellana*, s.v. "familia."

30. In this particular family, this is repeated on the level of both son and father. Just as the father can fight revolutions, the son can make money outside of the home (money needed in the home, to be sure) because the home and his needs are taken care of by the mother (and probably at some future point, by a wife).

31. Although the struggles of this family are specifically economic in nature, one wonders to what extent we might link Marucha's struggles with those of the Madres de la Plaza de Mayo (mothers of the Plaza de Mayo, mothers of the "disappeared" in Argentina during the "dirty war" in the late 1970s and early 1980s). While the goals of the latter were different, their activities brought females, particularly mothers, to the center stage of the political arena and eventually proved that women could exercise power, overcome larger forces without the apparent support of the system or men.

32. Nevertheless, for all practical purposes, a cooperative (if indeed not so named) was already about to be established, between mother and son, at the time of Saludador's first return.

33. This change in form that leaves the old ideological construct essentially intact is repeated outside the home, in Vicente's workplace. At the end of the play, Vicente has been made a *socio* (a partner, associate) in what ostensibly appears to be a promotion, until we realize that he is merely one of ten thousand *socios*, suggesting that little has changed except the name and the fact that Balestrini (the boss) has also built some huge, metal-roof *galpones* (sheds, but originally slave quarters) in which the ten thousand *socios* have lunch. Clearly, this is not much of a "promotion," and the previous exploitive structure remains essentially unaltered.

34. The term *amo/a* means master, owner, proprietor, boss. *Ama de casa* means housewife. *Dueño/a* means owner, proprietor, landlord.

35. My insistence on this notion of seduction is not gratuitous. In his dialogue with Pellettieri, Cossa himself proposes that theater is an act of seduction. Roberto Cossa and Osvaldo Pellettieri, "Diálogo de apertura," 22. He recurs to the same terminology in his interview with Martínez Landa and Mogliani. Lidia Martínez Landa and Laura Mogliani, "Entrevista a Roberto Cossa," 106.

36. Judith Butler, *Bodies That Matter*, 2.

37. Ibid., 13.

38. Sikora has also observed that Marucha's remarks to the audience do not break the illusion of reality but rather situate us as neighbors. Marina Sikora, "*El saludador* o la persistencia del realismo," 187.

39. For details of the stage, see Laura Mogliani, "*El saludador:* Del fracaso de las utopías comunitarias."

40. Significantly, the word in Spanish for audience is *público.*

41. Gabriel García Márquez, *One Hundred Years of Solitude,* trans. Gregory Rabassa (New York: Harper and Row, 1970), 422.

CHAPTER 5. *¿HOMO SAPIENS?*

1. Marcela del Río, *¿Homo sapiens? Suspenso familiar en dos actos,* in *Cien años de teatro mexicano,* CD-ROM (Mexico: Sogem, 2002) (hereafter referred to as *HS*). Subsequent quotations are cited parenthetically in the text; all translations from the Spanish are my own. Since the CD-ROM edition of this play does not include page numbers, I have indicated only the act in which each reference can be found. In recent years, Marcela del Río has lived in the United States, teaching at the University of Central Florida beginning in 1990. She began her career in theater as an actress and also worked in television for several years. In 1957 she decided to abandon the field of acting and began her career as a dramatist. She is the author of more than a dozen plays, most of which have been published and/or staged, although the play that concerns me here, *¿Homo sapiens?,* has not, and this in spite of its excellence. Her first play, *Miralina,* was written in 1964 and staged the following year. Her 1970 *El pulpo* [The Octopus] won the Juan Ruiz Alarcón prize for best play of the year. She has also written and published in the genres of poetry, novel, and short story. In the 1970s she was the Mexican cultural attaché in Czechoslovakia, and between 1958 and 1968 she published weekly articles and reviews on theater in *Excelsior,* Mexico City's major newspaper.

2. Although del Río has noted that her first play, *Miralina,* was not understood by the critics, she has made every effort here to be sure that the message of this play will be understood. Marcela del Río, "La vocación literaria en los años de la formación," *Alba de América* 11, nos. 20–21 (1993): 103. In the same article, she expresses disdain for television: in a reference to her childhood, she states that fortunately for her television did not exist at that time. Ibid., 99.

3. Although J.C. is a *funcionario* (government employee) rather than an elected official, he is a member of the "Party." For that reason, throughout this chapter I link him to politicians and often refer to him as one.

4. The initial stage directions also underline the play's link to television and melodrama by stating that it is important that there be music like that of television programs.

5. For an interesting discussion of framing that serves to hide or redirect one's attention, see Susanne Kappeler, *The Pornography of Representation* (Minneapolis: University of Minnesota Press, 1986).

6. Indeed, at one point J.C. wonders to which truth Pericles refers (*HS,* II).

7. In a technique that underlines the artificial division of nature and culture, the play begins as we hear the sounds of the television, juxtaposed with the roars, screeches, and so on, of the caged animals.

8. Throughout I have capitalized Man as del Río has in the play. It is important to emphasize, however, that although J.C. gives lip service to *man* as human beings, he ultimately means man, the masculine, and from his perspective superior component of the species.

9. The irony, of course, is that in some ways J.C.'s inclusion in this group is also a sham insofar as he does not come from the upper class but has had to

"climb" his way up. There are many suggestions throughout the play that he may not be as influential as the family perceives him to be. I discuss below the males' tendency to identify with, while serving as accomplice and collaborator for, those who are perceived as powerful.

10. The setting is described as a zoo at the end of the twentieth century that might be Chapultepec or any other. Chapultepec Park in Mexico City is home to a large zoo, an amusement park, Chapultepec Castle (now a museum of Mexican history), and the Museum of Anthropology as well as the home of Mexico's presidents.

11. For the first time since the 1930s a party other than the PRI won the presidency in the elections of 2000. But the PRI's power was already being challenged in the late 1980s and early 1990s. The presidential elections of 1988 were marked with charges of fraud. And, according to Hamnett, between 1988 and 1991 opposition parties secured 240 of the 500 seats in the Chamber of Deputies. Brian Hamnett, *A Concise History of Mexico* (Cambridge: Cambridge University Press, 1999), 284. Earlier, declining oil prices had placed significant stress on the Mexican economy. Then, in 1994, the PRI presidential candidate was assassinated, many said as part of a PRI conspiracy. Earlier rebellions in Chiapas also undermined the credibility of the PRI as well as its authority.

12. The lack of distinction between the Candidate and the President is not gratuitous insofar as in Mexico the PRI presidential candidate was effectively selected by the current president in what is known as the *dedazo* (finger pointing, the outgoing president points to the one he has selected to succeed him).

13. Interestingly, the Institution, which would unite the family, does so in the concrete sense only on the most superficial level. Early in the first act the members of the family are physically together in the cage/home but mentally and emotionally completely unconnected: Gloria watches television, Pericles reads, and Shakespeare works on his computer. There is no interaction.

14. Jacques Donzelot, *The Policing of Families,* trans. Robert Hurley (Baltimore: Johns Hopkins University Press, 1997).

15. In retrospect, and in light of Mexico's 2000 elections in which the PRI lost the presidential election for the first time in decades, one can read the play in direct reference to the political structure of Mexico and the PRI, just beginning to have its dominance questioned in 1988 and 1991 when the play was written. In addition, del Río emphasizes the fact that the gender structure whereby the males hold the keys, the pistol, and other symbols of power is not specific to the upper middle classes in a brief scene between Hombre and Mujer, in their roles as thieves, as they are waiting to rob the cage. Although from a lower socioeconomic class, he, like males of the higher classes, demands that she hand over to him the keys she has just found. When asked why, he responds merely, "just because"—implicitly because that is the way it is. Similarly, in spite of the fact that J.C. is not originally from the upper classes, he too has learned the patriarchal rules of power and how to be the one to hold the symbolic keys and the gun.

16. As Pericles notes, associating theater's lack of economic resources with the government, "Grandes proyectos, gran tecnología, pero cuando buscas trabajo: no hay presupuesto, no hay vacantes, como dice ese cómico, 'no hay,' 'no hay,' 'no hay'" (Big projects, great technology, but when you look for work: there's no budget, there are no openings, like that comedian says, "there isn't any," "there isn't any," "there isn't any") (*HS,* I). But again, this lack of work in theater is a direct reference to the realities of Mexican life. Theater spectatorship and productions declined in the 1980s and 1990s, due in part to Mexico's economic crisis and continually rising crime rates.

17. Similarly, Inés, who frequently functions as the family's audience and in many ways mimics a television audience, seldom manages to distinguish between the two.

18. The question, of course, is whether J.C. sees his father as "so good" because that is the way a father should be, because those are the words with which he has been taught to perceive and describe fathers (and thus cannot perceive him any other way), because that is the way he would have liked him to be so that his father would model the norm, or because that is the way he needs to perceive him since he imitates him. If he were to perceive the father as something other than "so good," he would perhaps have to view himself in a similarly negative light.

19. It is interesting that on a number of occasions characters employ expressions such as "hijo de tu puto padre" (son of your whoring father), "vaya a chingar a tu padre" (fuck your father), "chingado padre" (fucked father). All slang expressions of significant aggression and hostility, they are derivations from the more common Mexican expressions, *puta madre* (whore of a mother) and *chingar a tu madre* (to fuck your mother), replacing the much-maligned image of the mother with that of the father.

20. Yet, as del Río subtly suggests, this model family, the perfect Christian Trinity, is the exception rather than the rule. The other families evoked in the play do not follow this paradigm. As we learn, although J.C.'s family may initially have shared some similarity (although it is a poor family of multiple children), that family disintegrated after the death of the father. When Inés talks about her family, we are reminded of its parallelisms with the "original" Mexican family. Today's Mexico is often imaged as "born" of the violent meeting between two cultures, the native Indian culture and that of the Spanish conqueror. That "birth" is generally imaged as a product of the consented rape of the Indian interpreter, la Malinche, by Cortés. Inés's father, whom she never knew, was a colonel who apparently extracted a price from her mother for the release of her brother from jail.

21. Pericles apparently has forgotten that in the Institution of the Planetary Family he cannot hunt without killing other "family members." Significantly, Gloria also has a gift for Shakespeare: a trophy, like an Oscar, on which is engraved, "To the world's best Son" (*HS,* I), words that remind us of the theatrical nature of all our familial roles. It is surely relevant too that the gun Pericles gives Shakespeare comes specifically with a cowboy holster, a prop that would simultaneously evoke U.S. Westerns (art/theater) and a child's toy, and is accompanied by his assurance that Shakespeare needs to enjoy himself or have a good time (ibid.). Should we conclude then that from some perspectives, using a gun, killing, is fun?

22. It cannot be irrelevant that the term used by J.C. has not only sexual connotations, but specifically masculine ones.

23. For a discussion of the Mexican perceptions and usage of *chingón* and *chingada,* see chapter 4 of Octavio Paz, *The Labyrinth of Solitude: Life and Thought in Mexico,* trans. Lysander Kemp (New York: Grove Press, 1961).

24. Jacques Donzelot, *The Policing of Families.*

25. It seems relevant to point out the inversion of socioeconomic positions here. As children, Pericles was economically comfortable but J.C. was not, while the reverse is true in the present.

26. Interestingly, in recent years in Mexican usage, the adjective *padre* (father) has come to be used as an adjective meaning good or great.

27. Shakespeare refers to what he is writing with the term *obra.* While *obra* can refer to any work of literature (or art for that matter), it is also the term used to refer to a play.

28. Further highlighting the conscious theatricality of it all, at several points throughout the play, characters look directly at the audience, address their words to the audience, or make some reference to that audience.

29. As that story also demonstrates, good and evil are tied to perspective. From the perspective of the townspeople, it was good that he led the rats away, bad that he led the children away. The rats might see it differently. Nonetheless, the suggestion in the story (or at least some versions of it) is that he may have led the children off to a better life, away from the treachery of the town's patriarchy, the town council (fathers) who broke their promise.

30. When Inés wonders what Shakespeare's play is about and asks if it is about love, he acknowledges that ultimately there are no other themes: "Se escriba de la familia o de la justicia o de la libertad [all themes addressed here], siempre . . . se está hablando de amor" (Whether one writes about the family or about justice or about freedom, always . . . one is talking about love) (*HS,* I). Given the rest of the play, however, one wonders to what extent this love is self-love.

31. As a credit to del Río's ability to imply multiple messages with a single object or situation, this moment might well be read in more feminist terms as well. Gloria's statement that it must be exciting for J.C. to see all those people in front of him, cheering him, with banners and all (*HS,* I), might be understood as a reference to the fact that J.C. is a politician/government employee or to the fact that he is a male, and therefore applauded, acclaimed, and supported. Thus, in many ways the play posits that not only must one be male to be a politician, to participate in power (which is particularly true in Mexican society) but that to be a male is to be a politician, one who uses or takes advantage of the word/rhetoric and the power implied in it.

32. For a discussion of the political motivations behind various festivals and celebrations in Mexico (including parades), see Thomas Benjamin, *La Revolución: Mexico's Great Revolution as Memory, Myth, and History* (Austin: University of Texas Press, 2000). This notion of not always seeing what is in fact there is reinforced in the play by the folding screen, behind which one might do something one might not want to do in public. Because they are in a cage, the couple has requested the screen to provide privacy in their bedroom. They believe J.C. has forgotten to provide it as promised but later discover that it was there all along; they simply had not noticed it.

33. The stage directions note that the names could be changed according to the locale where the play is staged and in accordance with current events, again emphasizing the sociopolitical links the playwright would have us perceive. In addition, although those same directions note that the voice of the announcer might be substituted by slides or video, I find the invisible parade a particularly effective metaphor.

34. I have dealt in detail with the notion of the military academy in Sharon Magnarelli, "*La ciudad y los perros:* Women and Language," in *The Lost Rib: Female Characters in the Spanish-American Novel* (Lewisburg, PA: Bucknell University Press, 1985), 102–16.

35. Again, see Benjamin, *La Revolución.*

36. The dramatist herself describes the Coyoacán of her childhood as a semirural small town where streets were unpaved and cattle grazed in the parks. Juana A. Arancibia, "Entrevista con Marcela del Río," *Alba de América* 9, nos. 16–17 (1991): 395. Today Coyoacán is a populated, affluent section in the southern part of Mexico City.

37. Jacques Donzelot, *The Policing of Families,* xxv.

38. Ibid., 94.

CHAPTER 6. *ENTRE VILLA Y UNA MUJER DESNUDA*

1. Sabina Berman, *Entre Villa y una mujer desnuda* (Mexico: Milagro, 1994), hereafter referred to as *EV* and cited parenthetically in the text. Translated by Shelley Tepperman as *Between Pancho Villa and a Naked Woman, Theatre Forum* 14 (1999): 91–108, hereafter referred to as *PV* and cited parenthetically in the text. Except where otherwise noted, translations are from Shelley Tepperman. In the translation different names are assigned to some of the characters. While Gina retains her name, Adrián is renamed Alberto, and Andrea is called Paulina. In addition, doña Micaela, Villa's mother, is a role played by Gina in the translation, and doña Micaela, Andrea's maid, is eliminated completely. Berman was born in 1955 or 1956 or 1953 (sources differ) in Mexico City. *Esta no es una obra de teatro* [This Isn't a Play] (also known as *Un actor se repara* [An Actor Restrains Himself]) is generally considered her first play. She is one of the most successful playwrights, both commercially and artistically, in Mexico today. She was a student of Hugo Argüelles and has written on a wide variety of themes. Her early plays often fall into the category of documentary theater as she revisits themes from Mexican history. More recently she has examined relations between the sexes and the political situation in Mexico, among other focal points. She has won numerous prizes. *Entre Villa y una mujer desnuda* debuted in 1993 at the Teatro Hellénico in Mexico City under Berman's direction. I saw the performance in July of that year. Throughout this chapter I am indebted to Stuart Day's article on the play. Although we deal with very different aspects of the work, several of the theoretical texts he used were most helpful in my own analysis. Stuart Day, "Berman's Pancho Villa versus Neoliberal Desire," *Latin American Theatre Review* 33, no. 1 (Fall 1999): 5–23.

2. That family romance is evoked in the Freudian sense of the term, however, insofar as historian Adrián turns to the figure (myth) of Pancho Villa for a model and father figure, identifying with the latter while eliding any reference to his own father.

3. Jacques Donzelot, *The Policing of Families,* trans. Robert Hurley (Baltimore: Johns Hopkins University Press, 1997). Similarly, Laura Mulvey has viewed family as an icon of normality and conformity. Mulvey, "Melodrama In and Out of the Home," in *High Theory / Low Culture: Analysing Popular Television and Film,* ed. Colin MacCabe (New York: St. Martin's, 1986), 95.

4. See Jacqueline Eyring Bixler, "The Postmodernization of History in the Theatre of Sabina Berman," *Latin American Theatre Review* 30, no. 2 (Spring 1997): 45–60, for a discussion of postmodernism in Berman's works. It is interesting that although Bixler is discussing history in her article, much of what she says about history as employed by Berman also applies to the playwright's depiction of the family. For example, she notes that Berman distorts the already distorted, specifying, she "presents history not as a compendium of objective facts but rather as a narrative that is created according to the ideological motives of those who hold power" (ibid., 48); "history itself, like a staged play, is a text easily modified to suit the desires and the ideology of the historian/director" (ibid., 49); "history . . . has been homogenized much like the population itself was" (ibid., 50). Bixler further notes that Berman denaturalizes Mexican history (ibid., 53). In each case, we might well substitute the term *family* for *history.*

5. Sharon Magnarelli, "Masculine Acts / Anxious Encounters: Sabina Berman's *Entre Villa y una mujer desnuda,*" *Intertexts* 1, no. 1 (Spring 1997): 40–50;

Magnarelli, "Tea for Two: Performing Desire in Sabina Berman's *Entre Villa y una mujer desnuda," Latin American Theatre Review* 30, no. 1 (Fall 1996): 55–74.

6. Roland Barthes, *Mythologies,* trans. Annette Lavers (New York: Hill and Wang, 1972).

7. Ilene V. O'Malley, *The Myth of the Revolution* (Westport, CT: Greenwood, 1986), 141.

8. The text states, *"Villa se desploma, muerto por fin, de vergüenza" (EV,* 79) (*Villa collapses, dead at last, of shame) (PV,* 105). I agree with Martínez de Olcoz's premise that Berman turns to the ideal of the nation to show that it fabricates or conspires with the family romance. Nieves Martínez de Olcoz, "Escrito en el cuerpo: Mujer, nación y memoria," in *Performance, pathos, política de los sexos: Teatro postcolonial de autoras latinoamericanas,* ed. Heidrun Adler and Kati Röttger (Madrid: Iberoamericana, 1999), 59. This is an assertion that she does not further develop in either this or her other article on Berman, "Decisiones de la máscara neutra: Dramaturgia femenina y fin de siglo en América Latina," *Latin American Theatre Review* 31, no. 2 (Spring 1998): 5–16. Still, I cannot be as optimistic as she when she argues that along with Villa a figure of discourse, a national myth, an invention of identity with its politics of language dies onstage. "Decisiones," 10; "Escrito," 60. The fact that he reappears in the final act suggests that in mythic terms, he is still very much alive. Or in the words of Octavio Paz, paraphrased by Adrián in the play, "Villa still gallops through the north, in songs and ballads." Octavio Paz, *The Labyrinth of Solitude: Life and Thought in Mexico,* trans. Lysander Kemp (New York: Grove Press, 1961), 148; originally published as *El laberinto de la soledad* (Mexico: Fondo de Cultura Económica, 1959).

9. Paz, *Labyrinth of Solitude,* 143.

10. Indeed, several recent studies have emphasized the mythmaking involved in the contemporary perception of both the Revolution and the Revolution's heroes. According to Thomas Benjamin, *"La Revolución* [in reference to the image, not the historical event] was a product of collective memory, mythmaking, and history writing." Benjamin, *La Revolución: Mexico's Great Revolution as Memory, Myth, and History* (Austin: University of Texas Press, 2000), 19. Ilene V. O'Malley argues, "Mystification is central to the official ideology of the Mexican regime as well as to the political culture which supports it and is supported by it." O'Malley, *The Myth of the Revolution,* 4–5. O'Malley also observes that Villa was not officially added to the cast of national heroes until 1965. Ibid., 112. Throughout I have adopted standard Mexican practice by capitalizing Revolution when referring to the Mexican Revolution in specific, even when I omit the adjective. With a lowercase, the word refers to revolution(s) in general.

11. Barthes, *Mythologies,* 109 and 143.

12. Ibid., 143.

13. Interestingly, his desire in regard to his monograph and Villa parallels his erotic desire for Gina, for as these words are spoken, he is doing his best to get her into the bedroom and "mount" her.

14. One of the examples O'Malley gives of this exploitation of patriarchal attitudes, which links notions of family to those of government, is the typical Mexican association between a father and a leader or boss, an association reinforced linguistically by referring to both as "mi jefe" and one that reaffirms dominance and superiority. O'Malley, *The Myth of the Revolution,* 139.

15. Sandra Messinger Cypess, "Dramaturgia femenina y transposición histórica," *Alba de América* 7, nos. 12–13 (1989): 295.

16. O'Malley, *The Myth of the Revolution,* 145.

17. Paz, *Labyrinth of Solitude*. In what may be simple coincidence, both the gender issues and the class issues that underlie the narrative of the Conquest were replayed in Villa's own life. It is generally believed that he became first a bandit and then a revolutionary as a result of having avenged the rape of his sister by the landowner or the landowner's son. Of course, we cannot know to what extent this is fact or part of the mythmaking, but it seems significant that the story relies on the same gender and class exploitation that structure the narratives of the Conquest.

18. The validity or lack thereof of this perception of Malinche, doña Marina, is still open to debate among scholars. For a discussion of Malinche in general and in literature, see Sandra Messinger Cypess, *La Malinche in Mexican Literature: From History to Myth* (Austin: University of Texas Press, 1991). One might well argue also that the all too typical patriarchal (il)logic is at work here: if she was raped, she must have deserved it or wanted it. As Bartra has observed, "Mexican man knows that woman (his mother, lover, wife) has been raped by the *macho* conquistador, and he suspects that she has enjoyed and even desired the rape." Roger Bartra, *The Cage of Melancholy: Identity and Metamorphosis in the Mexican Character,* trans. Christopher J. Hall (New Brunswick: Rutgers University Press, 1992), 158, emphasis in the original. This is the same inversion or projection of desire and blame that Berman so effectively dramatizes in this play and that I discuss below.

19. Also pertinent to this discussion no doubt is the difference in the structures of the families of the two potential founding fathers. Villa's family is not clearly defined, nor neatly policed. Its genealogy is vague at best; the borders are loose and shifting. As depicted in the play, Villa cannot satisfy his mother's demand that he provide her with the names and addresses of his "wives" and children, responding that there are a number of women who love him and that his marriages to five of them have been blessed by the Church. The Calles family, on the other hand, is clearly defined. Members presumably know to whom they are related and how. It has a clear genealogical lineage, inheritance, etcetera. Its borders have been more neatly defined and rigorously policed. If there have been illegitimate children, their existence has been conveniently erased. Paradoxically, then, again it would seem that Adrián might well have much more in common with Calles than with Villa.

20. Paz, *Labyrinth of Solitude,* 176.

21. Ibid., 142–43.

22. Paz, *Laberinto de la soledad,* 133. In the Kemp translation we read, "By means of the Revolution the Mexican people found itself, located itself in its own past and substance." *Labyrinth of Solitude,* 148.

23. Judith Butler, *Bodies That Matter: On the Discursive Limits of "Sex"* (New York: Routledge, 1993).

24. Aztec mythology locates that founding moment in 1325 with the foundation of Tenochtitlán in Lake Texcoco; the Aztecs had been instructed by their tribal deity, Huitzilopochtli, to build their city where they found an eagle on a cactus, eating a serpent. See Henry Bamford Parkes, *A History of Mexico* (Boston: Houghton, 1969), 20. The Aztec tribe had been led by the evening star to their promised land in central Mexico. See Brian Hamnett, *A Concise History of Mexico* (Cambridge: Cambridge University Press, 1999), 48.

25. It might well be argued that the narrative of Malinche as mother of the mestizo and thus the Mexican nation has also served to keep Indians and mestizos in their places. Symbol of betrayal, she is a constant reminder to these groups of their implicit inferiority in relation to those of European descent. Her narrative has provided an even greater reminder to women of their inferiority and treacherousness,

especially when contrasted with the other icon of femininity, the Virgin of Guadalupe. It is as if society were saying to women, here is what you could be (the Virgin), and here is what you are (Malinche).

26. I do not mean to suggest here that the civilization that predated the arrival of the Spaniards in Mexico was unified, homogeneous, or nonexploitive. There were numerous distinct native groups, with different customs, often warring with each other.

27. Stuart Day, "Berman's Pancho Villa versus Neoliberal Desire," 11. The Day article also discusses the manipulation of the myth of Villa and touches on several of the points I discuss here. I would agree with his point (also made by O'Malley) that the manipulation of the myth of Villa "instead of being cultivated to improve the lot of the poor, can in fact serve as an excuse to ignore their plight." Ibid., 17.

28. Homi K. Bhabha, introduction to *Nation and Narration,* ed. Homi K. Bhabha (New York: London, 1990), 1.

29. Francis Mulhern, "English Reading," in *Nation and Narration,* ed. Homi K. Bhabha (New York: Routledge, 1990), 253, emphasis in the original.

30. Butler, *Bodies That Matter.*

31. O'Malley, *The Myth of the Revolution,* 8.

32. Judith Butler, *Bodies That Matter.*

33. I discuss the issues of desire and role playing in detail in my two articles on this play. Sharon Magnarelli, "Masculine Acts / Anxious Encounters"; Magnarelli, "Tea for Two."

34. I have discussed his attempted return in the final act in terms of a metaphoric return to the womb in "Masculine Acts."

35. As I discussed in chapter 5, the PRI has controlled Mexican politics since the 1930s, losing a presidential election for the first time in 2000.

36. Interestingly, the image of the Virgin has frequently been politicized, appearing on the banners of the fighters for Independence and invoked during the Revolution.

37. See the Meléndez article for a discussion of the play's title. Priscilla Meléndez, "Marx, Villa, Calles, Guzmán . . . : Fantasmas y modernidad en *Entre Villa y una mujer desnuda* de Sabina Berman," *Hispanic Review* 72, no. 4 (Autumn 2004): 523–46.

38. Although his immediate object of study is France, Donzelot's analysis of how government encourages and controls the family unit in order to control individuals and any deviance from the norm is surely applicable here. Jacques Donzelot, *The Policing of Families.*

39. Magnarelli, "Tea for Two," 59.

40. I am inclined to read her statement more as an indirect declaration of erotic desire (i.e., let's make love) than as desire for a child, the authorized desire. Insofar as society has declared her erotic desire nonexistent (or improper), she can express it only indirectly.

41. The stage directions are explicit that we are dealing here with "*el Villa mítico de las películas mexicanas de los años cincuenta, sesenta, y setenta*" (*EV,* 20) (the mythological Pancho Villa straight out of Mexican films from the 50s, 60s or 70s) (*PV,* 91), the years when Villa was finally, metaphorically, inducted into Mexico's hall of fame and recognized officially as a hero.

42. The paradox here is even greater than it first appears, for while Villa is often idolized for having stood up to the Americans in his 1916 attack on Columbus, New Mexico, in fact, in his earlier years he had been backed by the United States government.

43. In some ways, Villa's killing of the woman literalizes the metaphor Gina earlier employs when she refers to the sex act as "matar el deseo como un animal" (*EV,* 32) (killing desire like an animal) (my translation). I have discussed the symbolism of tea and the performance of gender roles in "Tea for Two."

44. Judith Butler, *Bodies That Matter,* 1–2.

45. Paz, *Labyrinth of Solitude,* 175–76.

46. As Cypess has noted, in her article on *Herejía* [*Heresy*], Berman "rereads the past to integrate into the official national record episodes that many would prefer to ignore or forget. *Herejía,* like *Águila o sol* [Heads or Tails], exposes the lie inherent in the concept that Mexican cultural identity is a single, monotone hegemonic voice." Sandra M. Cypess, "Ethnic Identity in the Plays of Sabina Berman," in *Tradition and Innovation: Reflections on Latin American Jewish Writing,* ed. Robert DiAntonio and Nora Glickman (Albany: State University of New York Press, 1993), 176–77. While Cypess refers to Jews in Mexico as a marginalized group, she also acknowledges that they have been "all but invisible in the official national history." Ibid., 169. Thus, my insistence that the various ethnic groups have been more than marginalized; they have been made invisible, nonexistent (the marginal is still somehow at least somewhat visible there at the margins). It is significant too that while national politics have officially recognized the mestizo element and valorized the indigenous as a part of a romanticized past, until recently (the Zapatistas in Chiapas) the indigenous populations of contemporary Mexico have been as marginalized and/or invisible as the other ethnic groups to which I have referred. A similar irony can be found in the fact that Mexico is said to view itself as a nation of mestizos, in a gesture that would reject or minimalize the socioeconomic impact of its European ancestors, but the fact is that, official rhetoric to the contrary, the majority of those in power (political and economic) are more European than mestizo. And, in another political, rhetoric sleight of hand, even the "valuation" of the mestizo paradoxically serves to devalue the indigenous insofar as what is valued in the mestizo is the presence of European traits. See Gabriela Cano, "The *Porfiriato* and the Mexican Revolution: Constructions of Feminism and Nationalism," in *Nation, Empire, Colony: Historicizing Gender and Race,* ed. Ruth Roach Pierson and Nupur Chaudhuri (Bloomington: University of Indiana Press, 1998), 106–20.

47. I am inverting Doris Sommer's argument here. In "Irresistible Romance" she reads "denial [of dependence, of literary genealogy] as a symptom of unresolved dependence." Sommer, "Irresistible Romance: The Foundational Fictions of Latin America," in *Nation and Narration,* ed. Homi K. Bhabha (New York: Routledge, 1990), 73. Following her lead of reading against the grain or with resistance, I here am arguing that insistence on homogeneity and similarity marks unresolved and irresolvable differences, even if unrecognized.

48. O'Malley, *The Myth of the Revolution,* 8.

Chapter 7. *De profesión maternal* and *La esfinge de las maravillas*

1. As Marianne Hirsch has cogently observed, "The mother became either the object of idealization and nostalgia or that which had to be rejected and surpassed in favor of allegiance to a morally and intellectually superior male world." Mari-

anne Hirsch, *The Mother/Daughter Plot: Narrative, Psychoanalysis, Feminism* (Bloomington: University of Indiana Press, 1989), 14.

2. Judith Butler, *Bodies That Matter: On the Discursive Limits of "Sex"* (New York: Routledge, 1993); and Butler, *Gender Trouble: Feminism and the Subversion of Identity* (New York: Routledge, 1990).

3. Hirsch notes "The ideology of motherhood as the ideal of femininity coincides with the institutionalization of childhood during the eighteenth and nineteenth centuries. As representations of the child's vulnerability and need for nurturing and protection became more prominent, motherhood became an 'instinct,' a 'natural' role and form of human connection, as well as a practice." Ibid. These statements are also borne out by the studies of Ann Dally and Jacques Donzelot. Dally, *Inventing Motherhood: The Consequences of an Ideal* (New York: Schocken, 1983); Donzelot, *The Policing of Families,* trans. Robert Hurley (Baltimore: Johns Hopkins University Press, 1997).

4. Dally, *Inventing Motherhood,* 17. For a discussion of the historical development of the concept of "mothering" in Argentina, see Donna J. Guy, "Mothers Alive and Dead: Multiple Concepts of Mothering in Buenos Aires," in *Sex and Sexuality in Latin America,* ed. Daniel Balderston and Donna J. Guy (New York: New York University Press, 1997), 155–73.

5. Griselda Gambaro, *De profesión maternal,* in *Teatro* (Buenos Aires: Norma, 2002), 45–80, hereafter referred to as *PM* and cited parenthetically in the text; Hugo Argüelles, *La esfinge de las maravillas,* in *Teatro vario II* (Mexico: Fondo de Cultura Económica, 1995), 251–321, hereafter referred to as *EM* and cited parenthetically in the text. All translations are my own.

6. Judith Butler, *Bodies That Matter,* 2 and 12.

7. Ibid., 7.

8. Interestingly, from the son's perspective his mother uses him, as do the other women (mostly prostitutes) in his life. Other characters, however, describe him as a womanizer, and his mother not only refers to his exploitation of those women but also clearly takes pleasure in the fact that he "atropell[a] a tanta 'polla' ganosa" (rides roughshod over so many hot chicks) (*EM,* 255).

9. Catherine Clément, *Opera, or the Undoing of Women,* trans. Betsy Wing (Minneapolis: University of Minnesota Press, 1988).

10. Surely, the insistence on mothers being wives is related to issues of ownership and paternity. The male cannot be assured that the child is his without the exclusiveness of the marital relation.

11. Apparently, Leonardo has chosen Lucía specifically for her submissiveness.

12. Hirsch has also noted the absence of the Sphinx from the Freudian developmental paradigm. Marianne Hirsch, *The Mother/Daughter Plot,* 2.

13. For a discussion of the issues of purity of blood, class, and so on in colonial Mexico, see Claudio Lomnitz, *Deep Mexico, Silent Mexico: An Anthropology of Nationalism* (Minneapolis: University of Minnesota Press, 2001).

14. The Argüelles play also includes conflict between mother and daughter but still revolves mostly (on the surface, at any rate) around the mother and the father and son.

15. Ironically, Leticia seems unwilling to acknowledge the role of her father's second wife in her upbringing, failing to conceive of the maternal other than in biological (rather than social) terms.

16. *Webster's New World Dictionary,* 3rd college ed. (New York: Simon and Schuster, 1989), s.v. "profession." A similar point is made in Diana Raznovich's *Casa Matriz* [*MaTRIX, Inc.*], which I discuss in chapter 9. In that play, a young

woman hires a professional to perform the desired maternal roles. Raznovich, *Casa Matriz* in *Defiant Acts / Actos Desafiantes: Four Plays by Diana Raznovich,* ed. Diana Taylor and Victoria Martinez (Lewisburg, PA: Bucknell University Press, 2002), 263–86.

17. Marianne Hirsch, *The Mother/Daughter Plot,* 14. The statements are further supported by the studies of Ann Dally and Jacques Donzelot. Dally, *Inventing Motherhood;* Donzelot, *The Policing of Families.*

18. Revealingly, in both cases the earlier times were already marked by a distinct theatricality: Matilde was a singer, a performer; Lucía's existence was centered on the movie house.

19. The unwitting control that the media exercise in our actions is perhaps best exemplified at the end of act 1 when a film persona literally "possesses" Lucía as she attempts to strangle her daughter. As she vehemently (and apparently sincerely) declares, "¡No fui yo! ¡Fue Lilia Prado en *Las mujeres de mi general!* ¡Se los [*sic*] juro! ¡Fue ese personaje de ella metida en mí! ¡Dentro de mí, no sé cómo!" (It wasn't me! It was Lilia Prado in *The Women of My General!* I swear it! It was that character of hers inside me! Inside me, I don't know how!) (*EM,* 287). Surely, her words might be understood as a reflection of the way in which we internalize the socially prescribed gender roles, without knowing quite how.

20. Judith Butler, *Bodies That Matter,* 2.

21. It is important to recognize that there is not just one single script for motherhood but multiple and contradictory scripts, scripts that vary somewhat from society to society, from one socioeconomic class to another, from one religion to another, and so on, but it seems likely that each individual woman, inscribed as she necessarily is by multiple axes of identity, has necessarily internalized more than one of these scripts.

22. John Berger, *Ways of Seeing* (London: Penguin, 1972), 29.

23. The opera is based on a trilogy of plays by French playwright Beaumarchais and thus in many ways is a translation in terms of both language and genre. At the same time, surely, it is not irrelevant that the subtitle of *The Barber of Seville* is *Or the Futile Precaution,* a clear indicator (intended or not) of the ending of the Argüelles play. It is probably also significant that Beaumarchais' *The Barber of Seville* is the first work of a trilogy. That play ends with Rosina successfully escaping from the oppressive household of Bartolo and marrying Almaviva. Interestingly, the third play of the trilogy is entitled, *The Guilty Mother.* It is the only play of the trilogy not converted into an opera (the second play is *The Marriage of Figaro*), but more important, the main character, "the guilty mother" is precisely Rosina, who lives in the now oppressive household of Almaviva (that same ideal hero and lover from the first play), and the principal source of the household disharmony is her earlier affair with another man and subsequent adoption of the child that was a product of that affair. Obviously, the Argüelles play demonstrates points of contact with *The Guilty Mother* insofar as the adopted son, Juan Carlos, was adopted precisely because he may be the son (by another woman, not Lucía) of Pedro Infante, whom Lucía had once kissed.

24. Luce Irigaray, *Speculum of the Other Woman,* trans. Gillian G. Gill (Ithaca: Cornell University Press, 1985), 98–99.

25. Indeed, Lucía seems to recognize the fantastic nature of her escape as well as why she withdraws into that fantasy. She says, "Un juego es un juego, y terminado éste, creo que sabré volver a mi realidad, que me parece horrenda y vomitiva, pero es la mía, ¡cómo no! Sólo que para contrarrestarla, jugar un poco" (A game is a game, and once this one is finished, I think I will know how to return to my

reality, which seems awful and revolting to me, but it's mine, of course! It's just that to counteract it, playing a little) (*EM,* 284).

26. Judith Butler, *Bodies That Matter.*

27. Not irrelevantly, Alfonso, the psychoanalyst, also blames her: "¿Te das cuenta de cómo en cuatro meses has venido desquiciando todo lo de tu hogar?" (Do you realize how in four months you have been disrupting everything in your household?) (*EM,* 305), words that are particularly revealing insofar as they reflect his support for status quo.

28. I have also discussed this tendency to see Freudian psychoanalytical models everywhere in chapter 1.

29. There is a sense in the play too that Isolda's dedication to controlling the family is related to her lack of interest outside the family circle. This in turn, the first scene suggests, is a result of the social structure that allows no possibility for change or democracy—hence her disillusionment with political activism and her decision after "la frustración del sesenta y ocho" (the frustration of sixty-eight) (*EM,* 252) to stay in the home and look after the father's interests.

30. To be sure, Alfonso does note that Leonardo is a "titán demoledor" (a devastating titan) (*EM,* 279) and that his approach to his family is oppressive; nonetheless, he never fails to "perform" in all senses of the word, on his side, in his "best" interests.

31. Judith Butler, *Bodies That Matter,* 189.

32. Alfonso's complicity with the patriarch as well as patriarchal society is subtly underscored in his final words of the play, directed to Leonardo, after he has confessed his love for the latter: "¡chinga a tu madre!" (go fuck your mother!) (*EM,* 316), words that degrade both women in general and the mother in specific and implicitly (if indeed unintentionally) underscore male superiority and privilege: the suggestion is that the male's superiority is so supreme and unquestionable that it could well lead to the extreme of sexually exploiting his own mother.

33. Interestingly, in the first scene, a conversation between Isolda and Juan Carlos, the printed version of the text designates the characters only as *Hija* (Daughter) and *Hijo* (Son). Although each character's name is mentioned in the lines they speak, I interpret the lack of names in the play text as a sign of the importance of familial roles and performances in the play. For the reader not familiar with the events of 1968 in Mexico, the army opened fire on a student protest in Tlatelolco (also known as the Plaza of Three Cultures) in Mexico City. Using tanks and machine guns, troops broke up the student demonstration, killing "about forty people, including many uninvolved residents, old folks, children. Unofficial estimates placed the toll of dead from five to ten times that figure." John A. Crow, *The Epic of Latin America,* 4th ed. (Berkeley: University of California Press, 1992), 728.

34. This is a clever play on words. *Dictadura* means dictatorship. *Dictar (dicta)* is etymologically related to *decir,* to say, and *dura* means hard, while *blanda* means soft. The wordplay suggests that family and government are in fact dictatorships, but they disguise it in "softness," hiding their real goals under the rhetoric of nurturing, care, and concern.

35. Judith Butler, *Bodies That Matter,* 12. Glickman has observed that Gambaro has used this conjugal situation (the lack of a male head of the household) to underscore the fact that daily conflicts have more to do with personality than with sex. Nora Glickman, "De *La malasangre* a *De profesión maternal:* Griselda Gambaro y el incómodo vaivén entre hija y madre," *Revista Hispánica Moderna* 55 (December 2002): 439.

36. Burgin is cited in Linda Kintz, *The Subject's Tragedy: Political Poetics,*

Feminist Theory, and Drama (Ann Arbor: University of Michigan Press, 1992), 108; Judith Butler, *Bodies That Matter,* 19.
  37. Judith Butler, *Bodies That Matter,* 14.
  38. Ibid., 13.
  39. Judith Butler, *Gender Trouble,* 122.
  40. Ibid., 91.
  41. Ibid.
  42. Catherine Clément, *Opera, or the Undoing of Women.*

CHAPTER 8. *VOLVIÓ UNA NOCHE*

The Spanish in the epigraph reads, "Tengo miedo del encuentro / con el pasado que vuelve / a enfrentarse con mi vida." "Volver," lyrics by Alfredo Le Pera, music by Carlos Gardel. Carlos Gardel and Alfredo Le Pera, "Volver," in *Todo Tango. The Library,* http://www.todotango.com/english/biblioteca/letras.
  1. Eduardo Rovner, *Volvió una noche,* in *Eduardo Rovner Teatro I* (Buenos Aires: Ediciones de la Flor, 1994), 9–104, hereafter referred to as *VN* and cited parenthetically in the text. Except where otherwise indicated, translations of the play are from Eduardo Rovner, *She Returned One Night / Volvió una noche,* trans. Charles Philip Thomas (Chula Vista, CA: Aventine Press, 2003), 1–66, hereafter referred to as *SN* and cited parenthetically in the text. Rovner (b. 1942) has had a distinguished career as a playwright, director, and professor of dramatic writing. He held the influential position of general and artistic director of the Teatro San Martín (arguably the largest and most prestigious in Buenos Aires) during the years 1991 to 1994. Rovner's first play, *Una pareja* [A Couple], was produced in 1976; he continues to write, and his plays have been produced almost annually in recent years. The play I analyze in this chapter, *Volvió una noche,* won the Montevideo City Council's prize in the Concurso Candeau in 1991 and received the Casa de las Américas prize the same year. It debuted in 1993 in the Teatro Stella in Montevideo (with the Teatro de la Gaviota group), a production that won the Florencio prize for the best production of 1993. In the fall of 2001 (and again in the spring of 2002), it was staged in New York City at the Repertorio Español with Daniel Marcove in the role of Manuel and Lilian Olhagaray in the role of Fanny, which she had played in the premiere of the play in Montevideo. In 2005 it was staged again in Buenos Aires at the Teatro Andamio '90; directed by Alejandro Samek (who also directed the New York production), it once again starred Daniel Marcove, but this time Fanny was played by the well-known Argentine actress Norma Pons. The play has had lengthy runs as far away as the Czech Republic and won numerous prizes around the world. George Woodyard has labeled it the most successful Rovner work to date. Woodyard, "Sombras y muerte: El teatro reciente de Eduardo Rovner," in *Tendencias críticas en el teatro,* ed. Osvaldo Pellettieri (Buenos Aires: Galerna, 2001), 210. For overviews of the dramatist's career and works, see George Woodyard, "Sombras y muerte," 209–15; and Osvaldo Pellettieri, "El teatro de Eduardo Rovner: Un mundo sentimental y satírico," *Ollantay* 10, no. 20 (2002): 97–111.
  2. Marina Sikora, "La remanencia del microsistema premoderno: Concepción de la obra dramática (1983–1998)," in *Historia del teatro argentino en Buenos Aires,* vol. 5, *Teatro actual (1976–1998),* ed. Osvaldo Pellettieri (Buenos Aires: Galerna, 2001), 432. Sikora refers, of course, to *Juan Moreira,* a novel by Eduardo

Gutiérrez from 1879, which was adapted by José Podestá and staged as pantomime theater in 1884.

3. As Bixler has noted, much of Rovner's work (*Volvió una noche,* among others) is "deceptively simple. The semi-comic dialogue and dramatic situations would seem to discourage the critic in search of complexity and *historico*-political relevance." Jacqueline E. Bixler, "Metaphor and History in the Theater of Eduardo Rovner," *Ollantay* 10, no. 20 (2002): 9 (emphasis in the original).

4. Sharon Magnarelli, *"Volvió una noche* de Eduardo Rovner: Recepción en Nueva York," *Teatro XXI* 8, no. 15 (Spring 2002): 75–78.

5. My thinking on culture in this chapter is indebted to studies on essentialism and identity formation by feminist scholars such as Diana Fuss, Elizabeth Grosz, Teresa de Lauretis, and those included in the anthology edited by Fraser and Bartky, all of whom in some fashion develop on Michel Foucault's notions. Diana Fuss, *Essentially Speaking: Feminism, Nature and Difference* (New York: Routledge, 1989); Elizabeth Grosz, *Volatile Bodies: Toward a Corporeal Feminism* (Bloomington: Indiana University Press, 1994); Teresa de Lauretis, *Technologies of Gender* (Bloomington: Indiana University Press, 1987); and Nancy Fraser and Sandra Lee Bartky, eds., *Revaluing French Feminism: Critical Essays on Difference, Agency, and Culture* (Bloomington: Indiana University Press, 1992). For example, my perception of what we call culture is parallel to Fraser's perception of "social identity." As she notes, social identities are not constructed once and for all; they are not fixed but rather alter over time. Furthermore, they are discursively constructed in specific social (and, I would add, historical) contexts. Fraser, "The Uses and Abuses of French Discourse Theories for Feminist Politics," in *Revaluing French Feminism: Critical Essays on Difference, Agency, and Culture,* ed. Nancy Fraser and Sandra Lee Bartky (Bloomington: Indiana University Press, 1992), 178.

6. For a different reading of the play, see Marina Sikora, "La comedia en Buenos Aires: Circulación y desplazamientos," *Teatro XXI* 1, no. 1 (Spring 1995): 22–26. My reading will differ from hers in that I read the play less as a love story than she does. I also do not agree that there is no critique of the social context. I do, however, concur with her that the play questions the tyranny of a Jewish mother who insists that her traditions be respected and that although Fanny is presented as a Jewish mother, she could represent any immigrant mother. Ibid., 24. In another article, the same critic cogently observes that the mother's tyranny is presented as the internalization of certain cultural mandates that one must overcome. Sikora, "La remanencia del microsistema premoderno," 433. As I will argue, her tyranny is in fact a metaphor of imperial or colonial power.

7. From this point on I employ the somewhat awkward term *(trans)culture* as a means of refuting the notion of a somehow originary, essential culture. What we call culture is always and already, to some degree, a transculture.

8. There are several references to the fact that the home was hers. When Manuel tries to get Fanny to go into the kitchen in scene 15, she responds, "Ni en mi propia casa puedo estar tranquila" (*VN,* 81) (I can't even find peace in my own home) (*SR,* 49). Later, when Manuel refers to it as his, she responds, "¿Así que tu casa? ¡Siempre fue mi casa y lo va a seguir siendo!" (*VN,* 87) (Oh, so it's your home? It was always mine and it's going to stay that way!) (*SR,* 54). It is revealing also that the home's character changes with the arrival of Fanny. In scene 3, the first one to take place there, it is described as *"una casa antigua . . . El clima es de cierta tristeza y algo lúgubre. Muebles antiguos y algunos otros objetos indican que la casa se mantiene en las mismas condiciones que hace muchos años"* (*VN,*

21) (*an old house . . . The ambience has a certain sadness and is somewhat fune-real. Antique furniture and some other objects indicate that the house has been maintained in the same condition as it was many years ago*) (*SR,* 7). Shortly there-after, and following some lighting adjustments and other changes on the part of Fanny, that same home is described as follows: "*El ámbito aparece ahora cálido y sugerente*" (*VN,* 22) (*The room now appears warm and suggestive*) (*SR,* 8). The use of the term *ahora* (now) accentuates the contrast.

9. Bill Ashcroft, Gareth Griffiths, and Helen Tiffin, *Key Concepts in Post-Colonial Studies* (New York: Routledge, 1998), 233.

10. Mary Louise Pratt, *Imperial Eyes: Travel Writing and Transculturation* (New York: Routledge, 1992), 6.

11. Ibid.

12. Ibid., 7.

13. My use of the term *child* here is less a reference to age (i.e., immaturity, childhood) and more an attempt to avoid the gendered terms *son* and *daughter.* I would add that the home also marks the contact zone as husband and wife (like all other family members) play out the same patterns, simultaneously influencing (modifying) the identity and attitudes of the others and being influenced (modified) by them. Once again, the slippage between the concepts, center and periphery, colonizer and colonized, is perceptible.

14. Mary Louise Pratt, *Imperial Eyes,* 7. While we often perceive of groups in homogeneous terms, that homogeneity is usually based on one or two essentialized qualities, and power relations are still asymmetrical. Certain groups within the primary group are marked by race, gender, religion, sexual preference, and so on, and still peripheral to or subordinated by the primary group.

15. Mary Louise Pratt, *Imperial Eyes,* 6–7.

16. For an overview of the history of this policing of the family in France, see Jacques Donzelot, *The Policing of Families,* trans. Robert Hurley (Baltimore: Johns Hopkins University Press, 1997).

17. I would point out here that my view of family as the colonial paradigm is borne out by the fact that colonial discourse has long employed tropes of family and home, characterizing the colonizer as the father (or on rare occasion, the mother) and the colonized people as children who need that parental guidance to develop and mature into proper adults. Thus, I am not imposing colonial discourse on the family so much as recognizing the family as its source.

18. John A. Crow, *The Epic of Latin America,* 4th ed. (Berkeley: University of California Press, 1992), 576; Frederick S. Stimson and Ricardo Navas-Ruiz, eds., *Literatura de la América Hispánica: Antología e historia; Tomo II: El siglo dieci-nueve (1825–1910)* (New York: Dodd, 1971), 13.

19. Ibid., 14.

20. Enrique Anderson Imbert and Eugenio Florit, eds., *Literatura hispanoame-ricana: Antología e introducción histórica* (New York: Holt, 1960), 294.

21. For in-depth analyses of the gaucho tradition in theater, see Raúl H. Castag-nino, "Dos siglos de teatro gauchesco," *Teatro* (Teatro Municipal San Martín) 4, no. 12 (June 1983): 4–9; and Osvaldo Pellettieri, *Cien años de teatro argentino: Del* Moreira *al Teatro Abierto* (Buenos Aires: Galerna, 1994).

22. Osvaldo Pellettieri, *Cien años de teatro argentino,* 16.

23. Ibid., 18.

24. For a summary of the pros and cons of the terms *hybrid* and *synergy,* see Bill Ashcroft, Gareth Griffiths, and Helen Tiffin, *Key Concepts in Post-Colonial Studies,* 299.

25. Although the type of music with which the play closes is not specified by Rovner, one might well imagine that the director would opt for the tango music with which the play began.

26. For an overview of the history of tango, see Julie Taylor, *Paper Tangos* (Durham, NC: Duke University Press, 1998); and Simon Collier, Artemis Cooper, María Susana Azzi, and Richard Martin, *Tango* (London: Thames and Hudson, 1995).

27. Simon Collier et al., *Tango,* 61.

28. Mary Louise Pratt, *Imperial Eyes,* 6.

29. Indeed, the Rovner play might itself be viewed as an ongoing product of transculturation. It is not irrelevant that the play has been as, if not more, successful outside of Argentina as inside. Add to this the fact that productions outside of Argentina have added some very interesting (and one might add, transcultural) twists to the production. In Finland, Sargento Chirino entered mounted on a real horse. Olga Cosentino, "Sentimientos argentinos, en muchos idiomas," *El CELCIT en acción* (Boletín electrónico del Centro Latinoamericano de Creación e Investigación Teatral) 3, no. 149 (March 16, 2003): 1 (repr. from *Clarín,* March 15, 2003), http://www.correo@celcit.org.arg. In the Czech Republic, he entered from the sky and had a black eye because the staff had checked the details of the original version of the Gutiérrez work. Ernesto Schoo, "Chirino, en sueco [*sic*]," *La Nación,* April 26, 2003, http://www.lanacion.com.ar/03/04/26/ds 491696.asp.

30. René Girard, *Deceit, Desire and the Novel,* trans. Yvonne Freccero (Baltimore: Johns Hopkins University Press, 1965).

31. Laura Mulvey, "Visual Pleasure and Narrative Cinema," *Screen* 16, no. 3 (Autumn 1975): 6–18.

32. In both the Teatro Repertorio Español production (2001–2) and the Teatro Andamio '90 production (2005), Manuel stands at the edge of the stage and looks down. At first it appears that he is looking at us, the audience, and speaking to us. Only as his monologue continues do we realize that he is looking down at the grave of his mother and speaking to her.

33. Mary Louise Pratt, *Imperial Eyes.*

34. Salo's words are not direct, but I believe that such is the suggestion: "¡Te lo pido por mí, Fannushka! Si él te llega a olvidar . . . yo . . . ¿Qué hago sin vos?" (*VN,* 97) (I'm asking you for me, Fannushka! If he manages to forget you . . . I . . . What will I do without you?) (*SR,* 61).

35. *El día de los muertos* (the day of the dead) is a day for remembering and honoring those that have died.

36. Interestingly, although she analyzes narrative rather than theater, Marianne Hirsch has noted that most literature about mothers is written from the perspective of the daughter (or in Rovner's case, the son) in a gesture that effectively silences the mother and fails to include her experience except as perceived, reported, rescripted, by her progeny. See the introduction to *The Mother/Daughter Plot.*

37. In the terminology of postcolonial theory, Manuel "colonizes" Fanny by speaking for her, in her place.

38. One indeed wonders if the obsession with the name and "law of the father" is not to some degree at least a reaction to and attempted denial of this very fact. As Barbara Johnson has argued, basing her comments on two citations from Judith Fetterley and Toni Morrison, "the text may itself be a 'response' to the reader it represses, marginalizes, or excludes." Barbara Johnson, *The Wake of Deconstruction* (Cambridge, MA: Blackwell, 1994), 36. What anxieties on the part of cultural texts and their authors does the insistence on patriarchy and the law of the father

ameliorate? To what extent is it an overcompensation for the perceived powers of the mother that Rovner addresses here?

39. Fanny is something of a single mother, which is not to suggest that she was not married, but to underscore the absence of the father in their family life. When she queries about Dolly and her son, "¿Lo crió ella sola?" (Did she bring him up by herself?) and receives an affirmative response from Manuel, she comments, "Como yo a vos" (*VN*, 100) (Like I did with you) (*SR*, 63). Earlier she refers to the fact that "Tu padre nos dejó hace mucho" (*VN*, 99) (Your father left us such a long time ago) (*SR*, 62). The lack of a father figure would, of course, render her even more powerful within the home and from the perspective of the child than she might otherwise be. This absence of a father figure in both cases might also be read as a commentary on the situation of the country, in terms similar to those of Mary Beth Tierney-Tello in her discussion of Diamela Eltit's *Por la patria*. Tierney-Tello, *Allegories of Transgression and Transformation: Experimental Fiction by Women Writing Under Dictatorship* (Albany: State University of New York Press, 1996), 79–127.

40. Mary Louise Pratt, *Imperial Eyes*, 6.

41. It cannot be irrelevant that in the scene at the cemetery, the audience does not immediately grasp where Manuel is or to whom he is speaking until he uses the term *mamá* after which the lights come up so that we can see where he is and he refers to her as *vieja*, a common term to refer to one's mother to be sure, but it can also be translated as "old woman," which emphasizes the past, the old, that which no longer fits current conditions.

42. In a different context, to be sure, Rovner himself evoked this difference within in a roundtable discussion, when he noted that Argentina is a country of immigrants, where everyone, more or less, looks outward and inward. "Mesa redonda: Los autores entre el acuerdo y la polémica," *Teatro XXI* 2, no. 3 (Spring 1996): 68.

43. Michel Foucault, *The Use of Pleasure*, vol. 2 of *The History of Sexuality*, trans. Robert Hurley (New York: Vintage, 1986).

44. This oscillation between domineering despot and misunderstood victim also echoes the manner in which colonial powers have often presented themselves—as merely wanting the "best" for their colonial "children" who neither understand nor appreciate them.

45. Interestingly, this too is a double-edged gesture. On the one hand, there is a certain suggestion that it is Manuel's fault that her feet are in bad shape: if he is a pedicurist he should have somehow taken care of them. But, on the other hand, it is an opening, a gesture of reconciliation that, in what is traditionally associated with motherly nurturing, allows him to demonstrate his skills to her. The scene ends with the following stage directions: "*[Fanny] va hacia una silla, se sienta, se descalza y apoya los pies. Manuel mira, primero sorprendido y luego feliz, toma un instrumento y comienza a trabajar sobre los pies de Fanny*" (*VN*, 67) (*[Fanny] goes toward the chair, sits down, takes off her stockings and puts up her feet. Manuel looks on, at first surprised and then happy. He gets an instrument and begins to work on Fanny's feet*) (*SR*, 38–39).

46. It is interesting that many of the rituals of orthodox Jewish faith tend to marginalize women. One wonders if the association of the Jewish mother with a certain power within the home might not be a compensation for this marginalization. Or perhaps it is vice versa: the marginalization within the rituals is a masculinist compensation for her perceived power within the home.

47. My overlapping of these terms (individual, culture, and society) is not un-

conscious. It is an intentional slippage that I believe stages and reflects a slippage in our lives. I would argue that there are no neat, clear-cut borders between the individual, family tradition, religious tradition, social tradition, and cultural tradition. For example, to what extent are family traditions interfused with and confused with cultural traditions, national traditions, and religious traditions? Is culture religious, ethnic, national, or familial? Obviously, I find it some supple combination of all of these. This permeability or instability, this quality of exceeding the boundaries of stable control, is perhaps epitomized in holidays. To what extent is a religious holiday (say, Christmas or Passover) a religious event and to what extent is it a family (or even national) event. Surely these celebrations vary from family to family, from region to region. The same might be said of national holidays/celebrations: independence days, celebrated differently in different parts of the world (but perhaps always a constant in the national[ist] repertoire), are often family celebrations and surely perceived as such long before the child recognizes (learns) the sociopolitical significance of the event.

48. Let us not forget, however, that as Butler has insightfully argued, these roles and identities are constructed, but they are not necessarily assumed consciously or at will. Although the following quote is specifically concerned with gender, I believe it might well apply to any aspect of identity: "The 'activity' of this gendering cannot, strictly speaking, be a human act or expression, a willful appropriation, and it is certainly *not* a question of taking on a mask." Judith Butler, *Bodies That Matter*, 7 (emphasis in the original). In *Volvió una noche* there are multiple examples of characters knowingly assuming a mask/role, but there are also multiple examples of unconscious performativity à la Butler, such as Manuel's reaction to wearing or not wearing the overcoat when Dolly appears, which I discuss in the next paragraph.

49. Homi K. Bhabha, introduction to *Nation and Narration,* ed. Homi K. Bhabha (New York: London, 1990), 1–7. Unquestionably, the gaucho here also functions as an indicator of the juxtaposition of temporal moments. His reaction to Fanny's response to his request, "¡Sólo necesito el nombre / de ese gaucho endemoniau!" (*VN,* 20) (I only need the name of that wretched gaucho) (my translation), demonstrates the newness or strangeness of the idea that an Argentine (i.e., gaucho in his words) might be Jewish. When she responds with his name, "¡Manuel Stern!" the stage directions note, "*Chirino se asombro*" (*Chirino is surprised*) (*SR,* 7). Obviously, in Chirino's day, to be a Jew and an Argentine was not a likely possibility (at least not from the gaucho's uneducated, rural subject position).

50. His first appearance onstage is in the world of the dead, when he appears to Fanny and her friends (who do not understand his archaic, poetic language), in what for me evokes the notion that like them, he belongs to another world, another time, place, and mentality.

51. Gay McAuley, *Space in Performance: Making Meaning in the Theatre* (Ann Arbor: University of Michigan Press, 2000), 233.

CHAPTER 9. *CASA MATRIZ*

1. First published in 1989, the play has undergone a number of rewritings. I have used the most recent version, published in *Defiant Acts,* since it is the only one the author herself claims to have authorized (personal correspondence). Diana Raznovich, *Casa Matriz,* in *Defiant Acts / Actos Desafiantes: Four Plays by Diana Raznovich,* ed. Diana Taylor and Victoria Martinez (Lewisburg, PA: Bucknell Uni-

versity Press, 2002), 263–86, hereafter referred to as *CM* and cited parenthetically in the text. The play was originally published in *Salirse de madre,* ed. Hilda Rais (Buenos Aires: Croquiñol, 1989), 163–86. All translations are from Diana Raznovich, *MaTRIX, Inc.,* trans. Victoria Martinez, in *Defiant Acts,* 99–127, hereafter referred to as *MT* and cited parenthetically in the text. Note that in the translation, Bárbara's name has been changed to Gloria. According to the author's Web page, *Casa Matriz* was produced in Rome in 1986, http://autores.org.ar/dianaraz/. Raznovich (b. 1943) had her first play, *Buscapiés* [Jumping Jack] produced in 1968. In 1981 her work was included as part of the Teatro Abierto (Open Theater) cycle of plays in Argentina, a series of one-act plays that were intended as gestures of resistance to the military dictatorship in power at that time. More than a dozen of her plays have been produced, but she is probably best known for the four plays anthologized in *Defiant Acts: Jardín de otoño [Inner Gardens]* (1983), *Desconcierto [Disconcerted]* (1981), *De atrás para adelante [Rear Entry]* (1995), and *Casa Matriz [MaTRIX, Inc.]*. She has won prestigious awards around the world, including a Guggenheim. Her works have been translated into several languages. For overviews of Raznovich's work, see Diana Taylor, "Fighting Fire with Frivolity: Diana Raznovich's Defiant Acts," in *Defiant Acts,* 23–39; Nora Glickman, "Parodia y desmitificación del rol femenino en el teatro de Diana Raznovich," *Latin American Theatre Review* 28, no. 1 (Fall 1994): 89–100; and David William Foster, "Recent Argentine Women Writers of Jewish Descent," in *Passion, Memory, Identity: Twentieth-Century Latin American Jewish Women Writers,* ed. Marjorie Agosín (Albuquerque: University of New Mexico Press, 1999), 35–57. Quote is from Marianne Hirsch, *The Mother/Daughter Plot: Narrative, Psychoanalysis, Feminism* (Bloomington: University of Indiana Press, 1989), 9.

2. Castellví deMoor explains the multiple referents of the title. She notes that, in addition to the double meaning of *Casa Matriz* as a center for the distribution of services, perhaps a metaphor of society, and as an organ of female reproduction, in the theatrical field the term also refers to "matrices of representativity" that exist within the virtual roles of the theatrical text. Magda Castellví deMoor, "Dramaturgas argentinas: Perspectivas sobre género y representación," in *El teatro y su mundo: Estudios sobre teatro iberoamericano y argentino,* ed. Osvaldo Pellettieri (Buenos Aires: Galerna, 1997), 276.

3. In addition to the *Magnificat* discussed below, the play includes Indian music, Italian music, a tango, a Yiddish lullaby, a love song, a rock song, and so on.

4. Castellví deMoor, "Dramaturgas argentinas," 276.

5. Judith Butler, *Gender Trouble: Feminism and the Subversion of Identity* (New York: Routledge, 1990), 138.

6. The "Aclaración" (Clarification) is not included in the version of the play published in *Defiant Acts,* although it was included in the version published in *Salirse de madre* and in earlier translations. My references to the "Aclaración" in this chapter are taken from the version of the play available through Raznovich's Web site, which includes most of the updates we find in *Defiant Acts.* See: http://autores.org.ar/dianaraz/Obras/Casa/texto.html. All translations of the "Aclaración" are my own.

7. Jean Baudrillard, *Revenge of the Crystal: Selected Writings on the Modern Object and Its Destiny, 1968–1983,* trans. and ed. Paul Foss and Julian Pefanis (Concord, MA: Pluto, 1990).

8. Claudia Villegas-Silva notes that the *Magnificat* is one of Bach's religious hymns and was written for Christmas in honor of the Virgin Mary, a symbol of

motherhood. In reference to its use in the Raznovich play, she posits that it has ironic connotations since it is played in a work whose central space is basically a brothel of women playing the role of mothers. Villegas-Silva, "Diana Raznovich: Dramaturga feminista," *Gestos* 16, no. 32 (November 2001): 110.

9. The only control Bárbara might be able to exercise is to start or stop the recording, but in the play, even that stops by itself as soon as she breaks the baton.

10. Diana Taylor, "Fighting Fire with Frivolity," 31.

11. Judith Butler, *Bodies That Matter: On the Discursive Limits of "Sex"* (New York: Routledge, 1993), 12.

12. Ibid.

13. Castellví deMoor, "Dramaturgas argentinas," 277.

14. For overviews of the history of motherhood, see Elisabeth Badinter, *Mother Love: Myth and Reality* (New York: Macmillan, 1981); Ann Dally, *Inventing Motherhood: The Consequences of an Ideal* (New York: Schocken, 1983); and Jacques Donzelot, *The Policing of Families,* trans. Robert Hurley (Baltimore: Johns Hopkins University Press, 1997).

15. For example, "Todos, pero absolutamente todos, necesitan verme en la más triste de las servidumbres. ¡Nunca me salvo de limpiarles la casa!" (*CM,* 280) (Everyone, absolutely everyone wants to see me in the most menial state of servitude. I'll never get away from having to clean the house) (*MT,* 119).

16. Kappeler, *The Pornography of Representation* (Minneapolis: University of Minnesota Press, 1986), 148–66.

17. Ibid., 152.

18. Marianne Hirsch, *The Mother/Daughter Plot,* 16.

19. David William Foster, "Recent Argentine Women Writers of Jewish Descent," 51.

20. Bárbara's words are perhaps particularly pertinent in light of Catherine Clément's analysis of opera as not only the least realistic of art forms but the one perhaps most pernicious to women. Clément, *Opera, or the Undoing of Women,* trans. Betsy Wing (Minneapolis: University of Minnesota Press, 1988).

21. As Diana Taylor has argued in reference to the work of Raznovich ("Fighting Fire") as well as that of others (*Theatre of Crisis*), even those theatrical works that most ostensibly appear to be works of sociopolitical criticism and resistance exhibit a tendency to deal with only those themes or motifs that the audience wants to witness. Taylor, "Fighting Fire with Frivolity"; Taylor, *Theatre of Crisis* (Lexington: University of Kentucky Press, 1991). As she notes in reference to Teatro Abierto, the Argentine theater project of the early 1980s that was designed to offer resistance to the military dictatorship, those playwrights who chose to focus on other sociopolitical problems were silenced or marginalized as "the social pact between power brokers and complicitous audiences [was] being negotiated." Taylor, "Fighting Fire with Frivolity," 27.

22. Ibid., 34.

23. Ibid., 29.

24. Griselda Pollock, *Vision and Difference: Femininity, Feminism and the Histories of Art* (New York: Routledge, 1988), 158.

25. Ibid.

26. Ibid., 165.

27. Ibid., 171.

28. Later, at the end of the play, Madre Sustituta in turn breaks the baton in what might appear to be an inversion of power (as the baton passes hands, so ostensibly does the power). But, in keeping with my earlier argument about Bárbara's

direction, the power that is being inverted is still a simulacrum and therefore the inversion is a sham.

29. Interesting, too, is the fact that Madre Sustituta does not like being objectified as a gift (*CM,* 274).

30. René Girard, *Deceit, Desire and the Novel,* trans. Yvonne Freccero (Baltimore: Johns Hopkins University Press, 1965).

31. Pollock, *Vision and Difference;* Kappeler, *The Pornography of Representation.*

32. Judith Butler, *Bodies That Matter,* 13.

33. Pollock, *Vision and Difference,* 6.

Works Cited

Adame, Domingo. "La teatralidad en la dramaturgia de Hugo Argüelles." Paper read at Las Cuartas Jornadas Internacionales de Teatro Iberoamericano in Puebla, Mexico, July 8–12, 1996.

Aisemberg, Alicia. "Una propuesta minimalista." *Teatro XXI* 5, no. 9 (Spring 1999): 45–47.

Anderson Imbert, Enrique, and Eugenio Florit, eds. *Literatura hispanoamericana: Antología e introducción histórica.* New York: Holt, 1960.

Andrade, Elba, and Hilde F. Cramsie. "Estudio preliminar." In *Dramaturgas latinoamericanas contemporáneas,* edited by Elba Andrade and Hilde F. Cramsie, 15–68. Madrid: Verbum, 1991.

Anouilh, Jean. *Medea.* In *Jean Anouilh,* vol. 3, translated by Luce and Arthur Klein, 57–87. New York: Hill and Wang, 1967.

———. *Médée.* Paris: Table Ronde, 1953.

Arancibia, Juana A. "Entrevista con Marcela del Río." *Alba de América* 9, nos. 16–17 (1991): 395–401.

Argüelles, Hugo. *Escarabajos.* Guadalajara, Mexico: Agata, 1992.

———. *La esfinge de las maravillas.* In *Teatro vario II,* 251–321. Mexico: Fondo de Cultura Económica, 1995.

———. *Medea y los visitantes del sueño.* In *Obras,* vol. 8, 225–78. Mexico: Gaceta, 1994.

Ashcroft, Bill, Gareth Griffiths, and Helen Tiffin. *Key Concepts in Post-Colonial Studies.* New York: Routledge, 1998.

Badinter, Elisabeth. *Mother Love: Myth and Reality.* New York: Macmillan, 1981.

Barthes, Roland. *A Lover's Discourse.* Translated by Richard Howard. New York: Hill and Wang, 1978.

———. *Mythologies.* Translated by Annette Lavers. New York: Hill and Wang, 1972.

Bartra, Roger. *The Cage of Melancholy: Identity and Metamorphosis in the Mexican Character.* Translated by Christopher J. Hall. New Brunswick: Rutgers University Press, 1992.

Barzilai, Shuli. "Reading 'Snow White': The Mother's Story." In *Ties That Bind: Essays on Mothering and Patriarchy,* edited by Jean F. O'Barr, Deborah Pope, and Mary Wyer, 253–72. Chicago: University of Chicago Press, 1990.

Baudrillard, Jean. *Revenge of the Crystal: Selected Writings on the Modern Object and Its Destiny, 1968–1983.* Translated and edited by Paul Foss and Julian Pefanis. Concord, MA: Pluto, 1990.

Benjamin, Thomas. *La Revolución: Mexico's Great Revolution as Memory, Myth, and History.* Austin: University of Texas Press, 2000.

277

Berger, John. *Ways of Seeing*. London: Penguin, 1972.

Bergson, Henri. "Laughter." In *Comedy,* edited by Wylie Sypher, 61–190. New York: Doubleday Anchor, 1956.

Berman, Sabina. *Between Pancho Villa and a Naked Woman*. Translated by Shelley Tepperman. *Theatre Forum* 14 (1999): 91–108.

———. *Entre Villa y una mujer desnuda*. Mexico: Milagro, 1994.

Bhabha, Homi K. Introduction to *Nation and Narration,* edited by Homi K. Bhabha, 1–7. New York: London, 1990.

Bixler, Jacqueline E. "Metaphor and History in the Theater of Eduardo Rovner." *Ollantay* (special issue dedicated to Rovner) 10, no. 20 (2002): 6–13.

———. "The Postmodernization of History in the Theatre of Sabina Berman." *Latin American Theatre Review* 30, no. 2 (Spring 1997): 45–60.

———. "Power Plays and the Mexican Crisis." In *Performance, pathos, política de los sexos: Teatro postcolonial de autoras latinoamericanas,* edited by Heidrun Adler and Kati Röttger, 83–99. Frankfurt: Vervuert, 1999.

Blau, Herbert. *The Audience*. Baltimore: Johns Hopkins University Press, 1990.

Boling, Becky. "Reyes y princesas: La subversión del signo." In *En busca de una imagen,* edited by Diana Taylor, 75–88. Ottawa: Girol, 1989.

Boorman, Joan Rea. "Contemporary Latin American Woman Dramatists." *Rice University Studies* 64 (1978): 69–80.

Booth, Wayne. *The Rhetoric of Fiction*. Chicago: University of Chicago Press, 1961.

Bulfinch's Mythology. New York: Avenel, 1978.

Bulman, Gail A. "El grito infinito: Ecos coloniales en *La malasangre* de Griselda Gambaro." *Symposium* 48, no. 4 (1995): 271–76.

———. "Humor and National Catharis in Roberto Cossa's *El saludador*." *Latin American Theatre Review* 36, no. 1 (Fall 2002): 5–18.

Butler, Judith. *Bodies That Matter: On the Discursive Limits of "Sex."* New York: Routledge, 1993.

———. *Gender Trouble: Feminism and the Subversion of Identity*. New York: Routledge, 1990.

Cano, Gabriela. "The *Porfiriato* and the Mexican Revolution: Constructions of Feminism and Nationalism." In *Nation, Empire, Colony: Historicizing Gender and Race,* edited by Ruth Roach Pierson and Nupur Chaudhuri, 106–20. Bloomington: Indiana University Press, 1998.

Caplan, Paula J. *The New Don't Blame Mother: Mending the Mother-Daughter Relationship*. New York: Routledge, 2000.

Carlson, Marvin. *The Haunted Stage: The Theatre as Memory Machine*. Ann Arbor: University of Michigan Press, 2001.

Carlson, Susan. "Revisionary Endings: Pam Gem's *Aunt Mary* and *Camille*." In *Making a Spectacle: Feminist Essays on Contemporary Women's Theatre,* edited by Lynda Hart, 103–17. Ann Arbor: University of Michigan Press, 1989.

Castagnino, Raúl H. "Dos siglos de teatro gauchesco." *Teatro* (Teatro Municipal San Martín) 4, no. 12 (June 1983): 4–9.

Castellví deMoor, Magda. "Dramaturgas argentinas: Perspectivas sobre género y representación." In *El teatro y su mundo: Estudios sobre teatro iberoamericano y argentino,* edited by Osvaldo Pellettieri, 271–85. Buenos Aires: Galerna, 1997.

Clément, Catherine. *Opera, or the Undoing of Women.* Translated by Betsy Wing. Minneapolis: University of Minnesota Press, 1988.

Collier, Simon, Artemis Cooper, María Susana Azzi, and Richard Martin. *Tango.* London: Thames and Hudson, 1995.

Corominas, J. *Diccionario crítico etimológico de la lengua castellana.* 4 vols. Madrid: Gredos, 1954.

Cosentino, Olga. "Sentimientos argentinos, en muchos idiomas." *El CELCIT en acción* (Boletín electrónico del Centro Latinoamericano de Creación e Investigación Teatral) 3, no. 149 (March 16, 2003): 1. Repr. from *Clarín,* March 15, 2003. http://www.correo@celcit.org.arg.

Cossa, Roberto. *El saludador. Teatro XXI* 5, no. 9 (Spring 1999): 107–17. Also published in *Diálogos dramatúrgicos México-Argentina,* edited by Felipe Galván, 37–61. Puebla, Mexico: Tablado IberoAmericano, 2000.

Cossa, Roberto, and Osvaldo Pellettieri. "Diálogo de apertura." In *Tradición, modernidad y posmodernidad (Teatro iberoamericano y argentino),* edited by Osvaldo Pellettieri, 15–23. Buenos Aires: Galerna, 1999.

Crow, John A. *The Epic of Latin America.* 4th ed. Berkeley: University of California Press, 1992.

Cypess, Sandra M. "Ethnic Identity in the Plays of Sabina Berman." In *Tradition and Innovation: Reflections on Latin American Jewish Writing,* edited by Robert DiAntonio and Nora Glickman, 165–77. Albany: State University of New York Press, 1993.

———. "La imagen del monstruo y su víctima en las obras de Griselda Gambaro." In *En busca de una imagen,* edited by Diana Taylor, 53–64. Ottawa: Girol, 1989.

Cypess, Sandra Messinger. "Dramaturgia femenina y transposición histórica." *Alba de América* 7, nos. 12–13 (1989): 283–304.

———. *La Malinche in Mexican Literature: From History to Myth.* Austin: University of Texas Press, 1991.

———. "Myth and Metatheatre: Magaña's Malinche and Medea." In *Perspectives on Contemporary Spanish American Theatre,* edited by Frank Dauster, 37–52. Lewisburg, PA: Bucknell University Press, 1996.

Dally, Ann. *Inventing Motherhood: The Consequences of an Ideal.* New York: Schocken, 1983.

Dauster, Frank. "La forma ritual en *Los huéspedes reales.*" In *Ensayos sobre teatro hispanoamericano,* 60–65. Mexico: SepSetentas, 1975.

———. "The Ritual Feast: A Study in Dramatic Form." *Latin American Theatre Review* 9, no. 1 (Fall 1975): 5–9.

Day, Stuart. "Berman's Pancho Villa versus Neoliberal Desire." *Latin American Theatre Review* 33, no. 1 (Fall 1999): 5–23.

de Lauretis, Teresa. *Technologies of Gender.* Bloomington: Indiana University Press, 1987.

del Río, Marcela. *¿Homo sapiens? Suspenso familiar en dos actos.* In *Cien años de teatro mexicano.* CD-ROM. Mexico: Sogem, 2002.

———. "La vocación literaria en los años de la formación." *Alba de América* 11, nos. 20–21 (1993): 99–106.

Derrida, Jacques. *Of Grammatology.* Translated by Gayatri Chakravorty Spivak. Baltimore: Johns Hopkins University Press, 1974.

Dolan, Jill. *The Feminist Spectator as Critic.* Ann Arbor: University of Michigan Press, 1988.

Donzelot, Jacques. *The Policing of Families.* Translated by Robert Hurley. Baltimore: Johns Hopkins University Press, 1997.

Elam, Keir. *The Semiotics of Theatre and Drama.* New York: Methuen, 1980.

Euripides. *Medea.* In *Ten Plays by Euripides,* translated by Moses Hadas and John McLean, 31–63. New York: Bantam, 1960.

Feal, Rosemary Geisdorfer. "Veiled Portraits: Donoso's Interartistic Dialogue in *El jardín de al lado.*" *Modern Language Notes* 103 (1988): 398–418.

Fetterley, Judith. *The Resisting Reader: A Feminist Approach to American Fiction.* Bloomington: Indiana University Press, 1978.

Foster, David William. "Recent Argentine Women Writers of Jewish Descent." In *Passion, Memory, Identity: Twentieth-Century Latin American Jewish Women Writers,* edited by Marjorie Agosín, 35–57. Albuquerque: University of New Mexico Press, 1999.

Foucault, Michel. *The Use of Pleasure.* Vol. 2 of *The History of Sexuality.* Translated by Robert Hurley. New York: Vintage, 1986.

Franco, Jean. "Death Camp Confessions and Resistance to Violence in Latin America." *Socialism and Democracy* 2 (1986): 5–17.

Fraser, Nancy. "The Uses and Abuses of French Discourse Theories for Feminist Politics." In *Revaluing French Feminism: Critical Essays on Difference, Agency, and Culture,* edited by Nancy Fraser and Sandra Lee Bartky, 177–94. Bloomington: Indiana University Press, 1992.

Fraser, Nancy, and Sandra Lee Bartky, eds. *Revaluing French Feminism: Critical Essays on Difference, Agency, and Culture.* Bloomington: Indiana University Press, 1992.

Fuss, Diana. *Essentially Speaking: Feminism, Nature and Difference.* New York: Routledge, 1989.

Gallop, Jane. *The Daughter's Seduction.* Ithaca: Cornell University Press, 1982.

Gambaro, Griselda. *Bitter Blood.* Translated by Evelyn Picon Garfield. In *Women's Fiction from Latin America,* edited by Evelyn Picon Garfield, 111–57. Detroit: Wayne State University Press, 1988.

———. "¿Es posible y deseable una dramaturgia específicamente femenina?" *Latin American Theatre Review* 13, no. 3 (Summer 1980): 17–21.

———. *La malasangre.* In *Teatro I: Real envido, La malasangre, Del sol naciente,* 57–110. Buenos Aires: Ediciones de la Flor, 1984.

———. *De profesión maternal.* In *Teatro,* 45–80. Buenos Aires: Norma, 2002.

———. *Teatro: Nada que ver, Sucede lo que pasa.* Edited by Miguel Angel Giella, Peter Roster, and Leandro Urbina. Ottawa: Girol, 1983.

García Márquez, Gabriel. *One Hundred Years of Solitude.* Translated by Gregory Rabassa. New York: Harper Row, 1970.

Gardel, Carlos, and Alfredo Le Pera. "Volver." In *Todo Tango. The Library.* http://www.todotango.com/english/biblioteca/letras.

Giella, Miguel Angel. "La metamorfosis individual de las utopías: *El Saludador* de Roberto Cossa." In *Itinerarios del teatro latinoamericano,* edited by Osvaldo Pellettieri, 121–25. Buenos Aires: Galerna, 2000.

Gilbert, Sandra M., and Susan Gubar. *The Madwoman in the Attic: The Woman*

Writer and the Nineteenth-Century Literary Imagination. New Haven: Yale University Press, 1979.

Giordano, Enrique A. "*La malasangre* de Griselda Gambaro: Un proceso de reconstrucción y recodificación." In *Teatro argentino durante el Proceso (1976–1983),* edited by Juana A. Arancibia and Zulema Mirkin, 57–74. Buenos Aires: Vinciguerra, 1992.

Girard, René. *Deceit, Desire, and the Novel.* Translated by Yvonne Freccero. Baltimore: Johns Hopkins University Press, 1965.

Gladhart, Amalia. *The Leper in Blue: Coercive Performance in the Contemporary Latin American Theater.* Chapel Hill: University of North Carolina Press, 2000.

Glickman, Nora. "De *La malasangre* a *De profesión maternal:* Griselda Gambaro y el incómodo vaivén entre hija y madre." *Revista Hispánica Moderna* 55 (December 2002): 435–46.

———. "Parodia y desmitificación del rol femenino en el teatro de Diana Raznovich." *Latin American Theatre Review* 28, no. 1 (Fall 1994): 89–100.

Graham-Jones, Jean. *Exorcising History: Argentine Theater under Dictatorship.* Lewisburg, PA: Bucknell University Press, 2000.

Grosz, Elizabeth. *Volatile Bodies: Toward a Corporeal Feminism.* Bloomington: Indiana University Press, 1994.

Guy, Donna J. "Mothers Alive and Dead: Multiple Concepts of Mothering in Buenos Aires." In *Sex and Sexuality in Latin America,* edited by Daniel Balderston and Donna J. Guy, 155–73. New York: New York University Press, 1997.

Hadas, Moses. Introduction to *Ten Plays by Euripides,* translated by Moses Hadas and John McLean, ix–x. New York: Bantam, 1960.

Halbwachs, Maurice. *On Collective Memory.* Translated and edited by Lewis A. Coser. Chicago: University of Chicago Press, 1992.

Hamnett, Brian. *A Concise History of Mexico.* Cambridge: Cambridge University Press, 1999.

Hernández, Luisa Josefina. *Los huéspedes reales.* In *Teatro mexicano del siglo XX,* edited by Antonio Magaña-Esquivel, 84–140. Mexico: Fondo de Cultura Económica, 1970.

Hirsch, Marianne. *The Mother/Daughter Plot: Narrative, Psychoanalysis, Feminism.* Bloomington: Indiana University Press, 1989.

Huyssen, Andreas. *After the Great Divide: Modernism, Mass Culture, Postmodernism.* Bloomington: Indiana University Press, 1986.

Irigaray, Luce. *Speculum of the Other Woman.* Translated by Gillian G. Gill. Ithaca: Cornell University Press, 1985.

———. *This Sex Which Is Not One.* Translated by Catherine Porter. Ithaca: Cornell University Press, 1985.

Johnson, Barbara. *The Wake of Deconstruction.* Cambridge, MA: Blackwell, 1994.

Kamuf, Peggy. *Fictions of Feminine Desire.* Lincoln: University of Nebraska Press, 1982.

Kappeler, Susanne. *The Pornography of Representation.* Minneapolis: University of Minnesota Press, 1986.

Kintz, Linda. *The Subject's Tragedy: Political Poetics, Feminist Theory, and Drama.* Ann Arbor: University of Michigan Press, 1992.

Knowles, John K. "Luisa Josefina Hernández: The Labyrinth of Form." In *Drama-*

tists in Revolt, edited by Leon F. Lyday and George W. Woodyard, 133–45. Austin: University of Texas Press, 1976.

Knowles, John Kenneth. *Luisa Josefina Hernández: Teoría y práctica del drama.* Mexico: Universidad Nacional Autónoma de México, 1980.

Laqueu, Thomas. *Making Sex: Body and Gender from the Greeks to Freud.* Cambridge, MA: Harvard University Press, 1990.

Larson, Catherine. *Games and Play in the Theater of Spanish American Women.* Lewisburg, PA: Bucknell University Press, 2004.

Larson, Catherine, and Margarita Vargas, eds. *Latin American Women Dramatists: Theater, Texts, and Theories.* Bloomington: Indiana University Press, 1998.

Lomnitz, Claudio. *Deep Mexico, Silent Mexico: An Anthropology of Nationalism.* Minneapolis: University of Minnesota Press, 2001.

Lyotard, Jean-François. *The Postmodern Condition: A Report on Knowledge.* Translated by Geoff Bennington and Brian Massumi. Minneapolis: University of Minnesota Press, 1984.

Magnarelli, Sharon. "Acting Women / Seeing Women / Seeing Nude: Griselda Gambaro's *El despojamiento.*" In *Latin American Women's Writing: Feminist Readings in Theory and Crisis,* edited by Anny Brooksbank Jones and Catherine Davies, 10–29. Oxford: Oxford University Press, 1996.

———. *"La ciudad y los perros:* Women and Language." In *The Lost Rib: Female Characters in the Spanish-American Novel,* 102–16. Lewisburg, PA: Bucknell University Press, 1985.

———. "El espejo en el espejo: El discurso reflejado/reflexivo en *Real envido* de Griselda Gambaro." In *En busca de una imagen,* edited by Diana Taylor, 89–102. Ottawa: Girol, 1989.

———. "Giselda Gambaro habla de su obra más reciente y la crítica." *Revista de Estudios Hispánicos* 20, no. 1 (1986): 123–33.

———. "Interview with Griselda Gambaro." *Hispania* 68, no. 4 (1985): 819–21.

———. *The Lost Rib: Female Characters in the Spanish American Novel.* Lewisburg, PA: Bucknell University Press, 1985.

———. "Masculine Acts / Anxious Encounters: Sabina Berman's *Entre Villa y una mujer desnuda.*" *Intertexts* 1, no. 1 (Spring 1997): 40–50.

———. "Roberto Cossa habla del teatro." *Latin American Theatre Review* 20, no. 2 (Spring 1987): 133–38.

———. "Tea for Two: Performing Desire in Sabina Berman's *Entre Villa y una mujer desnuda.*" *Latin American Theatre Review* 30, no. 1 (Fall 1996): 55–74.

———. *Understanding José Donoso.* Columbia: University of South Carolina Press, 1993.

———. *"Volvió una noche* de Eduardo Rovner: Recepción en Nueva York." *Teatro XXI* 8, no. 15 (Spring 2002): 75–78.

Martínez de Olcoz, Nieves. "Decisiones de la máscara neutra: Dramaturgia femenina y fin de siglo en América Latina." *Latin American Theatre Review* 31, no. 2 (Spring 1998): 5–16.

———. "Escrito en el cuerpo: Mujer, nación y memoria." In *Performance, pathos, política de los sexos: Teatro postcolonial de autoras latinoamericanas,* edited by Heidrun Adler and Kati Röttger, 55–68. Madrid: Iberoamericana, 1999.

Martínez Landa, Lidia, and Laura Mogliani. "Entrevista a Roberto Cossa." *Teatro XXI* 5, no. 9 (Spring 1999): 105–6.

McAuley, Gay. *Space in Performance: Making Meaning in the Theatre.* Ann Arbor: University of Michigan Press, 2000.

Meléndez, Priscilla. "Co(s)mic Conquest in Sabina Berman's *Aguila o sol.*" In *Perspectives on Contemporary Spanish American Theatre,* edited by Frank Dauster, 19–36. Lewisburg, PA: Bucknell University Press, 1996.

———. "Marx, Villa, Calles, Guzmán . . . : Fantasmas y modernidad en *Entre Villa y una mujer desnuda* de Sabina Berman." *Hispanic Review* (Autumn 2004): 523–46.

"Mesa redonda: Los autores entre el acuerdo y la polémica." *Teatro XXI* 2, no. 3 (Spring 1996): 67–78.

Milleret, Margo. *Latin American Women on/in Stages.* Albany: State University of New York Press, 2004.

Mitchell, Juliet, and Jacqueline Rose, eds. *Feminine Sexuality: Jacques Lacan and the école freudienne.* Translated by Jacqueline Rose. New York: Norton, 1985.

Mogliani, Laura. "*El saludador:* Del fracaso de las utopías comunitarias." *Teatro XXI* 5, no. 9 (Spring 1999): 35–38.

Moliner, María. *Diccionario de uso del español.* 2 vols. Madrid: Gredos, 1966.

Mulhern, Francis. "English Reading." In *Nation and Narration,* edited by Homi K. Bhabha, 250–64. New York: Routledge, 1990.

Mulvey, Laura. "Melodrama In and Out of the Home." In *High Theory / Low Culture: Analysing Popular Television and Film,* edited by Colin MacCabe, 80–100. New York: St. Martin's, 1986.

———. "Visual Pleasure and Narrative Cinema." *Screen* 16, no. 3 (Autumn 1975): 6–18.

Murray, Timothy. *Drama Trauma: Specters of Race and Sexuality in Performance, Video, and Art.* New York: Routledge, 1997.

O'Malley, Ilene V. *The Myth of the Revolution.* Westport, CT: Greenwood, 1986.

Parkes, Henry Bamford. *A History of Mexico.* Boston: Houghton, 1969.

Partridge, Eric. *Origins: A Short Etymological Dictionary of Modern English.* New York: Greenwich House, 1983.

Paz, Octavio. *El laberinto de la soledad.* Mexico: Fondo de Cultura Económica, 1959.

———. *The Labyrinth of Solitude: Life and Thought in Mexico.* Translated by Lysander Kemp. New York: Grove Press, 1961.

Pellettieri, Osvaldo. "Cambios en el sistema teatral de la gauchesca rioplatense." *Gestos* 2, no. 4 (November 1987): 115–24.

———. *Cien años de teatro argentino: Del Moreira al Teatro Abierto.* Buenos Aires: Galerna, 1994.

———. "Roberto Cossa y el teatro dominante (1985–1999)." In *Teatro argentino del 2000,* edited by Osvaldo Pellettieri, 27–35. Buenos Aires: Galerna, 2000.

———. "El teatro argentino del año 2000 y el teatro del futuro." *Latin American Theatre Review* 34, no. 1 (Fall 2000): 5–23.

———. "El teatro de Eduardo Rovner: Un mundo sentimental y satírico." *Ollantay* 10, no. 20 (2002): 97–111.

Pollock, Griselda. *Vision and Difference: Femininity, Feminism and the Histories of Art.* New York: Routledge, 1988.

Pratt, Mary Louise. *Imperial Eyes: Travel Writing and Transculturation.* New York: Routledge, 1992.

Raznovich, Diana. *Casa Matriz.* http://autores.org.ar/dianaraz/Obras/Casa/texto.html.

———. *Casa Matriz.* In *Defiant Acts / Actos Desafiantes: Four Plays by Diana Raznovich,* edited by Diana Taylor and Victoria Martinez, 263–86. Lewisburg, PA: Bucknell University Press, 2002. Also published in *Salirse de madre,* edited by Hilda Rais, 163–86. Buenos Aires: Croquiñol, 1989.

———. *MaTRIX, Inc.* Translated by Victoria Martinez. In *Defiant Acts: Four Plays by Diana Raznovich,* edited by Diana Taylor and Victoria Martinez, 99–127. Lewisburg, PA: Bucknell University Press, 2002.

Roster, Peter. "Griselda Gambaro: De la voz pasiva al verbo activo." In *En busca de una imagen,* edited by Diana Taylor, 43–52. Ottawa: Girol, 1989.

Rovner, Eduardo. *She Returned One Night.* Translated by Charles Philip Thomas. In *She Returned One Night / Volvió una noche,* edited by Charles Philip Thomas, 1–66. Chula Vista, CA: Avetine, 2003.

———. *Volvió una noche.* In *Eduardo Rovner Teatro I,* 9–104. Buenos Aires: Ediciones de la Flor, 1994.

Saavedra, Mario. "La visión trágico-burlesca en el teatro de Hugo Argüelles." Prologue to *Obras,* by Hugo Argüelles, vol. 8, 9–16. Mexico: Gaceta, 1994.

Schoo, Ernesto. "Chirino, en sueco [*sic*]." *La Nación,* April 26, 2003. http://www.lanacion.com.ar/03/04/26/ds_491696.asp.

Sikora, Marina. "La comedia en Buenos Aires: Circulación y desplazamientos." *Teatro XXI* 1, no. 1 (Spring 1995): 22–26.

———. "La remanencia del microsistema premoderno: Concepción de la obra dramática (1983–1998)." In *Historia del teatro argentino en Buenos Aires.* Vol. 5, *Teatro actual (1976–1998),* edited by Osvaldo Pellettieri, 430–36. Buenos Aires: Galerna, 2001.

———. "*El saludador* o la persistencia del realismo." *Gestos* 15, no. 29 (April 2000): 185–88.

Sommer, Doris. *Foundational Fictions: The National Romances of Latin America.* Berkeley: University of California Press, 1991.

———. "Irresistible Romance: The Foundational Fictions of Latin America." In *Nation and Narration,* edited by Homi K. Bhabha, 71–98. New York: Routledge, 1990.

Stapleton, Michael. *The Concise Dictionary of Greek and Roman Mythology.* New York: Peter Bedrick, 1982.

Stevens, Camilla. *Family and Identity in Contemporary Cuban and Puerto Rican Drama.* Gainesville: University of Florida Press, 2004.

Stimson, Frederick S., and Ricardo Navas-Ruiz, eds. *Literatura de la América Hispánica: Antología e historia; Tomo II: El siglo diecinueve (1825–1910).* New York: Dodd, 1971.

Stone, Lawrence. "The Rise of the Nuclear Family in Early Modern England." In *The Family in History,* edited by Charles E. Rosenberg, 13–57. Philadelphia: University of Pennsylvania Press, 1975.

Taylor, Diana. *Disappearing Acts: Spectacles of Gender and Nationalism in Argentina's "Dirty War."* Durham, NC: Duke University Press, 1997.

———. "Fighting Fire with Frivolity: Diana Raznovich's Defiant Acts." In *Defi-*

ant Acts / Actos Desafiantes: Four Plays by Diana Raznovich, edited by Diana Taylor and Victoria Martinez, 23–39. Lewisburg, PA: Bucknell University Press, 2002.

———. *Theatre of Crisis.* Lexington: University of Kentucky Press, 1991.

Taylor, Diana, and Roselyn Costantino, eds. *Holy Terrors: Latin American Women Perform.* Durham, NC: Duke University Press, 2003.

Taylor, Julie. *Paper Tangos.* Durham, NC: Duke University Press, 1998.

Tierney-Tello, Mary Beth. *Allegories of Transgression and Transformation: Experimental Fiction by Women Writing Under Dictatorship.* Albany: State University of New York Press, 1996.

Trastoy, Beatriz. "Madres, marginados y otras víctimas: El teatro de Griselda Gambaro en el ocaso del siglo." In *Teatro Argentino del 2000,* edited by Osvaldo Pellettieri, 37–46. Buenos Aires: Galerna, 2000.

Valdés, María Elena de. "Luisa Josefina Hernández." In *Escritoras de Hispanoamérica,* edited by Diane E. Marting, 246–58. Bogota: Siglo Veintiuno, 1990.

Villegas-Silva, Claudia. "Diana Raznovich: Dramaturga feminista." *Gestos* 16, no. 32 (November 2001): 107–10.

Waldman, Gloria Feiman. "Three Female Playwrights Explore Contemporary Latin American Reality: Myrna Casas, Griselda Gambaro, Luisa Josefina Hernández." In *Latin American Women Writers: Yesterday and Today,* edited by Yvette E. Miller and Charles M. Tatum, 75–84. Pittsburgh: Latin American Literary Review, 1977.

Warner, Rex. *The Stories of the Greeks.* New York: Farrar, Straus, and Giroux, 1967.

Webster's New World Dictionary. 3rd college ed. New York: Simon and Schuster, 1989.

Weedon, Chris. *Feminist Practice and Poststructuralist Theory.* New York: Basil Blackwell, 1987.

White, Hayden. *Tropics of Discourse: Essays in Cultural Criticism.* Baltimore: Johns Hopkins University Press, 1978.

Woodyard, George. "Rovner's Theater: Questions of Value with Humor." *Ollantay* 10, no. 20 (2002): 15–22.

———. "Sombras y muerte: El teatro reciente de Eduardo Rovner." In *Tendencias críticas en el teatro,* edited by Osvaldo Pellettieri, 209–15. Buenos Aires: Galerna, 2001.

———. "The Theatre of Roberto Cossa: A World of Broken Dreams." In *Perspectives on Contemporary Spanish American Theatre,* edited by Frank Dauster, 94–108. Lewisburg, PA: Bucknell University Press, 1996.

Index